A
VICTOR HUGO
ENCYCLOPEDIA

John Andrew Frey

Foreword by ARNAUD LASTER

Greenwood Press
Westport, Connecticut • London

Library of Congress Cataloging-in-Publication Data

Frey, John Andrew, 1929–
    A Victor Hugo encyclopedia / John Andrew Frey ; foreword by
Arnaud Laster.
        p.   cm.
    Includes bibliographical references and index.
    ISBN 0–313–29896–3 (alk. paper)
    1. Hugo, Victor, 1802–1885—Encyclopedias.   I. Title.
PQ2292.F73   1999
848'.709—dc21   97–33139

British Library Cataloguing in Publication Data is available.

Library of Congress Catalog Card Number: 97–33139
ISBN: 0–313–29896–3

First published in 1999

Greenwood Press, 88 Post Road West, Westport, CT 06881
An imprint of Greenwood Publishing Group, Inc.
www.greenwood.com

Printed in the United States of America

The paper used in this book complies with the
Permanent Paper Standard issued by the National
Information Standards Organization (Z39.48–1984).

10 9 8 7 6 5 4 3 2 1

Contents

Note to the Reader

Shortly following the unexpected death of John Andrew Frey, my esteemed colleague and oldest friend since college days, I immediately agreed to review, at the request of Peter Louis Morris, the manuscript of this now completed encyclopedia of Victor Hugo. Initially it was with a heavy heart that I began to read his text as I could hear his now stilled voice resonate in my ear. As I continued, however, my sorrow was assuaged because that resonant voice seemed more and more as if he and I were engaging in a dialogue of the kind we so often had had. This task thus became a source of solace. Whatever contribution I have made to the publication of this book has been done in tribute to my friend, affectionately known by all as "Jack."

James F. Burks
Professor Emeritus of French
George Washington University

Foreword

I knew John Frey for too short a time, but long enough to regard him as a friend and to feel the sorrow of his sudden death. The story of our friendship can be told in a few words: I was happy to make acquaintance with a true American "Hugophile" who, in his book about *Les Contemplations*, had adopted an original point of view. I was deeply honored to be asked to write a foreword for his Encyclopedia. Finally, we met in Paris and I discovered his gentleness and simplicity, which I appreciated very much.

Now let me explain why John Frey's Encyclopedia is so useful. Mainly written for a majority of American or English readers who consider Victor Hugo, above all, and sometimes exclusively, as the author of *The Hunchback of Notre-Dame* and *Les Misérables*, Frey's work will teach them the genius and the universality of the poet. I hope that, at the same time, it will remind the French of the importance and international glory of the novelist, since in the French *lycées* he is taught primarily as a poet, which is hardly less reductive. To me this is the primary interest of a survey of Hugo's entire life and work.

John Frey, who has much admired and carefully analyzed the great collection of poems which Victor Hugo presented as *Les Mémoires d'une âme* (The memorial of a soul), has introduced them with entries of the highest quality. This should draw attention to a book of inexhaustible richness which Victor Hugo left to us as a "mirror," reflecting not only his personal history but ours also, composed, like his, of joy, love, struggle, dreams, and mourning—hopes alternating constantly with doubts. But, even if Frey manifests preference for this lyrical masterpiece of exile, which Hugo entitled *Les Contemplations*, he neglects none of the other collections and gives each of them a substantial entry. The sole exception is a book which nevertheless was surely dear to Frey, *Les Quatre Vents de l'esprit*, published in 1881 and in which Hugo gathered the four great forms of poetry he practiced: satirical, dramatic, lyrical, and epic. Had Frey not died before the revision of his Encyclopedia, he would have caught sight of this unintentional gap and would have perspicaciously filled it up.

I also would have asked him to detail further the presentation of the *Théâtre en liberté* and perhaps to particularize each of its plays, not only the one he wisely celebrates: *Mangeront-ils?*—the most Shakespearean of Hugo's comedies—but others such as *L'Intervention*, so modern in its subject and tone, or *Mille Francs de récompense*, a drama whose hero (or antihero) is a sort of prefiguration of the character popularized by Charlie Chaplin. Even in France these plays are only known by a "happy few." And all of Hugo's dramatic works, in spite of the frequence and success of their revivals, remain underrated by most critics, who often simply admit the poetic value of the verse dramas. Therefore, because there is agreement on the difficulty, if not the impossibility, of translating Hugo's poetry, the situation is worse in Great Britain and the United States; there, Hugo's dramas are never played, except incognito by the medium of libretti. But is the audience who is thrilled by *Rigoletto* or *La Gioconda* conscious that both operas owe a part of their power to the Hugolian sources: *Le Roi s'amuse* and *Angelo, tyran de Padoue*? The prose dramas should find more favor in foreign countries, but it appears as if these works were victims of their bad reputation in France; they are considered inferior to the verse dramas, by implicit reference to the traditional model of the classical tragedies, written in alexandrines. The time for justice has come. Anglophones should at least be grateful for all that Hugo did to promote Shakespeare in France! Furthermore, American and English directors, less imprisoned than the French by the religion of seventeenth-century classicism, may better understand the Hugolian mixture of styles and genres, the coexistence of the grotesque and the sublime which is still frequently lacking in Hugo's stage productions, probably because its potentially subversive dimension is misunderstood.

So, Hugo's plays are still largely to be discovered. They will be rightly appreciated only if they are not taken for purely historical dramas; Hugo never intended to write history by the medium of theatre, novels, or poems. *A fortiori* when he entitled *La Légende des siècles* (*La Légende* and not *L'Histoire*) a collection of "petites épopées" (short epic poems). It is equally absurd that he has been blamed for inexactitudes in the presentation of historical facts or characters. Unjustified, too, were the complaints about his lack of verisimilitude, complaints which were based on a classical requirement he had specifically rejected. Other critics denigrated his theatrical output as melodrama, a genre classified as inferior.

This is an unfair amalgam which neglects the fact that Hugo respects neither the typology of characters nor the optimism of happy conclusions, characteristics of traditional melodrama. By making Hugo's conception conform with the codes of melodrama, Disney's recent adaptation of *Notre-Dame de Paris* unintentionally confirms its originality. By reducing the character of Claude Frollo to a stereotype, it helps to reveal the character's complexity in the novel. Prefigurations of modern psychology and psychoanalysis, rarely recognized because of judgments based on classical criteria, can be found in Hernani's obsessions or in the description of Jean Valjean's most intimate feelings. Hugo's last drama enables us to understand the terrifying logic of fanaticism in the person of the Great Inquisitor, Torquemada, whose name gives the play its title. Hugo published *Torquemada* in 1882 as a protest against the bloody pogroms in Russia. At the end of the twentieth century, when fundamentalism still makes victims, this drama is more timely than ever.

It is necessary to break from all the prejudice against Hugo, including the biographical clichés. For instance, he is often represented as a womanizer, but he had no extramarital affairs until his wife was unfaithful to him; moreover, he approved, shared, and upheld feminist claims, demanding for women the same juridical and political rights as those of men. He has been reproached for the violence of his attacks against Louis-Napoléon Bonaparte, whom he had formerly supported, and he has even been accused of being angry merely because he had hoped to be one of Bonaparte's ministers. No one has ever been able to prove the accusation. The elected president of the Second Republic restored the Empire for his own profit, as Hugo suspected, and the banished poet spent nineteen years in exile, refusing the opportunity for an honorable repatriation. In addition, Hugo is often considered a bourgeois, though he was neither a landlord nor an heir to a rich family. Lacking estate or fortune, for years he had no civic rights, and during his entire life he owned only his house of exile on the island of Guernsey, which he purchased in the hope that it would make his expulsion more difficult. He is sometimes believed to have been a naïve and confident adept of spiritism, particularly when he questioned the "speaking tables" for a time. But he never strayed far from his critical position, and after two years he abandoned the experiment. Having published *L'Art d'être grand-père* (The art of being a grandfather), he was regarded as an old man bordering on senility but, even in the most anecdotic poems of this collection, he was subtly pleading for the amnesty of those who were persecuted for having taken part in the insurrection of the Commune of Paris in 1871. His patriotism has been emphasized but, in fact, it never drifted into nationalism, and he was very pleased when some critics declared that he was out of step with so-called "French taste." Furthermore, he publicly encouraged the Mexican people's resistance to the French imperial army and regarded himself as a brother of all victims of oppression throughout the world.

One must reject the clichés of hostile critics who, hating Hugo's political, social or anticlerical messages, tried to discredit his works under aesthetic pretexts. Far from giving way to verbosity, Hugo admired the conciseness he found in Tacite's work, for example, and cultivated it in his own writings, especially in his prose. This may seem paradoxical for a writer who is not known for his brevity, but the greatest specialist of Hugo's manuscripts, René Journet, was fond of defining the author's style as "an accumulation of concisions." To be convinced of the aptness of Journet's definition, it suffices to read *Le Dernier Jour d'un condamné*, *L'Homme qui rit* (the extraordinary novel which inspired an admirable expressionist film directed in the United States by Paul Leni), or the notes Hugo wrote about contemporary life, published after his death under the title *Choses vues*. Even when it was in vogue to show disdain toward Hugo and to distance themselves from the popular admiration his works still retained, fashionable critics made an exception of *Choses vues*. Had there been a new *Dictionnaire des idées reçues*, Hugo might well have been considered as the model of journalists. At the same time, and in other milieux, two posthumous collections of poems, *La Fin de Satan* and *Dieu*, were privileged; they were erroneously thought to have been produced in the last years of the author's life and therefore were believed to have been testaments. Finally, to declare that Hugo's drawings were precursors of the surrealist experiments and formed the only portion of his output of any worth was the supreme snobbery. And yet, the various ways in which critics followed the prevailing fashion helped to shed light upon less visited parts of Hugo's world.

May John Frey's Encyclopedia, by the comprehensiveness of its investigation of Victor Hugo's life and works, incite further explorations and lead many anglophone readers, spectators, directors, film-makers, actors, painters, musicians, and singers toward one of humanity's greatest and most generous geniuses!

Arnaud Laster

Introduction: The Focus and Use of This Encyclopedia

The Greenwood encyclopedia on Victor Hugo is designed to meet the needs of the English-speaking community—those with no knowledge, or a limited one, of the French language and its literature as well as those adept in French. It is its focus that differentiates it from its antecedents in France, namely the *Dictionnaire de Victor Hugo* (Paris, Librairie Larousse, 1970) by Professor Philippe Van Tieghem, and the more recent comprehensive study by Professor Arnaud Laster, *Pleins Feux sur Victor Hugo* (Paris, publications of the Comédie-Française, 1981), roughly rendered in English as *A Spotlight on Victor Hugo*. The Greenwood compilations are in no way designed to compete with the French studies, which were created for the Francophone world and differ in methodology; they are complementary texts, and any reader interested in Hugo should consult all three works.

DICTIONNAIRE DE VICTOR HUGO

If the separate entries of a broad-based dictionary on a particular writer or subject are useful as a reference tool, in their entirety they give a whole picture of the person or subject. In reading the Van Tieghem dictionary, it becomes clear that it is his sense of history that pinpoints his methodology; it could be considered diachronic in a very loose sense of the word, for Van Teighem is interested in linguistic and literary change in the texts of Victor Hugo. The dictionary, monumental in its scope, is indispensable to any scholar or informed lay reader. It is factual in orientation and punctiliously exact in determining precise datings, manuscripts, and evolution of texts, but it is little concerned with questions of aesthetics. His entry on *Les Misérables* is a fine example of his approach. He places the text within Hugo's general concern with social

problems, poverty, crime, and punishment; and he returns to earlier
Hugo texts and discusses an earlier version of the 1862 novel, entitled
Les Misères, which will inevitably, in the thought of Hugo, move from
the embryonic state to the birth of *Les Misérables* in 1862. Briefly, Van
Tieghem worked with literary history in its most external form, based
on factual information uncovered while editing, publishing, revising,
and comparing related themes. He is not working in the sense of René
Journet and Guy Robert (*Autour des "Contemplations*," published by the
University of Besançon in 1955), who employed a more scientific approach to the problem of appropriately dating texts (for Hugo, especially
in the 1856 poetry collection *Les Contemplations*, rearranges not only dates
of composition, but also places). Van Tieghem's vast erudition is much
to be admired; it has, however, about it the odor of nineteenth-century
positivism.

PLEINS FEUX SUR VICTOR HUGO

A more refreshing, more modern interpretation of the phenomenon
called Victor Hugo is found in the work of Arnaud Laster. In thirty-four
chapters, written with verve, humor, and obvious admiration for the
entire corpus of Hugo's writings, Laster demonstrates the total scholarly
commitment of the Parisian Hugophiles. He has revised, modernized,
even revolutionized the nineteenth-century "L'Homme et l'oeuvre" (The
writer and his work) developed primarily by the critic Charles-Augustin
Sainte-Beuve. The chapters can be read as separate entities. Read as a
whole they form a new insight into Hugo, the man and his works, made
possible by the methodologies offered by modern criticism. His work is
indispensable for those wishing to deepen their knowledge of Hugo. The
chapters cover a vast field, starting with Hugo within the context of his
time. Other chapters highlight Hugo's familial relationships, including
his family, brothers, wife, children, grandchildren; his lifelong companion Juliette Drouet; his many amorous adventures; his disciples, admirers, and enemies; and his homes, trips, political evolution, and political
combats. Also treated are Hugo's ideas on religion and careful critical
readings of Hugo's relationship with the Comédie-Française and other
Parisian theatres. Chapters or sections are devoted to Hugo's critical
writings, his drawings, and his influence within France and abroad. Concluding chapters attest to Hugo's presence in the twentieth century with
materials on recordings, radio, film, and television. The breadth and
depth of Laster's work is almost gargantuan in its exploration of every
nook and cranny of Hugo. His organization of the materials, synthetic
in nature, resurrects Hugo and puts him together again. For these reasons, his work serves the purpose of a dictionary or encyclopedia, but it
may also be read as a biography.

THE GREENWOOD *VICTOR HUGO ENCYCLOPEDIA*

This work follows the A to Z format found in Van Tieghem's dictionary, but it has a totally different orientation. Its basic intent is to provide an interpretation of Hugo's works and, to a lesser degree, an interpretation of some debatable or questionable aspects of Hugo's personality without, however, trying to compete with *Psychoanalyse de Victor Hugo* by Charles Baudoin (1943). The historical materials are present and complete to the degree necessary to gain a comprehensive view of the life and times of Victor Hugo; however, above all, this encylopedia considers questions of aesthetics, stylistics, poetics, and rhetoric as found in Hugo's writings and provides an overview of his own poetic arts theory.

A unique feature of this work is the inclusion of poems from Hugo's youth, maturity, and old age so as to provide a corollary to the evolution of Hugo's social and political thought across the nineteenth century. The poems selected may be considered representative and will guide the reader to related poetical materials. While not of the nature of classical French textual explanation, they are indeed interpretive.

The same may be said for the entries on Hugo's novels and theatre. They are, of course, viewed within the context of the existential issues of Romanticism, but they must also be seen outside of history as meaningful unto themselves, that is, the text reading the text.

Above all, the Greenwood encyclopedia is comparative in methodology. Hugo is read first within his own French tradition, which is not limited to the nineteenth century, and attempts have been made to put Hugo within a larger aspect of the Western cultural tradition. References are made to English, German, and American writings that should make this work more accessible to the English-speaking world.

USE OF THE GREENWOOD ENCYCLOPEDIA

1. To the degree possible, titles and citations have been translated into English, except when they are obvious; for example, *dictionnaire* is clear to anyone as "dictionary."

2. The individual entries complement the short biographical essay. A reading of all the entries would provide a biography. The reader, however, is directed to a pertinent list of biographies both in French and in English.

3. Where necessary, bibliographical item(s) will follow. Some entries, however, do not need a bibliography at the end of the entry. Pure historical fact, such as the drowning of Hugo's daughter in 1843, need not have after its text a bibliography, although bibliographical references to historical events can be found in the general bibliography.

4. At the end of the text will be found a selected bibliography, includ-

ing a description of Hugo's manuscripts, as well as a listing of the major editions of the complete works of Hugo, and some reference to single editions of works.

5. An asterisk (*) within an entry will guide the reader to another entry pertinent to the one being read.

I wish to thank Greenwood Press and Dr. George Butler of its editorial section for help with this project as well as Professor Arnaud Laster, at the University of Paris III; Professor Henri Cazemayou, former curator of the Hugo sites and archives in Paris and the Channel Islands; and the encouraging staffs at the Bibliothèque de la Comédie-Française, the Bibliothèque nationale, the Library of Congress, and the Columbian School of Arts and Sciences of George Washington University for their sustaining enthusiasm, both moral and financial.

Biographical Sketch

HUGO AND NINETEENTH-CENTURY FRANCE

Any evaluation of the nineteenth century in France would be incomplete, indeed even false, without a solid evaluation of Hugo's role in determining not only its literary directions, as undisputed head of the Romantic movement, but also as prophet of future literary efforts not just in poetry but also in the novel and in the theatre, especially the publication in 1886, one year after his death, of *Le Théâtre en liberté* (Free theatre) which contains plays started during the exile and which, by their form, announce modernistic trends of the twentieth century. Hugo's impact, however, was not limited to literature. In the mainstream of nineteenth-century intellectual thought, he was a cultural giant who dominated political, religious, and humanitarian ideas throughout the century.

The years of his life span (1802–1885) indicate that he spanned nearly the entire century, and his writings in both literary and nonliterary domains reflect the penchants of those times. If for some, the nineteenth century does not end until the beginning of World War I, for others it can be said to conclude with Hugo's death in May 1885. This is the point of view of Roger Shattuck who offers a brief but accurate description of the public wake held for Hugo, when his sarcophagus was placed atop a great urn under the Arc de Triomphe, and the long funeral procession the following day to the Panthéon. Shattuck seizes the meaning of the burial of Hugo as the great doors of the Panthéon closed on the remains of the poet: "The church had to be specially unconsecrated for the occasion. By this orgiastic ceremony France unburdened itself of a man, a literary movement, and a century" (Roger Shattuck, *The Banquet Years*, New York, Vintage Books, 1968, pp. 4–5).

This introductory sketch will capture only the essential features of the life of Victor Hugo, his origins, writings, love affairs, and political causes. A detailed discussion can be found in any one of the biographical recommendations listed at the end of this chapter, in the individual entries included in this encyclopedia, and in the general bibliography found at the end of this work.

EARLY YEARS

Born on February 26, 1802, Victor Hugo was the third son of the union of General Léopold Hugo and Sophie Trébuchet. Because of his father's engagement in the Napoleonic wars, the child Hugo was taken to both Italy and Spain, memories of which can be found in his letters, his drawings, and many of the poems of *Les Orientales* and some in *Les Contemplations*. When the Hugo marriage came to an end, Sophie established herself in Paris in the former Feuillantines convent whose garden is recalled in many of Hugo's most lyrical poems. Hugo's mother saw to the proper education of her sons, and that is the first remarkable thing to be noted about Hugo. His innate genius was enhanced by an exposure to classical languages and authors, and at a very early age he began writing poetry, mainly imitative, which gained him unusual notice in French poetry competitions both in Toulouse (the famous *Jeux Floraux* competition) and even in the French Academy.

At the age of seventeen, Hugo met and fell in love with Adèle Foucher, whom he married in a religious ceremony performed in the church of Saint-Sulpice in Paris. The marriage itself brought to a head the question of Hugo's religious formation and beliefs. Hugo, it would seem, had never been baptized, but a false certificate was obtained through his father. Under the influence of the Abbé Lamennais, Hugo, already an ultraconservative royalist, seemed to be an orthodox Catholic. Time would only prove the contrary as Hugo became radical, almost socialist, while developing his own brand of personal religion, a type of Romantic deism.

The romantic fervor of Hugo's marriage to Adèle did not last more than a few years. Adèle fell under the spell of their friend Charles-Augustin Sainte-Beuve with whom she had a brief flirtatious and probably adulterous relationship.

HUGO AND THE ROMANTIC MOVEMENT

Meanwhile, Hugo's reputation as the leader of the new Romantic movement was gaining momentum, partly due to his presence in the salon of Charles Nodier at the Bibliothèque de l'Arsenal, but also because of his dazzling output of theatrical and poetic works in the new style, of which he can be considered the inventor. Starting with the series *Odes et ballades* in 1820, there is then the famous Romantic manifesto *Préface de Cromwell* (1827), which sets down Romantic principles of art as opposed to the seventeenth-century codification of classicism as found in Nicolas Boileau-Despréaux's *Art poétique*. Hugo's first major collection of new poetry, *Les Orientales*, was published in 1829, and the same year saw the triumph of the first truly Romantic play, Hugo's *Hernani*. In 1831 his first great Romantic novel, *Notre-Dame de Paris* (The hunchback of Notre Dame), was issued.

THE FRUITFUL YEARS OF THE 1830s

1833 was a crucial and determining year in the life of Hugo, for it was then that he met a second-rate, but beautiful, actress, Juliette Drouet who became, in a way, the second Madame Hugo, since their affair was sustained, in spite of many obstacles, to the end of their lives. In Hugo's own family, he and Adèle had sons and daughters. Insanity was an everpresent factor in Hugo's family. His brother Eugène apparently went mad when Victor married Adèle Foucher, and he died at an early age. Adèle, Hugo's last-born daughter, went mad as a result of an unreasonable and unrequited love for an English lieutenant named Pinson. His elder daughter was named Léopoldine. Readers are referred to the second poem of *Les Contemplations* entitled *Mes deux filles* (My two daughters), a tribute to Hugo's abiding sense of family that continued unabated until the last days of his life when he was left with only his two grandchildren, the record of which can be found in the late lyrics of *L'Art d'être grand-père* (The art of being a grandfather). The drowning death of Léopoldine and her husband Charles Vacquerie in the Seine river at Villequier, just three months after their marriage, in 1843, was to be but the beginning of the mental and spiritual suffering of the poet. It was while on a walking tour in southwestern France that Hugo learned of the death of his daughter when he read about the incident in a newspaper at Rochefort.

The years before the exile were filled with intense literary and political activity, and meditations (later to be amplified in his poetry and novels) on capital punishment, the plight of the poor, and social injustice.

The death of Léopoldine silenced the literary Hugo of the 1830s, a period noted for intense literary activity in poetry, novel, and theatre. In poetry, he produced the following volumes: *Les Feuilles d'automne* (Autumn leaves) in 1831; *Les Chants du crépuscule* (Twilight songs) in 1835; and *Les Voix intérieures* (Interior voices) and *Les Rayons et les ombres* (Light and shadow), both in 1840. In the theatre, on the heels of the triumph of *Hernani* came *Marion de Lorme*, 1831; *Le Roi s'amuse* (The king has a good time), 1832, which is the basis of the opera *Rigoletto; Lucrèce Borgia*,

1833; the same year, *Marie Tudor*; and *Ruy Blas*, 1838, which many consider to be Hugo's greatest play. 1843 saw the failed production of *Les Burgraves*; many manuals of literature regard this as the end of Romanticism in the theatre. In prose, Hugo was busy during the 1830s bringing out new editions of earlier works, such as *Le Dernier Jour d'un condamné* (The last day of a condemned man); *Bug-Jargal*, expressive of Hugo's abolitionist tendencies; another edition of the early novel *Han d'Islande*, and a new work concerning capital punishment, *Claude Gueux*.

POLITICAL ACTIVITY

At first a supporter of Louis Napoléon-Bonaparte for the presidential election of 1848, Hugo became more and more suspicious of this man, especially after the coup d'état of 1851 which installed him as Napoléon III (Second Empire 1851–1870). Hugo had especially objected to the passage of the Falloux act (Loi Falloux) which gave special monetary privileges to private (mainly Catholic) schools. Increasingly seen as an enemy of the establishment, Hugo realized that he had to face arrest or flee Paris; he went first to Brussels and then to the Channel Islands of Jersey and Guernsey.

EXILE

Hugo's exile lasted until the end of the Franco-Prussian war with the defeat of France and the fall of Napoléon III's empire. Hugo returned, almost like Voltaire, in triumph, to a country he had not seen for almost a generation. The exile years, although filled with grief and political anguish, did have a positive side, for in the solitude of the Channel Islands he was able to create some of his finest poetry as well as his enormously successful novel *Les Misérables*. The sorrow came in part from his efforts to contact his dead daughter Léopoldine through table turning. He was encouraged in this activity (which was then fashionable) by his friend Delphine Gay, a Romantic poet and spiritist who came to Jersey and introduced the Hugo clan to this form of poltergeist contact. Hugo became convinced, and, during two years, if we are to believe the diaries of his daughter Adèle, he thought himself to be in communication, not only with Léopoldine but also with William Shakespeare and other celebrities. After protesting the visit of Queen Victoria to the Emperor Napoléon III, Hugo moved from Jersey, where he produced his satirical indictment of Napoléon III *Les Châtiments* (1853, The punishments) and wrote the major part of *Les Contemplations* (1856), to Guernsey, where he purchased Hauteville House, now the property of the city of Paris and a literary touristic spot for Hugophiles, and produced the first volume of *La Légende des siècles* (The legend of the centuries), 1859.

The Hugo family was not at all content with the island exile. His wife frequently left for Paris. His daughter Adèle chased her unrequited love first to Canada and then to the Caribbean from whence she had to be returned years later, totally deranged, and confined to an asylum in Paris where she died in 1915. Son François-Victor spent his time translating Shakespeare. Hugo, himself, spent his time writing, supervising the renovation of Hauteville House, visiting Juliette Drouet who was put up in an apartment a short distance up the hill, and hiking from one end of the island to the other. The poet's promenades on the islands and previously in France attest to a taste for walking, a type of Romantic activity engaged in by many nineteenth-century people. Upon his return to Paris, now too old to do much walking, he could be seen riding the new double-decker omnibuses around the city.

RETURN TO PARIS, FINAL YEARS, AND DEATH

The return to Paris was triumphal. Hugo played an important role in the establishment of the Third Republic. He grew old reluctantly, living with Juliette Drouet who had fits of jealousy over his continual sexual adventures. He became a national hero, and he was feted on his eightieth birthday by a procession of Parisians who promenaded by his home, on the avenue now named after him, while he greeted them from his balcony. Though becoming physically frail, and giving the appearance of dozing at literary banquets, he made it clear that he understood all that was happening. He died in 1885. His last words were: "Je vois une lumière noire" (I see a dark light).

Hugo wanted no religious ceremony. His will indicated a deep belief in God but a total rejection of organized religion. In the spirit of charity, which characterized his entire life, he left one hundred thousand francs to the poor.

SUMMATION

To this day, Victor Hugo is recognized as one of the greatest French poets, whose poetic genius and intuition practically created the new Romantic vision. At the same time, because of his strict control of versification, his work became a model for the Parnassian school of poetry. Furthermore, many of his poems, especially *Mazeppa* from *Les Orientales*, anticipate symbolic devices, especially as found in the poetry of Arthur Rimbaud.

While the Romantic theatre, where the battle of Romanticism vs. Classicism was fought, is often supposed to be not of the same high quality as his poetry, a play such as *Hernani* is worthwhile precisely because of its soaring poetry. As for his novels, in spite of an earlier twentieth-century criticism (Percy Lubbock) that would downplay the "engaged" novelist in favor of the impersonality of a Gustave Flaubert or a Henry James, the tide seems to be turning, and it may be that criticism will soon regard *Les Misérables* as the greatest nineteenth-century French novel. Thus when André Gide answered the question of who was his favorite poet with his enigmatic "Victor Hugo, hélas," we might now also say that he was also one of the greatest novelists of that period.

RECOMMENDED BIOGRAPHIES

French and English Biographies

It is acknowledged both in France and in the English-speaking world that the André Maurois biography is the most professional and inclusive. Therefore this item is listed separately from the others, in spite of their high merits.

Maurois, André. *Olympio, ou, la vie de Victor Hugo*. Paris: Hachette, 1954.
Maurois, André. *Olympio: The Life of Victor Hugo*. Translated by Gerard Hopkins. New York: Harper and Brothers, 1956.

French Biographies

Barbou, Alfred. *La Vie de Victor Hugo*. Paris: Charpentier, 1886.
Barrère, Jean-Bertrand. *Victor Hugo, l'homme et l'oeuvre*. Paris: Hatier, 1967.
Decaux, Alain. *Victor Hugo*. Paris: Libraire académique Perrin, 1984.
Gregh, Fernand. *Victor Hugo, sa vie, son oeuvre*. Paris: Flammarion, 1954.
Juin, Hubert. *Victor Hugo*. 3 vols. Paris: Flammarion, 1984–1986.
Venzac, Géraud. *Les Origines littéraires de Victor Hugo*. Paris: Bloud et Gay, 1955.

English Biographies

Houston, John Porter. *Victor Hugo*. New York: Twayne, 1974.
Richardson, Joanna. *Victor Hugo*. New York: St. Martin's Press, 1976.
Swinburne, Algernon. *A Study of Victor Hugo*. Philadelphia: R. West, 1978.

A

Abrantès, Laure Junot, Duchesse d'. Laure Junot Abrantès (1784–1838) was, by her life and her memoirs, an important figure during the Napoleonic era. Her husband, General Junot, was military governor of Paris in 1806. Upon the death of her demented husband, who committed suicide, brought on by a nervous depression after a defeat in battle in Portugal, she became, for some time, the mistress of Honoré de Balzac (*See* Balzac, Honoré de). Reduced to a precarious financial existence, she published her memoirs, with Balzac's aid, which recount political and social events occurring in France during the First Empire through the early years of the reign of Louis-Philippe. The work enjoyed a considerable success.

Hugo's poem in *Les Rayons et les ombres** (poem XII) was inspired by the poet's rightful indignation at the callousness of the city of Paris which refused this daughter of the First Empire a burial site in Père-Lachaise cemetery. Hugo's poem directly confronts this insult: Could not France do its duty and provide a grave for this noble casket (strophe 1); and the concluding strophe 11 sees this refusal of a burial site as an affront to the Napoleonic Empire. It concludes with a recall to Hugo's own plea for the Vendôme column to be dedicated to Bonaparte, and for the city to give this noble lady a decent burial. His poem is a monument to this woman who was much maligned by indifferent bureaucrats who had quickly forgotten the meaning of the Empire.

Académie Française and Victor Hugo. The origins of the Academy go back to a literary circle that met in the home of Valentin Conrart (1603–1675), the Academy's first secretary, and received official approbation in 1635 from Cardinal Richelieu. Richelieu saw a political advantage in having a literary society subject to royal supervision, a type of censorship that would foster works favorable to the government. Since 1639 it has been limited to forty members called the "Immortals." Membership is not limited to literary figures but includes lawyers, doctors, statesmen, and religious leaders, as well. A candidate for election must so declare and make official lobbying visits. The main task of the Academy, which also bestows literary and film awards, is to write the official dictionary of the French language and compile a grammar. Conservative and conciliatory in nature, it has frequently denied admission to some of France's most important writers, Molière, for example. Only recently did the Academy accept women, starting with Marguerite Yourcenar (1903–1987) in 1983, and intellectuals not born in France (for example, Léopold Senghor, the first president of Senegal).

The conservative bent of the Academy manifested itself during the formative years of the Romantic movement. As in the time of Richelieu, when at his request it intervened in the quarrel about *Le Cid*, Corneille's tragicomedy of 1636, the Academy, which was dominated by eighteenth-century neoclassicists, fulminated against the new literary trends found in such new journals as *La Muse française** in which Hugo was publishing, in the salons of Charles Nodier* (1780–1844) at the Arsenal Library, as well as at Hugo's own literary gatherings held during the 1820s.

Hugo's relations with the Academy began during his early years and continued through his unsuccessful attempts to be elected to that body until he was successful in his bid in 1841, when he was thirty-nine years old. In 1817, when Hugo was fifteen years old, the Academy set as the subject of its poetry prize the theme: "Happiness as Dependent on Study in All Aspects of Living." Young Hugo entered the competition, submitting a poem of 394 lines (an early mark of his tendency toward exuberance). He received an honorable mention for this entry, and a part of the poem was read during an open (public) meeting of the Academy. The committee had found it difficult to believe that such a poem could be written by such a young adolescent.

Hugo, who knew that the peerage he desired would depend on his election to the Academy, presented himself, in 1834, for a seat left vacant. He lost this election to Mercier Dupaty, a writer of farces. Upon the death of Michaud, the historian, he made another attempt in 1839, but because of the indecisive balloting the election was put off for three months. In December 1839, the death of the Archbishop of Paris, Monsignor de Quelen, created another vacancy. A double election was held on February 20, 1840, and again Hugo was defeated. With the death of Népomucène Lemercier (1771–1840), a writer of tragedies based on national subjects, the path seemed clear, and indeed, he was elected to the Academy on January 7, 1841.

Hugo's reception speech of June 3, 1841, which betrayed his political astuteness and motivation, was pleasing perhaps to conservatives, even some liberals, and certainly to the Bonapartists. Opening with a pane-gyric to Napoléon-Bonaparte,* regarded by Hugo as the possessor of a providential power, the speech stressed Napoléon's genius, a consistent idea in Hugo's set of ideas. Shakespeare was, according to Hugo, another example of genius illuminating and directing mankind. The speech contains what historically appears to be a startling reference to Bonaparte's triumph, a position Hugo repudiated eleven years later in the conclusion of his diatribe against Napoléon III,* L'Expiation* (Book V, poem XIII of Les Châtiments* (1852). There is a long meditation on the events of 1793, in which Hugo saw a divine plan, as he did with Napoléon and out of which he would elaborate his novel, Quatrevingt-treize.* The speech concluded with a trite praise of the superiority of French literature. The reply of M. de Salvandy, director of the Academy, which matched some of Hugo's truisms and platitudes, warmly congratulated Hugo for his Notre-Dame de Paris.*

Hugo's acceptance speech is not only true Hugo in style and structure, but also a well-planned document of conciliation. He wanted the peerage and the power that went with being a member of the Academy. The French press interpreted Hugo's election as a mere stepping stone to a parliamentary career, and such was to be the case.

BIBLIOGRAPHY

Souday, Paul. Les Romantiques à l'Académie. Paris: Flammarion, 1928.
Trois Siècles de l'Académie Française par les Quarante. Paris: Firmin-Didot, 1935.

A Chateaubriand. This is not one of Hugo's great poems. Written in 1824 and placed as Ode Two in Book Three (1824–1828) of Odes et Ballades,* when Hugo was just twenty-two years old, it is filled with idolatrous admiration for the middle-aged Chateaubriand, then fifty-six. If Jean-Jacques Rousseau can rightly be regarded as the founding father of French Romanticism, then Chateaubriand and Mme. de Staël can be considered the second generation, which is commonly called pre-Romantic. Chateaubriand knew all about the turmoil and vicissitudes of the French Revolution. His ardent defense during the restoration of conservative politics and Romantic Catholicism were greatly appreciated by the young Hugo. Hugo had declared at the age of fourteen (July 10, 1816, in his diary): Je veux être Chateaubriand ou rien (I want to be Chateaubriand or nothing), a type of fervor and adulation that occasionally surfaces in French literary circles; for example, the cult of homosexuality that surrounded André Gide* in the twentieth century, or the imitations of the creation of Alfred Jarry (1873–1907) in the personage of Ubu roi, created in 1896.

This ode is divided into three parts all of which say more or less the same thing, namely that Chateaubriand's genius thrives on turbulence and discord; it is a genius that prefers tempests to sea breezes. This description must refer to Chateaubriand's fanatical defense of the Bourbon restoration. Its concluding three lines offer an interesting twist on Chateaubriand's ascendancy to the heights of glory, but with the use of the verb *tomber* (to fall): *Quand le sort t'a frappé, tu lui dois rendre grâce,/ Toi qu'on voit à chaque disgrâce/Tomber plus haut encore que tu n'étais monté!* (When fate struck you, you obligingly thanked him/You whom we see at each instance of disgrace/Fall still higher than you had already climbed).

The *Odes et Ballades* do not stand out as the best examples of Hugo's poetry. Perhaps because of a strict adherence to royalist and conservative principles, but also by the desire to get ahead in the official literary establishment, which of course Hugo succeeded in doing.

Ad majorem dei gloriam. This satirical piece (poem seven from *Les Châtiments*,* dated November 1852), composed of sixty-six lines divided into eleven strophes takes as its title the Jesuit motto: "All for the Greater Glory of God." It depicts the Society of Jesus as an evil and cunning bunch of religious politicians, the enemies of justice and freedom. By giving them the narrative voice, except for the last two lines where God speaks, the Jesuits are condemned by their own evil fanaticism, as interpreted by Hugo.

The Jesuits, founded by Ignatius of Loyola in Paris in 1534, are generally credited with being the agents of the Counter-Reformation, and, indeed, they recovered whole countries (Austria, for example) from the Reformation. The Jesuits have always been known for producing priests of superior mental ability in all fields of literature and science. Their involvement in politics, however, frequently got them into trouble with secular authority. Without truly deserving a derogatory name, nonetheless they came to have one. Thus, a secondary meaning for Jesuits found in dictionaries is that of practitioners of casuistry (deciding, in a most lenient manner, particular cases of conscience) and also those who are seen as crafty and engaged in secret intrigues. Having become the most numerous and popular of the religious orders, especially because of their work in education, scholarship, and foreign missions, the Jesuits provoked much hostility, especially in the rationalistic eighteenth century which, in France, was known for its anticlerical and antipapal stances. The group was suppressed by Pope Clement XIV in 1773 but was restored in 1814 by Pope Pius VII.

Hugo's anticlericalism, which surfaces throughout his poetry, often is coupled with a scorn for certain pedantic schoolmasters. This is an apt coupling since the Jesuits tried to control education all over Europe; the founding of secondary schools and colleges was one of their main projects.

The poem displays the same fanaticism found in Hugo's play *Torque-mada** (1869), where extreme notions submerge any authentic religious faith. As the narrator speaks, a chilling effect seizes the reader, probably akin to hearing the ravings of a mad but charismatic dictator, such as Adolf Hitler. The narrator states that the Jesuits will conquer, they will be masters, using military tactics (Ignatius was a soldier, and the Jesuits are commonly referred to as the pope's troops). The poem states that they are opposed to liberty, progress, law, virtue, rights, and talents, surely a hyperbolic and unjust remark. Their casuistry is displayed in the second strophe in which war and execution are justified. The Jesuits appear as obscurantists opposed to the spirit of the times.

References are made to the burning of the reformer Jan Hus.* Since he was burned in 1415, they cannot put him to the stake, so it is proposed they burn Gutenberg (1399–1468) who also died before the time of the Jesuits. Gutenberg, however, invented the printing press, a main prop of the Reformation. The Jesuit narrator proposes putting the arch anarchist Jean-Jacques Rousseau in prison because of his liberal and undisciplined methods of education, as opposed to their own rigorous methods, and suggests putting Voltaire in a dog kennel: *Mettons Jean-Jacques au bagne et Voltaire au chenil*. Voltaire, of course, educated by the Jesuits, became their arch enemy. Voltaire's biting wit is displayed in his short poem concerning a snake that bit a Jesuit: *L'autre jour, au fond d'un vallon,/Un serpent piqua Jean Fréron,/ Que pensez-vous qu'il arriva?/ Ce fut le serpent qui creva*. (The other day, down in a valley/ A serpent bit Jean Fréron,/ What do you think happened?/ It was the serpent who died.)

In the conclusion of the poem, God tells the Jesuits that, although they might succeed in scaling the highest mountain, he would remove them from it.

A good part of Hugo's criticism of the Jesuits had to do with their involvement in education in France, and with the famous Falloux Act* which granted special monetary rights to Catholic schools, a law opposed by Hugo.

Aïrolo. Aïrolo is the protagonist of Hugo's published play *Mangeront-ils?** (Will they eat?) from the 1886 edition of plays written during his exile, entitled *Théâtre en liberté* (Free theatre), an obvious reference not only to the political suppression of theatre in France during the nineteenth century, something of which Hugo had often been a victim, but also, of course, to his vituperative, revengeful spirit against Napoléon III.*

Aïrolo is a type of clown or tramp, a stock figure, a mocker of conformity and social mores. Aïrolo's humor goes beyond the Gallic spirit, *l'esprit gaulois*, which takes a tongue-in-cheek attitude toward authority, especially for Hugo the bourgeois authority of the nineteenth century.

Such a type harkens back to the medieval poetry of François Villon, but it also has affinities with the personage of the street gamin Gavroche of *Les Misérables*.*

Aïrolo as a personage is an antiestablishment creation with a long tradition in France which reasserts itself starting with the Figaro figure in the late-eighteenth-century theatre of Beaumarchais.

***Album de 1869*.** This work is centered about Hugo's trip to the International Peace Conference in Lausanne,* Switzerland, in 1869. It contains seven poems, all dated from October of that year, written after Hugo's return to Brussels. In the edition of the *Imprimerie Nationale*, these poems were tucked away between the *Nouveaux Châtiments* and *Les Années funestes** (The dreadful years). They are now placed properly in volume 2 of the Pléiade (Gallimard) edition of Hugo's poetry.

Alcibiados, Don. This pretentious protagonist of a verse fragment found in Hugo's *Comédies cassées* epitomizes bourgeois social values. In Hugo's fragment, Don Alcibiados seems to fuse Spanish concepts of honor, a subject about which Hugo knew a lot (*Hernani**) with *comme il fautisme*, a French concept about how things should be. Don Alcibiados' wife has been unfaithful, but rather than turn her over to the civil authorities for punishment (a subject Hugo personally knew about from his affair with Léonie d'Aunet*), he decides to punish her himself. Is Hugo mocking the double standards of the nineteenth century? Such may be the case. Hugo himself, partly bourgeois despite his political radicalism, often mocked the middle class, especially its wish to keep women in second-class civil status. This fragment dates from 1853.

This theme seems to be a derivative of the middle-class dramas of Diderot (1713–1784): *Le Fils naturel* (The bastard), 1757, and *Le Père de famille* (The father), 1758, both of which are rather pompous in construction, revealing Diderot's budding bourgeois values. Another source could be the tradition of the late-eighteenth-century *comédie larmoyante* (tearjerkers).

***Amy Robsart*.** This prose drama in five acts was partly composed in 1822, further completed in 1827, and given one performance at the Odéon theatre on February 13, 1828. It was a total failure and Hugo withdrew it. Alexandre Soumet* had proposed this topic to Hugo, based on *Kenilworth* (1821), one of the best of Sir Walter Scott's historical novels.

Hugo's play loosely follows Scott's narrative: it depicts Queen Elizabeth I's displeasure upon learning of the news of the marriage of one of her favorites, the Earl of Leicester. In Scott's novel, Leicester's bride, Amy Robsart, is hidden in the home of Richard Varney, who was dependent upon Leicester's patronage. An entanglement of lies causes Edmund

Tressilian (who had also courted Amy) to believe, falsely, that Amy is Varney's mistress, and he attempts to persuade Amy to return to her parents' home. Tressilian informs the queen that Varney has seduced Amy. All these bits of false information result in Amy's death.

Hugo takes a great deal of license with this narrative. In his play, Amy's father, Sir Hugh Robsart, is concerned about the reputation of his noble family. He is confused through most of the play, as is the queen, as to whom Amy is or is not married. Hugo adds a subtext of speculation on Elizabeth's interest in Leicester, thus casting the virgin-queen as potential wife to Leicester. The action then centers on suspicions cast by Richard Varney to Amy (Act III) as to Leicester's interest in the queen, perhaps his ambitions to be king. Bewildered, Amy becomes convinced by Varney that her marriage to Leicester will be annulled so that he may marry the queen. Furthermore, it is Leicester's wish that she marry Varney. Varney is thus portrayed as a villain, despised by Amy who considers him nothing more than Leicester's valet.

Another important deviation from the Scott text is the role played by Fibbertigibbet (also known in the Scott text as Dickie Sluddge). Because Amy's pleading once spared his life, he is her devoted follower. He tries on several occasions to aid her, first by making sure she does not drink the potion prepared by Alasco, the magician-astrologer, and then by attempting to free her from her tower prison where she had been sent by Elizabeth. The play concludes with Amy's death, which was caused by her falling through a trap door in the prison, and a final immolation of both Varney and Alasco when they die in a fire set by Flibbertigibbet.

This play is notable for its many scene changes (characteristic of the new *drame**) and for its reliance on what are to become stock characters of the new Romantic historical theatre. The personage of Alasco the astrologer, for example, anticipates the role of a similar predictor of good and bad fortune, Côme Ruggieri, the astrologer in Dumas père's drama *Henri III et sa cour* (Henri III and his court), 1829.

The play aims at a kind of quotidian realism with much discussion of the latest fashion models and digressions on the accuracy of astrology in predicting the future. This may be considered as impeding the movement of the dramatic action. Thus the first three acts drag on and on; the concluding ones move rapidly; and act 5, too quickly, as if Hugo were anxious to get the thing finished.

The role of Flibbertigibbet is of special interest. He is cast as a *lutin*, that is, a mischievous sprite, imp, elf, or goblin. Indeed, early in the play, he does frighten his former partner Alasco by playing the role of a ghost, for Alasco had thought him dead. While he truly has no magical powers, he comes to the rescue in amusing ways, recalling the Puck tradition in English literature, a type that extends from the Middle Ages through the Elizabethan period. Puck is above all famous for his role in Shakespeare's

A Midsummer Night's Dream where he is, of course, more impish than the character in either Hugo or Scott.

The plot line of *Amy Robsart* is cluttered. The historical novel has more time to explain character motivation and action.

'ANÁΓKH. Destiny or fate* in Greek, the concluding prefatory remark of Victor Hugo explains the motif of his 1831 novel *Notre-Dame de Paris:* *C'est sur ce mot qu'on a fait ce livre* (This work is built on that word). Romantic obsession with the concept of fate is present elsewhere in Hugo's writings and can be discerned in most of the major Romantic writers. It even penetrates the character of Charles in Gustave Flaubert's *Madame Bovary* (1857). After Emma's suicide, Charles learns through letters that she had been adulterous, and he exclaims, "*C'est la faute de la fatalité*" (It is the fault of fate), proving that Romanticism has even filtered down to a country bumpkin. In Hugo's historical meditations, the concept of fate shifts to a kind of Marxian determinism—hence, for Hugo, the inevitability of the French Revolution, the Reign of Terror, and the advent of Napoléon Bonaparte.

Ane, L'. In this very long, satirical poem of 3,000 lines, Hugo fulminates, not against his political enemies as in *Les Châtiments,* * but against philosophers and academic pedants. Published in 1880, the same year as *Religions et Religion,* * the poem testifies to an anger that dates back to the exile, for *L'Ane* was written in 1857–1858. Hugo, prophet of a new democratic society, demonstrates an iconoclastic mood in this work: mankind's enemies, philosophers and theologians, are under attack. The general public was somewhat amazed with his prolific poetic production during these last years: *La Pitié suprême** in 1879; *Les Quatre Vents de l'esprit* in 1881; and *Torquemada* in 1882. The truth is that all these works had been written long before; only a few editorial additions were made at the time of publication.

Satire mixed with black humor best describes *L'Ane*. The donkey, Patience, first criticizes Immanuel Kant, then reviews science and philosophy, stressing contradictions. Hundreds of names of philosophers, theologians, and scholars are cited in a negative evaluation when compared with the positive image of theology and philosophy found in *Les Mages* (poem twenty-three of Book Six of *Les Contemplations**. This poem, however, places heavy emphasis on ancient religious and philosophical systems while stressing the primacy of the poet as leader of mankind: *Pourquoi donc faites-vous des prêtres/Quand vous en avez parmi vous?* (Why do you create priests when you already have them amongst you?). *Les Mages*, almost equal in length to *L'Ane*, should be considered its positive corollary.

The fifth part, a well-deserved attack on nineteenth-century pedagogical pedants who deform the hearts and minds of children, corresponds to *A Propos d'Horace* (poem thirteen of Book One, *Aurore, of Les Contemplations*): *Marchands de grec! Marchands de latin!, cuistres, dogues! Philistins! Magisters! Je vous hais, pédagogues*! (Sellers of Greek and Latin, watch dogs, pedants, Philistines, schoolmasters, I hate you pedagogues). Since *L'Ane* was composed on the heels of the publication of *Les Contemplations*, it is natural that there is a connection between the vehemence of the poem reserved for publication until 1880 and several other poems in *Les Contemplations* against a too rigid, but formless and heartless type of education. In both *L'Ane* and *Les Contemplations*, we find Hugo as defender of the young against a societal perversity disguised as education. Here he is in the best tradition of the *Emile* of Jean-Jacques Rousseau, outdoing him because of his poetic power.

In French the word for donkey or jackass also has the pejorative meaning of a limited, ignorant blockhead. Hence the figurative intent would be comprehensible to any French reader.

Angelo, tyran de Padoue. This play in five prose acts was performed with success on April 28, 1835, with two famous actresses, Mesdemoiselles Mars and Marie Dorval. The play was such a success that it was reprised by Rachel* in 1850 and then later by Sarah Bernhardt.* It was also the inspiration for Amigo Borto's libretto *La Gioconda*. This opera by Amilcare Ponchielli was first performed at La Scala, Milan, on April 8, 1876. Under this form, Hugo's drama still enjoys popular success.

Hugo's attempts at prose drama do not have the high reputation of his verse plays which, enhanced by their soaring poetry, help the spectator ignore the frequent use of melodrama and sensationalism. *Angelo* is built on two premises: Venice's absolute domination over smaller northeastern Italian principalities, such as Padua, and romantic love interests, the more important of the two elements. Angelo, who represents Venice in Padua, is in love with an actress, La Tisbe, who in turn loves Rodolfo, who is in love with Catarina, who is married to Angelo against her will. The agent of Venice, Homodei, seems also to be in love with Catarina, but he seeks, as does everyone else in this play, vengeance, and then death. La Tisbe, a well-known actress, has perhaps the best dramatic lines in the play; she has character and depth. It is not often that Hugo gives such a powerful role to a woman.

The play stresses Romantic absolutism, eternal love, or death.

It is astonishing how Victor Hugo's theatre remains today so successful in spite of the hostility of numerous critics.

Animals. Victor Hugo exhibited empathy for all living creatures, beautiful or not, for example: *J'aime l'araignée et j'aime l'ortie* (I love the spider and I love the nettle; poem twenty-seven of Book Three, *Les Luttes et les* *rêves*, of *Les Contemplations**) or *Je payai le pêcheur qui passa son chemin*, (I paid the fisherman who passed on his way; poem twenty-two of Book Five, *En Marche*, of *Les Contemplations*) in which the crustacean which he had just purchased tried to bite him, and which he releases back into the sea: *Sois béni, pauvre maudit!* (Blessing on you, poor cursed one). In this short poem, Hugo acknowledges the ugliness of this crab with its awful mouth. Had this crab been larger it would have been a hydra; smaller, a wood louse. Hugo contemplates ugliness, be it in man or animal, with sympathy and without repugnance (as he does with Quasimodo* in *Notre-Dame de Paris**). Such poems contrast with exaltation in the varieties found in the animal world; here, all across Hugo's poetry, can be found praise in the manner of Saint Francis of Assisi to all creation. This is particularly true in regard to Hugo's poems about birds, which are numerous, and can be explained only in terms of their freedom which is expressed in their ability to fly.

Hugo cannot tolerate persecution of either man or animal. Thus he reacts to the pillory of Quasimodo. In one of the longest poems of *Les Contemplations, Melancholia* (poem two, Book Three, *Les Luttes et les rêves*), Hugo places cruelty to animals in the same category as other alienations within the human family. Thus, in this poem, we are given illustrations of man's cruelty to man—a poor woman with starving children and an adulterous husband, a poor working girl who finally sells herself into prostitution, a poor man sent to prison for stealing a loaf of bread (anticipating Jean Valjean*)—and the terrible vision of a horse being beaten to death by a drunken drayman. Hugo gives the "unthinking" horse a profound psychology, a fear born from confusion. The horse has no way of understanding who or what is beating him, the block of stone he is hauling, or the whip: *Ce que lui veut la pierre et ce que lui veut l'homme?* (What does the stone want from him, what does the man want from him?). The scene in this poem is reminiscent of one attributed to the philosopher Friedrich Nietzsche, who tried to stop another drunken drayman from beating a horse to death in Turin. Nietzsche, it is reported, embraced the horse and fainted in a romantic exaltation.

Pierre Albouy, in the Pléiade edition of *Les Contemplations*, cites Hugo's thoughts (derived from the document *Alpes et Pyrénées*) on this subject, which can be summarized as follows: Hugo worked out of a sentiment of universal pity which extends the law of love, announced by Jesus, to animals. Furthermore, the poet doubted that man could, without violating some secret and paternal intention of the creator, make oxen, donkeys, and horses the convicts of creation. Another poem from *Les Contemplations, La Chouette*, enables the reader to come closer to Hugo's penetration of the mysteries of animal life. This becomes a means of fusing aesthetic Romanticism into a moral Romanticism. Hugo, in both his prose and poetry, is trying to decipher the hieroglyphics of the animals. The signs are there for those who know how to decipher them. The noble language of the lion and the eagle is forgotten for a moment, and the *patois* of the dispossessed—the crab, owl, pig, bat, and toad—is to be heard.

Hugo gives to the beasts of the earth the possibility of telling man something about good and evil, vice and virtue. If man lost his ability to communicate with nature and the animals at the Fall, the animals who share the Fall, but with less culpability, are capable of teaching man the road back to God, according to Hugo.

On another level, leaving philosophy aside, Hugo's exaltation in all of creation, nature, and the animal world had more practical ramifications. An important aspect of the nineteenth century, engendered by Romanticism, was a concern for, and the protection of, animals. In this regard we note the founding, in England in 1824, of the animal welfare society which was given the royal seal in 1840 at the request of Queen Victoria. In France, the Société Protectrice des Animaux was founded in 1845 by Jacques Delmas de Grammont. Ironically, legislation for the protection of minor workers, although inaugurated quite early in England, lagged behind the protection of animals. In any case, for the first time in Western history, concern for animals was taking hold; the spirit of Francis of Assisi, long ignored by the medieval church, was coming into play.

Hugo's prose and poetry make specific references to animals, especially to dogs. In this regard, he is anticipating the work of the Franciscan-spirited Francis Jammes (1868–1938) whose poetry gives equality in his Christian eschatalogy to animals and man, as for example in his poem *Prière pour aller au paradis avec les ânes* (Prayer to go to heaven with the donkeys). Hugo sensed the intuitive intelligence of animal life; specifically, this can be found in his evaluation of his own dog Ponto,* who figures in *Les Contemplations*; in the dog Rask* in the early novel *Bug-Jargal*; and in the character of the tamed wolf Homo* in *L'homme qui rit*.* In these examples, the animals mimetically reproduce the spiritual and humanitarian urges of their masters, in the case of Ponto, metaphysical speculations on Channel Island walks; with Rask, the ability to carry out humane missions in the manner of Bug-Jargal. The only twentieth-century realization of what Hugo intuited is found in the training of seeing-eye dogs to aid the blind.

Année terrible, L'. This very long collection of poetic meditations on the Franco-Prussian War and France's defeat at Sédan is divided into one calendar year from August 1870 through July 1871. It is Hugo's aesthetic equivalent of the historical event, not just of the war, but of the siege of Paris and the events of the Paris commune. It is poetically the equivalent of Emile Zola's *La débâcle*, with less of the spirit of vengeance felt by the naturalistic writer who had chronicled the entire Second Empire* in a spirit of vituperation. Indeed, it could be said that Hugo, in his personal political reactions, through debate and speeches, and in the poems themselves, seeks reconciliation and pardon especially for the Parisian communards. But this pity is extended also to the Prussian enemy.

While the greater part of the collection was written first at Vianden in Luxembourg after Hugo's expulsion from Belgium for public expression of his sympathy for the Parisian communards, and then in Paris, the study of the manuscripts reveals that some poems or portions thereof date back to the late 1850s, giving Hugo an almost prophetic voice. *L'Année terrible* is of enormous importance in evaluating what Hugo lived through, and which by his long life and poetic production make him a true symbol of the nineteenth century in France. He was born on the heels of the French Revolution, was a childhood witness to the Napoleonic wars, grew politically and philosophically from conservatism to liberalism to a type of socialism. *L'Année terrible* is indicative of a full-blown charity for suffering humanity, a saintly characteristic that was a mark of his declining years.

The collection is dedicated to Paris, Capital of the People. Written before the events of 1870–1871, the extremely long prologue is indicative of Hugo's evolution as a thinker. He arrives, as did the historian Jules Michelet, at a belief in the goodness, solidarity, and leadership of the masses. Thus the conservative Hugo, who became the liberal of the revolution of 1830, with its motto of Louis-Philippe "King of the French," as opposed to the ancien régime concept of the "King of France," now avows the role of the "people" (not unlike the spirit that was supposed to govern the Communist revolution in Russia). After reviewing human history from the Greeks, Romans, and forward in time, he concluded: *Je veux la république et je chasse César* (I want a republic and I expel Caesar). The republic for Hugo is the path to the single most important element in mankind's trajectory, the concept of liberty.

L'Année terrible, then, can be read as a poetic history of the Franco-Prussian War, the defeat of France at Sédan, the siege of Paris, and the events of the commune. The poem entitled *Sédan* ponders the surrender of France and Napoléon III. *Its spirit is milder but it has some of the intent, if not the poetic vigor, of *Expiation** in the section that evokes the battle of Waterloo. Another poem, entitled *Après Sédan* and dedicated to the France of 1872, asks both France and Prussia to engage in a moral purification. Read as a sequential narrative, the Paris poems give us realistic images such as "Paris blockaded," "Paris slandered in Berlin," "Paris on fire," "The executions," and "On seeing Prussian cadavers floating in the Seine." While the poet still reclaims Alsace and Lorraine for France, he supports reconciliation between the countries, and within France. He desires a general pardon for the atrocities committed by both the Versailles government troops and the communards who had held hostages, among them the archbishop of Paris whom they executed (see the poem *Pas de représailles* [No reprisals]).

Throughout we not only hear the very personal voice of Victor Hugo, but we also sense his central stage appearance in the events of 1870–1871. A poem dedicated to his granddaughter Jeanne creates a family myth which parallels that of the city of Paris. In the birthday poem, *A petite Jeanne*, we find the lyricism found earlier in the young father Hugo concerning Léopoldine Hugo* and Adèle Hugo* in such poems as *Lorsque l'enfant paraît* (When the child comes) or *Mes deux filles* (My two daughters*). Jeanne was born on September 29, 1869, and for Hugo the innocence of childhood is contrasted with the horrors of war. Another poignant note is found in the poem *Une bombe aux Feuillantines* (A bomb in the Feuillantines). The former Feuillantines convent, where Hugo and his brothers had lived with their mother, had been a joyful place during the Napoleonic period. Visiting there now, in the company of Juliette Drouet, he discovers that the house and garden are gone. What the modern world had contributed to the obliteration of that lyrical spot by paving it over was completed by the bomb that fell on it. However, the memory remains in his heart: *Le passé devant lui, plein de voix enfantines, Apparaissait; c'est là qu'étaient les Feuillantines* (The past before him, filled with children's voices/ appeared; that's where the Feuillantines were). This type of recall of the past is a consistent motif in Hugo's poetry; here it equals a similar procedure found in the bucolic idyll *Tristesse d'Olympio* (Olympio's sadness).

L'Année terrible is not the greatest of all of Hugo's poetic works, but it stands out singularly for its historical narrative of the events that took place during the collapse of the Second Empire and the ushering in of a new world order, the Third Republic.

Années funestes. The *Années funestes* (The dreadful years), a lyrical and satirical collection of verse, was published in 1898, thirteen years after Hugo's death. This collection is more personal and even more severe in terms of the exile years than *Les Châtiments.** Hugo had no interest in publishing this work; the wisdom of old age was advising the poet to forget the past and to work toward healing the wounds of France, in a manner similar to Emile Zola's* final volume of the *Rougon-Macquart* series, *Docteur Pascal*. The collection contains a very long poem (556 lines, each in five syllables) dedicated to Giuseppe Garibaldi,* entitled *Mentana*. In this poem Hugo continued the verbal acrobatics he had mastered as early as 1829 (*Les Djinns** in *Les Orientales**).

Antisemitism. On a personal level, Victor Hugo, like Emile Zola* in France, or Charles Dickens in England, are all known as defenders of individual rights and the liberty of all. Hugo's concept of the United

States of Europe is visible evidence of this stance. A superficial reading, however, of some of Hugo's fiction, might convince some modern sensitivities of a current of antisemitism in his thought. Such a conclusion should be dismissed as false. Thus, Jewish people are depicted as weak and sniveling in *Torquemada,** which is set in the time of the Catholic kings of Spain in the fifteenth century. But this very play has been published by Hugo as a protest against the Russian antisemitic "pogroms." Another problem arises from the French language which uses the same word for both noun and adjective (*juif, juive*) as opposed to English which clearly differentiates the adjective, Jewish, from the noun, Jew. The antisemitism found in the work of nineteenth-century writers is a cultural inheritance, not all of whose origins are clear. It can be stated that the whole society of the time took this prejudice in its cultural stride; Jews were seen as existing out of the mainstream. It is in such a light that what appears to be overt antisemitism in Dickens's *Bleak House*, or in Hugo or Zola (for example his novel *L'Argent*), is a cultural given. The prejudice, if it is there, is passive, almost unconscious.

More blatant forms of antisemitism, such as Charles Baudelaire's* poem *Une nuit que j'étais près d'une affreuse Juive* (During a night that I spent near a horrible Jewess) from *Les Fleurs du mal*, seems more intentional and mean-spirited than anything to be found in Hugo. Hugo, therefore, must be considered within his cultural context.

A.Q.C.H.E.B. (A quelque chose hasard est bon). This lighthearted work, written by Hugo at the age of fifteen, was described by the author as a "Vaudeville," a term that is fulfilled in the twenty-four scenes of this play. It not only contains "spontaneous" songs inspired by the action, but also dialect in the speech and the poems of Maître Jacques, proprietor of the rooming house. In this it recalls French medieval farce. It is farcical also in the introduction of a rogue character, Rognespèce, a village judge who tries to swindle Saint Léger of his rightful monies. The total nonsense of this work is furthermore based in linguistic absurdities, such as Rognespèce's wooing speech to Céline: *Pour vous je deviens hypocondre* (For you I am becoming a hypochondriac). He claims to have loved Céline for the last twenty years; yet she is but sixteen. His sidekick, the court clerk, is referred to as Monsieur Polygraphe. The linguistic somersaults found in *A.Q.C.H.E.B.* hark back to the medieval *Farce de Maître Pathelin*, and to Molière and anticipate the linguistically based theatre of the absurd of the twentieth-century playwright Eugène Ionesco.* The plot is ridiculously simple. Saint-Léger, a soldier on the run from civil and military authorities, instantly falls in love with Céline, daughter of M. d'Escour and sister of Saint-Léger's best friend, Armand, an old army buddy. Unfortunately, M. d'Escour has planned a marriage for young Céline with Dorval, Saint-Léger's officer in the army. Throughout, Saint-

Léger is unaware that Armand is Céline's brother; in fact, at one time, he takes him for a rival. All ends well, however, with the guilty Rognespèce punished, and the father and the ex-suitor Dorval wishing the couple well.

In this vaudeville, the young Hugo continued certain French theatrical traditions, namely the rococo love and chance themes developed by Pierre Marivaux (1688–1763), especially in his *Le Jeu de l'amour et du hasard* (1730), which as in this play of Hugo, ends with the characters singing the essential meaning of the work. But these are Romantic modifications of the rococo spirit, maintaining the spirit of wit and humor, minus the rococo cynicism. It is good to see some humor in Romanticism, for it is not too frequently found there, perhaps with the exception of the drawing-room comedies of Alfred de Musset* (1810–1857), especially his *On ne badine pas avec l'amour* (Do not trifle with love) (1834), which, while incarnating the wit found in Hugo's early vaudeville, does end on an ambiguous but tragic note. Hugo's work, written at such an early age, is worthy of attention.

Art d'être grand-père, (L'). By the time Hugo had published *The Art of Being a Grandfather* (1877), all but one of his own children had died: Léopold died during the first year of his life, Léopoldine (*see* Hugo, Léopoldine) drowned in 1843, Charles died in 1871, and François-Victor died in 1873. For all practical purposes, Adèle Hugo,* who was confined to a home for the deranged, did not die before 1915, but in her alienation she could be considered dead to any family life. Hugo now had only his two grandchildren, born to Charles and his wife Alice Lehaene. These personal losses probably only augmented a strong, bourgeois familial poetry centered around the children, dating back to such early poems as *Lorsque l'enfant paraît** (When the child comes) and to the touching lyrics found in *Les contemplations*,* *Mes deux filles* (My two daughters*), or the entire section dedicated to Léopoldine in the same collection, *Pauca meae*, where the poems of grief *Demain, des l'aube** (Tomorrow at dawn) and *A Villequier* are not able to crush totally the joyful memories of his children, as well as such poems as *Pure innocence! Vertu sainte!* (Pure innocence! Holy virtue!) and *Elle avait pris ce pli dans son âge enfantin* (She got into that habit at an early age).

The Art of Being a Grandfather, therefore, is but the crowning achievement of the aging poet, who proclaimed to the end of his life his love of and belief in the innate goodness of children. These poems, which come from the daily observations of the behavior of his grandchildren, insist upon one fundamental idea: the child is man before he is corrupted. Hugo further believed that a child's prayer goes directly to God, and that it is the most efficacious type of prayer. Furthermore, the love of the child is the remedy for man's impurity.

The poems, of course, center on Hugo's two grandchildren: Georges II, born on August 16, 1868, and Jeanne, born on September 29, 1869. Hugo saw them for the first time on June 7, 1870. Some of the poems, however, predate their births. One poem goes back to 1846: *J'aime un groupe d'enfants* (I like a group of children), two to 1855, others to 1857, 1859, 1864, 1865, and then from 1868 until the poems were published by Calmann-Lévy.

The collection of seventy-one poems is divided into eighteen parts as follows: 1. *Guernesey*; 2. *Jeanne endormie* (Jeanne asleep); 3. *La Lune* (The moon); 4. *Le poème du jardin des plantes*; 5. *Jeanne endormie II*; 6. *Grand âge et bas âge mêlés* (Old age and young age mixed together); 7. *L'Immaculée Conception*; 8. *Les Griffonnages de l'écolier* (The scribblings of the school boy); 9. *Les Fredaines du grand-père* (Grandfather's pranks); 10. *Enfants, oiseaux et fleurs* (Children, birds, and flowers); 11. *Jeanne lapidée* (Jeanne stoned); 12. *Jeanne endormie*; 13. *L'Epopée du lion* (The lion's epic); 14. *A des âmes envolées* (The flight of souls); 15. *Laus puero* (Praise to the child); 16. *Deux chansons* (Two songs); 17. *Jeanne endormie*; and 18. *Que les petits liront quand ils seront grands* (What the little ones will read when they grow up).

The following discussion will attempt to give the reader some idea of the flavor and intent of this highly original collection of lyric poems. In the first section, poetic scenes situated on the Channel Island of Guernsey, poem three, *Jeanne fait son entrée* (Jeanne makes her entrance), is almost impressionistic in its desire to capture the naive discourse of a child. Albouy remarks in his notes to the following poem, *Victor, sed victus* (Conqueror but conquered), that its fundamental thesis is that of the most powerful man, here the poet, being conquered by the weakest, the child. Poem five of this section, *L'Autre* (The other one), is the first poem dedicated to grandson Georges: *Viens, mon Georges, ah! les fils de nos fils nous enchantent* (Come now, my Georges, Ah! the sons of our sons enchant us). Poem six joins together Georges and Jeanne much as in an earlier work: *Mes deux filles*, which photographs Léopoldine and Adèle sitting on a threshold at twilight: *Moi qu'un petit enfant rend tout à fait stupide/ J'en ai deux; Georges et Jeanne; et je prends l'un pour guide/ Et l'autre pour lumière* (Me, made totally stupid by a little child/ I have two of them, Georges and Jeanne, and I take the one for a guide and the other for light). Poem eleven, *Fenêtres ouvertes* (Open windows), is a magical piece of sound impressionism. With windows open, the poet hears voices, the bells of the parish church of St. Peterport, the cries of the bathers in the Channel, the sounds of birds, a cock's crowing, and the voices of Jeanne and Georges.

The second part, which opens with the siesta of Jeanne, is appropriately entitled *Jeanne endormie*. There is no doubt that this is the motif of the entire collection because it repeats in variants three more times throughout the collection.

The poem most appreciated by Hugo's French contemporaries was the charming *Jeanne était au pain sec dans le cabinet noir** (Jeanne was put on dry bread in the dark pantry). Jeanne had misbehaved, and her grandfather comes to visit her in her "prison" bringing her a pot of confiture. She promises to be good, and she informs him that if he has to be punished she too will bring him a pot of jam. This is a very subtle manner of speaking for the amnesty of the commune's partisans.

The section on the *Jardin des plantes* in Paris combines many motifs of Hugo. First, it is a wonderful place to take a child and set his imagination free. Poem four of this section, dedicated to Georges, speaks of a visit to Buffon's park. Paraphrased it looks as follows: "My sweet Georges, come see a menagerie, any one, at Buffon's place, at the circus, anywhere, without leaving Lutetia (Paris), let's go to Syria, and without leaving Paris, let us depart for Timbuktu." In poem six, the poet tells Jeanne: *Je ne cache pas que j'aime aussi les bêtes* (I won't hide from you that I love animals). The Lion's Epic (Section 13) is dedicated to fantastic storytelling, a prime amusement for little children whose imaginations have not as yet been suffocated by reason.

On a more somber note, *A propos de la loi dite liberté de l'enseignement* (Concerning the law on the so-called liberty of education) is important in understanding Hugo's stance on education. Very early he supported the concept of mutual education (the better educated helping those in need of tutoring), and his opposition to subsidies for private, mainly Catholic, schools was the start of his first problems with the government of Louis Napoléon-Bonaparte.* In this strongly anticlerical poem, Hugo opposes the so-called Dupanloup (Archbishop of Paris) law on higher education. His protest was in vain, and it was this law which led to the founding of the Institut catholique in Paris.

Thus, from the beginning of this collection, memories of his exile in the Channel Islands, to this anticlerical poem (there are also two poems against the dogma of the Immaculate Conception), these serious matters frame the lyrical exaltation of childhood and the joy it brings to a grandfather.

Hugo's poems praising childhood find parallels in late nineteenth-century painting: some poems evoke the paintings of Mary Cassatt, other poetic equivalents of the children in the garden paintings of Auguste Renoir. The opening line of *La Lune* is a literary equivalent of a Renoir: *Jeanne songeait, sur l'herbe assise, grave et rose* (Jeanne was dreaming, seated on the grass, grave and pink); also poem three from *Enfants, oiseaux et fleurs*, entitled *Dans le jardin: Jeanne et Georges sont là. Le noir ciel orageux/ Devient rose, et répand l'aurore sur leurs jeux* (Jeanne and Georges are there. The black stormy sky/becomes pink and spills dawn onto their games).

The Art of Being a Grandfather, which is at times very sentimental, promulgates the innocence of children, which some twentieth-century writers, including Jean-Paul Sartre* or Jean Cocteau* (*Les Enfants terribles*,

1929) would refute. It is perhaps easy to project innocence onto children, giving the adult the possibility of believing that at one time he too was innocent. All the same, this family poetry touched the hearts of a nineteenth-century France intent on family values; as a collection of poetry, it was entirely original in its day and remains unique.

Art of Being a Grandfather, The. See *Art d'être grand-père, (L').*

Athélie ou les Scandinaves. This fragment of a tragedy was begun and abandoned in 1817. Hugo tried to be inspired by Scandinavian materials, but his heart did not seem to be in the work. Consequently, he turned to his vaudeville *A.Q.C.H.E.B. (A quelque chose hasard est bon),* which he presented to his mother as a New Year's Day present.

Only the first two acts of *Athélie* are complete, but there is a schema for the remaining three acts. The play carefully respects the unities of time and place. Nordic motifs return with the publication of Hugo's novel *Han d'Islande** (1823).

Au Lion d'Androcles. This meditation on Roman perversity comes from Part Eight, *Décadence de Rome* in the first series of *La Légende des siècles.** This poem, which consists of ninety-six lines, without break, of rhymed alexandrine couplets, dates from February 28, 1854. The title is significant in that the lion plays a most insignificant part in the body of the poem; it appears in the last nine lines when the poet drops the descriptive portion of his text and makes a direct appeal to the lion.

The source is twofold. First, it is based on the legend of Androcles, the fugitive slave condemned to be killed and devoured in the arena by wild beasts. The lion, recognizing that this is the man who removed a thorn from his paw, spares him. The emperor, impressed, pardons Androcles and gives him the lion as a pet. This, in itself, could have been sufficient for contrasting goodness with evil, as it was for British playwright George Bernard Shaw who wrote the play *Androcles and the Lion*, consisting of a prologue and two acts (1912, performance in Berlin; 1916, publication) with a meditation on the theme of life having meaning only when it has an end outside itself. This surely is also the intent of Hugo, but it is complicated by the spiritism* practiced by Hugo and his exiled family on the Channel Islands. Hugo claimed to have made contact with the lion in the spirit world, which adds a dimension that many would find dubious. For Hugo, however, who believed in many levels of intelligence for man, animals, and even inanimate nature, such as stones and rocks, it was not inconceivable that he could speak with a spirit lion, and in verse form at that.

The poem has nothing to do with Androcles at all, and the lion makes a surprise appearance in the poet's apostrophe to the lion in the conclusion, for after all the lion is generally considered not just noble, but king of the jungle—quite a contrast with the decadent Roman emperors who have turned life in the city into a perpetual orgy.

The major portion of the work is given to an indictment of decadent Roman civilization; the eagle has been replaced by the scorpion: *Rome buvait, gaie, ivre et la face rougie;/Et l'odeur du tombeau sortait de cet orgie* (Rome was drinking, gay, drunk, flushed-faced;/And the odor of the tomb was coming forth from this orgy). Horrible scenes are presented— scenes in which parents are killed by their children; a woman of means displeased with the way her hair has been set pierces the woman hair- dresser's breast with a golden pin; six thousand crucified people are seen along the highways; and above all, the arena games where pregnant women, weak old men, babies at the suckling stage, captives, gladiators, and Christians are all thrown to the beasts for the enjoyment of sadistic ticket holders.

From the very beginning, Hugo had pondered the question of good and evil in his poetry, and he found evil personified in the decadence of the Romans. The poem concludes with an address to the lion. Born in the wild desert, the lion, a true dreamer ("mystic" could just as well be read here), is brought to the city. He shudders at seeing so much dark- ness and so many abysses. The lion is stirred to virtue, to love and pity, and he shakes his mane at Rome. A typical Hugolian antithesis, the last line tells us who is the real man and who is the monster: *Et l'homme était le monstre, o lion, tu fus l'homme* (And, man was the monster, o lion, you were the man).

This poem aptly captures Hugo's belief in the innocence found in the world of animals.* Acting mainly out of instinct, they are incapable of moral disorder. In this case, we have a thinking and meditative lion who is able to pass God's judgment on a wicked city.

D'Aunet, Léonie. Victor Hugo's affair with Léonie d'Aunet (Madame Biard) cheapened his public reputation and created havoc in his amorous world. For a period of time, he seemed to be maintaining three house- holds; one for his wife, one for Juliette Drouet, and one for Léonie. It was a difficult and embarrassing juggling act.

Léonie d'Aunet was an authentic member of the lower aristocracy. As a young girl she went to live with a painter, François-Auguste Biard, whose main title to fame are the grandiose historical scenes commis- sioned by King Louis-Philippe for Versailles. Through a mutual friend, Fortunée Hamelin, Hugo made the acquaintance of Léonie, and an am- orous affair soon developed. Unfortunately for the lovers, Léonie's hus- band made a formal complaint at the police station in the Vendôme neighborhood of Paris, and Léonie and Hugo were caught in flagrante delicto. Adultery was then considered a very serious crime, and Léonie was arrested and hauled off to the Saint-Lazare prison. Hugo, recently made a peer of France, claimed immunity, and he was allowed to go free. The scandal, however, hit all the newspapers. Hugo confessed everything to his wife, and it is said that Adèle Hugo went to visit Léonie in prison. Afterward, Léonie's marriage was legally annulled, and at this point she pressured Hugo to abandon Juliette Drouet. She threatened blackmail, saying that she would send all the love letters she had received from Hugo to Juliette. She temporarily backed off from this position, but in 1851 she did send the letters to Juliette who was stung to the heart when she learned that this affair had been going on since 1844. In a maudlin move, more worthy of a modern romance novel or a soap opera, Juliette devised a plan by which there would be a period of four months in which the poet could see the three women in his life, but after that he would have to choose between Léonie and Juliette. Juliette quickly gained ground. Among other things, she would invoke the spirits of her own dead daughter Claire and of Léopoldine Hugo.* Finally, and mostly, she saved Hugo's life during the coup d'état of December 1854. Thus Juliette won.

This was by no means the end of the presence of Léonie d'Aunet. Throughout the years, even during the exile, she was a force; first she demanded money and then she planned trips to visit Hugo. It was Mme. Hugo who had to intervene constantly to prevent new disasters.

Hugo sent Léonie a copy of *L'Homme qui rit** with the simple dedication, *hommage*. She can be seen as a model for a main character of the novel *Josiane*. While the work itself is a serious social commentary, the title may have another ironic sense, that of the poet with a guilt-ridden grin on his face, like his hero, Gwynplaine. The love affair with Léonie is not a "decent" episode in Hugo's life. He temporarily appears weak, like Gwynplaine seduced by Josiane.

BIBLIOGRAPHY

Guimbaud, Louis. *Victor Hugo et Juliette Drouet*. Paris: Auguste Blaizot, 1914.
———. *Victor Hugo et Madame Biard*. Paris: Auguste Blaizot, 1927.
Maurois, André. *Olympio ou, la vie de Victor Hugo*. Paris: Hachette, 1954.

Auverney. This pseudonym was used by Hugo to sign certain pieces of poetry and prose, works of his young years which he published in the *Conservateur Littéraire*. It could be speculated that this might explain the social ambivalence of Captain d'Auverney,* the white protagonist in Hugo's first novel *Bug-Jargal** (1818), who slowly learns the lessons of social justice in the confrontation of the white European with an African prince made slave. It may be a clue to Hugo's own social evolution which moved rapidly through the 1820s. Authors frequently assume other names, a kind of projection of the ego into other dimensions. Hugo also referred to himself as Olympio, hence the title of the poem *Tristesse d'Olympio** (Olympio's sorrow). In similar fashion, Emile Zola* assumed as a pseudonym the name of the protagonist of the last novel in his *Rougon-Macquart* series, Doctor Pascal, when he sought refuge in London after his trial in the French courts (Dreyfus Affair). Such pseudonymities are common with major writers in the nineteenth century. The meaning may be obscure, but it is worth pondering.

Auverney, Captain d'. The narrator and protagonist in Hugo's novel *Bug-Jargal*,* Captain d'Auverney recounts to other military personnel his misadventures when stationed on Santo Domingo during the slave insurrection in 1791. This military officer is by nature compassionate, even passive in personality as compared with his equivalent, the slave-prince Bug-Jargal.* Through a series of events which pitch him for and against white supremacy as practiced on the island, he becomes the friend, indeed the "brother," of Bug-Jargal whom he has frequently protected, and in turn he is protected by the regal slave. Captain d'Auverney, as the narrative ends, is stoically depicted as the victim of multiple tragedies: the loss of his friend Bug-Jargal who was executed, the destruction of the plantation of his uncle, and the death of his uncle and that of his fiancée Marie. Back in France he recounts the events of Hispaniola to a group of entranced officers. Shortly thereafter he is killed in the line of duty.

Aux arbres. In Victor Hugo's nature poems at least four points seem paramount: water (the sea); rocks, stone, and masses (mountains); trees; and bird song, reminding the modern reader very much of the spiritual quality found by the French organist and composer Olivier Messiaen in such works as *Le Réveil des oiseaux* (The awakening of the birds, 1953), *Oiseaux exotiques* (Exotic birds, 1956), and *Catalogue d'oiseaux* (Catalogue of birds, 1959). Hugo found deep spirituality in nature's geology and vertebrates, and in the mighty arborescent forms known as trees. Unlike the sentimental rendering of the American poet Joyce Kilmer (1886–1918), in his poem *Trees* (1913), Hugo's *Aux arbres* (In praise of trees) and other poems in which trees appear as central motifs stress their apparent silent witness to God their creator, with a very solemn and religious tone enveloping the poems.

Pierre Albouy, in his notes to the Pléiade edition of *Les Contemplations* (NRF Gallimard, 1967), cites the critic Vianney who has seen in this poem an inspiration derived from a rather obscure French poet, Victor de Laprade, whose poems *A un grand arbre* (To a high tree) and *La Mort du chêne* (The death of the oak tree) had both appeared in the *Revue indépendante* in December 1841. Hugo's poem dates from 1843. According to Albouy, *Laprade exalte la leçon de calme et de patience que les arbres donnent aux hommes* (Laprade praises the lesson of calm and patience which trees give to men) (Albouy notes, p. 1499).

Hugo's poem of forty lines, divided into two parts, with no apparent logical or poetic justification, does indeed echo Laprade's religious sentiments about nature, but the sentiment is widespread in European Romanticism, and therefore the "influence" idea should either be minimized or even rejected.

The poem is striking in the way in which Hugo continued one of his main stylistic devices, that of dialogue and dialectic. In this case, it is a question of a conversation with trees that know him well: *Vous connaissez mon âme! Vous me connaissez, vous!* (You know my soul . . . You indeed do know me). Out of this intimacy, religious in nature, is born the poet's desire to finish his days and then be buried under the trees' branches, at peace with the world, and with God, about whom he has learned something from the trees.

Hugo's poem is high Romantic pantheism, filled with a religious feeling partially formed by a Catholic thought practically unknown to his important predecessor, Jean-Jacques Rousseau (1712–1778) in such works as *Les Rêveries d'un promeneur solitaire* and *Confessions de foi d'un vicaire savoyard*. Hugo's trees are religious, as he wishes to be, and they invite mankind to engage in the act of contemplation. Romantic pantheism, therefore, moves close, through Hugo, to the meanings of monastic silence.

B

Balzac, Honoré de. It would be difficult to imagine two more antithetical literary figures than Balzac (1799–1850) and Victor Hugo, save for the eclecticism of nineteenth-century France which attempted to reconcile opposites. Balzac, who lived a scant fifty years, represents the quickly burned-out energy of the nineteenth century. Hugo, despite his own personal and aesthetic energy, was a slower candle, outliving Balzac by thirty-five years. Their viewpoints are contrary but not hostile. Hugo began his adult life as a Catholic conservative who moved rapidly into liberalism and socialism. Balzac remained faithful to a traditional Catholicism and pined for the ancien régime, France before the French Revolution. While Hugo's novels first reflected Romantic historicism with *Notre-Dame de Paris** (1831), he moved on to a humanitarian view of the nineteenth century in *Les Misérables** (1862). Balzac became the historian of the France in which he lived. His first contemporary novel, *Les Chouans* (1829), depicts the insurrection of royalist Catholics in the Vendée against the trends of the French Revolution. His *Comédie humaine*, or *The human comedy*, depicts French life from the fall of Napoléon almost to the events of 1848, but this is a France he viewed with a jaundiced eye, with sorrow for what he saw and wrote about.

Nothing seems more awkward than Balzac's personal and literary perception by the new Romantic generation. With the exception of the open and tolerant Delphine Gay,* he was poorly received in person at various Romantic gatherings, such as his participation in an 1829 reading of Hugo's play *Marion delorme,** and by the new Romantic criticism which, in its own way, was as nearsighted as the previous Neoclassical criticism. It was not possible for this new generation to understand what Balzac was all about. He was the first writer in France to report on contemporary society, he was the first realist.

Balzac's own peculiar conservatism, frequently at war with his desire to make a fortune, puts him at odds somewhat with Victor Hugo who must have appeared to him to be the living example of what could be wrong with the nineteenth century in France. André Maurois has suggested that the character of Baron Hulot in Balzac's *La Cousine Bette* (1846) has similarities with that of Victor Hugo, in the depiction of sexual meanderings (Maurois, *Olympio*, French ed. 538). The reference, of course, is to Hugo's publicly discovered affair with Léonie D'Aunet.*

In spite of artistic and political differences, Hugo remained, to the end, a person known for his civility and also for his intuition of what was great. The biographical details underline Hugo's comprehension of the genius of Balzac. Hugo had supported Balzac's candidacy for the chair vacated by the death of Chateaubriand (July 4, 1848) in the French Academy (*See* Académie Française and Victor Hugo), and during Balzac's final days Hugo visited the ailing author. He subsequently went to view the corpse (see Hugo, *Choses vues,** vol. 2, ed. of the Imprimerie nationale, Paris, 1913). Hugo, who formed part of the funeral cortège, delivered the oration at Père-Lachaise cemetery.

It is arguable that Balzac and Hugo best represent the energies of the nineteenth century. Quite different in viewpoint and in literary conceptual manifestations, there were, nevertheless, common denominators. Both had strong beliefs in the Swedenborgian principle of "correspondances," that is of the relationship between quick and inanimate matter. His pondering of the nature of the universe is apparent in most of the mature poetry of Hugo, starting with *Les Contemplations** (1856). Similar themes are found in several Balzacian novels: *La Peau de chagrin* (The wild ass's skin, 1831); *Séraphita* (1832), and *Le Lys dans la vallée* (The lily in the valley, 1836). The common bond, therefore, is a Romantic yearning to comprehend and unify the physical and spiritual realms.

Bande Noire, La. This group of Restoration speculators would be known only to specialists of that period were it not for the third ode of Hugo in the second group of the *Odes* (*see Odes et Ballades*) of 1822–1823. This group of entrepreneurs knew how to take advantage of the chaos and anarchy of the French Revolution and the Restoration. They bought confiscated or abandoned châteaux and abbeys, tore them down, and sold the materials. This destruction of the French patrimony particularly enraged and compelled to action Charles Nodier* and, under his influence, Victor Hugo. The ruins of the past became a central motif of French Romanticism, and it fired Hugo's sensibilities. The iconoclasm of the Revolution never appealed to Hugo's French pride, and many of his works evoke a past where there is nothing but ruins, those he had observed at the abbey of Jumièges in the Seine-Maritime, or the ruins of the Benedictine abbey of Cluny in Lamartine's Burgundy, destroyed at the beginning of the nineteenth century. Meditation on the relics of the past is the cornerstone of *Notre-Dame de Paris,** not ruined, but almost. Stones of the past are not just relics for Hugo, but a means of physically touching that which had been.

Baudelaire, Charles. Charles Baudelaire (1821–1867), with Victor Hugo, Arthur Rimbaud, and Stéphane Mallarmé,* is one of the most important French poets of the nineteenth century. Baudelaire's position is unique because his poetic production looks both to the past, Romanticism, and to the future, Symbolism. He was dependent upon Hugo's intuitions on the directions of modern poetry, and he developed, even more than Hugo, the interdependency of Romantic imagination, the objectivity of Parnassian poetry,* and deep Symbolist probings of the unconscious. His *Les Fleurs du mal*, or *Flowers of Evil*, published in 1857, reveals these three dominant tendencies. The ensuing civil trial charging Baudelaire for corrupting morals in certain poems made him a sympathetic soul for Hugo, who had had more than his share of problems with censors.

Through a modest exchange of letters between the two poets, of the most flattering variety, Baudelaire kept in literary contact with Hugo, and during his lecture tour in Belgium in 1865, he frequently visited the Hugo clan in July, August, and October while they were living in Brussels.

Les Fleurs du mal went on sale on June 25, 1857, and on August 20 the authorities brought Baudelaire to trial. Hugo quickly responded, writing to the poet on August 30 from Guernsey: *Vos* Fleurs du mal *rayonnent et éblouissent comme des étoiles* (Your *Flowers of Evil* shine and dazzle like the stars).

Hugo had every reason to be pleased with Baudelaire. Baudelaire, in the section entitled *Tableaux parisiens*, had dedicated three of the poems to Hugo: *Le Cygne* (The swan); *Les Sept vieillards* (Seven old people); and *Les Petites Vieilles* (The little old ladies), the third of which was quite similar in form, length, and metaphorical development to Hugo's own work. *Les Sept vieillards*, however, metamorphosed out of one old man is a far cry from the *Le Mendiant** found in *Les Contemplations.**

Concerning the swan poem, Baudelaire wrote to Hugo stressing the suffering of animals* as the point of departure for a meditation on suffering in general: *la vue d'un animal souffrant pousse l'esprit vers tous les êtres que nous aimons, qui sont absents et qui souffrent* (the sight of a suffering animal directs our thoughts toward all beings whom we love, who are absent and who suffer). Baudelaire had hit upon a chord dear to the heart of Hugo, namely the suffering of all creation. Hugo's reply, in the same month of 1859, is symbolic and shows that he understood the poem well: *Votre Cygne est une idée. Comme toutes les idées vraies, il a des profondeurs. Ce cygne dans la poussière a sous lui plus d'abîmes que le cygne des* *eaux sans fond du lac de Gaube. Ces abîmes, on les entrevoit dans vos vers pleins d'ailleurs de frissons et de tressaillements.* (Your Swan is an idea. Like all true ideas it has depths. This swan in the dust has underneath or beneath him more abysses than the swan of the bottomless waters of Lake Gaube. These chasms can be intuited in your poetry filled with shudders and quivers.) While on one level the poem appeals to both poets' humanitarian sensibilities, on the other, its theme of exile must have touched Hugo who finds himself alienated from France. On a deeper level the swan poem joins together the Romantic and Symbolist movements, leading directly to Mallarmé's famous swan sonnet *Le vierge, le vivace et le bel aujourd'hui* (The virginal, the vivacious and the beautiful day).

Baudelaire's critical essays offer insights into his positive evaluation of Hugo the man and writer. In his essay on Théophile Gautier,* Baudelaire calls Hugo "great, terrible, immense, like a mythic creation, representing the forces of nature and their harmonious struggle." More incisive are his remarks in *L'Art romantique* in a two-page portrait of Hugo. It is clear, not just from this passage, but from multiple sources that Hugo was a great walker. Baudelaire seizes upon this point, recalling seeing Hugo crossing the city of Paris. He wonders how the head of the Romantic school had any time to write poetry, but concludes that Hugo was a disciplined person who had need of these promenades for his reveries and contact with the exterior world. Hugo, according to Baudelaire, had a deep spiritual constitution which permitted him to work while walking or to walk while working. Baudelaire imagines the solitary walks on the island of Guernsey, hearing now only the roar of the ocean: *Mais là-bas comme ici, toujours il nous apparaît comme la statue de la Méditation qui marche* (But over there, as here, he always seems to us to be the statue of Meditation walking).

Formal comparisons speak of Hugo's ability to transcend other arts, particularly painting. Thus in his *Salon of 1846*, in which Baudelaire compares Hugo and Delacroix, he affirms that Hugo is a painter in poetry. In the *Salon of 1859*, he proclaims that Hugo is a landscape artist.

Baudelaire's essays on *Les Misérables** also discuss *Les Contemplations* and *La Légende des siècles** and underline Hugo's spirit of justice and charity. Hugo was touched by these articles and wrote a note of thanks to Baudelaire in April 1856, with the astonishing avowal that the two are poets from the same mold.

It is clear, then, that on all levels Baudelaire understood the thematic thrust of Hugo's poetry, and he also understood Hugo's particular spirituality. Baudelaire's affirming portrait of Hugo the man and poet is in sharp contrast to the negative assessment of Paul Claudel,* the arch-Catholic poet who had emerged from the Symbolist movement.

BIBLIOGRAPHY

Baudelaire, Charles. *Oeuvres complètes,* texte établi presente et annoté par Claude Pichois. 2 vols. Paris: Editions Gallimard, 1975–1976.

Bazan, Don Cesar de. This principal character, who brings comic relief to Hugo's 1838 Spanish drama *Ruy Blas*,* was derived from Hugo's imagination concerning vagabonds, people on the margin of society. Such a stock figure of Romanticism cannot be confined to a single play. Don Cesar de Bazan dwelled for a long time in Hugo's mind and he appears in sketches for the *Théâtre en liberté* (Free theater*). It has been assumed that Hugo wanted to write a picaresque novel or play about this character, and indeed, as type, he has the qualities of the hero found in Spanish Golden Age picaresque novels.

The Beggar. See Mendiant, Le.

Bernhardt, Sarah. One of the best known of the nineteenth-century French actresses, Bernhardt was noted for her interpretations not only of French classical theatre, but also of nineteenth-century works, including the plays of Victor Hugo. Rosine Bernard, known as Sarah Bernhardt (1844–1923), made a noticeable impression on Hugo who was impressed not only by her voice, but also by her beauty, and a flirtatious relationship developed between the poet and the actress. Bernhardt is important in Hugo dramaturgy for her interpretation of Doña Maria de Neubourg, queen of Spain, in the 1872 revival of *Ruy Blas** at the Odéon theatre where she had started acting in 1866. She was also a great success in the 1877 revival of *Hernani** in the role of Doña Sol de Silva* at the Comédie-Française where she had returned in glory, years after her contract there had been canceled, in 1863, for an intemperate display of anger toward another actress.

Bertin family. The Hugo family had close ties of friendship with the family of Louis-François Bertin, usually called Bertin l'aîné (Bertin the elder). Although the poetry and correspondence refer directly or indirectly to his sons, Edouard the painter and Armand the journalist, the two figures important in understanding Hugo's relationship with the Bertins are the father, Louis-François (1766–1841), and his daughter, Louise (1805–1877).

Louis-François was a considerable publicist. He made the *Journal des Débats* the mouthpiece for constitutional royalism. We note both in letters and in poetry Hugo's affection and respect for this conservative patriarch.

It is to the daughter, however, that we should turn our attention. Louise Bertin had an affinity for the arts, first for painting, and then for music, where, unfortunately, she was not much of a success outside of family gatherings. Rather plain looking and paralytic she had a balanced personality and gave a willing ear to Hugo's daughter, Léopoldine Hugo*, and it seems, if we read the poetry correctly, that she was some sort of spiritual advisor to Hugo in his moments of doubt and despair.

Louise wrote a series of operas all of which failed, including her opera based on the Sir Walter Scott novel of 1816 *Guy Mannering*, as well as her *Le loup-garou* (The werewolf) and *Faust*. Hugo willingly prepared a libretto for her *La Esmeralda*,* based on the gypsy girl of *Notre-Dame de Paris*,* but this too was panned by the critics in 1836.

Louise, however, was not a failure in the Bertin household at Les Roches in the Vallée de la Bièvre* where the Hugos frequently summered and where Victor Hugo spent several autumns. Louise was an intimate of Léopoldine, and, despite their great difference in age, she acted like an older sister and confidante. That she was much admired by the poet is made evident in the poems dedicated to her, plus those in which she is directly addressed, and in Hugo's letters. Intelligent and discreet, she seems to have played the role not only of confidante, but also of psychotherapist and mother-confessor.

Louise makes several appearances in Hugo's poetry starting with *Les Chants du crépuscule** (Songs of twilight, 1835). In this collection, poems thirty-seven and thirty-eight are dedicated to her. Poem thirty-seven underlines Romantic anguish over the flight of time, but in part 2, a pre-Proustian resolution is offered because Louise knows how to conquer time through works of art. Both Dante and Mozart, poetry and music, are cited as immortal citadels against the exterior temporal storms. Poem thirty-eight pits Hugo's increasing metaphysical doubts against his desire to believe. This poem contains the famous description of Louise as being *Homme par la pensée et femme par le coeur* (Man by thought and woman by the heart). The narrator complains of the enemy within his soul, "doubt," caused perhaps by his passions, but Louise is contemplative and all serene almost in a Buddhist sense. The poet speculates about whether love will lead to an enlightenment. The theme of doubt is continued in the next collection, *Les Voix intérieures** (1837). In another poem dedicated to Louise, the poet sees doubt as normal for the human condition, and he concludes with the parable of the just man living in the country, retiring for the night filled with doubts. *Sagesse* (Wisdom), the last poem (forty-four) of *Les Rayons et les ombres** (1840), is also dedicated to Louise. In the poem, divided into six parts, the poet decries the vile century in which he lives. He recalls his innocent childhood and contrasts it with the human condition. Mankind is in a fallen state, which is attributed to Eve and to Cain. Louise is invited to hear these complaints, which she does, calmly with a smile, out of her *bonté séraphique* (angelic goodness). She is thus an agent of calm and balance for the disturbed poet.

Finally, two poems from *Les Contemplations** (1856) merit our attention. Poem twenty-one in Book Three, *Les Luttes et les rêves: "Ecrit sur la plinthe d'un bas relief antique"* (Struggles and dreams: Written on the plinth of an ancient bas-relief) is aptly dedicated to Louise if only because of the opening line: *La musique est dans tout* (Music is in everything). More important, from the same collection, is poem five of Book Five, *En Marche* (On the way), which is a nostalgic recall of the days spent at Les Roches with the Bertin family. This poem looks like a letter to Louise about the good days, with warm memories of Bertin l'aîné, the evenings of song, and the laughter of children. Now all is gone and most of the actors in that bucolic scene are dead. The critic Jules Janin,* in his *Histoire de la littérature dramatique*, vol. 3, evoked the days of Les Roches in almost the same terms we find in the Hugo poem. Hugo wrote to Janin (December 26, 1854) to thank him for remembering those happy days: *Cela nous ramène aux Roches, Notre grand viellard et notre bon Armand sont là qui jasent* (That takes us back to Les Roches; our great old fellow and our good Armand are there chattering away). Hugo's wife Adèle, in *Victor Hugo raconté par un témoin de sa vie*, chapter 49 (if she truly wrote it), gives similar testimony: *on apercevait le maître de la maison, levé dès l'aube, dirigeant le travail des jardiniers, ou assis sur un banc un livre à la main quelquefois endormi* (We would see the master of the manor, up since dawn, directing the work of the gardeners, or seated on a bench, a book in hand, and sometimes sound asleep). This last citation is practically a paraphrase of strophe 4 of poem five of *En Marche*.

Victor Hugo knew how to make poetry from real life experience, and he made no effort to disguise the realities behind the poems. Furthermore, he joined the personal with metaphysical ponderings concerning death, doubt, belief, and immortality. This is done in the form of dialogue or correspondence with Louise Bertin, and it would not be incorrect to speak of these poems as the Louise Bertin cycle in the poetic opus of Victor Hugo.

BIBLIOGRAPHY

Hugo, Adèle Foucher. *Victor Hugo raconté par un témoin de sa vie*. Brussels: A. Lacroix Verboeckhoven et Cie, 1863.
Janin, Jules. *Histoire de la littérature dramatique*. 6 vols. Paris: Michel Lévy, 1853–1858.

Biassou. This former slave was the leader of a faction during the 1791 slave insurrection in Hugo's novel *Bug-Jargal.** Biassou is a true historical figure, unlike Bug-Jargal,* who was fashioned entirely from Hugo's imagination. The fictional portrayal of Biassou, however, removes him from history as it does any historical figure represented in fictive form. In the novel, Biassou is represented as egocentric, self-indulgent (especially concerning food), cruel, and perverted in his devising of unusual punishments for his captives. He is also crafty and very intelligent, yet a certain cultural inferiority is suggested in hints made by the narrator Captain d'Auverney* that Biassou is unsure of his French grammar which he wants corrected in a document that he is sending as a conciliatory move to the provincial government. When Captain d'Auverney refuses to perform this secretarial task, he is handed over to Habibrah,* the dwarf "chaplain" of the rebel army. Biassou's parody of white manners, military parades, and the Catholic Mass can be interpreted by modern standards as a desire for liberty but with the unexpressed acquiescence to so-called white supremacy. Hugo's humanitarian urges, found in *Bug-Jargal* and elsewhere, frequently express a paternalism that was a part of nineteenth-century progressive thinking. Were Biassou not free and head of a rebel army, his psychology would be seen as reflecting passive slave thinking, and would be characterized by twentieth-century standards as Uncle Tomism.

Bienvenu, Bishop. Hugo could not have chosen a better name, Bishop "Welcome," for the person who begins the salvation of Jean Valjean. In giving Bishop Bienvenu the silver candlesticks, which Jean had stolen, he tells Jean that he has purchased his soul for God. Valjean, in time, becomes a laicized saint, helping and protecting many people, including Fantine,* Cosette,* and Marius.*

Hugo's anticlericalism did not blind his eye to transcendental religious urgings. Bishop Bienvenu, whose character scandalized orthodox Catholic readers of the nineteenth century, is nearly considered a saint by twentieth-century measures.

Bièvre, La Vallée de. The Bièvre, which flows into the Seine in Paris, gives its name to a valley and to a village not far from the property of the Bertin family* at Les Roches where the Hugo family spent their summer vacations. Victor Hugo had met Louis-François Bertin, founder of the *Journal des Débats*, in 1827, and a strong friendship developed between the two families. The happy days spent at the Château des Roches are recalled in Hugo's poetry and in many items of correspondence. The general picture that evolves from the time spent at Les Roches is of a family idyll, a gathering of children, adults, and the old, a scene right out of a Greuze painting. Center stage in this Rousseau-like paradise is Louise Bertin, an accomplished musician. Even the modern reader can feel a nostalgia for the summer evenings enjoyed there, with Louise at the piano, the children playing, the adults singing and listening.

However, there is yet another side to the Bièvre Valley in the lives of the Hugos and in Hugo's poetry. Conjugal alienation had driven Adèle Foucher Hugo into an amorous relationship with Charles-Augustin Sainte-Beuve,* an affair in which Adèle seemed to defy convention, or at least was indifferent to her husband's jealousy. While on vacation at Les Roches in 1834, Adèle frequently and unabashedly strolled with Saint-Beuve around the Bièvre. On the other hand, Hugo himself evoked the Bièvre Valley in what is perhaps the most important love poem of French Romanticism, *Tristesse d'Olympio** (Olympio's sadness) in *Les Rayons et les ombres.** In the manuscript of this poem, which Hugo gave to Juliette Drouet, we find the following dedication: *Pour ma Juliette, écrit après avoir visité la vallée de Bièvre en octobre 1837* (For my Juliette, written after having visited the valley of the Bièvre in October 1837). (See annotated notes of Pierre Albouy in Victor Hugo, *Oeuvres poétiques*, vol. 1, Paris: Bibliothèque de la Pléiade, 1968, p. 1576).

Thus, the Bièvre, important in both biography and poetry, forms a contrast of Romantic bucolic settings, far from the bustle of Paris, but also witnesses the disintegration of Hugo's marriage and the nostalgia of the poet for a love that is not lost but has lost its setting (a dominant fixed idea with Hugo) and the idea that the exterior world changes (similar to the loss of Les Feuillantes).* In *Tristesse d'Olympio*, the place of love has been destroyed: *Ma maison me regarde et ne me connaît pas* (My house looks at me and doesn't know who I am).

Likewise, Hugo recalls in a letter to Louise Bertin on May 14, 1840: *Si l'on pouvait ressaisir les années envolées, je voudrais recommencer un de ces ravissants étés où nous avions des soireés si exquises près de votre piano, les enfants jouant autour de nous et votre excellent père nous échauffant et nous éclairant tous* (If we could seize again the years which have flown away, I would like to begin again one of those wonderful summers in which we had such exquisite evenings around your piano, the children playing around us and your wonderful father warming and illuminating everyone).

The Château des Roches and the Bièvre Valley are sites equal in importance to Jersey and Guernsey to Hugo, and they should be kept in mind when evaluating Hugo's life and his poetry.

Biré, Edmond. Edmond Biré (1829–1907), a negative biographer of Hugo who began his career under the Second Empire, published voluminously on the French poet: *Victor Hugo avant 1830* (before 1830), *Victor Hugo après 1830* (after 1830), and *Victor Hugo après 1852* (after 1852). Biré as a nineteenth-century critic and biographer seems to have been obsessed with Hugo, mainly in a chronological manner.

Biscarrat, Felix. Biscarrat, the master of studies at the pension Cordier where Eugène and Victor Hugo were enrolled, was a mentor, counselor, and good friend to the Hugo boys. Although he left Paris for Nantes in

1817, he stayed in touch by letter with both Eugène and Victor, and was, with Alfred de Vigny,* the official witness to Victor Hugo's marriage.

Biscarrat saw in Hugo the potential of a very great poet, which probably evoked a certain amount of jealousy in the unstable Eugène. He corrected both boys' translations and offered advice on their poetic output, all with the affection of a big brother.

It was Biscarrat, charged with the mandatory walks of the students around Paris, who arranged a stop in front of the Institute, seat of the French Academy (See Académie Française and Victor Hugo). While the other pupils admired the architecture of the building, Biscarrat and Victor slipped inside to deposit Hugo's poem in the poetry contest of 1817 on the topic: *Sur le bonheur que procure l'étude* (On happiness derived from study). Hugo's poem, 324 lines long, received honorable mention, placing ninth in the competition.

It was Félix Biscarrat who expressed genuine concern about the mental instability of Eugène, which was openly manifest at Victor's marriage ceremony. The following day, Biscarrat had to alert Victor to the fact that his brother had had a severe mental breakdown. Eugène's father decided to take Eugène to his property in Blois where he improved temporarily. There was a relapse, however, and this time he required confinement to an institution in Paris.

Biscarrat is to be remembered as an early and important influence on Hugo's poetic development, a kindly Mr. Chips type, who had the qualities of a superior teacher who combined knowledge with encouragement, devotion, and affection.

BIBLIOGRAPHY

Barret, Paul. "L'Elève Victor Hugo." *Revue des Deux Mondes*, 15 janvier 1928.

Black Group, The. *See* Bande Noire, La.

Blanche. Blanche-Marie Zelia, called Blanche and later Madame Emile Rochereuil, was only twenty-two when she was sent to Hauteville House on Guernsey, where she was engaged by Juliette Drouet as a linen maid. Blanche, who was to become the last passionate lover of Victor Hugo, attached herself to him with an obstinacy equaled only by that of Hugo's daughter Adèle for the English lieutenant Alfred Pinson.* Blanche had some degree of aesthetic sensibility, having memorized poetry, including some of the poems of Hugo. Her parentage was unknown, but she was raised by the Lanvin family as their own daughter. Alone at Hauteville House with her, Hugo's passion was aroused, and his notebooks of 1873 attest to his desire to resist the allure of this young girl. He soon came to call her "Alba," and an affair quickly developed. When Juliette discovered what was happening, she sent Blanche back to Paris where she was supposed to be married. Hugo himself returned to Paris and soon established Blanche in an apartment. Frightened by a warning that Hugo could, at his advanced age, die in her arms, Blanche was persuaded to marry Emile Rochereuil, and the wedding took place on December 2, 1879, in the 20e arrondissement followed by a religious ceremony held in the church of Saint-Jean Baptiste, witnessed by a hairdresser and a pork butcher. Blanche's marriage was most unhappy. Her husband, a mean-spirited scoundrel wanted to take advantage of Blanche's liaison with the famous poet by bringing out an edition of poems Hugo had written to her. The enormous scandal that would have resulted would have tarnished Hugo's few remaining years. In 1881, when Hugo turned eighty, it was the occasion of a national holiday. Blanche was seen mingling in the crowd and afterward walking about the Hugo mansion. After Juliette's death, she hoped to reestablish the liaison, but her letters were intercepted, and it appears that the aging poet may have completely forgotten about her. She separated from her husband, and the last record we have of her is of her living in a garret on the Ile Saint-Louis.

Blanche is an important figure in Hugo's amorous biography. She was his last opportunity to play out once again the passionate romance with Juliette Drouet so many years before. An important poem from *La Légende des siècles*, entitled *En Grèce* (In Greece), and dated July 12, 1873, is addressed to Blanche. In intent it is similar to the amorous evasion proposed by Charles Baudelaire* in his *L'Invitation au voyage*, but it is 131 lines long. Part of its structure is to play on variants of "whiteness"; thus we encounter aube (dawn) and alabaster. For this reason, classical Greece seems the ideal voyage for the aged lover and his young mistress. This motif, however, had been well treated in a sensual poem of Théophile Gautier,* *Symphonie en blanc majeur*. With its geographic pinpointing of famous sites in Greece, it is close to the prose spirit of *La Nuit de mai,* by Alfred de Musset,* which mixes poetic inspiration and love yearnings with sights to inspire both.

Finally, the poem seeks a reconciliation of spirituality and carnality, a principle of Hugo's poetry from his earliest days: *Car l'hostie et l'hymen, et l'autel et l'alcôve/ ont chacun un rayon sacré du même jour/ La prière est la soeur tremblante de l'amour* (For the Eucharistic host and hymen, and the altar and the bedroom/ each has a sacred ray of the same day/ prayer is the trembling sister of love). This must be seen as an erotic mysticism, an idea that is gaining popularity in some theological circles at the end of the twentieth century.

Boaz Asleep. *See Booz endormi.*

Boîte aux lettres. Composed of approximately 200 fragments of satirical verses, possible rhyme schemes, and prose sections, the *Boîte aux lettres* (mailbox) was written on the heels of the exile, begun in 1853 and dating mainly from 1854–1855. They are very difficult to unravel and somewhat confusing; it is a haphazard collection of vitriolic short pieces, rougher in intent than the polished finished product of *Les Châtiments*.* What clarity is to be found is due to the work of René Journet and Guy Robert in their second *Cahiers de Victor Hugo* plus the notes of Pierre Albouy in the Pléiade edition of *Les Châtiments*. Most of the invectives are aimed directly at Napoléon III,* for example: *Qui? toi! Napoléon? avec ton aigle en paille/ Avec tes goûts de sport, de gin et de ripaille!* (Who? You! Napoléon? with your straw eagle? with your taste for sports, for gin, and for feasting!).

Hugo was especially harsh with writers and philosophers who craved the approval of the Empire. In this category are found Louis Veuillot (1813–1883), editor of the ultraright Catholic journal *L'Univers*. Veuillot had been attacking Hugo since the publication of *Le Rhin** in 1842 as well as Barbey d'Aurevilly (1808–1889) whose name Hugo transformed into *Barbet* (spaniel). Later Barbey d'Aurevilly led a campaign to reestablish the Empire in the journal *Le Public*. He was also a contributor to the Bonapartist organ, *Le Pays*, in which, in June 1856, he unmercifully criticized *Les Contemplations*.*

One of the most satirical and amusing pieces makes references to a senator, Raymond-Théodore Troplong (too long), a name inviting ridicule. Hugo seems obsessed with this pompous politician. In his *Histoire d'un crime* IV, xviii (1852–1877), we find this satirical portrait of Senator Troplong: *légiste glorificateur de la violation des lois, jurisconsulte apologiste du coup d'état, magistrat flatteur du parjure, juge panégyriste du meurtre* (Glorifying jurist for the violation of laws, apologetic legal expert for the coup d'état, perjured magistrate, panegyrist judge of murder).

Playing with rhyme schemes in preparation for poems forms part of the *Boîte aux lettres. Troplong . . . cette brute/choisi Ham/Siam/per Dei gratiam* (Troplong . . . this brute chosen Ham/Siam/Thanks be to God) or *ce groin neveu d'une hure/furie/ahurie/charcuterie* (this pig snout nephew of the head of a pig/fury/dumb-founded/delicatessen). The translations, of course, do not reveal the deep resentment being expressed by Hugo as he searches for demeaning rhymes.

The *Boîte* is of limited value for the general reader of Hugo. It should be reserved for one specializing in *Les Châtiments*. It remains striking in its direct accusations, by name, of the conspirators, as Hugo would see them, of the Second Empire.* While fragmentary in form, it probably has been equaled in name-calling only by the medieval testaments of the poet François Villon. Finally it shows the close affinity between form (here rhyme), and meaning, with meaning directing the search for the most demeaning rhyme scheme possible.

Booz endormi. *Booz endormi*, one of the most brilliant modern evocations of Jewish scripture, based on the Book of Ruth, is found in the mythical and legendary section of *La Légende des siècles** (first series, II, 6, 1859). Hugo's collection, which fits neatly into Romantic historicism, seeks to establish, step by step, humanity's progress. This particular poem is pivotal in understanding Hugo's poetic processes, consisting of a truly magical and uplifting rendering of the events in one of the shortest books of the Bible, making of this poem of twenty-two stanzas, each typically of four lines, a modern pastoral, for indeed that is the setting. Second, the poem highlights the advent of Jesus Christ as one of the most important figures in human myth or history, a Jesus born into the House of David which issues forth from the union of the old Boaz and his relative, the young widow Ruth.

The poetic narrative proceeds across the motif of the sleeping patriarch Boaz and the watchful Ruth, a Moabite woman, who with Naomi had come to glean in Boaz's fields. The poem reiterates the idea of the peaceful sleep of Boaz across its sections: *Booz s'était couché de fatigue accablé* (Boaz went to sleep overwhelmed with fatigue); *Donc, Booz dans la nuit dormait parmi les siens* (Thus, Boaz in the night slept amidst his own). In his sleep, he has a dream of an oak tree coming forth from his belly, a genealogical tree at the base of which is found a singing king (David) and at the top, a dying God. This prophetic dream announcing Boaz's role in creating a new royal Judaic line is complemented by Ruth's vigil as she lies next to the old patriarch. Ruth sees in the sky, above the peaceful landscape of Ur and Jeerahmeel, the golden sickle of some harvester of an eternal summer.

Booz endormi may be considered one of the happiest lyrics of Romanticism. Hugo had carefully read the Book of Ruth, the story of Ruth and of Naomi her mother-in-law, and of Ruth's marriage to the aged Boaz. It has many of the qualities of the Song of Songs and captures the celebrations found in Jewish scriptures.

Boulanger, Louis. Louis Boulanger (1806–1867), a French painter, gained a high reputation among the Romantics, especially with the group gathered about Victor Hugo in the 1820s and 1830s. Today he is hardly remembered, but his long friendship with Hugo perhaps brought him more merit than his paintings and watercolors. Boulanger came onto the scene with his painting of *Mazeppa** (*see* Mazeppa, Ivan Stepanovich), which he entered into the salon of 1827. This painting, now in the Rouen museum, is a nearly perfect complement to the Hugo poem found in *Les Orientales** (1829). Although Boulanger drew much of his inspiration from the work of Hugo, he also used Shakespeare as a source, particularly *Othello* and *King Lear*. But it is in the shadow of Hugo and Hugo's work that Boulanger will be slightly remembered. In 1833 he presented a series of watercolors based on *Notre-Dame de Paris*.* Other watercolors were inspired by Hugo's play *Lucrèce Borgia*. As late as 1866, he was still drawing inspiration from *Notre-Dame de Paris* with his *Vive la joie*! (Long live joy).

Hugo dedicated a number of poems to Boulanger in the collections published before the exile, namely in *Odes et ballades*,* *Les Feuilles d'automne*,* *Les Chants du crépuscule*,* and *Les Rayons et les ombres*.*

In 1860 Boulanger was named director of the School of Fine Arts in Dijon (Burgundy), a post he held until his death. This provincial appointment fits with Boulanger's early success which was followed by basking in the light of Hugo as his friend and protector.

Brown, John. A militant and messianic abolitionist, John Brown (1800–1859) headed the insurrection at Harper's Ferry in 1859, taking the federal armory and local hostages in a move which he believed would lead to a general rebellion of American slaves. Brown was finally defeated by a group of U.S. Marines, taken prisoner, condemned to death, and hanged on December 2 of the same year. Brown, perhaps the last and most important American abolitionist, has entered profoundly into American mythology in both song and legend. The long narrative poem of Stephen Vincent Benét (1898–1943) entitled *John Brown's Body* (1928) is a symbolic interpretation, somewhat in the tradition of Henry Wadsworth Longfellow, on the meaning of the American civil war.

Brown's bold incursion at Harper's Ferry stirred the imagination of the world and incited Victor Hugo's own humanitarian and pacifist impulses. Hugo wrote an impassioned plea asking for Brown's pardon which, of course, was to no avail. Hugo's own abolitionist sentiments, part and parcel of the general humanitarian thrust of the Romantic movement, can be traced back to his earliest works, indeed to the first rendering of his novel *Bug-Jargal** dating from 1818 when Hugo was only sixteen. Hugo's abolitionist sentiment is acutely tied in with his strong sentiment against capital punishment,* which was best expressed in *Le Dernier Jour d'un condamné* (The last day of a condemned man) in 1828, or in his strong reaction to the execution on Guernsey of Mr. Tapner (1854), which provoked his long letter of protest to Lord Palmerston against the death penalty (*see* Tapner, the execution of Mr.). In the cases of both John Brown and Mr. Tapner, the reaction of Hugo shows him to be an engaged and daring writer, unafraid to confront authority in the name of justice.

Bucolic settings. *Les Chansons des rues et des bois** (Street and woodland songs) of 1865 depicts many nineteenth-century excursions out of Paris into the suburbs which, unlike now, were part of the countryside. This volume of poetry vaunts both admiration and love for the simple joys of the burgeoning proletariat, the flirtations and loves of the grisettes, coquettish young working girls who had left the provinces for the attractions of Paris and their beaux. Herein, Hugo is rendering what had been done earlier by Henri Murger (1822–1861) in his *Scènes de la vie de bohème* (1847–1849), which was later turned into Giacomo Puccini's popular opera *La Bohème* (1896).

What Hugo has done in this collection of poetry is repeated in *Les Misérables** (Part One, Book Three, *In the Year 1817*, chapters 2 through 9, pp. 120–44, in the new English translation, New American Library, 1987). Thus the novel of 1862 and the poems of 1865 complement each other chronologically and frequently thematically.

The chapters in *Les Misérables* recount the off-and-on flirtations of four grisettes—Favourite, Dahlia, Zéphine, and Fantine*—with four students—Blachevelle, Listolier, Fameuil, and Tholomyès.* The day in the country for these couples begins at five in the morning with a coach ride to Saint-Cloud. The country idyll is recounted in small but accurate detail, joining nature and physical love with psychological portraiture. The physical details, which represent a type of romantic fetish as ogling, is a characteristic trait found in such Romantic writers as Hugo (see *Sara la baigneuse* from *Les Orientales*,* 1829), Théophile Gautier,* and Alfred de Musset.* Such voyeurism is found in many of the poems of *Les Chansons des rues et des bois* (see poem seven, *Jeunesse—Choses écrites à Créteil* (Youth—Things written at Créteil). Créteil is located to the southeast of Paris in the department of Val-de-Marne.

While the pastoral scenes of *Les Misérables* and of *Les Chansons des rues et des bois* do not have the pictorial shock of Edouard Manet's (1832–1883) *Le Déjeuner sur l'herbe* (Lunch on the grass), in which two nude women are picnicking with two fully clothed men, the same kind of contrast is found in *Les Chansons des rues et des bois* between classical mythology and modernity.

The proletarian women in the poetic and prose renditions announce a type of war of the sexes with the women as passive objects. In the idyll of *Les Misérables*, the young women are offered a surprise which turns out to be their abandonment by the young men who leave them in a restaurant to return to filial duties; they are returning to society, leaving behind the rustic interlude. The girls laugh at this surprise, but it is a false mirth for Fantine (recalling the melancholia of *La fête chez Thérèse* from *Les Contemplations**) who will bear Tholomyès' child, Cosette.* Only the American-born French symbolist poet Stuart Merrill can approach Hugo in the representation of the walk east of Eden.

Bug-Jargal. This novel, in its most primitive form, was written in 1818 when Hugo was only sixteen years old. The guests at one of the Edon banquets* proposed that each one write a military story, and the collection would be published under the title *Les Contes sous la tente* (Stories told under the tent). Hugo was the only one to fulfill this obligation. This version was published two years later (1820) in *Le Conservateur Littéraire*. The final fifty-eight-chapter version was published in 1826. Important changes were made in the final version: the narrator's name was changed from Delmar to Captain d'Auverney,* and an important new character was added, the mulatto dwarf Habibrah, who plays an important role in the denouement.

The central action concerns the slave insurrection that occurred on Santo Domingo in 1791, an insurrection inspired both by the cruelty of the slave masters and the news that filtered in from France about the events of the French Revolution as well as ensuing events (the Convention). There is a strong emphasis in the novel on the slogan Liberty, Equality, Fraternity; in fact, the last word was used as a motif in this short novel. The plot is simple enough. Rich plantation life, especially on the estate of d'Auverney's uncle, is contrasted with the plight of the slaves. Into this Caribbean idyll is added the dimension of d'Auverney's love for Marie, the uncle's eldest daughter to whom he is engaged to be married. It is learned that Marie has an anonymous suitor who sings to her in the garden. This inspires the jealousy of d'Auverney, who speculates that the would-be Lothario might be a slave: *la révoltante supposition d'avoir un esclave pour rival* (the revolting supposition of having a slave as a rival). Thus is introduced into the sequence the possibility of interracial contacts on the amorous level and, later, on the fraternal level.

The insurrection, which begins on August 22, 1791, the very day of d'Auverney's marriage to Marie, is led in part by Pierrot (Bug-Jargal*), an African prince who was sold with his father, the king, into slavery. Pierrot had saved Marie from a menacing crocodile, and throughout the narrative the reader is presented with heroic deeds on the part of d'Auverney and Bug-Jargal, saving each other's lives and living by a high code of honor.

The narrative moves rapidly with battle skirmishes in one of which d'Auverney is captured. He is released by the command of Bug-Jargal. In the final chapter, Bug-Jargal nobly takes the place of ten of his men who are about to be executed as a reprisal, and he is then executed. Meanwhile Marie has perished in the forest fire set by the insurgents. With the insurrection put down, and his family all destroyed, Captain d'Auverney returns to France with his aide Thadée and Bug-Jargal's dog Rask,* and he participates in French military campaigns in one of which he dies courageously next to his friend Thadée and the dog Rask.

This early novel of Victor Hugo brings together disparate elements of French Romanticism: global social issues—slavery and the need for its abolition—and two other fundamental aspects of Romanticism, the use of local color and innovative linguistic structures preluding Realism.

As for local color, Hugo is in the tradition of Chateaubriand's *Atala* (1801). What Chateaubriand had done for the North American continent, Hugo did for the Caribbean. A new lexicon was introduced. As Chateaubriand explained the nuances of Indian rituals, so Hugo explores, with brief explanatory notes, Creole expressions and Spanish dialects. This is done to explain various food products and customs of the slaves, customs brought with them from Africa. While the nature described is less exotic and hyperbolic than that which is found in the Chateaubriand text, the reaction of the narrator to this new world nature is, all the same, in the manner of Chateaubriand. While the young Hugo cannot at this point match the descriptive genius of Chateaubriand, there are approximations, such as the description of setting fire to the plantations by the rebels. Again, while not equaling the fires at the Napoleonic retreat from the walls of Moscow in another Chateaubriand work, the style is similar: *C'était un spectacle affreux et imposant* (It was an imposing and frightening spectacle). The New World to both writers was seen as virginal and very ancient: *des grands arbres centenaires de la forêt* (the high centenary trees of the forest). Romanticism also invades the characterizations of the two male protagonists, Captain d'Auverney and Bug-Jargal. Captain d'Auverney swoons when he is overwhelmed with emotion; the African is often moved to tears. The two former enemies have become not only friends, but brothers (a fraternity of black and white), and they both live by their word which they keep and by a high Cornelian sense of honor. They both love the same woman, Marie, but Bug-Jargal's high moral sense urges him toward heroic renunciation. Had he been just a simple "savage," he could have taken Marie away for himself. However, he is not a savage but a princely romantic. Hugo's text, for all its apparent simplicity foretells racial tensions and relationships as they would be experienced in the twentieth century, especially in the United States. When he is taken prisoner to the camp of the leader Biassou,* d'Auverney witnesses a parody of white civilization. The black leader imitates white military stances; a mock Catholic Mass is performed by the witch doctor; and a military parade and inspection are conducted. Underneath the mask of Biassou there seems to be a desire to please the whites (who will soon be victorious) if not to be white himself. Its racism, unintended by Hugo, looks like an American minstrel show of yesteryear. It should be added, however, that the whites also have their own pretensions. Marie's father, the plantation owner, dresses his dwarf like the jester of a medieval feudal lord with whom he secretly identifies. Although the dwarf is treated well by his master, he is regarded as a favorite dog, which will cause him to seek revenge on the entire family.

The black-white tensions, either stated explicitly or as subtext, antici-pate many literary aspects of interracial contacts and conflicts in the twentieth century. In this regard, we can consider this early work of Hugo as a step toward modernity. His novel anticipates twentieth-century texts that articulate similar themes, including Eugene O'Neill's *The Emperor Jones* (1920), Jean Genet's *Les Nègres* (1958), Lorraine Hans-berry's *Les Blancs* (1972), and William Styron's *The Confessions of Nat Turner* (1967). These four works all deal with the violence engendered by racism as well as the motifs of domination and fear, revenge and mutilation. The texts of Hansberry and Styron, however, while appre-ciating the need for violence and revenge, also underline a message of reconciliation and brotherhood. All of these ideas are present in the text of the young Hugo, and it can be said that contemporary literature on race relations lifts the Hugo text above the triteness of melodramatic Romanticism of which it has often been accused.

Bug-Jargal. Bug-Jargal, or Pierrot (his slave name), is the protagonist of Hugo's novel of the same name, which was published in 1826. The char-acter of Bug-Jargal is very complicated. He is an African prince sold into slavery with his father, the king, and he has a remarkable European and Romantic education; he is adept in both French and Spanish, and he has a remarkable command of ballad literatures, especially of the Spanish *romanceros*. What is striking is for Hugo to present a black slave hero who stands up for his rights, who considers himself the equal if not the superior of his white masters. Throughout the narrative, there are dra-matic instances of actions taken to save either his own life or that of the other protagonist, Captain d'Auverney,* or the heroine Marie, who is engaged to marry Captain d'Auverney, but who is amorously pursued by Bug-Jargal. Bug-Jargal renounces his love for Marie with deference to the captain and also with recognition of the impossibility of open inter-racial liaisons within a slave culture. In a final act of heroism, he surren-ders his own life to the authorities in order to spare the lives of other slaves.

Bug-Jargal is an overriding presence in the novel, but he always is seen somewhat in the background. This situation is caused by the fact that Captain d'Auverney is recounting his adventures in Santo Domingo. Therefore, it is his story, but a story that cannot be told without reference to Bug-Jargal and his upright character, honesty, and role in the slave insurrection. His presence comes in the form of several tableaux or scenes such as the serenading of Marie, the rescue of Marie from a crocodile attack, a confrontation with a plantation owner, interviews with Captain d'Auverney while in prison, and the rescue of the captain from a rival insurrectional force headed by Biassou.* Finally, we witness Bug-Jargal's courageous acceptance of death at the hands of the authorities.

Bug-Jargal is the first of several original types forged in the imagination of Victor Hugo. This creation of Hugo forced his contemporaries to take a second look at the dehumanization caused by the institution of slavery.

***Bug-Jargal* (theatrical adaptation).** Hugo's antislavery novel of 1826 had one theatrical adaptation, in 1880, which was made by Hugo's secretary, Richard Lesclide, and Lesclide's nephew, Pierre Elzéar. The play was performed in seven scenes or tableaux. The text was radically modified by the introduction of new characters and the changing of names. Textual modifications reflect the evolution of theatrical conventions and changing attitudes toward the slavery question since, by 1880, the question had legally been resolved, at least in the United States. Bug-Jargal's* dog Rask* disappears completely to be replaced by Zora, the sister of the leader of the revolt. Zora plays the traditional French role of confidante, a person to whom one entrusts the secrets and emotions of the soul. What is striking is the amplified role of Habibrah*—a role that combines feigned subservience, a desire for revenge and justice, and a curious function as a sorcerer or witch doctor who fuses all sorts of occult practices brought from Africa with the rites of Roman Catholicism, a trait that is true to anthropological studies of Latin America, particularly the Caribbean. Habibrah is an ugly dwarf, a type found also in Hugo's use of German legends (see *Le Ciel et l'enfer*, which is a theatrical adaptation of letter twenty-one of Hugo's *Le Rhin*,* which recounts the Legend of Pécopin and Bauldour*). In a thoroughly dramatic contrast, Habibrah speaks a French dialect called *petit nègre* with his masters, but he utilizes a perfect French with the other blacks.

As in all theatrical adaptations of novels, a careful comparison of narrative and dramatic text and action yields primary clues as to the nature of each genre.

Burgraves, Les. *Les Burgraves* of 1843 is Hugo's last major play to have been created on stage during his life. It exhibits the same promises, premises, and mistakes of his *Cromwell* of 1827, bringing to closure that which had begun just fifteen years earlier. If French literary history misidentifies French Romanticism in terms of the theatrical triumph of *Hernani** (1830), it likewise reduces Hugo's theatre and hence Romanticism, to a very short vibrancy, especially if measured by the public's negative reaction to *Les Burgraves*.

The year 1843 promised much happiness for the young leader of the Romantic rebellion. Just two years after his election into the French Academy (*see* Académie Française and Victor Hugo) at the age of thirty-nine, with enormous literary successes behind him in his published novels, poems, and theatrical acclaim (*Ruy Blas*,* for example, was a great success, just on the heels of *Hernani*), *Les Burgraves* could have been the capstone of a promising and dazzling career for Hugo as the most important French writer since Jean Racine. The year itself, however, proved both personally and professionally fatal. His beloved daughter Léopoldine Hugo,* married in February 1843, drowned in the Seine river near Villequier with her husband Charles Vaquerie* (September 1843). The news came to Hugo while he was reading a newspaper in a café on the Atlantic coast of France at the conclusion of a walking tour with his mistress Juliette Drouet. Between Léopoldine's wedding in February and her death in September, the production of *Les Burgraves* took place on March 7 and continued for thirty-seven performances in spite of the success of François Ponsard's neoclassical play *Lucrèce*.

The history of the failure of *Les Burgraves* is not the end of Romanticism, but of Romanticism's theatrical mode. Romanticism entered into the literary battle through the theatre; the theatre, however, did not remain its strongest asset.

The play did not live up to what was promised in Hugo's historical meditation on its meaning. Indeed, the preface had led many critics to see its format in terms of history or epic, but not as dramaturgy. Its division into parts rather than acts may be the clue to this conclusion.

In the preface, Hugo invites the reader to consider Teutonic history as a modern parallel and parable to ancient Greek mythology. The struggles between late Medieval Rhine barons and the Holy Roman Emperor are portrayed as a new historical "myth," intertwining the tensions between Fate (symbolized by Guanhumara) and Providence (the all-forgiving Emperor Frederic). The play underlines in ways never explained by the playwright, nor perhaps for the audience, the modern urge toward nationalism, seen in France much earlier with the Fronde wars, and soon to be seen in Germany as it moved toward unification in the nineteenth century.

Despite the lack of any classical verisimilitude in *Hernani* or *Ruy Blas*, poetry and plausibility did win out. *Les Burgraves* is filled with surprising presentations. Venerable personages with exceptional longevities, a sensational dramatic representation staged on several levels with personages, a slave in chains walking back and forth across the scene, magical incantations, and magic potions are also used. One of these potions saves the Countess Regina from a mortal illness but then puts her into a somnambulistic state, followed by immediate resurrection and reunion with Otbert, her love, who also happens to be old Job's last son of the first generation. The plot is difficult to follow, and these melodramatic elements frequently submerge the intent clearly announced in the preface. Indeed, this may have been the source of the play's failure. However, two anniversary productions were given in the twentieth century (in

1902 and in 1943) and two modern productions (on French television in 1968 and in 1977).

Its dramatic dialogue must have left its audience bewildered. A few examples demonstrate the clash between Hugo's high poetry and his, at times, pedestrian attempt at realistic dialogue (traits which are also present in his best plays, such as the opening scene of *Hernani*). In *Les Burgraves*, Guanhumara's suicide is hardly in the tradition of Racine's *Phèdre*: her dying words seem almost comical for a modern reader: *Donato, ce poison est rapide . . . Adieu!* (Donato, this poison works fast . . . Goodbye). The venerable Job's pathetic description to the Countess Regina of the kidnapping of his son Georges (Otbert) becomes banal with his advice to Regina that once she becomes a mother she should not let her children wander out of her sight: *Oh! quand tu seras mère,/ Ne laisse pas jouer tes enfants loin de toi!* (When you become a mother don't let your children play far from you). The most famous line in the play, however, is one that has acted as a parody of it for generations of superficial critics who don't understand Hugo's humor. Job's famous address to his son Magnus (second generation of these ancient sages): *Jeune homme, taisez-vous* (Young man, shut up), could only have provoked laughter in 1843 as it does today, for Magnus, the younger, is over sixty years old.

The play concludes with the emperor's pardon to all the bandit Burgraves. His constant concern, expressed when he first appears as a poor beggar, is that Germany has no leader. This is the whole point of the play: it expresses its satisfactory conclusion for the personages, if not for the audience or classical readers, who have found this thesis submerged in melodramatic subplots and mysterious motivations which certainly are the sources of its failure.

Byron, Lord. George Gordon Byron, 6th Baron Byron (1788–1824), is the universal Romantic poet who had an influence on the Continent at least equal to that of Sir Walter Scott. Lord Byron's revolutionary themes and new poetic forms and his commitment to idealistic causes provoked enthusiasm and admiration among the French Romantics, including Hugo. Byron was passionately engaged in the struggle of the Greeks for their independence from Turkey, a sentiment echoed by Hugo in *Les Orientales** of 1829. Through his enormous psychological and aesthetic energy he seems at first, although in quite a different manner, the equivalent of an Honoré de Balzac,* and then of a Victor Hugo. His writings and assertiveness seem to have frightened the more passive and fragile Alphonse de Lamartine* who, in a poem addressed to Lord Byron, counseled moderation in all things and faith in God.

The young Victor Hugo, from about 1819 to 1824 (ages seventeen to twenty-two) had not yet totally established his own aesthetic principles.

Thus he adhered first to the writing of the executed poet André Chénier*
(1752–1794), then the novelistic influence of Sir Walter Scott, already
translated into French, and then to Lord Byron.

Through the English writers Hugo came to understand the pan-
European nature of Romanticism which would include authors he could
never read because of his lack of knowledge of the English language.

By 1830, however, he seems to have understood the message delivered
earlier by Madame de Staël concerning contemporary literary revolutions outside of France, mainly in Germany and England. His comprehension of the meaning of northern European Romanticism was
enhanced during the exile when his son translated the theatre of Shakespeare.

BIBLIOGRAPHY

Rosenblum, Robert. *Modern Painting and the Northern Romantic Tradition: Friedrich
    to Rothko*. New York: Harper and Row, 1975.

C

Capital punishment. Hugo's views on capital punishment should be understood as an aspect, a very important one, of his leadership in the humanitarian movement of French Romanticism. Writing about war (the poems on Napoléon Bonaparte's battles) or the Reign of Terror, *Quatrevingt-treize*,* for example, convinced him of the horror of hostilities and abetted his general pacifism. The early novel *Bug-Jargal** is witness to his opposition to slavery, and his advocacy for the abolition of capital punishment echoes across his life and work, especially in *Le Dernier Jour d'un condamné* (The last day of a condemned man) and the subsequent *Claude Gueux*.* After having written these two short novels, he begins to meditate a vast one, *Les Misères* which became *Les Misérables** in 1862, a humanitarian inquiry into the injustices of the penal system, the courts and laws, not unlike the work of Charles Dickens in England, especially *Bleak House.* Hugo's humanitarian vision, like that of Emile Zola,* was utopian and messianic inasmuch as he imagined a brave new world in the future. In the grounds of his home, Hauteville House on Guernsey, he planted an oak tree dedicated to the future United States of Europe in which there would be no more war, and totalitarian forces, such as the papacy, in his opinion, would have ceased to exist. The papacy is still there, but the oak tree is growing, the United States of Europe exist and there are no more totalitarian governments in this part of the world.

Hugo's call for the abolition of capital punishment should be read with the abolitionist movement of the French and English enlightenment, starting with Montesquieu and Voltaire in France, Caesar Beccaria in Italy, and Jeremy Bentham in England.

Although the forty-one poems of *Les Orientales* do not bear directly on the question of capital punishment, they do, nevertheless, underline the struggle for freedom and revulsion at the devastation of war, particularly in regard to the Greek wars of independence from the Ottoman Empire (1821–1832). The ode *Les têtes du sérail* (The heads of the harem) in honor of the Greek hero Canaris is given a Shakespearean citation: *O horrible!, O horrible! most horrible* from *Hamlet*. Poem eighteen, *L'enfant*, from *Les Orientales* contrasts the poet's lyrical feeling for the young with the massacre at Chio: *Les Turcs ont passé par là. Tout est ruine et deuil* (The Turks went through there. Everything is ruin and mourning).

As with the involvement of intellectuals and writers during the Spanish civil war (1936–1939), writers and painters were existentially engaged in the struggle for Greek independence. In addition to aesthetic value, the paintings and poems act as a kind of *reportage* of contemporary events of vital interest to the impassioned Romantic generation. It would seem improbable that Hugo would not have been aware of Eugène Delacroix's paintings of the Greek insurrection, works such as *Scènes des massacres de Chios* and *Scènes de la guerre actuelle entre les Turcs et les Grecs*, of 1826.

Hugo is consistent in his humanitarian beliefs, and resistance to capital punishment is found in later works, such as *Les Misérables* and in certain poems of *Les Contemplations*,* for example, *La nature*, poem twenty-nine, Book Three, written in 1854 after Hugo's fruitless intervention against the hanging—the last one to take place on Guernsey—of Mr. Tapner (*see* Tapner, the execution of Mr.). This poem spells out in the dialogue of the good tree and the good wood cutter the ideal relationship that should exist between man and the rest of creation. Thus a curious metaphysical position leads to a poetic reverie in dialogue form. The tree is willing to undergo any number of positive transformations: to become the Christmas log and go as flame to heaven, to be the blade of a plough to make the earth fruitful, to be the supporting beam of a man's dwelling, or to form the mast of a ship, but never to be made into a gallows. The longer poem, also from Book Three, *Melancholia*, contrasts the carefree crowd, dancing, singing, and drinking on top of a huge prison, with the meaning of the gallows in their midst, a poetic rendering of which is also found in *Le Dernier Jour d'un condamné*.

Executions have always served as a type of entertainment to the public, especially since the Reign of Terror. Hugo, while totally republican in spirit, could not and would not accept the idea of execution as a solution to man's moral transgressions.

Carlos, Don. Don Carlos is the king of Spain and then Holy Roman Emperor in Hugo's drama *Hernani** (1830). Hugo's characterization reveals a rather profound psychological, if not dramatic, insight into the human personality upon which an enormous responsibility has been thrust. If Don Carlos, as king of Spain, is somewhat of an amorous adventurer, in the sense of the Spanish myth of Don Juan, more transformation seems possible when destiny chooses him to head the latter-day Christian Roman Empire. Despite the lack of verisimilitude in much of French Romantic theatre, the poetry in this drama, and the psychological reasoning behind it, especially in the role of Don Carlos, is to be acknowledged. Act 4 begins in the tomb of Charlemagne at Aix-la-Chapelle (Aachen) where the king is named emperor, an event that radically changes his personality. His wanton love for Doña Sol de Silva,* heroine of the play, is forgotten and his animosity toward Hernani,* the outlaw nobleman, is erased when he pardons Hernani. In the celebrated monologue of scene 2 of this act he acknowledges, as would a pope or a president, the duties bestowed upon him by his new office. It certainly equals, for Romantic drama, the monologues of French Classical theatre of the seventeenth century, for example the celebrated *récit* (narration) of Théramène in the conclusion of Jean Racine's *Phèdre* (1677). While Romantic drama is usually faulted for lacking the psychological depth of the classical tradition, it can be said that, in spite of woefully unbelievable theatrical coincidences, it sometimes reaches deep truths on human motivation and personality transformation. Such is the case of the role of Don Carlos in Hugo's *Hernani*.

Centenary celebration of Victor Hugo's birth. The centenary of the birth of Victor Hugo in 1902 was not limited to Paris, or even to France. It was an international celebration. In France important festivities were held in Cambrai, Melun, Lyons, and Marseilles, among other sites. Elsewhere in Europe there were commemorations in Brussels, Bucharest, Prague, Athens, Geneva, Lisbon, London, Madrid, Rome, Istanbul, Oran, and Saint Petersburg. The adulation of the public in 1902 seems almost to have equaled the fanatical reception Hugo received upon his return from exile.

There was a spectacular honoring of Hugo in the Panthéon, the former church of Sainte-Geneviève. The event was preserved in a picture by Théobald Chartran which is now housed in the national museum of the château of Versailles. Newspaper headlines boasted of the celebrations, and there were more pictures of white-robed girls and ladies paying homage to the poet in front of his home at the Place des Vosges.

It was upon the occasion of this centenary that François Paul Meurice* suggested turning the Hugo sites into national museums. The city of Paris agreed to turn the property at the Place des Vosges into a museum, and other sites were thereafter acquired: Hauteville House on Guernsey in 1925 and the Villequier home in 1956.

The fervor of the 1902 activities can be attributed, in part, to the fact that the poet had been dead for only seventeen years. Many of the participants had known Hugo personally; most people throughout the world had read his works. He was, in a sense, a living presence.

The enthusiasm for marking Hugo anniversaries diminished as the twentieth century moved along, and so the fiftieth anniversary of his death in 1935 was less noticed.

A true commemorative appreciation of Hugo seemed to gain momentum in the 1950s with expositions at the Hugo museum in his apartment on the Place des Vosges and at the Bibliothèque nationale, located on the rue de Richelieu. In France, interest in the life and work of Hugo only increases as the twentieth century comes to a close. The centenary celebration of Victor Hugo's death* in 1985 was officially, publicly proclaimed, and backed by the superb scholarship of a new, large population of Hugo scholars.

BIBLIOGRAPHY

Le Centenaire de Victor Hugo, relation des fêtes (Paris, province, étranger), discours, hommages au maître, documents graphiques. Paris: Larousse, 1902.
Le Centenaire de Victor Hugo, relation officielle des fêtes organisées par la Ville de Paris du 25 février au 2 mars 1902. Paris: Imprimerie nationale, 1903.
Fêtes du centenaire de Victor Hugo. Association générale des étudiants de Besançon, août, 1902. Besançon, 1903.
La Gloire de Victor Hugo. Paris: Editions de la réunion des musées nationaux, 1985.

Centenary celebration of Victor Hugo's death. The centenary observances in 1985 of Hugo's death were quite different from the public and popular manifestations of the centenary celebration of Victor Hugo's birth* in 1902. Although the celebration of his birth also had its dignified and scholarly aspect, it paid homage to a popular living legend, and thus the population as a whole participated.

The year 1985 presented a new scenario. The perennial institution of yearly expositions held at the Grand Palais continued with a Hugo exposition from October 1, 1985, through January 6, 1986, assisted by the American Express Company. The catalog of this exposition was the focal point for the centenary activities.

Like the 1902 celebration, there was emphasis on popular and student participation. The most important late twentieth-century Hugo scholars were at the heart of this activity: Henri Cazaumayou, who was then the director of the Victor Hugo museums; Jean Gaudon, an internationally acclaimed Hugolian, especially for his work on Les Contemplations*; Professor Arnaud Laster, the leading critic of the dramaturgy of Hugo from the University of Paris III; Professor Guy Rosa from the University of Paris VII and Professor Jacques Seebacher from the same university; and Professor Anne Ubersfeld from the University of Paris III. More names could be cited, but these are the leading Hugo scholars of today, and they gave a university orientation, rigorous in its scholarship, to the centenary observance of Hugo's demise.

In organizing the exhibit at the Grand Palais, the committee in charge was able to assemble materials from around the entire globe. Included in the exhibit were materials from Argentina, Australia, Belgium, Denmark, and the United States, as well as multiple holdings in various French provincial museums.

The success of the 1985 celebration should be seen as the fruit of a Hugo revival which started in the 1950s and continues unabated in France today. On a popular level, the worldwide success of the musical *Les Misérables*, which has been applauded in countries as far away as Japan, may account, in some part, for the Hugo revival occurring in the latter half of the twentieth century.

On the serious, scholarly level this has meant a reevaluation not only of Hugo's theatre, which was the battleground of the young Romantics, but also of his poetry which seems to announce the Parnassian and Symbolist movements which were to follow Romanticism (*see* Parnassian poetry and Symbolism and Victor Hugo). In the area of the novel, Hugo's work seems to be dethroning that of Gustave Flaubert,* pitting Flaubert's impersonal approach against the social engagement found in Hugo, particularly in *Les Misérables*. 1902 was the adulation of a personality; in 1985, there was a profound appreciation of a writer whom some would consider the greatest ever produced by France.

BIBLIOGRAPHY

La Gloire de Victor Hugo. Paris: Editions de la réunion des musées nationaux, 1985.

Ce que dit la bouche d'ombre. This very long poem, twenty pages in the Pléiade edition, is the next to the last of the poems included in *Les Contemplations** (Book Six: *Au bord de l'Infini*, or At infinity's edge), placed just before the concluding Léopoldine Hugo* piece, *A celle qui est restée en France* (For she who remained in France), thus marrying Hugo's religious and philosophical quests with his deep grief over the death of his daughter, the two basic threads of this collection.

The poem is mesmerizing in its confrontation with death, interment, and dark night scenes, probably occasioned by Hugo's habit of walking about, often for great distances, on the islands of Jersey and Guernsey during his exile. The poem is derived from a rather small dolmen found near Rozel Bay on Jersey, on a bluff which looks out to the sea toward France, visible twelve kilometers away. The dolmen seems to speak, to explain to the poet and to the reader, the haunting question of good and evil. The *Bouche d'ombre* suggests that death will give the answers to the questions that man poses throughout a lifetime: *One day, in the tomb, sinister vestiary,/you will learn it, for the tomb is built for your understanding*. The shadow mouth (*bouche*) then becomes a type of Dantean escort through the underworld; Hugo has only the *bouche*. Dante works out of a recognizable theological tradition; Hugo's is eclectic. His theological speculations are sometimes difficult to follow.

In the conclusion, Hugo attempts to reconcile the problem of good and evil by reinterpreting the meaning of the mythical fall of the angels. The same was attempted by Hugo's friend and fellow poet Alfred de Vigny* in his *Eloa,* in which God and Lucifer are reconciled. Hugo too tries to build a reconciliation of the warring forces described in Jewish and Christian traditions. His final image, however, of Lucifer walking hand in hand with Christ before the throne of almighty God could be considered by some Catholic readers to be exaggerated if not distasteful, and the whole poem is naive and full of theological meanderings.

Ce qu'on entend sur la montagne. This poem, one of Hugo's best-known nature poems, is found in the 1831 collection of *Les Feuilles d'automne* (Autumn leaves). *What's Heard on the Mountain* is but another example of Victor Hugo's early but sustained meditation on the natural world, a trait of Romanticism more appreciated perhaps in Germany and England, but also manifest in France mainly in the works of Hugo and Alphonse de Lamartine.* The poem expresses the awe felt by a Romantic hero while contemplating some European mountain, perhaps some peak in the Alps, in a vision not unlike a painting by the German Romantic Caspar-David Friederich (1774–1840). Hugo brings to French Romanticism an uncanny, almost Germanic meditation on things final. The poem is built simply enough on a contrast between the sounds of nature, filled with harmony, and the cacophony or babel of the human race.

Chansons des rues et des bois, Les. The *Chansons des rues et des bois* was published in 1865 and divided into two parts: *Jeunesse* (Youth), with fifty-seven poems, and *Sagesse (Wisdom),* with nineteen entries. The collection is a lyrical recall to the poet's amorous youth, to the love and seeking out of young women in a bucolic setting, thus combining nature and even sexuality, for the latter is always present in Hugo's love poetry. The collection is in marked contrast with the long historical collection that precedes it, *La Légende des siècles**; the tone is no longer totally serious. The work seems to anticipate Stéphane Mallarmé's* *Afternoon of a Faun*: the idea of spying on and ogling mythological nymphs. For Hugo, these nymphs would simply be real Parisian girls; in this collection, they are the *grisettes* or working girls.

The whole collection is done with the octosyllabic form, lyrical in contrast to the formal alexandrine. The idea contrasts city life (Paris) with the country suburbs, such as Saint-Cloud, which in the nineteenth century was truly out in the woods. Similar sentiments will be found in sections of *Les Misérables** (*see also* Bucolic settings). These poems certainly are Romantic continuations of the bucolic tradition first experienced in modern French literature in the writings of Jean-Jacques Rousseau. There is, however, an undertone of melancholy that emanates from postcoital confrontations in the countryside. The atmosphere is not unlike that found in the pastoral paintings of Antoine Watteau (1684–1721), for example, *The Departure and Return from Cythera*. It reveals a Victor Hugo who is not totally emancipated from ethical questions about love and human sexuality. A different expression of Romantic conflict between sex and respect is found in *La Fête chez Thérèse* (Theresa's party), one of the great erotic poems of *Les Contemplations*.* The carpe diem message of the Renaissance poet Pierre de Ronsard (1525–1585) is tempered in Hugo with echoes back to the painting *Shepherds of Arcadia* of Nicolas Poussin (1594–1665), in which the frolicking shepherds (city aristocrats in Arcadian costumes) discover the tomb of an amorous ancestor, with the inscription: *Et in Arcadia ego* (I, too, lived in Arcadia). The modern Virgilian pastoral of the *Chansons des rues et des bois*, then, is not destroyed but pondered with restrictions both by the classic painter, and by the satyr Victor Hugo, as he sometimes thought of himself.

BIBLIOGRAPHY

Gide, André. *Poussin*. Paris: Au Divan, 1945.

Chants du crépuscule, Les. This collection, published on October 25, 1835, is the second of four volumes commonly referred to as the July Monarchy collections. *Les Chants du crépuscule* (Twilight songs) includes a short preface, a prelude poem, and thirty-nine additional pieces. If the title suggests doubt, anxiety, and misgivings on the personal, religious, and political levels, the series of poems dedicated to Juliette Drouet, whom Hugo had met on January 2, 1833, suggest a hope found in a new day; as a second thought, we could entitle some of these poems morning songs.

The preface is filled with perplexity and doubt. Hugo asks if things are good or bad and what will be accomplished by the nineteenth century. Truthfully the poet seems to be confused.

This collection of poetry is characteristic of Hugo's tendency toward length leading to discursiveness and variations of focus. This may be a reflection of the poet's distraction, going in multiple directions at the same time. Thus the poem entitled *Prélude* contains 100 lines; poem 1, 260; poem 2, 240; poem 5, 216; poem 12, 112; poem 15, 174; poem 20, 136; poem 26, 138; and poem 32, 218. Long poems tend to dampen the lyric spirit, but it must be said in Hugo's defense that the love lyrics are not unreasonably prolonged.

Thematically, the collection can be reduced to approximately ten focal points, with some overlapping. The groupings would be as follows: (1) political pieces, (2) cult of Napoléon, (3) patriotism, (4) the rich and the poor, (5) materialism, (6) poetry and art, (7) nature, (8) God and the religious question, (9) Juliette Drouet, and (10) Madame Hugo.

Under the rubric of politics should be mentioned the first poem which attempts to explain the meanings of the July Revolution. As an aside, it should be stated that the Monarchy of July is not a source of great inspiration for the poet which may, in relation to the "twilight" of the title, explain the lackluster quality of many of the political poems. They seem forced, and some are written as a rehash of an older inspiration. Such is the case with two poems dedicated to the hero of the Greek wars for independence, Canaris, who had already properly figured in *Les Orientales** of 1829 (poem 2). Now two more Canaris poems appear in *Les Chants du crépuscule* (poems 8 and 12) leaving the impression that these are leftovers, and are being used as fillers. European political issues, such as the fate of Poland (poem 9) or the political betrayal of the Duchesse de Berry because of her political conservative activity in the Vendée region (site of the original insurrection against the French Revolution (see Hugo's novel *Quatrevingt-treize**), are aspects of Hugo's political vision which call for respect even for the conservative fallen. Finally, Hugo's fixed idea on bad kings versus the people crops up in poem 16 with Hugo marching with history and giving his approval to the downfall of bad leaders (kings).

Some patriotic verses seem perfunctory, for example, poem 3, *Hymne*, which was sung by a choir at the Panthéon to celebrate the revolutionary days of the July Monarchy. Poem 7 is Hugo's prayer to God to save France from political upheaval, inspired, no doubt, by the worker insurrections that were beginning to surface in the 1830s.

The cult of Napoléon is a main feature of Romanticism in general and specifically of Victor Hugo. Poem 2, *A la colonne*, follows in the tradition of *A la colonne de la Place Vendôme* which appeared in *Odes et Ballades.** This latter poem expresses Hugo's indignation at the refusal of the Chamber of Deputies to allow the return of Napoléon's ashes to France to be placed under the Vendôme column. This forms a strange alliance in Hugo of his liberal streak with a fervent, if reserved, admiration for the genius of Bonaparte. Poem 5, *Napoléon II*, concerns the king of Rome, born in 1811, who was named by Bonaparte as his successor, a succession never accepted by the allies. The young boy died in 1832. The poem expresses Hugo's scepticism as to what the future can hold for anyone, especially politicians. Nothing, he states, is for sure or predictable in this world.

Many poems reveal Hugo's humanitarian bent. The contrast between the haves and the have-nots is revealed in poems 4, 11, 14, and 15, especially in poem 11, which is addressed to Ferdinand Philippe, Duke of Orleans, the eldest son of Louis-Philippe. Ferdinand Philippe, a good friend of Hugo, performed an act of charity at Hugo's request, thus satisfying the poet's quest for and approval of a good prince.

Poems 6 and 13 speak out against the materialism and debauchery of the nineteenth century, a fitting prelude to a dominant theme to be found later in Emile Zola's* *Rougon-Macquart* series, in which Zola accuses the Second Empire* of Napoléon III* of excessive attachment to the world and the flesh. Hugo's concern for the poor of the earth is well known, and poem 6, entitled *Sur le bal de l'Hôtel de Ville*, depicts silly and giddy women at a state dance totally unaware of the suffering around them. The poet speaks of feeding the hungry, abolishing capital punishment,* and providing adequate housing. Poem 13 addresses debauchery in the line of Alfred de Musset's* *Rolla*. It depicts the death of a young man who turned from virtue to live a life of excess, burning his candle at both ends. For Hugo, the idea of poetry cannot be separated from that of virtue.

On a more positive note are the poems dedicated to nature, almost always a consolation to Hugo (see poems 20, 27, 28, 31), and the poems that ally nature and art (19, 34, 37). Particularly fetching is poem 37, dedicated to Louise Bertin (*see* Bertin family), which stresses the Romantic theme of the flight of time, mitigated by a sustaining belief in the value of Art. It is thus that Louise Bertin, surrounded by Dante and Mozart, remains serene and unaffected by the passage of time, a Romantic prelude to the central idea of Marcel Proust in *A la recherche du temps perdu* (In search of lost time).

The poems concerning religious belief, which are perhaps the most poignant of the collection, reveal Hugo's desire to believe in God and Providence, yet show him to be beset by doubt (poems 30, 32, 33, 38). Some of these poems are very sentimental, maudlin, and filled with a weak religiosity. The most famous, poem 38, *Que nous avons le doute en nous* (There is doubt within us), again dedicated to Louise Bertin, expresses Hugo's need to believe and his desire to deny. He evaluates his religious conflict as derived from his passionate nature. By contrast, Louise Bertin remains contemplative. This poem has the famous description of Louise as having the mind of a man and the heart of a woman.

Finally, there are the ten love poems dedicated to Juliette Drouet, she who brings morning hope into the life of the poet (poems 21, 22, 23, 24, 25, 26, 28, 29, 31, 33). The most famous of these is poem 25, *Puisque j'ai mis ma lèvre à ta coupe encore pleine** (Since my lips touched your still full cup), which combines what would appear to be a highly erotic, if not pornographic, poem with an appeal to the spiritual redemptive qualities of a pure love. This love is not affected by time, and it will be eternal.

It seems almost an ironic travesty that Hugo should conclude the collection with three poems dedicated to his wife (33, 36, 39). Adèle Hugo is his port of safety. When the poems to Juliette Drouet and those to Adèle are compared, one gets the feeling that Hugo was engaging in some sort of polygamous relationship that satisfied two contrary aspects of his personality: passion with Juliette Drouet; domestic tranquillity with Adèle. It does not seem to occur to him that his position is equivocal.

There are some great poems and some fine lines in *Les Chants du cré-puscule*, but in general the collection is not judged to be among Hugo's best. Aside from the passionate tones of love for Juliette and the anguish of his religious doubts, this book may seem lukewarm, written without much enthusiasm or inspiration.

Châtiments, Les. *Les Châtiments* (The punishments) was published first in Brussels, in 1853, in two forms, an underground but complete edition, and an expurgated edition from which more than half of the poems had been excised since it was against Belgian law to inflict verbal assault on a foreign head of state, in this case Napoléon III.* These editions were forbidden in France until the collapse of the Second Empire,* but they were fairly well known by travelers returning to Paris from England and Belgium, some of whom had even memorized certain poems. Furthermore, some copies of *Les Châtiments* were smuggled into France. The complete French edition appeared in 1870 with additions. If we put together all of the poems concerning the Second Empire, we are overwhelmed by the sheer quantity which must have matched Hugo's obsessive drive for revenge, which though mitigated and generalized, is all the same apparent in reading these works as an indictment of Napoléon III and his entourage.

The original *Les Châtiments* comprises 97 poems. The *Boîte aux lettres,** an auxiliary collection, containing direct name-calling and vituperative utterings, is composed of 218 poems. The *Nouveaux Châtiments*, appended posthumously to the original work, offers 96 pieces. The total then is 411 poems, some subtle and mitigated in tone, others truly confrontational. The total number is indicative of Hugo's bitter mood on a personal, but also on a patriotic, level.

Les Châtiments are the most important political satires of the nineteenth century, perhaps equaled only by Honoré Daumier's (1808–1879) biting satirical lithographs against the French bourgeoisie and its social institutions (the class of lawyers, for example) during the Romantic period. In *Les Châtiments*, however, Hugo attempts to avoid personal attack, realizing it could look petty and degrading to both art and the political fortunes of France.

The collection is framed by two poems, *Nox* (Darkness) and *Lux* (Light), which indicate an optimistic progression, a prophecy about the doomed Second Empire. *Nox* has the feverish pitch of the French national anthem, *La Marseillaise,* a call to arms against tyranny. The portrait of Napoléon III at Notre-Dame cathedral is particularly chilling: *Sur une croix dressée au fond du sanctuaire/ Jésus avait été cloué pour qu'il restât./Cet infâme apportait à Dieu son attentat./Comme un loup qui se lèche après qu'il vient de mordre,/Caressant sa moustache, il dit: J'ai sauvé l'ordre.* (On a cross at the back of the sanctuary/ Jesus had been nailed so that he would remain there/This infamous person was bringing to God his criminal act./ Like a wolf licking himself after having bitten,/Twisting his mustache, he says: I have saved order). Two lines later, Napoléon exclaims: *J'ai sauvé la famille et la religion*! (I have saved the family and religion).

These are apt introductions to the seven parts of the collection in which Hugo's biting satire is manifest.

Book One, entitled *La Société est sauvée* (Society is saved), contains many a bitter satire. Poem Six, *Le Te Deum du 1ᵉʳ janvier, 1852,* (The Te Deum of January 1, 1852), is addressed to the Archbishop of Paris, Monseignor Sibour, who, in addition to his ecclesiastical rank, desired political power, which he received when he was named a senator on March 27, 1852. Hugo points out to the prelate that his altar is built from the marble slabs of death (the morgue): *Archevêque, on a pris, pour bâtir ton autel,/Les dalles de la morgue.* Another piece attacks the Jesuits, favorite whipping boys for French liberals going back to Voltaire (*Ad majorem dei gloriam,** slogan of the Society of Jesus).

Book Two, *L'ordre est rétabli* (Order is reestablished), creates a new dimension for this collection. The poem *Souvenir de la nuit du 4* (Memory of the night of the fourth) is not satirical but sentimental as it tells of the death of a seven-year-old boy caught in the crossfire when Napoléon III consolidated his power. Satire has been replaced by a sentimental family scene, an idyll in the manner of the painter Jean-Baptiste Greuze (1725–1805) turned tragic.

Book Three, *La Famille est restaurée* (The family is restored) stresses the bourgeois nature of the Second Empire with such entries as poem six, *Un bon bourgeois dans sa maison* (A good middle-class man in his home), in which certain key words stand out: *boutique* (shop), *la rente* (revenue), *le coupon* (dividends), *La Bourse* (the stock market). Poem ten, *L'empereur s'amuse* (The emperor has a good time), describes the daily life of Napoléon III: *Pour les bannis opiniâtres/La France est loin, la tombe est près,/ Prince, préside aux jeux folâtres,/Chasse aux femmes dans les théâtres,/Chasse aux chevreuils dans les forêts; Rome te brule le cinname,/Les rois te disent: mon cousin,-/Sonne aujourd'hui le glas, bourdon de Notre-Dame,/Et demain le tocsin!* (For the obstinate exiles/France is far away, the tomb is close by,/ Prince, preside over frolicsome games,/Chase after women in the theatres,/Chase the roe-deer in the forests/Rome burns aromatic herbs for you/Kings call you cousin,/Today sounds the knell, great bell of Notre-Dame,/And tomorrow the alarm signal).

Book Four, *La Religion est glorifée* (Religion is glorified), brings up the submotif of the role of the people, the proletariat, and their suffering. In *Sacer esto*, a paraphrase of strophe 5 would go as follows: Because of this man, ephemeral emperor, the son no longer has a father, and the child no hope, the widow, kneeling, cries and sobs, and the mother is only a ghost seated under a long black veil.

Book Five, *L'Autorité est sacrée* (Authority is sacred), with its thirteen poems, has some of the most often cited poems of the collection: *Le sacre* (The coronation), *Le manteau imperial* (The imperial cloak), *Ô drapeau de Wagram! ô pays de Voltaire* (Oh flag of Wagram! oh country of Voltaire); and it concludes with the celebrated *L'Expiation** (Expiation). *Le sacre*, with the refrain in each of the eighteen strophes: *Paris tremble, ô douleur, ô misère* (Paris trembles, oh sorrow, oh misery), mocks the coronation of Napoléon III as that of bandits who have stolen and raped French liberties. The third poem, *Le manteau imperial*, focuses on the bee icon which was found on the imperial cloaks, sullied now by Napoléon III. The bees recall France's glorious past, and the hope is expressed that the usurper will be chased from his office by a swarm of black flies. Poem five, *Ô drapeau de Wagram! ô pays de Voltaire*, with its thrilling exclamatory lyrics pays tribute to France's liberal tradition and also to the glory brought to France by Napoléon Bonaparte (Voltaire for the liberal tradition; Wagram, site in Austria of Napoléon's victory over the archduke Charles of Austria, July 5 and 6, 1809). This is one of the earlier poems of the collection, written in 1849 when Hugo entered the camp of the opposition to Napoléon III. The poem hurls invectives at the new regime, these poor conquering dwarfs: *Ce pays de lumière en un pays de honte* (changing this country of light into one of shame). Napoléon III is depicted as a lost soul.

Finally comes *L'Expiation*, whose title appropriately explains Hugo's own ambivalences about Napoléon I. Unlike Napoléon III, who seems damned, Napoléon I must expiate his sin, which involves the events of *Dix-huit Brumaire*, the events of November 9, 1799, when Bonaparte forced the Directory to resign, to be replaced by his consulate.

Book Six, *La Stabilité est assurée*, looks to a future of hope symbolized by the sun. *L'Expiation* of Book Five seems to conclude with a look at a pessimistic present time. The opening poem, however, does not resist a further literary lapidation of Napoléon III, calling him a *nain immonde* (a filthy midget). Poem eight, *Aux femmes* (To women), looks to the heavens, as does poem seven, *Luna*. *Aux femmes* concludes with the apparition in the sky of a female angel symbolizing glory and liberty: *Nous disons: c'est la Gloire et c'est la Liberté!/Et nous croyons, devant sa grâce et sa beauté,/ Quand nous cherchons le nom dont il faut qu'on le nomme/Que l'archange est plutôt une femme qu'un homme!* (We say; It is Glory and Liberty!/And we believe faced with her grace and beauty,/When we seek a name by which it must be called/That the archangel is rather a woman than a man). This could also be interpreted as part of Hugo's ongoing adoration of women.

Book Seven, *Les Sauveurs se sauveront* (The saviors will run away), announces the victory of the people, symbolized as a lion, the guardians of liberty, over Napoléon III. Pierre Albouy (in *Victor Hugo. Oeuvres poétiques*, vol. 2, Paris, Gallimard, 1967) states that the walls of Jericho will come crumbling down (p. 1143). The last poem, the famous *Ultima verba* (Last words), highlights Hugo's defiant opposition to the Second Empire. Two notes are joined together: love of France and liberty, and firm opposition to tyranny: *Patrie, ô mon autel! liberté, mon drapeau!* (Fatherland, my altar! liberty, my flag!). The poet would always prefer exile to submission, and he will remain in the opposition be there but a thousand, or even a hundred, or just ten, or just one; he will be there until Napoléon III is sent to his *cabanon* (his small hut or prison or a lunatic's padded cell). *Si l'on n'est plus que mille, eh bien, j'en suis! Si même ils ne sont plus que cent, je brave encore Sylla;/S'il en demure dix, je serai le dixième;/Et s'il n'en reste qu'un, je serai celui-là.* (If there are no more than a thousand, well, I am among them! If even there are no more than a hundred, I brave Scylla still;/If ten remain, I shall be the tenth;/And if there remains only one, I shall be he.)

As *Nox* introduced *Les Châtiments*, so *Lux* concludes it. According to Pierre Albouy, "*Lux* is distinguished by its messianic songs, which after the denunciation of evil, celebrates the ineluctable and total triumph of good" (p. 1183).

It is certain that Hugo in *Les Châtiments* has succeeded in transforming his personal rancor against Napoléon III into an aesthetic battlecry in the name of liberty and true French patriotism. All the same, the picture drawn of Napoléon III in these poems and in the novels of Emile Zola* may be only partially true. Historians are divided in their evaluations of the Second Empire; some find many positive accomplishments. In any case, Napoléon III was not an Adolf Hitler. Hugo's extremism, out of which he creates high poetry, is all the same myopic, historically speaking. The exile was real, but also somewhat brought about by Hugo's own stubbornness and exacerbated by increasing anger as he looked across the Channel to a France in chains. For indeed, there were executions, deportations, jailings, and censorship, and the Second Empire did come to a justifiable end at Sédan when Napoléon III fell into the traps set by Bismarck. Napoléon I also had his faults, but they were partially excused by Hugo.

History aside, the modern reader derives aesthetic pleasure in the satirical verses of *Les Châtiments* with its contrasting epithets, icons standing for liberty and oppression, good and evil.

Chenay, Paul. Paul Chenay (1818–1906) married Adèle Foucher Hugo's sister, Julie Foucher. If he had any fame, it was as the brother-in-law of

Victor Hugo and engraver of a collection of his drawings. The marriage to Julie was a very unhappy one due to Chenay's warped temper and sad disposition. He visited Guernsey and had published, in 1902, a book entitled *Victor Hugo à Guernsey*, in which there is much backbiting. Chenay, mean-spirited and jealous in temperament, but having married into a most illustrious family, appeared only to wish to use the Hugo clan for his own advancement.

Chénier, André. Perhaps the most important poet, if not the only real poet of the eighteenth century, André Chénier (1762–1794) is remembered today as the writer who tried to bridge classicism and the budding movement of Romanticism with the famous citation: *Sur des pensers nouveaux, faisons des vers antiques* (Let us make old time verses based on new thoughts), thus electing to preserve classical forms by enlarging the thematic field, basically a position of compromise.

Born in Constantinople, Chénier, who had biographical interests as well as a true penchant for Hellenic civilization, anticipated the mid–nineteenth century thrust of Parnassian poetry.* Chénier, outraged by the excesses of the French Revolution, harshly criticized it in his collection *Iambes* (1794) which was written during his imprisonment in Saint-Lazare penitentiary. Chénier was executed.

Hugo had a lifelong interest in this poet. In many ways, although he approved of the revolution and of its historical necessity, he, like Chénier, was aware of its excesses and regretted them. In 1819 Hugo wrote a favorable article for *Le Conservateur Littéraire* (*see* Periodicals) on the newly published edition of Chénier's works by H. de Latouche. He concentrated on the elegaic aspects of Chénier's work. In the *Odes et Ballades**of 1821 he sees Chénier as a royalist victim (keeping in mind that, at that time, Hugo was a royalist and a conservative) of the Reign of Terror. Later in his life, starting around 1850, Hugo came to appreciate the pagan (Hellenic) and epicurean nature of Chénier's poetry. In a poem published in *La Dernière Gerbe*, a curious poem entitled *A André Chénier*, the classic poet is seen as the fulfillment of the erotic fantasies of the adolescent Hugo. In *La Légende des siècles*,* poem twenty-two of *Le groupe des idylles*, Chénier is regarded as the poet of joyful love. Although he is not mentioned by name in the body of the text, this tribute to Chénier coincides with the hortatory imperatives to heed the call to love, in a bucolic setting, inhabited by gods and goddesses. Love makes the world go round according to Hugo. Its equivalent is the "charming scandal of the birds in the trees" (*le charmant scandale des oiseaux/Dans les arbres*); "Let the birds sing and the brooks murmur" (*Laissons dire/Les oiseaux et laissons les ruisseaux murmurer*). All of nature is not just happy, but joyful: "The star-filled sky seeks the meeting of mouths, a lioness seeks a lion on the mountains" (*Le ciel étoilé veut la rencontre des bouches;/Une lionne cherche un lion sur les monts*).

If in other places Hugo finds heaven giving its assent to physical love, here it is the unity of all nature—plant, animal, and human life—which is joined in the call of love. It is doubtful that Chénier would have written in such an explicit manner, but the citations from this poem give us some idea of Victor Hugo's interpretation of the neoclassic, quasi-Romantic poet of the time of the French Revolution.

Childhood and adolescent poetry of Victor Hugo. The earliest works of Hugo are discussed and annotated in the Pléiade edition of the *Oeuvres poétique*, vol. 1 (*Avant l'Exil*, 1802–1851), edited by Pierre Albouy for Editions Gallimard, 1964. The materials presented herein follow the divisions established by Albouy and other Hugo scholars. While most of this early verse was written in the classical style of the eighteenth century, the works in themselves have little importance in understanding the genius of Hugo's mature poetry. The interest, then, is primarily historical.

HUGO'S FIRST TWO LINES OF POETRY

Professors René Journet and Guy Robert found in the Victor Hugo house, Place des Vosges in Paris, some sheets of the *Journal de l'Exil* of Hugo's younger daughter, Adèle Hugo.* Despite her cryptic handwriting, they were able to decipher what she had written. If it is true or simply anecdotal cannot be determined. Dated on August 6, 1855, Adèle claimed that these are the first two lines ever written by her father: *le grand Napoléon/Combat comme un lion* (Great Napoleon/fights like a lion).

TROIS CAHIERS DE VERS FRANÇAIS

These three sections contain a total of 158 short poems and fragments, works Hugo had recopied between 1815 and 1818 when he was in the pension Cordier. They can be classified as epigrams, fables, riddles, madrigals, translations or imitations of Latin texts, odes, satires, romances in the Spanish manner, and anniversary pieces.

Notebook 1

This notebook includes several anniversary pieces, mainly for his mother (there are six in all in the three notebooks). The eclectic and conservative nature of the collection indicates to what degree Hugo at this stage is merely an imitator, albeit a young and learned one. There are fables: "The City Rat and the Country Rat" and "The Two Lions." There are patriotic pieces: "Long Live the King, Long Live France," and there are historical portraits: "Richard the Lion-hearted." An epigram entitled *Imitation d'Owen* was published in *Le Conservateur Littéraire* in April 1820 under the pseudonym J. Sainte-Marie. Its vein is satirical, and it is quite witty for such a young writer. The "Paul" at whom this four-line piece is aimed has not been identified: *Vous vous aimez avant tous,/ Paul, vous n'aimez que vous même;/Mais si vous n'aimez que vous/Il n'est que vous qui vous aime* (You love yourself above everyone,/Paul, you only love yourself,/There is only you who loves you). The title makes reference to a Welsh poet of the sixteenth century, John Owen, or Ovenus, who wrote, in imitation of Martial, three books of epigrams. Some poems reflect the classical education that Hugo was receiving, such as "Caesar Crosses the Rubicon." In sum, the diversity and the subject matter demonstrate that Hugo was developing an encyclopedic knowledge of ancient and contemporary history.

Notebook 2

Entitled *Diverse Poetry*, the same eclecticism found in the first notebook is also present here. One interesting short entry, entitled "Concerning an Atheist," demonstrates Hugo's early and official Catholicism. He derides the atheist and concludes by saying: *Penses-tu nous réduire à ne croire qu'en toi?* (Do you hope to reduce us to only believing in you?).

Notebook 3

These entries reflect a young and ambitious Victor Hugo anxious to please political, academic, and literary authorities. Some of the titles are very pompous such as: *Bonheur que procure l'étude dans toutes les situations de la vie* (Happiness which study rewards in all of life's situations); however, this topic was proposed by the French Academy* (See Académie Française and Victor Hugo). There is also a poem on the death of Louis XVII.

What conclusions can we draw from reading these juvenile pieces? First, and most important, Hugo had not yet found his own way. He was dependent upon inherited forms, both classical, particularly Latin ones, and the legacy of French Classicism, which was already dying out. Hugo, of course, was the one to place the final nail in its coffin, toward the end of the 1820s. These poems do not indicate yet the evolution to come. Second, they demonstrate the conservative thought of the young Hugo in matters of government, religion, and aesthetics. This viewpoint disappeared when the poet matured. Finally, they reveal ambition, mainly literary, but with some hints of political roles yet to be played. The ambition remained throughout his career, of course, and Hugo figured prominently in the politics of France, but more and more in a leftist manner.

ACADEMIC POEMS: POEMS SENT TO THE FRENCH
ACADEMY

1. *Bonheur que procure l'étude dans toutes les situations de la vie,* 1817.

2. *Institution de jury en France* (Institution of the jury system in France), 1819. This very long poem, in dialogue form, consists of conversations between Voltaire and Malesherbes (1721–1794). Malesherbes, a secretary in the household of the king, tried to initiate reforms, especially in the area of censorship, but he was forced to resign in 1776. After defending the king before the Convention, he was executed during the Reign of Terror. The tone of the poem is that of a royalist Voltairianism, in its opposition to political and judicial excesses.

3. *Avantages de l'enseignement mutuel* (Advantages of mutual teaching), 1819. This is a commentary on a liberal pedagogical method in which those with more instruction would teach those with less learning, thus allowing the teacher to have larger classes of children. It is a prelude to Hugo's interest in educational issues, the most important of which was his opposition to the Falloux Act* which made him a leader of the left wing.

4. *Le Dévouement de Malesherbes* (Malesherbes' devotion), 1819. Ernest Dupuy published this poem in *La Revue de Paris* in 1902. Hugo received second mention from the Academy for this work. This poem and the preceding ones, as well as those sent to the Academy of Jeux Floraux* of Toulouse, come out of a psychology described by the abbé Venzac, *Les Origines religieuses de Victor Hugo*, as Hugo's *royalisme voltairien*, that is a liberal stance that is reluctant to see radical transformations of society, as those proposed by Jean-Jacques Rousseau, for example. The young Hugo, before his very formal and Chateaubriand-like Catholicism, is seen as a kind of deist, a rationalist, harboring anticlerical sentiments (which will resurface in his maturity), but standing in horror of the excesses of the French Revolution. Since all of the poems sent to the Toulouse Academy eventually were included in the *Odes et Ballades** of the 1820s, there is no need for any further comment here.

5. *Le Télégraphe* is a satirical poem of 1819 whose rhythm is similar to Edgar Allan Poe's *Raven: Tandis qu'en mon grenier, rongeant ma plume oisive,/ Je poursuis en pestant la rime fugitive,/ Que vingt pamphlets nouveaux, provoquant mon courroux,/ Loin d'échauffer ma veine, excitent mes dégoûts,/ Que tour à tour j'accuse, en ma rage inutile,/ Et ce siècle fécond et mon cerveau stérile,/ Ce maudit télégraphe enfin va-til cesser/ D'importuner mes yeux, qu'il commence à lasser?* (While in my attic, chewing on my lazy pen/ I continue to rage against the fugitive rhyme/ While twenty new pamphlets, provoking my anger/ Far from warming my luck, excite my disgust/ While in turn I accuse, in my useless rage, both this fruitful century and my sterile brain/ this accursed telegraph will it finally stop/ pestering

my eyes which it is beginning to tire?). The optical telegraph, invented by Claude Chappe, was mounted on the towers of the church of Saint-Sulpice, just 300 feet from the pension Cordier where Hugo, as a student, could see it and be annoyed by it.

6. *L'Enrôleur politique* (The political recruiter) is a satirical political poem from 1819 in the form of a dialogue between the recruiter and the *adepte* (the follower).

7. *Epître à Brutus* (Epistle to Brutus) was published in *Le Conservateur Littéraire* in 1820 and signed "Aristide." Hugo later published it in *Littérature et philosophies mêlées.**

8. *Le 4 novembre, 1820.* This poem gives the voice to the Duc de Berry's widow (he was assassinated in February 1820), the Duchess of Berry, Caroline of the Two Sicilies.

Choses vues. These materials were gathered from Hugo's papers and published first in 1887, two years after the poet's death; another group of odds and ends was brought out in 1900. In sum, they represent Hugo's impressions of cultural and political events in France from 1838 through 1877. Not everything recounted here was witnessed by Hugo, for example, the execution of Louis XVI. Other entries do bear the mark of an eyewitness account, such as the court of Louis-Philippe, the revolution of 1848, and some remembrances of Chateaubriand (*see A Chateaubriand*), who had been Hugo's ideal during his conservative, royalist youth.

Ciel et l'enfer, La. *See Heaven and Hell.*

Claque, La. Plays in the nineteenth century were seldom judged on their individual merit. A success or a failure often depended on the esteem in which the leading actors were held by the theatre-going public. There is no doubt that the premiere of *Hernani** was prejudged by the new Romantic generation, and it was booed by the entrenched classicists. Thus, *Hernani* was at one and the same time an innovative play pioneering new directions and a political-literary battle beyond the play's inherent structure. Actors and actresses also had their own egos, fueled by petty jealousies. While it can be conceded that Juliette Drouet was a second-rate artist, her replacement in Hugo's *Marie Tudor** was instigated by Mademoiselle George,* who would tolerate no rival.

The triumph of *Hernani* was due to the acceptance of new dramaturgical tastes; in like manner, the failure of *Les Burgraves** can be attributed to a shift in public interest, to the return of a classical taste that could be attributed to the genius of a superb new actress, Elisa Félix Rachel,* and to the ephemeral success of François Ponsard's (1814–1867) *Lucrèce* (1843), the same year *Les Burgraves* was staged. It is recorded in Théophile Gautier's* *Histoire du Romantisme* (Paris: Charpentier, 1874) that

Hugo's friends August Vacquerie* and François Paul Meurice* rounded up the Romantic troops to ensure the success of *Les Burgraves*, for Hugo himself had presentiments of doom. Hugo wanted to be supported by sincere friends. He always refused "la claque." What was to be their task? Simply to applaud vigorously, hence the term *La claque* (applaud). The dictionary meaning of this term is "a group of persons paid to applaud at the opera or theatre."

Vacquerie and Meurice wanted 300 young men to do the applauding but, as André Maurois aptly observed, "There was no longer any young Romantic generation to fulfill what had been accomplished at the premiere of *Hernani*" (Maurois, *Olympio*, Paris: Librairie Hachette, 1954, p. 309).

The *claque*, it would seem, was taken from any level of society, and also from the ranks of political and literary theorists. At the bottom rank of society we learn that Gavroche, the street urchin of Paris, attends theatre and opera. Speaking to the frightened Thénardier brothers (*see* Thénardier family), he speaks of future adventures: "After that, we'll go to the Opera. We'll go in with the claque. The claque at the Opera is very select. I wouldn't go with the claque on the boulevards. At the opera, just think, some pay twenty sous" (Hugo, *Les Misérables*, New York: New American Library, 1987, p. 961).

A play or an opera then, as now, could be made a success or a failure by the whim of a critic. In nineteenth-century France, the *claque* was an informing factor. Juliette Drouet was convinced that the hooting and whistling that led to the failure of *Les Burgraves* was provoked by a cabal against Hugo (Drouet, *Mille et une lettres d'amour à Victor Hugo*, Paris: Gallimard, 1951, p. 248). *Les Burgraves* closed after thirty-three performances, and Hugo ceased writing in this genre for ten years, except for short sketches.

Claude Gueux. Published in 1834, this work sprang from Hugo's obsession with the question of capital punishment.* The narration is based on a true episode recounted in the *Gazette des Tribunaux* (March 19, 1832). Documentation from real life is a characteristic of Romantic prose, whether it is historical or contemporary (Honoré de Balzac's* *Les Chouans*, 1829). Hugo's work evidences this regard for truth as a basis of fictional transformation which will inform the work of major novelists of the nineteenth century (Stendhal,* *Le Rouge et le noir*, 1831; Gustave Flaubert,* *Madame Bovary*, 1857).

As in other major expressions of Hugo's revulsion at the idea of execution, *Le Dernier Jour d'un condamné** (1829) or *Quatrevingt-treize** (1874), subjectivity in favor of the condemned prisoner is evident. Crime is seen as the result of unfavorable social conditions; the criminal is less to blame than the society that formed him. Here Hugo joins Charles Dickens in castigating nineteenth-century society which gives priority to ownership (thus the gravity of stealing and poaching as infringements on the rights of proprietorship). The text of *Claude Gueux* anticipates the appearance of Jean Valjean* in *Les Misérables** (1862).

The story of the protagonist, Claude Gueux, is that of a man of honesty and integrity who is the victim of circumstances. After being arrested for stealing in order to feed his mistress and child (keeping in mind that poverty often made marriage impossible), Claude is befriended by a fellow convict, Albin, who shares his food with Claude who has a robust appetite. Claude threatens the petty inspector who has separated him from Albin, his only friend. Becoming in a way the judge of his masters, Claude can be seen as a type of existential hero, *avant la lettre*. Passing sentence on Monsieur D, Claude gives him a deadline by which he must return Albin to him. The deadline passes, Claude kills the inspector with an axe, and then attempts suicide.* Claude's heroism is underlined by the devotion of one of the nursing nuns who urges him to appeal his sentence and by fellow prisoners who wish to abet his escape.

Claude walks to his execution, his eyes firmly fixed on the crucifix held by the chaplain. It is striking that Hugo, who believes in God, but not in organized religion, can so convincingly conjure up the symbols of Christian suffering in these accounts of capital punishment. He is, perhaps, making an appeal to a sense of justice which might be comprehended by a more-or-less believing Catholic readership.

As in *Le Dernier Jour d'un condamné*, Hugo stresses the role of the mob at the execution; it seems to be a festive occasion. The idea of public execution, related also in his account of the hanging of Mr. Tapner (*see* Tapner, the execution of Mr.) on Guernsey, is another aspect of Hugo's horror at the guillotine as an instrument of cruel death.

The work concludes with an appeal to the conscience of France, an appeal to aid the poor through education and to bring the poor up the ladder of progress. The government, according to Hugo, has an obligation to succor the poor, the weak, and the helpless. Truly Claude Gueux is seen as a victim of society by the author.

***Claude Gueux* (theatrical adaptation).** *Claude Gueux*, the 1834 thesis novelette against capital punishment* (similar to *Le Dernier Jour d'un condamné**) had one theatrical adaptation at the end of the nineteenth century (1884). Both the novel and the dramatic version are important as Victor Hugo's humanitarian views grow in popularity during the nineteenth century. Hugo, in this regard, is representative of the best humanitarian urges of the French Romantics. The play, written by Gadot-Rollo played first at the Théâtre Beaumarchais in February 1884, then at the Théâtre de la République in April 1895. Both productions were very successful.

An important dramatic modification was to give three of its five acts over to the life of Claude Gueux before going to prison, as opposed to the novel in which life before prison is presented only in a slight opening paragraph.

This modification is important in underlining the essential goodness of Claude, and of workers in general, who seem persecuted by an indifferent affluent capitalist society. Hugo's leftist or socialist leanings, while playing the role of subtext in the novel, become explicit in the play. Claude is both illiterate and naive, and at first he responds to his persecutors before and in prison by turning the other cheek. Finally his sense of justice and his solidarity with other workers (the rise of the proletariat) are awakened.

The last act, in which Claude is led in a cart to his death at the guillotine with masses of Parisians leaning from their windows, and another crowd gathers about the scaffold, is of course inspired by the last moments of *Le Dernier Jour d'un condamné*. It also anticipates, however, the closing pages of the existential and humanitarian novel of Albert Camus, *L'Étranger* (The Stranger), a denouement of which Claude would not be capable. Claude hopes to the end for some sort of pardon; Camus' hero, Mersault, welcomes the hatred of the crowd assembled for his execution. Both as novel and play *Claude Gueux*, along with *Les Misérables*,* shows Hugo's abiding interest in the humanitarian issues facing the nineteenth century; namely, capital punishment, slavery, poverty, and the abuse of children and workers. Some of these themes will be picked up by Emile Zola,* but certainly without the intense Romantic emotionalism of Victor Hugo.

Claudel, Paul. French poet, dramatist, and diplomat, Paul Claudel (1868–1955) was one of the most important writers of the first half of the twentieth century. His literary roots, found in the French symbolist movement, merged with his Catholic faith after his conversion in Notre-Dame cathedral during Christmas Eve Midnight Mass. Despite positive and even at times erotic feeling in both his poetry and plays, strict Catholic orthodoxy is present for most of his career, and he could be harsh on those he wanted to convert, for example, André Gide,* displaying a fundamental intolerance for those who deviated from his sense of a well-organized world. It is not surprising, then, that he not only misunderstood Victor Hugo's special brand of spirituality, but also assigned to the Romantic poet a special existential anguish, which was present at times, given the multiple tragedies that occurred during Hugo's life. Hugo's personal tragedies, however, would not be reasons Claudel would offer to explain the poet's existential anguish.

Claudel's evaluation of Hugo is negative, in stark contrast with that of Charles Baudelaire.* In Claudel's mind, Hugo remained gripped by fear, living in shadows, metaphysically almost blind. In his *Digressions sur Victor Hugo*, Claudel described how he had studied a marble bust of Hugo in a Copenhagen museum, trying to discover within the artifact Hugo's spirituality. The evaluation, which looks like a Balzacian physiognomy, is written in the hyperbolic style associated with Honoré de Balzac*: *Le tout sous le poids énorme du front a je ne sais quoi de tassé, de comprimé, de colérique, de bouché, de mesquin, d'hostile et de méchant* (The whole structure under the enormous weight of the forehead has I do not exactly know what of being dumpy, compressed, choleric, plugged up, shabby, hostile, mean). The claustrophobic description actually fits in with many of the poems in *Les Contemplations*.* After looking at the eyes of Hugo in the bust, Claudel compared them to the sealed-house cavities of Hugo's novel *Les Travailleurs de la mer** (Toilers of the sea).

Hugo's contemplation of the firmament can frequently be seen as having inspired the emotion; it leads also to doubt, similar to that found in Matthew Arnold's (1822–1888) contemplation of the sea in his poem 'Dover Beach' or Paul Valéry's* (1871–1945) sea poem *Le Cimetière marin*. Sea and sky in modern poetry can produce fear and doubt. With Hugo there is a positive side, a feeling of awe inspired by nature's forces. It leads to an acknowledgment of man's insignificance in the plan of the universe. This sentiment was certainly derived from the ideas of Jean-Jacques Rousseau, and it was enhanced by Chateaubriand's (*see A Chateaubriand*) cosmic commentaries derived from his viewing of Niagara Falls and the volcanic Mount Etna. Hugo was not out of step with his times, but perhaps Claudel was.

Claudel should be refuted for imposing a single aspect of Hugo's poetic spectrum on the whole; there are other notes that are more optimistic. Sarcastically, Claudel dismissed Hugo's spirituality: *La Religion sans religion de Victor Hugo, c'est quelque chose comme le vin sans alcool, le café sans caféine et le topinambour qui est le parent pauvre de la pomme de terre* (The Religion without religion of Victor Hugo, it is something like wine without alcohol, coffee without caffeine and the Jerusalem artichoke which is a poor relative of the potato).

Claudel concluded by seeing in Hugo the total absence of God, an absolute negation of Christian existentialism in which the abyss of Blaise Pascal becomes an inexhaustible negation. Needless to say, Claudel emphasized what he wanted to, out of his own doctrinaire Christianity.

BIBLIOGRAPHY

Claudel, Paul. *Oeuvres complètes*. 26 vols. Paris: Gallimard, 1959, vol. 15.

Claustrophobia. The dictionary defines claustrophobia as an abnormal dread of being in closed or narrow spaces. It would be insufficient to describe the atmosphere of confinement that pervades Hugo's poetry and to some extent his novels. Hugo was obsessed with caves and caverns, underground passages, and grottoes. Indeed, a recurrent noun in his writing is *antre*, meaning den, lair, or a retreat for animals. It seldom has any positive feeling of blissful retreat in the writings of Hugo, at least not in the sense of escape from the turmoil of an active city life. For many nineteenth-century writers, it was, in the tradition of Jean-Jacques Rousseau, the antithesis between commotion and tranquility. It appears to be an obsessive preoccupation with the possibility of conscious and living interment, such as being buried alive, which was sometimes a true, if somewhat irrational, concern of nineteenth-century society, at least as expressed by many European and American writers.

His work abounds with such figurative burials, out of which some are resurrected. The example of Gilliatt,* protagonist of *Les Travailleurs de la mer** comes to mind. After his victory over the octopus in the undersea grotto, Gilliatt rises to the surface exhausted, but alive. Likewise, there is the scene in *Les Misérables** in which Jean Valjean* is buried alive in order to escape arrest by Javert* in the convent (see Book Four, chapters 4, 5, 6 ["In His Narrow Box"] and 7, pp. 543–63 in *Les Misérables*, new English translation, New York: New American Library, 1987). These are not exactly the Lazarus themes that were so popular in nineteenth-century France, especially in *La Joie de vivre* (The joy of living) of Emile Zola,* but Hugo's claustrophobic scenes are allied to it in a hyperbolic sense.

The most significant examples are found in some of the poems of *Les Contemplations*,* which, when viewed collectively, would seem to be based on the poet's extreme grief over the death of his daughter Léopoldine Hugo.* It has been seen, however, by many critics—Pierre Moreau, Michael Riffaterre, and John Frey—as more symptomatic of Hugo's obsession with what perhaps is life after the conscious material life. Hugo, for example, believed that all life is animated or quickened. For him, even stones had souls (we would say atoms) and some slight perceptions. He also imagined evil persons being imprisoned for eternity within rocks, a type of Gustave Moreau reinvention of hell or purgatory as might be found in the *Divine Comedy* of Dante. For those interested in these aspects of Hugo's imagination, the best example would be in the very long poem entitled *Pleurs dans la nuit* (Tears during the night) from *Les Contemplations*, derived from the Romantic Gothic imagination, somewhat akin to Mary Shelley's *Frankenstein* or *The Modern Prometheus* (1818).

The motif of confinement, however, is not limited to Hugo. It is also found in the poetry of Charles Baudelaire,* an excellent example of which is the second tercet of the sonnet *La Cloche pêlée* (The cracked bell). In this tercet, the narrator seems to find himself buried underneath a large pile of dead persons with the impossibility of escaping from his interment: *Semble le râle épais d'un blessé qu'on oublie/Au bord d'un lac de sang, sous un grand tas de morts,/ Et qui meurt, sans bouger, dans d'immenses efforts* (Seems to be the thick death rattle of a wounded person who has been forgotten/ At the edge of a lake of blood, under a great pile of dead,/ And who dies, without moving, in immense efforts).

Similar feelings are expressed in the paintings and lithographs of the Norwegian painter Edvard Munch (1863–1944), especially in his illustrations of Baudelaire's *Les Fleurs du mal* (Flowers of evil). His plastic images parallel the claustrophobic imagery found in both Baudelaire and Hugo. That this sentiment of confinement continues in Hugo's poetry can be confirmed by the poem *Je me penchais*,* from *La Légende des siècles*, probably composed around 1875, in which the poet peers into holes in the ground, "abysses" as Baudelaire would say. This is part of the Romantic staring at crevices whether they are volcanos, such as Mount Etna, or places for depositing the dead. *Les Contemplations*, however, is the best example of Hugo's fascination with cavities.

BIBLIOGRAPHY

Barrère, Jean-Bertrand. *La Fantaisie de Victor Hugo*. Paris: José Corti, 1949, 1950.
Claudel, Paul. *Oeuvres complètes*. Vol. 15. Paris: Gallimard, 1959.
Frey, John Andrew. *Les Contemplations of Victor Hugo: The Ash Wednesday Liturgy*. Charlottesville: University Press of Virginia, 1988.
Moreau, Pierre. *Les Contemplations de Victor Hugo ou le temps retrouvé*. Paris: Archives des Lettres Modernes, 1962.
Riffaterre, Michael. *Semiotics of Poetry*. Bloomington: Indiana University Press, 1978.

Cocteau, Jean. Jean Cocteau (1889–1963) explored and exploited many aesthetic media during his intense effete life. A forerunner of the artistic interdisciplinary approach he worked in prose, poetry, essays, painting, theatre, and film. His minimal relationship with the work of Hugo came mainly through his collaboration with Hugo's great-grandson Jean Hugo* (1886–1984), a painter and scene designer (he also did the costume sketches for Cocteau's celebrated *Les Mariés de la Tour Eiffel* (1921). Hugo's descendant, however, was not pleased by Cocteau's reinterpretation of *Ruy Blas*,* the 1838 play redone by Cocteau in 1947. The great-grandson saw in Cocteau's interpretation of Hugo's play nothing more than a vehicle for Cocteau's lover Jean Marais to play the dual roles of Don Cesar and Ruy Blas.

Cocteau's interest in Victor Hugo is peripheral to the corpus of his work, and it should not be considered significant. His few remarks about Hugo seem silly and sophomoric, too giddy to be of interest except in the history of arts and letters in France in the early years of the twentieth century. The best known of Cocteau's bons mots on Hugo comes from a 1934 essay defending the painting of Giorgio de Chirico against attacks made by the surrealist André Breton. In this work, entitled *Le Mystère laïc*, is found Cocteau's famous aphorism: "Victor Hugo was a madman who thought he was Victor Hugo."

The only connection, then, to Victor Hugo came through his adaptation of *Ruy Blas* and his personal and professional relationship with Jean Hugo.

Collections: Works and iconography. Within France, the Hugo collections, as to be expected, are enormous. In Paris there are Hugo archives to be found at the French Academy (*see* Académie Française and Victor Hugo), the Forney library, the Bibliothèque Nationale (soon to be incorporated into the new Bibliothèque de France), the library of the Opéra, the library of the Comédie-Française, the Cabinet des Estampes, the Cabinet des Médailles, the Victor Hugo house at the Place des Vosges,* the Carnavalet museum which is dedicated exclusively to all aspects of the city of Paris, the drawing section of the Louvre, the Museum of Film and French Cinematography, the Pompidou Center at Les Halles, the nineteenth-century museum at the Quai d'Orsay, and many others. Outside Paris there are important collections in the following cities: Angers, Avignon, Besançon (city of Hugo's birth), Dijon, La Rochelle, Marseilles, Nantes, Nice, and Nîmes.

Outside of France there are important collections in Argentina, in the Museo Nacional de Bellas Artes; Australia, in the Art Gallery of New South Wales in Sydney; in Belgium, in the Royal Museum of Fine Arts and also in the Antoine Wiertz Museum; in Maribo, Denmark, in the Fine Arts Museum of Lalande-Faister; in the United States, in the Philadelphia Museum of Art; in Italy, in the Gallery of Modern Art in Turin; and in Suwar, Japan, in the Kitazawa Museum.

The important sources, of course, are French and mainly Parisian, but the existence of important collections outside France attest to the universal genius of Hugo and the respect given to him by the entire world.

Comprachicos. *Comprachicos* (literally, Spanish for children buyers), is a central motif of Hugo's novel *L'Homme qui rit** published in 1869, and it is an important, if hideous practice for those interested in studying the literature of childhood. In this work, Hugo traced the European origins of the phenomenon of child buying back into the seventeenth century, but he did not limit himself to Europe. Children were purchased and then physically deformed (with concomitant mental results) through a variety of mechanical and surgical means. Such children, who became freaks, were used in circuses and traveling sideshows; they also became household pets, especially among the aristocracy. They were particularly favored by popes as the singing castrati. They made useful beggars; people offered alms to them out of human pity or just to get them out of sight. Of the many cases cited by Hugo, the Chinese example is the least repugnant and thus easiest to report. In a society known for binding the feet of female children, the formation of jar-shaped humans was easily accomplished. A child was placed in a jar without a bottom so that the feet as well as the head were free. During the day, the jar was upright; at night, for sleeping, the jar was put on its side. As the child grew, the body, encased in the jar, took on more and more of the jar's shape. Finally, the jar was broken and the product was finished—a human shaped like a jar.

The *comprachicos* were responsible for the physical mutilation of the protagonist of *L'homme qui rit*, Gwynplaine.* They enlarged his mouth to such a degree that he gave the impression of always smiling, an ironic twist to such a perverted, Byzantine practice.

Hugo devoted six introductory chapters to the *comprachicos*. Finally outlawed in both England and France, child buying was part of society's general repression of loitering, poaching, and stealing, all affronts to a society established on the basis of property and money.

Conscience, La. The famous Cain poem, written in 1853 and appearing in the 1859 first edition of *La Légende des siècles*,* is an apt rendering of Victor Hugo's moral preoccupations, in this case, the first recorded Biblical murder, when Cain killed his brother Abel. Hugo's short narrative (sixty-eight lines) traces the itinerary of the fleeing Cain who, with his family, seeks asylum from the powerful wrath of Jehovah. The motif of a long voyage, filled with suffering, already exploited by Hugo in the *Mazeppa* poem of *Les Orientales** (1829) is here reiterated as a frightening exodus, as Cain, his family, and his descendants seek calm and peace. But for Cain there is none, for he is pursued by the Eye of God (a symbol that can be found on the American one-dollar bill). Thus, even when he attempts to bury himself underground, the eye is always there, menacing and judging: *L'oeil était dans la tombe et regardait Cain* (The eye was in the tomb and kept looking at Cain). This poignant and persistent symbol of a bad conscience, hence the title of the poem, is somewhat akin to similar symbolisms found in the writings of Edgar Allan Poe (1809–1849). Helmut Hatzfeld in his *Initiation à l'explication de textes français* (Munich: Max Hueber, 1957) speaks of Hugo's success in fusing history and symbolism, making Cain's murder of Abel a very typical Romantic and visionary text.

Contemplations, Les. Published in 1856, this collection adds to the brilliance of French letters of the 1850s, which included Théophile Gautier's* *Emaux et Camées* (1852), Gustave Flaubert's* first realistic novel *Madame*

Bovary (1857), and Charles Baudelaire's* *Les Fleurs du Mal* (Flowers of Evil), (1857). It can be argued that *Les Contemplations* is Hugo's best collection of poetry because of its poignant remembrances of his dead daughter Léopoldine Hugo,* its many tributes to family and friends, its political and religious invectives, and finally its ardent search for God and the resolution of theological difficulties encountered by nineteenth-century persons of deep thought. The title, indeed, implies a mystical surge, a contemplation in either the sense of Eastern mysticism or that of the Spanish mystics of the sixteenth century. Although this goal may not have been achieved—some observers feel that Hugo had only arrived at a lower level (albeit a prayerful one) of spirituality—it is evident that Hugo searched deeply for spiritual illumination, even though the search is frequently intertwined with erotic expressions. For Hugo, these two aspects of body and soul were not incompatible, but fused.

At first glance, the reader might be tempted to think that the collection is centered on his daughter Léopoldine who tragically died three months after her marriage in a boating accident in the mouth of the Seine river. Important as it was, the Léopoldine sequence, however, was transcended, as has been pointed out by the eminent French Hugo scholar Jean Gaudon. The daughter's death seems to have engendered a more encompassing poetic meditation on man's mortality, an existential meditation on the meaning of life.

The work is scrupulously orchestrated and its divisions merit review. The preface is filled with symbolic hints as to what is to come within the body of the text. Hugo announces that it could be read as the book of a dead person, or as the memories of a soul. He concludes his introduction by making a temporal reference to *Autrefois, aujourd'hui* (Formerly and now); *Autrefois*, meaning the years between 1830 and 1843, and *Aujourd'hui*, the year of Léopoldine's drowning and thereafter.

In what may appear to the modern reader as a trite introduction to the collection is found a short allegorical poem about the passage of life, seen as a ship on a vast ocean, tossed by the waves, but always with a view of the stars. The sea is seen as God, and the boat as mankind.

The work is divided into six books, each of which needs some small description. Book One, entitled *Aurore* (Dawn), contains an eclectic mixture of paternal, political, and nature-oriented items, plus a recall to adolescent erotic feelings (the poems entitled *Lise** and *La Coccinelle*, or Lady bug). Especially beautiful and highly erotic is the rococo piece *La Fête chez Thérèse* (Theresa's garden party), a nocturnal event filled with covert sexual nuances. This section contains twenty-nine poems.

Book Two, *L'Ame en Fleur* (The budding of the soul), mixes intoxication with nature, especially trees and birds, with deep amorous sentiment, obviously directed toward Juliette Drouet. Some of these poems give a narrative voice to the woman who suggests that she is not just an object of desire, but also an intellectual creature, seeking cerebral equality with her lover.

Book Three, *Les Luttes et les Rêves* (Struggles and dreams), is increasingly melancholic and pessimistic, concentrating in such poems as *Mélancholia* (Melancholy) on social injustice in the nineteenth century— women forced into alms seeking or prostitution and the corruption of the judicial system (similar to what is found in Charles Dickens's *Bleak House*)—concluding, however, with the magnificent *Magnitudo parvi** in which the poet and his young daughter walk by the sea at night, contemplate the stars, and ponder eternity.

The fourth book, *Pauca Meae*, is dedicated almost entirely to the loss of Léopoldine: lyrical recalls of the happy days of a young father with his daughters, and then to the horrible tragedy of the 1843 drowning. Two of the most famous of all of Hugo's poems are found in this section. The first, the long poem *A Villequier*, concerns the town where Léopoldine lived with her new husband, on the Seine, which was also the site of the death of the newly married couple, the news of which Hugo received while on a walking trip on the Atlantic coast near Rochefort with Juliette Drouet when he read about the deaths in a newspaper. The poem seems to defy critical definition that lyrical emotion cannot be sustained across many verses. In this case, it seems to work. The father's grief should overwhelm even the most insensitive reader, and in French literature its only equivalent is the elegy of the early seventeenth-century writer François de Malherbe, in his *Consolation à Monsieur du Perier sur la mort de sa fille* (Consolation to Sir Perier on the death of his daughter). *A Villequier* is complemented by an equally famous, but very short, poem, *Demain, dès l'aube* (Tomorrow at daybreak), in which the poet makes a visit to the gravesite of his daughter.

Book Five, *En Marche* (On the Road), is too eclectic to classify with any ease. One unifying device is the oblique references made to the exile on the island of Guernsey. Particularly interesting is the poem *Pasteurs et troupeaux* (Shepherds and flocks) which combines Virgilian pastoral settings with the dangerous forces of the sea, especially as seen from the Corbière lighthouse on Guernsey.

The final book, *Au Bord de l'Infini* (Close to infinity), is principally metaphysical in intent. Here Hugo combines the two central motifs of the collection: the death of Léopoldine and the search for God. This is manifest in the two concluding poems. The first, *Ce que dit la bouche d'ombre** (What the mouth from the shadow says), is a very long meditation on good and evil and the final destiny of mankind. The so-called shadow mouth is a rather insignificant dolmen found near Rozel Baly on Guernsey, which is paleolithic in origin (with the primitive religious speculations that always surround these prehistoric monuments of mankind). Hugo makes of this pile of stone slabs—open at the front, viewed, it would seem, in the darkness of the night—a modern-day oracle that can resolve Manichean struggles, unify and absolve not only all of mankind from sin, but also resolve the Dantean and Miltonian dichotomy between heaven and hell. In its final stanza, Jesus Christ and Ballial (Satan) walk hand in hand before the throne of God. The final poem, *A celle qui est restée en France* (To she who remained in France), gives the clue to the entire collection. "She" is Léopoldine, who was buried in 1843. The intent seems to be how to get Léopoldine resurrected, thus marrying theology (belief in the immortality of the soul) with his desire to have his daughter back, whole and intact. The poet asks her to come out of the tomb, which of course cannot happen. Thus the lyrical and quasi-theological aspects of this great collection of poetry are joined in a manner that can almost be seen as a type of motif symbolism.

Les Contemplations is quite different from the earlier poetic works of Victor Hugo and from those that follow. It is not hard to understand why many readers and most Hugo scholars consider it his major poetic achievement, and a hallmark of the new poetry of the nineteenth century in France.

BIBLIOGRAPHY

Frey, John A. *Les Contemplations of Victor Hugo: The Ash Wednesday Liturgy*. Charlottesville: University Press of Virginia, 1988.
Gaudon, Jean. *Le Temps de la contemplation*. Paris: Flammarion, 1969.
Nash, Susan. *Les Contemplations of Victor Hugo: An Allegory of the Creative Process*. Princeton, N.J.: Princeton University Press, 1976.

Cosette. One of the principal personages of Hugo's *Les Misérables*,* Cosette is considered an adopted daughter by Jean Valjean.* The daughter of Fantine,* she is farmed out, while a mere child, to the Thénardier family,* who run an eating house near Paris. After being mistreated and forced to do menial and difficult work, she is rescued by Jean Valjean, who fulfills his promise to Fantine to look after the child. While hiding out with Jean Valjean in a convent garden, she grows into beauty and wisdom. When she is walking in the Luxembourg gardens, she is noticed by Marius* whom she eventually marries. The young couple later witness the death of Jean Valjean.

A sequel to *Les Misérables*, the novel *Cosette*,* written by Laura Kalpakian (New York: Harper Collins, 1995), provoked a huge controversy in France among Hugo followers. With much imagination, Kalpakian's novel carries Cosette and Marius through many adventures in the name of republican principles—the revolution of 1848 and the Second Empire.* An epilogue dated March 1867 brings this imaginative continuation of Hugo's novel to a conclusion.

Cosette. It is unusual and somewhat rare, but understandable, that a great novel touches not just the general public, but any sensitive writer who would prolong the pleasure of the original experience. Such is the case, for example, with Margaret Mitchell's *Gone With the Wind* and, it is understood, for E. M. Forster's gay novel *Maurice.*

Laura Kalpakian has written a sequel to *Les Misérables** entitled *Cosette* (New York: Harper Collins, 1995). Her heroine, obviously Cosette, is married to Marius,* and they continue the leftist struggle against totalitarianism that is depicted during the insurrection of 1832 in *Les Misérables.* With her husband, Cosette starts a leftist newspaper entitled *La Lumière* (The Light) which is central to the intrigue of the important revolution of 1848, sixteen years after the events in Hugo's novel. With the coup d'état of Napoléon III,* ill winds blow toward these new revolutionaries. Familial alienation, such as might be found in television's daily soap opera, is present with Cosette's son Jean-Luc who egotistically prospers during the days of the Second Empire.*

Laura Kalpakian certainly wants to continue at least the social strata found within Hugo's novel. Thus there is a mixture of stock characters reminiscent of *Les Misérables*—street urchins (like Gavroche), actors, printers, painters, and so on. Six hundred and fifty two pages long, it almost matches the epic length of Hugo's work.

A basic idea, transformed more than in the original, is the relationship between virtue, the qualities of being a human being, and freedom and justice.

The novel, of course, produced a typical French negative reaction, with an important premise, namely that *Les Misérables* is complete unto itself with no sequel possible or necessary. In other words, it should not be considered a *roman fleuve* as the French call novels that seem to vie generationally with real genealogies, as found, for example, in the works in France of Georges Duhamel (1884–1966) in his *Chronique des Pasquier* (1933–1944), the story of a family during the Third Republic, or the ten-volume novel *Les Thibault* (1922–1940) of Roger Martin du Gard (1881–1958), which portrays the lives of two bourgeois families during the years preceding World War I. In England, there is the example of the *Forsythe Saga* (1906–1921) of John Galsworthy (1881–1933). Some French critics may have thought that such was the intention of Laura Kalpakian, but the evidence of a single sequel until otherwise proven does not lead to the conclusion of an ongoing literary activity engendered by Hugo. In fact, *Cosette* can be read without attaching it to *Les Misérables* in any strict sense.

A more important criticism from France might have to do with style. Obviously the style is not Hugo's, nor is the language. In defense of Kalpakian, it would be fair to say that she saw a magnificent seed planted in *Les Misérables*, and her imagination led her to further specu-

lations about what could have happened to Cosette and Marius following the death of Jean Valjean.* Her work is indebted to Hugo, but not
in any slavish manner. When characters do not die at the end of a novel,
the imaginative mind wonders what happened afterward. It could be
assumed that Victor Hugo would have been pleased that a late-
twentieth-century American writer would have such a high opinion of
his work that she would want to send it forth into the revolution of 1848
and into the years of the Second Empire of Napoléon III.

Cow, The. *See Vache, La.*

Cravatte. The story of the bandit Cravatte is found in Book One, *Fantine:*
An Upright Man (chapter 7) of Victor Hugo's *Les Misérables.** Bishop Myriel (*see* Bienvenu, Bishop), the introductory hero of this novel, is
presented as the epitome of sanctity, a goal of perfection that will be
transmitted to Jean Valjean* in the famous episode of the silver candlesticks. The opening pages of *Les Misérables* pit good against evil in an
eternal struggle; bad intent is shockingly recognized in the figures of
authority, the higher clergy, the nobility, and magistrates. Goodness, or
morality, is recognized by Hugo the narrator where it might least be
expected to exist, within the cadre of social and political outcasts. It is
thus that, in the early chapters of this 1862 humanitarian novel, there are
presented not only the idealism of "G" the conventionalist,* but also the
moral integrity of the bandit named Cravatte.

The bishop, en route to making a pastoral visit in a mountainous terrain, has been warned of the dangers should he encounter the famous
outlaw Cravatte who had just recently robbed the sacristy of the cathedral of Embrun. Bishop Myriel, always trusting, for he never locked his
doors, proceeds on his mission and spends two weeks administering to
his distant flock. While he sings a *Te Deum* for the accomplishment of
his mission, it is noted that there is no ecclesiastical finery for the occasion. It is then that the miracle of the thieves takes place. A chest is
delivered, filled with the finery stolen from Notre-Dame d'Embrun with
a note: "From Cravatte to Bishop Bienvenu." The bishop did not return
the ecclesiastical "booty" to the cathedral; instead, it was sold for the
benefit of the poor, a central motif in Hugo's ideology. The episode of
Cravatte is indicative of a higher morality in Hugo's epistemology. It is
premised that thieves perhaps have a code of honor superior to that of
official morality. It is a higher and more valid form of casuistry which
is illustrated not just in the work of Hugo, but in other nineteenth-
century writers, including Prosper Mérimée and Guy de Maupassant,
and twentieth-century writers, such as Jean Genet in France and Alan
Burgess (*The Inn of the Sixth Happiness*, 1957), who uphold this tradition
of the Good Thief which thematically reverberates back to the crucifixion

of Christ. Stealing and retribution are essential ingredients of *Les Misérables*; the bishop's silver candlesticks are the catalyst for the redemption,
perfection, and sanctification of Jean Valjean.

Cromwell. This huge play is much less known than its famous *Préface*,
which has been acknowledged as the culmination of Romantic emanci-
pation from the tenets of French classic dramaturgy, especially from the
mediocre classical forms persisting at the end of the eighteenth century
(*see Cromwell, Preface to*). Literary historians are correct in assuming that
this document serves as a conclusion to the seventeenth-century Quarrel
of the Ancients and the Moderns. The triumph of Romantic theatre is
not manifest in *Cromwell*; it occurs in *Hernani*.* The play *Cromwell* is more
important politically than aesthetically, for it acts as a document revealing Victor Hugo's historical meditations on governance, and the rise,
continuation, and collapse of royal and noble prerogatives. The play,
therefore, should be considered in its relationship with Hugo's other
political dramas: on Spain, *Hernani*, 1830; *Ruy Blas*, 1838; England, *Marie
Tudor*, 1833; and Germany, *Les Burgraves*, 1843.

Hugo's choice of Oliver Cromwell as a subject for a tragedy or drama
is difficult to comprehend. It has something to do with the idea of revolution and the replacement of royalty by a kind of self-made man who
appears like a prototype of Napoléon.

Cromwell was never entirely performed and may be considered for
1826 as an ambiguous presentation of questions concerning the highest
form of government. It concludes with the enigmatic meditation of
Cromwell: *Quand donc serai-je roi?* (When then shall I be king?), which
may be a political statement not only for England, but also for France
before the revolution of 1830.

Cromwell as a historical figure remains problematic in both Europe
and America. He is viewed as a tyrant, a persecutor of nonconformists,
the subjugator of Ireland, and an antisemite, all of which issues are
touched upon in Hugo's play. Biography and bibliography, however, do
not substantiate this opinion. To the credit of Hugo, Cromwell seems
less of a dictator and more of an astute prime minister, almost a Richelieu
for England.

The play's format need not be discussed in detail. It holds to a mixture
of prose and poetry which was to be Hugo's new formula. Its alexandrines are in rhymed couplets, but other verse forms intervene and battle
somewhat with the prose. In five "classical" acts, it follows Cromwell's
meditations on the murder of Charles I and his paternal concerns for his
daughter and son, who first appeared as a possible traitor. The final
dramatic portrait is that of a shrewd and intelligent leader, capable of
forgiveness and understanding.

Charles-Augustin Sainte-Beuve's* evaluation of the play, after sitting through its reading, was correct from a French point of view. Sainte-Beuve was not yet thinking about the Shakespearean model Hugo had in mind. Therefore, his reference was to Molière, and thus for him, Hugo's play seemed more like the work of Beaumarchais, especially with its hundreds of asides recalling melodrama or some eighteenth-century operas. Hugo had read Shakespeare through the Letourneur and Guizot translations, both of which are marred and present to the French an inaccurate view of the Bard. Hugo, later on, did profit from his son's assiduous task of translating Shakespeare while in exile on Guernsey.

Cromwell reveals Hugo's Romantic modernity, specifically its almost Hegelian concept of human progress, moving away from the divine rights of kings to something close to the egalitarian ideas of Jean-Jacques Rousseau.

BIBLIOGRAPHY

Cortez, Wilbur. *A Bibliography of Oliver Cromwell.* Cambridge, Mass.: Harvard University Press, 1929.
Howel, Robert, and R. C. Richardson. *Images of Oliver Cromwell.* Manchester, England: Manchester University Press, 1993.
Morril, John. *Oliver Cromwell and the English Revolution.* New York: Longman, 1990.

Cromwell, Preface to. Hugo's *Préface de Cromwell,* 1827, was not composed in a vacuum but was, rather, the culmination of Romantic foment and polemics on the meanings of the new Romantic school as it was defining itself in the first quarter of the nineteenth century, mainly in Germany, but also in France under strong German influence. England and Germany were both providing examples of what form the literature could take. From England, the models were Shakespeare and Lord Byron.* German examples were the young Johann Wolfgang von Goethe (1749–1832), Friedrich von Schiller (1759–1805), and Friedrich Gottlieb Klopstock (1724–1803). Theoretical postulations were also being elaborated in Germany, and then imitated in France in the works of Benjamin Constant (1767–1830) and Madame de Staël (1766–1817). Key words in the new literary argument are nationalism, Middle Ages, and Shakespeare. These three perspectives finally led to a condemnation of classical tragedy, especially as it was practiced in France by the generation of 1660, notably by France's greatest writer of tragedies, Jean Racine (1639–1699).

Among Hugo's critical antecedents then were August Wilhelm von Schlegel (1767–1845), Madame de Staël, Benjamin Constant, Charles Nodier* (1783–1844), Alessandro Manzoni (1785–1873), and Stendhal* (1783–1842). Schlegel and his brother Friedrich von Schlegel (1772–1829) were in the forefront of German Romanticism—August von Schlegel for his translations of Shakespeare and for his unfinished translations of the Spanish playwright Pedro Calderón de la Barca (1600–1681), both of which interests reveal a penchant for theatre derived from the idea of the nation. August von Schlegel's *Lectures on Dramatic Art and Literature* (1809–1811) had a profound impact, especially in France, and helped spread the new Romantic gospel across Europe. The model for Schlegel was Shakespeare with a concomitant negative criticism of French classical tragedy.

Benjamin Constant was the major vehicle for the dissemination of German dramaturgical theory in France, and as a friend and lover of Madame de Staël, certainly influenced the writing of her *De l'Allemagne* (On Germany, 1813).

Moreover, Charles Nodier, the librarian at the Bibliothèque de l'Arsenal, was instrumental in enlarging the literary horizons of his time, making room for non-French literature. Nodier stated that paying homage to German or English literature would in no way defame the French canon. Starting in about 1801, with his *Pensées de Shakespeare extraites de ses oeuvres* (Thoughts of Shakespeare extracted from his works), he insisted on the primacy of genius over the classical unities, thus allying himself with the position of Wilhelm von Schlegel. The same can be said for the Italian Alessandro Manzoni, who was more famous for his novel *I promessi sposi* (The betrothed) and for his patriotic appeal to the budding *Risorgimento* movement in Italy. Manzoni, however, can also be remembered for two historical tragedies that were influenced by his reading of Shakespeare: *Il conde de Carnagnola* (1820) and *Adelchi* (1822). Shakespeare, therefore, was now regarded in Germany, Italy, and France as the supreme model for the new theatre.

Shakespeare, who had received a poor and hostile reception in France at the time of classicism, was on the rebound during the Romantic movement. The Letourneur translation was amended by François Guizot in 1821. Hugo, who did not know English well enough to appreciate Shakespeare in the original text, and aware of the deficiencies of the Letourneur translation, was fortunate enough to have, at a later date, the benefit of the translations made by his son François-Victor.

These translations are the point of departure for Hugo's own positive assessment of Shakespeare, the "man of genius," as found in Hugo's *William Shakespeare* (1864). English actors performed Shakespeare in Paris in 1822 and 1877, and thus the road was being paved for a supposed Shakespearean model to replace a moribund classicism.

What remained to be accomplished was found in the work of Madame de Staël and Stendhal, all of which culminated in the *Préface de Cromwell* of Hugo, and, of course, was the very example of Hugo's new theatre.

Two documents of Madame de Staël need brief explanation. *De la Littérature* (1800) presents a simplistic dialectic argument not unlike that of

Hugo in his *Préface*. She presents an either-or world of literature, determined by race and geography. There is southern and northern literature: the south includes the literature of the Greeks, Latins, Italians, Spaniards, and French of the period of Louis XIV. Northern literature, coming from the pseudo-Ossian, is more melancholic and Christian. Madame de Staël derived many of these ideas from Wilhelm von Schlegel and indirectly from Constant. She decided that northern literature was the wave of the future, a theatre liberated from the laws of the ancients. Tragedy would treat modern subjects, not just kings and nobles; it would be based on national or indigenous concerns. The model for the new theatre would be Shakespeare and Schiller.

Her *De l'Allemagne* more radically amplifies the ideas of her previous document. Her essay on Gotthold Lessing (1729–1781), which attacks French theatre, underlines the importance of a national taste, with no need to imitate the ancients. The essay on Goethe, the incarnation of German genius, praises the presence of the "natural" in Goethe as opposed to the artificiality of the French writers. The essay on poetry stresses the importance of religion, poetry's association with Christianity, and the positive role of the Middle Ages. Her comparison of Romantic and classical poetry presents a strong argument against classicism. Her key words were troubadours, Christianity, north, Middle Ages, character, meditative spirit, abstraction, divine providence, inspiration, and indigenous literature. She opposed classical literature as being artificial when imposed upon contemporary society. Finally, her ideas on *drame*,* the same as those expounded by Stendhal and demonstrated by Hugo, pushed the new literature toward a pseudo-psychological modernism.

Stendhal, taken with things both Italian and English, tells us that it was a capital date in his intellectual life when he took out a subscription to the *Edinburgh Review* (1823–1829), which was establishing the norms for modern literary criticism. Stendhal, who was allied with liberal Romanticism, presented not only a radical political concept of Romanticism (the banishment, for example, of poetry, meaning the absence of simile and metaphor), but also opted for the new literature as an emulation of Shakespeare, to the detriment of Racine. These arguments are presented in the two parts of his *Racine et Shakespeare* (1823–1825). Stress is put on the absurdity of the classical unities, particularly those of time and place.

All of the above should be seen as preparation for Hugo's *Préface de Cromwell*, a document of some seventy pages written several days after he finished writing the play. Hugo's aesthetic reading of history is as simplistic as that of Madame de Staël. The argument, entitled *The Development of Poetry*, divides human literary evolution into three distinct periods. It is not always possible to follow Hugo's argument, but it seems to go as follows: Primitive time (this may mean prehistory) has the ode as its primary form; it is thus lyrical uniting personal emotion and general meditation. The ode, says Hugo, is naive in character, singing of things eternal. Next comes the period of classical antiquity which gave gravity to history through its epic forms. The modern period has as its primary form dramatic art; it paints real life (the push toward realism), and its form is neither tragedy nor comedy, but *drame* (drama). If prehistory was naive, the historians of antiquity are known for their simplicity, whereas modern writers are not historians, but chroniclers. This would seem to mean the recording of particular histories within general histories, and would thus fit well into Hugo's dramaturgy. Spanish history, for example, is seen through the personages of Hernani* and Ruy Blas (see *Ruy Blas*), English history, through the perspective of Oliver Cromwell. Furthermore, contemporary literature, through the vehicle of the *drame* presents playwrights as critics and judges of events—the playwright as a seeker of truth. The role of personages reinforces some ideas found already in Madame de Staël. Prehistory texts, especially Jewish scriptures, present colossal individuals (Adam, Cain, Noah), and the Bible is the source of this literature of mankind's youth. Classical antiquity portrays the grandiose through epic heroes (Achilles, Orestes); the model is Homer. Modern literature, through the *drame*, presents the real. Primitive times reflect mankind's dreams; classical times, man's exploits; the modern period, mankind's thoughts. Primitive literature sings, classical literature recounts, modern literature paints. It no longer separates tragedy and comedy but freely mixes the sublime and the grotesque.

The whole argument is concluded with a slogan that announces clearly what the Romantics, and Hugo in particular, are about. They want to be realists, without knowing what such a word would mean. The slogan is *Tout ce qui est dans la nature est dans l'art* (All that is in nature is in art). This is decisive for it means that art has no limitations as to subject matter, contrary to the restrictions of the seventeenth-century theoretician Nicolas Boileau-Despréaux (*Art poétique*); it assails the arbitrary limitations of genre and with ease mixes with both verse and prose.

While Shakespeare may indeed be the theoretical model for the new German and French Romantic theatre, it would be presumptive and even naive to consider the new drama on a par with that of Shakespeare.

Hugo's manifesto, however, and the triumph of *Hernani** bring to a conclusion the old seventeenth-century dispute over imitation of Greek and Roman models as opposed to modern subjects. The seventeenth-century quarrel over the proper classification of Pierre Corneille's *Le Cid* becomes irrelevant with the triumph of the theatre of Alexandre Dumas père, Alfred de Vigny,* Prosper Mérimée, and above all Victor Hugo. It is, however, a triumph that will be short-lived, for there will be no more creations of Romantic dramas on stage, after the so-called failure of Hugo's *Les Burgraves** in 1843.

D

David d'Angers, Pierre-Jean. Pierre-Jean David d'Angers (1788–1856), a French sculptor of the Romantic period, is known particularly for the ornamental façade of the Panthéon in Paris. He is also celebrated for his medallion portraits and busts of many of the Romantics and important historical figures of his time. Hugo made his acquaintance in 1827, and the following year David d'Angers cast a medallion of the poet.

Hugo admired the art of David d'Angers, and it offered him the possibility of making comparative statements on the arts in his poetry. The first poetic mention of the sculptor is found in poem seven of *Les Feuilles d'Automne** (1831); again in poem twenty, *Au statuaire David*, in *Les Rayons et les Ombres** (1840); and finally a dedicatory piece in part of *Toute la lyre* of 1872. The 1831 poem is pure adulation as is that of the 1840 collection. The 1840 poem is a very long poem of 214 lines, divided into seven parts. Both poems place David d'Angers at the rank of the great Italian artists of the Renaissance.

The poem rambles here and there through history and up to the present time, particularly as it seeks a poetic of inspiration. A close reading of the poem makes it difficult to justify Hugo's poetic divisions; there is no logical sequence, and connectives are missing. An interesting aside is Hugo's allusions to "bad" kings, a lifelong preoccupation of the poet.

The friendship with David d'Angers is but another instance of Hugo's intermingling in other art forms such as sculpture and music. At this time, only dance (ballet) seems to be missing from Hugo's attention. Hugo's meditation and tribute to all the arts seems to fall within the theoretical field proposed by Théophile Gautier* (1811–1872) with his theory of *transposition d'art* (transposing art). It also has some kinship with Charles Baudelaire's* theory of the unity of all the arts found in his *Correspondances* sonnet.

Hugo's approach, however, may seem exterior and discursive when compared with the more sophisticated theories of Gautier and Baudelaire, both of whom approach Romantic theories of poetic (meaning the arts in general) imagination as expressed in Germany and England, especially in the theoretical writings of Samuel Taylor Coleridge. It is also leagues away from the synesthesia phenomenon (evolving out of the ideas of Gautier and Baudelaire) found in the poetry of Arthur Rimbaud (1854–1891).

Dea. Dea is an infant found by the equally abandoned Gwynplaine* in the opening pages of *L'Homme qui rit*.* Gwynplaine's plight is bad enough. He is barefoot and practically without clothing and has no idea where he is since being abandoned by the *comprachicos*.* In the wintery snow, he stumbles upon the corpse of a woman who is holding an infant who is trying to suckle the dead woman's breast. Gwynplaine takes her on a journey without destination. They arrive at the wagon of Ursus,* an itinerant medicine man, a peddler of low-class vaudeville, but a man with a conscience and ideals. He takes them in, and they quickly become part of his act. Dea is blind, and as time passes, she relies mainly on her spiritual intuitions of the reality about her. She is deeply dependent upon the ugly and deformed Gwynplaine, and a strong love develops between them. When Gwynplaine is "abducted," since his identity as a nobleman has been discovered, Dea has pangs of jealousy and abandonment. These fleeting feelings are dissipated when Gwynplaine returns to the itinerant flock as they are boarding a ship destined for Holland. Unfortunately, Dea, for unknown but romantic reasons, announces that she is dying, and indeed she does. The quick and determined suicide of her would-be lover soon follows.

Not many blind heroines are found in French literature; Dea is an early example. Hugo seems to want to stress her faith and confidence in those about her, which prohibits any bewilderment at being blind. The narrator gives the reader the impression that Dea is not only calm and confident, but also perhaps filled with sanctity. She sees what others with vision do not see. While different in intent, Dea has affinities with the blind heroine of André Gide's* *La Symphonie pastorale* (The pastoral symphony) (1919) in which blindness sees through the good and bad actions of those with sight.

Unlike *Les Travailleurs de la mer*,* *L'Homme qui rit* has not enjoyed immediate success in France. Both are important novels in which Hugo presents to his readers truly new and original characterizations. Dea has to be counted among them. Sweet and innocent, like some of Hugo's heroines, she possesses an old-fashioned passivity which may be considered in relation to Hugo's idea of femininity. But she is not the only woman in the novel and should not be studied without the complementary figure of Josiane.

Deluge, Le. *See Flood, The.*

Demain dès l'aube. *Demain dès l'aube* (Tomorrow at daybreak), poem sixteen of *Pauca meae* from *Les Contemplations*,* is a very brief piece of three strophes, with a scheme of abab, four lines each. It is clearly the antithesis of the longer poem of grief over Léopoldine Hugo's* drowning, *A Villequier.** This short poem is so well known in France that most schoolchildren can recite it by heart. The poem portrays the narrator-father (Hugo) in his traditional dialogue with his dead daughter.

While the poem fixes lyrically on nature's horizon, with a brief glance, almost realistic, at nearby Honfleur, the feeling is solemn, the grief of a father whose back is bent with it. The poet-father sees nothing of that which he has so briefly described; his gaze is only on the tomb to which he lyrically brings almost resurrectional gifts of green holly and flowering heather.

Dernier Jour d'un condamné, Le. Le *Dernier Jour d'un Condamné* (The last day of a condemned man), an early text of Hugo's (1829), indicates Hugo's early conversion to liberalism in art and politics. Written within the context of the modern fervor for the abolition of executions, the arguments of Cesare di Beccaria in Italy and Jeremy Bentham in England, it is above all a witness to Hugo's horror at the ineffective method of the guillotine, which was used for executions in Paris at the Place de Grève* (now the site of the city hall in Paris). Young Hugo's novel betrays his stand on the question of capital punishment* to which he adhered throughout his life.

This work, mostly composed of sensations but sometimes sentimental (in which the prisoner is saying goodbye to his daughter who does not seem to know who he is), is written as the narration of the man about to be executed. The reader follows the last moments of the prisoner while he is being taken from his cell to the place of execution. The final narration is interrupted when the man loses his head.

See also Hugo's arguments concerning the execution of Mr. Tapner (*see* Tapner, the execution of Mr.) on the Channel Islands and that of John Brown,* the American abolitionist, after Brown's insurrection at Harper's Ferry.

Dieu. This long (eight thousand lines) but incomplete philosophical poem should be read complementarily to *Religions et religion** and also to *The End of Satan*. The work expresses Hugo's thirst for knowledge of

God, if there is one, for he is not totally certain, in spite of affirmations made elsewhere. He claims in parts of his writings that he spent some time each day in prayer, and that is to be believed. His poetic theological inquiries, however, show him to be embedded in bibliographical historicism, seeking answers from books and history. Thus the poem *God* takes the reader through a review of atheism, skepticism, Manicheanism, paganism, and Christianity, all accompanied by an almost Balzacian analogy to the animal world. In this way, atheism is represented by a bat, Manichean beliefs by a crow, and Christianity by the griffon. In the case of Christianity, Hugo neglects the fundamental iconography created by the Christians themselves, namely Christ represented as the lamb. An angel exposes the message of the turning tables and "alight" Hugo's belief; but the search for the truth has no end.

This poem is very much praised by modern critics and has even inspired a vast "action of words and music" by the composer Pierre Henry.

Djinns, Les. *Les djinns*, about the malevolent spirits of the Arabian nights, is perhaps the most sensational of the sensational poems of *Les Orientales** (1829), an extraordinary poetic acrobatic piece which anticipates what will be done as avant-garde in the early twentieth century in the cubist poet Guillaume Apollinaire.

Les Djinns, despite its Western mythology about Islamic thought, practice, and superstition, does indeed convey a universal feeling about natural disasters; in this case, a tornado or hurricane. In primitive times, it was assumed that natural disasters were the work of a punishing god, a deity seeking some sort of revenge, reparation, or sacrifice. In modern times, an inheritance from the Greco-Roman tradition, natural phenomena are not just interpreted as divine interventions, but are frequently portrayed as gods or goddesses in the form of natural turbulence, thus the naming of hurricanes.

This poem is important for its dazzling metrical formation, giving it typographically the shape of a tornado. In fourteen verses the poem appears in the form of a funnel. Verse 1 is limited to two syllables, verse 2 to three syllables, verse 3 to four, verse 4 to five, verse 5 to six, verse 6 to seven, and so on as the poem diminishes back to a conclusion in two-syllable lines, as the storm passes away.

Les Djinns is the most important poem of *Les Orientales* if we think of this collection in terms of what the Parnassian poets of the mid-century wanted to do—that is, to create a kind of objective, melodic poetry— and also that which was to be found in cubism in the pre–World War I world of the twentieth century.

Documentation. Research by novelists into the past in order to write historical novels, and accounts of works depicting contemporary life, frequently of a journalistic nature, characterize the mode of the nineteenth-century French novel. This trend started with the example set by Sir Walter Scott (1771–1832) whose historical novels were very much in vogue in the first quarter of the century in France.

Hugo's novels represent a serious effort at historical or contemporary documentation. The notes, for example, to *Bug-Jargal** show that the author had firsthand knowledge of the abolitionist movements not only in France but also around the world. In Chapter 4 of this novel, for example, the author, in a footnote (history intruding upon fiction), explains the Massiac club: "The Massiac club . . . was an association of *négrophiles* (abolitionists). This club, founded in Paris at the beginning of the revolution, probably provoked slave insurrections which erupted in the colonies."

Two other noteworthy examples of Hugo's use of documentation come from *Notre-Dame de Paris*.* First of all, there was his historical research into medieval Paris, especially its architecture, specifically that of the cathedral. Such library work is supported by Hugo's historical meditations from atop the towers of Notre-Dame. This combination of historical research with on-the-spot visits is also characteristic of *Les Misérables** which can be cited for the documentation necessary for the re-creation of the battle of Waterloo, the site of which Hugo visited.

This kind of documentation done by Hugo and then meditated and finally turned into fiction would also be done by such other writers as Honoré de Balzac,* Stendhal,* Prosper Mérimée, Gustave Flaubert,* and Emile Zola* as the century moved along.

Most of Hugo's prose pieces and much of his theatre are based in historical research, out of which he sought history's message, which is demonstrated in the prefaces to his historical dramas.

A final type of documentation that remains almost unique to Hugo is the study of the language and speech of a people. Thus, in *Les Misérables* as in *Notre-Dame de Paris*, we find archival research into medieval argot and the urban slang of such revolutionary young heroes as Gavroche. *Les Misérables, Les Travailleurs de la mer,** and *L'Homme qui rit** abound in proof that Hugo did much research into the nature of individual languages, dialects, argot, and slang. Hugo's novels and plays are more easily comprehended if the essential role of documentation is kept in mind as the background of the aesthetic performance.

This indeed is a question of turning either past history or contemporary history into fiction which vies with history in its authenticity because of the behind-the-scenes scholarly inquiry.

Donkey, The. *See Ane, L'.*

Drame. Hugo's ideas, expressed in the preface to his play *Cromwell** (*see also Cromwell, Preface to*), place emphasis on stage settings, costumes, and above all historicism, all of which convey the intent of the work.

This is, of course, in direct opposition to the principles of French classic tragedy as enunciated by Nicolas Boileau-Despréaux in the *Art poétique* of the seventeenth century.

Whether or not the three unities of time, place, and action are derived from Aristotle across Italian Renaissance interpretations is unimportant. The three unities, seen as a barrier by both Hugo and Stendhal,* push dramaturgy into the direction of an inner, cerebral, psychic theatre, based in mythology and not in history. Thus, unity of place can, for the classicists, mean any place, not dependent upon a particular historical locale. This would facilitate the representation of Jean Racine's *Phèdre*, for example, in Japan, for the "place" is not determined simply by one identifiable historical place. The unity of time likewise absolves classic theatre from the historical march of time, making the action timeless. The argument against a so-called twenty-four-hour limit is extreme. Racinian tragedy becomes timeless; the spectator or the reader is not aware of any clock time but senses that the unity of time is a manner of abetting the single action of the drama. The unity of action, while spotlighting the central motif or paradox of classical theatre, does not preclude subplots, but it insists that these subordinations make psychological sense only to the degree that they are intrinsically tied to the main action.

Both Hugo and Stendhal are opposed to the principles enunciated above. The new drama, historically based, seeks to be historically realistic. Thus the action of the play can cover many months or years, with appropriate set changes, and the subplots are not always inherently tied to the main action. Not all is essential in the Romantic *drame* whereas the tightness of structure in classical tragedy, which never mixing prose and poetry as the Romantics do, makes it impossible to remove any element without destroying its aesthetic, almost hermetic, unity.

Drawings. There is a strong rapport between the pictorial arts and literature in France, starting in the eighteenth century, intensifying in the nineteenth, and continuing to this day. Denis Diderot (1713–1784) is considered the first modern art critic, and Charles Baudelaire* continued the tradition of Diderot with his reviews of the annual art salons, notably those of 1845–1846. Some literary movements in the nineteenth century competed with both sculpture and painting, for example, the Parnassian poetry.* Individual writers tried their hand at both serious drawing and at caricature, and the poet and novelist Théophile Gautier* announced that he would have preferred to have been a painter.

Within the last half century, literary criticism has become very much aware of the affinities of the arts. The classic work of Helmut Hatzfeld, *Literature through Art* (1954), was a wholesale attempt to evaluate French literature from its origins to the present day in terms of the interdependency of the arts.

Hugo was what the French call a *dessinateur*, a sketcher or drawer, a black-and-white artist. During his lifetime he produced somewhat more than two thousand drawings which can be found reproduced and catalogued in the Jean Massin edition of Hugo's complete works. Many editions of Hugo are illustrated with his own drawings; a good example is the work of Victor Brombert on *Victor Hugo and the Visionary Novel* (1984). Brombert utilizes twenty-seven illustrations in his work, some of which are related to *Les Travailleurs de la mer** (Toilers of the Sea).

A good number of Hugo's drawings are housed either in the Bibliothèque Nationale or in the Maison Victor Hugo, Place des Vosges; others remain in private collections.

Duarte, Doña Josefa. In the Spanish culture of the golden age, a *dueña* was usually an elderly spinster who was entrusted with protecting the morals of a young woman in an aristocratic household. Hugo seized upon this stereotypical personage as almost a comic relief in his drama *Hernani** (1830). In act 1, Don Carlos,* enamored of Doña Sol de Silva,* makes a rapid incursion into the chambers of the young princess, who has been awaiting the visit of Hernani.* Confused by the arrival of an unexpected visitor, Doña Josefa is hostile but then accommodating to Don Carlos, first because he has threatened to kill her, but more because he offers her a purse of money. She accepts this bribe and agrees to hide Don Carlos in a wardrobe. This action posits Hugo's ability to break with classical tradition and to establish a theatre built on intrigue as well as a narrative plot line that would have been absolutely forbidden in classical French theatre. The same interdiction would be found also in the historical tragedies of Shakespeare, which never could have been dependent on the haphazard. In this manner, then, Hugo broke with centuries of theatrical tradition, but also by his introduction of a comic type, such as Doña Josefa, who would be more in the late-eighteenth-century style of Beaumarchais, in *The Barber of Seville* or *The Marriage of Figaro*. Such comic figures, here the somewhat nutty or eccentric but shrewd old lady, make their appearances in nineteenth-century operas. Hugo must have had an insight into the histrionic possibilities of such a role. It certainly derives from his concept, elaborated on in the *Préface de Cromwell* (*see Cromwell, Preface to*), of the mixture of the sublime and the grotesque, the tragic and the comic: a type of artistic imitation of the same mixture, anticipating the realism found in real life.

Duvidal, Julie de Montferrier. The art teacher of Hugo's wife Adèle, Julie Duvidal was the victim of the young Victor Hugo's absurd Catholic morality: since she was an art teacher, she was an artist, and thus she was a bad influence. This recalls Hugo's own hypocritical insistence on "purity" before marriage as recorded in his *Lettres à la fiancée*.

As Hugo's moral and political conscience evolved, so did his tolerance for the unorthodox. This may have been influenced by the marriage of his eldest brother Abel to Julie Duvidal in 1827. In the last *Odes* (Book Five, 1819–1828) two poems are dedicated to Julie. The first, *Le Portrait d'une enfant*, is written in gratitude for a portrait executed by Julie of Hugo's daughter Léopoldine Hugo,* which was compatible with Hugo's obsession with the beauty, innocence, and purity of children, The second, dedicated to the newlyweds, acknowledges Julie as the new Countess Abel Hugo, but it is written with a certain degree of obsession with hymen, virginity, and deflowering by either Romantic or modern standards. This last poem is indicative of the fusion in Hugo's thought, at the time, of human sexuality and the bourgeois concept of the role of marriage, as well as the subservience of women to men.

E

Eclecticism. It would be inappropriate to use the word "mannerism" to describe the disparate tendencies of nineteenth-century French writers; a better term would be "eclectic." This applies not just to Hugo, but to most of the writers of the Romantic and so-called pre-Romantic schools of literature. Chateaubriand's *Le Génie du Christianisme* (1802) is hardly a defense of Catholicism; it seems to be a code word for Romanticism.

Hugo is the best example among the French Romantics of a direction-less assembly of ideas and yearnings. In retrospect he seems confused about religion, human sexuality, and the passage of time in history. His deism, in spite of his own anticlericalism, is influenced by a form of Catholicism, partially derived from the abbé Lammenais* who himself seems to have had a mixed-up potpourri notion of Roman Catholicism, which he finally renounced. Victor Hugo's new personal religion is a derivative of his Romantic Catholicism fused with historical occult read-ings and his so-called contact with the spirit world, encouraged by his friend, the poet Delphine Gay,* on the island of Jersey. The theology, or even theosophy, expressed in *Ce que dit la bouche d'ombre** (What the mouth from the shadow says) at the conclusion of *Les contemplations** indicates a new and muddled form of religion, far from any Catholic, Jewish, or Protestant orthodoxy.

Hugo is a modern nineteenth-century man, seeking answers from those who went before him. He finds few answers in the sages of classical antiquity, or in the evolution of Western thought since the advent of Christianity.

Edon Banquets. In addition to the literary salons of Romanticism, such as those held by Charles Nodier* at the Bibliothèque de l'Arsenal, a pop-ular forum among literary Romantics was the dinner meeting. The Edon reunions were held in the restaurant of the same name in the rue de l'Ancienne Comédie. Organized by Hugo's brother Abel, the meetings began on July 5, 1818. Aside from eating, this first generation of Romantics discussed literature and read their works. It was during one of these enthusiastic meetings that Hugo, then only sixteen years old, announced his intention to write what would turn out to be his first novel, *Bug-Jargal*.* Like so many other projects born of the enthusiasm of the moment, the Edon banquets came to a close just a few short months after the first meeting was held.

Eighteen hundred and forty-three. This was not a good year in the life of Victor Hugo, although it started off well enough with the marriage of his elder daughter, Léopoldine Hugo,* to Charles Vacquerie* on February 14–15. On March 7, however, the premiere of Hugo's play *Les Burgraves* was a failure. Traditional literary history signals this failure as the end if not of Romanticism then, at least, the end of Romantic theatre.

On September 4, 1843, Léopoldine and her husband drowned in the Seine river. Hugo received this news in a newspaper account. The family had arranged this manner of alerting him since they knew only that he was somewhere in southwestern France on a walking tour. This tragedy and the failure of his play, while not diminishing his political activity, did seem to silence the poet within him, and there was to be no more literary publication until the moment of his exile from France. Nevertheless, he began to write poems about his daughter's death and a novel, which was to become *Les Misérables*.

L'Enfant. *L'Enfant* (The child) is poem eighteen from *Les Orientales** (1829). This six-strophe lyrical evocation of the devastation of the island of Chio during the Greek wars for independence from Turkey struck a chord in contemporary readers as it does today in its portrayal of the tragedy of war as it affects children and their innocence. Hugo appears in this poem as a type of Romantic journalist, reporting to the French on what he had seen during the rebellion. The poem looks somewhat like Eugène Delacroix's reporting as found in his painting of 1824, *Les Massacres de Scio* (see Helmut Hatzfeld, *Literature through Art*, Oxford University Press, 1954, p. 146).

The poem's somber narrative tone—*Les Turcs ont passé là. Tout est ruine et deuil* (The Turks went through there. All is ruin and sorrow)—contrasts with the lyrical vision of Hugo, spotlighting the blue-eyed Greek boy found among the ruins. How to comfort the child is the poet's only concern. Thus he offers to the *bel enfant* (beautiful child) a list of possible comforts, almost like a Christmas list: Perhaps a blue lily from Iran, or more important, a fruit from the gigantic Tuba tree (found in the Koran). All these enticements from the poet/father, who deeply loves children, are in vain. The poem ends with a Romantic sensationalism, demonstrating that the boy is no longer a boy, but a man who seeks ways to avenge what has happened to the Greeks. The boy tells the poet: *Ami . . . je veux de la poudre et des balles* (Friend, give me powder and gunshot).

This poem is important in demonstrating how Victor Hugo could fuse aspects of his lyrical inspiration—here a pictorial representation of a contemporary tragedy with his highly inspired vision—perhaps Romantic and naive but all the same sincere about the beauty and innocence of childhood.

Enjambement. Enjambement is the continuation of the sense, its grammatical structure, in a poem past the end of a line, couplet, or stanza. It is also called *rejet* when the continuation is short (for example, just one word). In prosody this is a rhythmic procedure consisting of putting into the new line of verse one or several words dependent on the meaning of the preceding line. Enjambement creates a discordance between syntax and rhythm. The syntactical element that is projected into another rhythmic unit is given an extraordinary prominence. Whereas in ordinary lines of poetry the voice falls at the end of each line, the voice remains sustained and suspended at the end of the line which syntactically is being carried over to the next line. While not strictly forbidden during the classic period, except by classicism's codifier Nicolas Boileau-Despréaux, it was almost exclusively reserved for comedy and fable. Although found in Jean Racine's comedy *Les Plaideurs*, there are nearly no examples in all of his tragedies. Jean La Fontaine's fables present excellent examples, such as: *Un astrologue, un jour, se laissa choir/Au fond d'un puits* (An astrologer, one day, let himself fall/To the bottom of a well).

Enjambement becomes a characteristic of English and French Romantic prosody, and for France the best examples are found in the poetry of Victor Hugo. The new Romantic *drame*,* or drama mixing the formerly separated classical genres of comedy and tragedy, utilized enjambement as a structural support for the antitheses found in the thematic materials. The premiere of Hugo's *Hernani*,* on February 25, 1830, pitched the battle between the Romantics and the classicists with the very opening lines (act 1, scene 1) spoken by Doña Josefa Duarte,* with its daring enjambement. Someone is knocking at the door of the secret staircase, and Doña Josefa cries out: *C'est bien à l'escalier/Dérobé* (It is indeed at the staircase/hidden). Enjambement and the mixture of prose and poetry found in *Hernani* are hallmarks of the new Romantic style, and they would be practiced by Hugo and the other Romantic poets.

Enjambement becomes characteristic of all of Hugo's poetic production, as the following example from his 1852 poem *L'Expiation** illustrates: *Il neigeait, il neigeait toujours! La froide bise/sifflait; Sur le verglas, dans les lieux inconnus,/On n'avait pas de pain et l'on allait pieds nu* (It was snowing, it was always snowing. The cold north wind/was whistling: On the glazed frost, in unknown places,/There was no bread and they were walking without shoes). In this example, *sifflait* would constitute the *rejet*.

BIBLIOGRAPHY

Grammont, Maurice. *Petit Traité de versification française*. Paris: Armand Colin, 1961.

Eponine. The best, with Gavroche, of a bad family, the Thénardier family,* Eponine shows herself in the concluding pages of *Les Misérables*,* during the episode of the insurrection and barricades, to be a person of good will and intention, who saves the life of Marius,* whom she loves desperately, but who cannot reciprocate her love because of his commitment to Cosette.* Her link to the events of the Paris insurrection comes through her brother Gavroche, whom no one would have suspected, given his good will, as being a member of the Thénardier clan.

Eponine, dressed in male attire, is found, dying, by Marius. To protect him from a stray bullet, she had put her hand out, and the fire had passed through her hand into her bosom. In a recall, worthy of Romantic opera, the dying Eponine recounts her long-held feeling of love for Marius, feelings she interprets as both moral and physical defects making her unworthy. Here remembrance of past encounters with Marius seem almost to be diary entries. She receives a kiss from Marius as she dies. Somewhat like the plight of La Maheude in Emile Zola's* *Germinal*, she hypothetically thinks about the possibility that they could have been lovers. What she receives is a farewell kiss, and the narrator writes: *He kissed that livid forehead beaded with an icy sweat. This was not infidelity to Cosette; it was a thoughtful, gentle farewell to an unhappy soul* (*Les Misérables*, New American Library, 1987, p. 1144).

Eponine is symbolic of redeemed types found in Hugo's work—the Mary Magdalene fallen woman redeemed by a deep, albeit romantic and impossible love.

Esmeralda. Other than Quasimodo* (better known in the English-speaking world from the Dieterle movie with Charles Laughton, *The Hunchback of Notre Dame*), Esmeralda is the main character in Victor Hugo's medieval reconstruction, *Notre-Dame de Paris*.* She anticipates a whole series of Near-Eastern heroines who fire the imagination of the French Romantics from Eugène Delacroix to Gustave Flaubert* (Salammbô), and she may even have been the source of the mid-century refinement of the Spanish gypsy Carmen, in the Prosper Mérimée novella (1845) of the same name. Mérimée's heroine is more anthropologically correct in both complexion and temperament, but Esmeralda has not been born a gypsy. Hugo's Esmeralda is more the product of a Romantic imagination, reflecting a depiction of the ideal woman of early Romanticism as found in the poetry of André Chénier* and Alphonse de Lamartine,* among others, but including some realistic characteristics. She symbolically represents Hugo's antithetical worldview—beauty contrasted with physical deformity (Quasimodo), charity and grace when confronted with the rapacious cruelty of the demonic priest Claude Frollo,* and an unusual goodness in the face of the Parisian mob (certainly as important a collective characterization in this novel as the Gothic cathedral itself). Esmeralda represents an ideal if foreign character, and she held the attention of the readers of 1831.

At the behest of Louise Bertin (*See* Bertin family), a very close friend of Hugo, he consented to do a libretto for her musical score based on the novel. The opera was presented in November 1836, but it failed after only eight performances for both musical and political reasons.

Euphrasie. Euphrasie is the real name of Cosette,* heroine of *Les Misérables.** In Book Four, Chapter 1, Fantine,* ignored and then abandoned by her lover, hands over her child, born from her illicit sexual relationship with Tholomyès,* to the Thénardier family.* The narrator (Hugo) speaks of Fantine's desire to call the infant girl Cosette, not unlike the habit in Spain of changing Josefa to Pepita, but he remarks that such maternal rebaptizing confuses and disconcerts the entire science of etymology.

L'Expiation. *L'Expiation* (November 1852) is the most cited in anthologies of all the satirical poems directed against Napoléon III* in the vituperative *Les Châtiments* (1853). It is not just a diatribe against the new usurper of the name Napoléon, but it is also a chastisement against Napoléon I, who was at one time admired by the young Romantic poet. That he now has reservations can be seen in the concluding statement of this poem concerning Bonaparte's progressive coup d'état starting with the events of November 9, 1799 (Dix-huit Brumaire). In this sense, the poem takes on epic dimensions, seeing in the triumph of Napoléon III the tragic flaw of Bonaparte who had made himself emperor. Hugo's democratic and socialist beliefs of the late 1840s and 1850s show a turnabout from his early conservative, Catholic ideas.

The poem, divided into seven parts, highlights the important events in Napoléon's career: the disastrous invasion of Russia; the battle of Waterloo; and the emperor in exile on the island of Elba, mulling over past victories in Egypt and evoking names of famous battles such as Marengo. In Part 4 is evoked the death of Napoléon, and in the concluding sections, the return of his remains to France. From his sepulchre in the Invalides, the dead emperor hears the raucous merrymaking of Napoléon III and his followers.

These seven sections are held together by an extraordinary poetic style in which Napoléon, as personage, interrogates God as to which event is his expiation, always receiving the answer, "No," until the poem's conclusion. Napoléon was not defeated by the Russians but by the snow on the steppes of Russia: *Il neigeait. On était vaincu par sa conquête* (It was snowing. We were defeated by its conquest). The battle of Waterloo opens with an epic lyrical cry: *Waterloo! Waterloo! Waterloo! morne plaine!* (Waterloo! Waterloo! Waterloo! sorrowful field), followed by a poetic narrative, almost cinematographic (or Flaubertian) in recounting the battle maneuvers and the ultimate defeat of the French.

The quieter tones of the fifth part are poetically relieved by a marked change from the classic alexandrine, which had been used throughout, to the octosyllabic form in the abab pattern, a type of lyrical respite from the previous grandeur of the work.

The concluding section—starting with *Une nuit, c'est toujours la nuit dans le tombeau* (One night, it is always night in the tomb)—finds the emperor awakened by the vulgar fun-making crowd of the Second Empire.* This is finally his expiation, and these words (similar to those seen by Balthazar in the Biblical passage), *Dix-huit Brumaire*, explain where the sin occurred, with the usurpation of power by the coup d'état of that date on the revolutionary calendar (November 9–10, 1799).

L'Expiation is rightfully considered one of the most masterful of Hugo's poetic achievements, above all for its almost Biblical tone of vengeance, revenge, and expiation.

Expressionism. This term is usually defined as an artistic, and then literary, tendency of the twentieth century marked by its intensity and unique, singular expressiveness. In painting the precursors of expressionism would be Vincent Van Gogh, Edvard Munch, and Mentor. The movement had more force in Germany than elsewhere. In literature, as well as in painting, expressionism and symbolism reject realistic and naturalistic approaches to reality, replacing it with abstraction, distortion, and hyperbolic exaggeration. While the movement in both painting and literature is basically associated with Germany, traces of expressionism have been found or suggested to be present in some texts of the nineteenth century in France. Syntactically it could be argued that the typical Flaubertian sentence, for example, contains realistic, impressionistic, and expressionistic elements. The animation and distortion of everyday objects also seem to be characteristic. Victor Hugo can be viewed as an expressionist both in his drawings and in the disintegrating images found in his novel *Les Travailleurs de la mer** (Toilers of the sea).

F

Falloux Act. This act was named after its author, Frédéric Comte de Falloux (1811–1886), a writer, politician, and leader of the French Catholic liberal party. Falloux served as secretary of education from 1848 to 1849 and wrote the Falloux Act, which passed in 1850, authorizing state subsidies for religious education and subjecting all education through the university level to the control of administrative and religious authorities. This act can be regarded as a counterrevolutionary response to the upheaval of 1848 which had brought the presidency of France to Napoléon III* (Charles Louis Napoléon Bonaparte). This law, along with other legislative deliberations concerning capital punishment and universal suffrage (which had been established by the Republic of 1848), were forces that drove Victor Hugo into the liberal camp, away from his previous support of Louis Napoléon-Bonaparte whom he had originally considered a liberal. The Falloux Act was one of the origins of Hugo's evolution toward the left, which finally led him to exile (December 11, 1851, to the collapse of the Second Empire*), first in Belgium, then on the Channel Islands of Jersey and Guernsey from which he assailed the reign of Napoléon III, the usurper, "the little one," in his brilliant satirical collection *Les Châtiments** (1853).

Fantine. The character Fantine, the mother of Cosette,* is an example of how women of the proletariat were brutalized in nineteenth-century France. Fantine had been seduced by Tholomyès,* a "rich" bohemian student, who abandoned her and her child. Leaving Cosette with the Thénardier family* was a psychological and financial mistake which, with the addition of other causes, forced Fantine into prostitution, a common solution to poverty among abandoned women in the nineteenth century. She is, fortunately, rescued by Jean Valjean,* then known as

Monsieur Madeleine (a name derived from the famous prostitute of the Christian gospels), but she soon dies and entrusts her child to his care.

Fantine represents Hugo's deep compassion for human suffering, especially for women born into low estate. Not a major character in *Les Misérables*,* she is, nevertheless, an important one in Hugo's evaluations of the moral concepts of the nineteenth century.

Fate (destiny). Fate is a recurring theme, if not a motif, in the writings of Victor Hugo; above all, it is the cornerstone of his 1831 novel *Notre-Dame de Paris*.* Such a preoccupation with fate should be considered within the general context of philosophical, theological, and literary speculation on man's destiny in terms of his free will or lack of it (determinism). What was basically a theological debate in seventeenth-century France (Jansenist versus Jesuit) was transformed in the nineteenth century into an almost existential meditation on man's fate. Later in the century the Romantic argument would be transformed into a scientific determinism by the philosopher Hipolyte Taine (1828–1893) and more or less put into literary fashion in the novels of Emile Zola.* With the Romantics, however, especially with Hugo, the question has appeared Manichean; this is certainly the case with his first important novel, *Notre-Dame de Paris*, in which forces of good and evil are played out on the *parvis* (the square in front of the church) and in the mysterious labyrinths of the cathedral's interior. The central role in this study of destiny must go to the almost diabolical priest Claude Frollo,* whose insatiable passion for the gypsy dancer Esmeralda,* brings Romantic tragedy to most of the main characters. Hugo's initial speculation on destiny, incarnate in the beautiful gypsy girl, becomes part and parcel of a more authentic gypsy woman, Carmen, of Prosper Mérimée's novella *Carmen* (1845). She is resigned to her destiny as it will be determined by her passionate Basque lover Don José. Gustave Flaubert's* *Madame Bovary* (1857) makes a spoof of Romantic fatality as observed in Hugo's masterpiece by having Emma Bovary's husband Charles, upon learning of his wife's adulterous liaisons, exclaim: *C'est la faute de la fatalité!* (It is fate's fault).

Feuillantines. The Feuillantines convent is historical as well as nostalgic for the Hugo family. The former convent became a home for Madame Hugo and her sons during the Napoleonic period. Hugo's poetry is filled with lyrical recalls to its garden, the adventures of young boys seeking out birds and insects, and climbing trees. The memory of those days, which stayed with Hugo to the end of his life, permeates many of his poems throughout his long poetic career.

Hugo visited the property at the end of the Franco-Prussian War, seeking a past that had been forever destroyed, as he had earlier found in his poem *Tristesse d'Olympio** (Olympio's sadness). The house and garden were gone, destroyed by a Prussian bomb. He and Juliette Drouet turned away, filled with melancholy and sadness, crossed the Luxembourg gardens, and left the past behind them.

Feuilles d'automne, Les. This collection of forty poems, considered melancholic and elegiac in tone, is the first volume in the tetralogy generally referred to as the collections of the July monarchy: *Les Feuilles d'automne* (Autumn leaves), *Les Chants du crépuscule** (Twilight songs), *Les Voix intérieures** (Interior voices), and *Les Rayons et les ombres** (Light and shadows). If we seek biographical confirmation of the poet's sad recall of days gone by, we have only to look to a series of dolorous events in Hugo's life at that time; he had just lost his mother, father, and first-born child. Furthermore, his brother Eugène had fallen deeper into insanity.

Some have seen in Hugo's previous volume, *Les Orientales*, a penchant toward art for the sake of art. This is partially true and explains why some regard *Les Orientales* as the antecedent volume to Parnassian poetry.* There is, however, in *Les Orientales* more than just a pyrotechnic display of poetic virtuosity (the poem *Les Djinns** for example) for the whole mode of orientalism. French Romanticism's fascination with the Middle East is on display here, as well as a truly engaged poetry concerned with the Greek wars of independence against Turkey. In this regard, Hugo vies with Lord Byron.* It would be unfair to put in opposition *Les Orientales* and *Les Feuilles d'automne*.

Indeed, the preface to *Les Feuilles d'automne* does suggest a poetry working for the cause of liberty, a poetry for the people and against kings and all kinds of dictatorships. The preface speaks of the bad state of affairs in Europe: Ireland is a cemetery, Italy is a convict prison. Nevertheless, art thrives amidst political and social unrest. By comparing the sixteenth and nineteenth centuries, Hugo contrasts the upheavals of the Reformation with the creative spirit of Michelangelo. Revolutions change all but the human heart; art is eternal because the human heart cannot be destroyed. He concludes by stating that there is no room in this collection for political poetry for such would destroy the serene if melancholic and peaceful lines found therein. The preface then rightfully indicates what is to follow: family verses, family values, poetry of the interior of the soul, and a mournful regret for times gone forever, mainly youth. Finally, across the collection, the primacy of art will be reiterated in specific poems given to this topic, but also as subtext within other thematic structures.

Although he disclaimed politics as inappropriate to this volume, politics, at least in the form of the Napoléon myth, is present in the very famous opening poem *Ce siècle avait deux ans* (This century was two years old), underlining the fact that Hugo and the nineteenth century have practically the same age. Hugo's mother's conservative politics and his father, a general in the Napoleonic armies, are put in contrast, and the poem stresses the importance of Bonaparte as a leader who shook up the world. Likewise, poem three, *Rêverie d'un passant à-propos d'un roi* (Thoughts of a passerby about a king), is a political work, calling on kings (Louis-Philippe?) to roll with the times and establish democratic monarchies. The concluding poem, *Amis, un dernier mot!* (Friends, a final word), insists on the militant role of the poet with the narrator boasting that he is a child of the century who believes in the holy fatherland and holy liberty.

It is specifically, however, the elegiac poems that dominate. Persistent themes in this collection which recur throughout Hugo's work are: happiness occurred only in the past (a typical Romantic fallacy); places of bliss (the Bievre Valley,* for example); regret for a lost youth (Hugo was only thirty-three years old when he wrote this collection); memories of his father's home in the Loire valley; death in general, and that of his mother in particular, *Quand je pense à tous ceux qui sont dans le tombeau* (When I think of all those who are in the grave), poem 13.

Although most of the elegiac poems underline faith in God, doubt does creep into the story. Thus *A mes amis* (To my friends), poem twenty-seven, expresses an uncertainty along the lines of Matthew Arnold's *Dover Beach*.

There are consolations in this life; however, they are not found in the giddy life of Paris, but in bucolic settings. Nature is pure and in harmony with the will of God. Of the six poems given over to the theme of a consoling nature, perhaps the most famous, *Ce qu'on entend sur la montagne** (What's heard on the mountain) contrasts nature's musical harmonies with the noise and din of humanity. Other consolations are found in domestic and conjugal bliss, the love and adoration of woman, and especially the purifying and soul-inspiring presence of children. The most famous of these poems is *Lorsque l'enfant paraît* (When the child comes into the room), poem nineteen, and also poem fifteen, *Laissez,-Tous ces infants son bien là* (Leave them be, the children are fine here), which looks like an echo to the famous scene of Christ surrounded by little children. Poem thirty-seven, *Prière pour tous* (A prayer for everyone), stresses the idea that the purity of a child's prayer is a mediation between earth and heaven for sullied adults. The poet exalts his daughter Léopoldine Hugo* to pray for him, but also for the dead (the souls in purgatory), and for all suffering humanity.

Finally, eight of the poems of *Les Feuilles d'automne* are dedicated to the primacy, munificence, and efficacy of art, with Hugo conjoining music and poetry, but also the plastic arts as in poem eight, which is dedicated to the work of Pierre-Jean David d'Angers.* In this world of Hugo, art has equivalency to the value of nature and the virtues derived from family life.

While by contemporary standards *Les Feuilles d'automne* may seem very sentimental and at times maudlin in its imagery, it is modern inasmuch as it announces the work of Charles Baudelaire,* Stéphane Mallarmé, and Arthur Rimbaud. For example, poem nine, dedicated to Alphonse de Lamartine,* describes the mission and the fate of the poet, a common enough theme in the nineteenth century, to a voyage of discovery, to a land of poetry. As the poets return to shore, because of a nostalgia for the native soil, we think of the famous *Bateau ivre* of Arthur Rimbaud which returns, after a terrible poetic ocean journey, to a mud puddle in Paris. The voyage of poetic discovery in this poem also anticipates Mallarmé's famous *Prose pour des Esseintes*. Furthermore, the six poems making up poem thirty-five, *Soleils couchants* (Setting suns), with its metamorphoses of clouds in the firmament as the sun goes down, turning meteorology into poetic fancy (clouds as alligators, clouds as palaces), while exalting in the spectacle of a sunset, leads directly to Rimbaud's contention that he could visually turn a factory into a mosque. In addition, Hugo's *Soleils couchants* anticipates items found in the Parisian tableaux of Baudelaire, in such poems as *Soleil* and *Le Crépuscule du soir* (Evening twilight). Although not abstract in the sense of Mallarmé's sunset sonnet *Victorieusement fui le suicide beau* (Victoriously fled the beautiful suicide), Baudelaire's and Mallarmé's works certainly stand on the back of these Hugo sunset visions.

The collection lives up to the purpose announced by Hugo in his preface. There are minor deviations, but the tone of melancholy, the evocation of bygone days and family idylls, the positive value of nature, and the importance of art are all well developed.

Fin de Satan, La. This theological epic of Victor Hugo redefined Judeo-Christian history by reinterpreting Biblical texts. This poem, started in 1854, was put aside (as is frequently the case with Hugo's monumental literary productions), continued in 1856, 1857, 1859, and 1860, but not published until 1886, a year after his death. As in *Religions et religion** (Religions and religion), or in the concluding poem of *Les Contemplations, Ce que dit la bouche d'ombre** (What the mouth from the shadow says), the same old Romantic story emerges of reconciling good and evil with the salutory reintegration of the fallen angel Satan into a heavenly accord. This idea had been batted about by the Romantics since the publication of Alfred de Vigny's* *Eloa* poem of 1824. Hugo's theological treatises, in poetic form, such as *Dieu** (God), published in 1891, are part and parcel of a Romantic religiosity which tries to refashion French Catholicism into radically new ways. Even such an orthodox believer as Chateaubriand seemed to participate in this poetic rewriting of traditional theology.

All of these new interpretations of traditional Catholicism seem curious to the modern secular reader, but they do indicate to what degree the Romantics, especially Victor Hugo, were wrestling with Catholicism, in spite of their frequent disclaimers.

Flaubert, Gustave. Gustave Flaubert (1821–1880), father of a French realism that emanated from his own and his century's Romanticism (*Madame Bovary*, 1856; *Sentimental Education*, 1869), had like most nineteenth- and even twentieth-century writers, an admiration, respect, and opinion (not always positive) of Victor Hugo and his influence on modern French letters.

Flaubert's early enthusiasm for the writings of Hugo are what should be expected from a brilliant provincial Romantic, who was striving to be in the vanguard of what was happening in Paris. It is through reading Flaubert's correspondence and critical responses to it that we discern his positive, but at times ambivalent, attitudes toward Victor Hugo. As an adolescent student in Rouen, Flaubert joined others of his generation in the unmitigated and passionate reading of the poetry and plays of Hugo. His early letters accentuate this point: Victor Hugo is, like Napoléon, a son of the century (letter of August 24, 1835); at sixteen, Flaubert announced that he would give all to be either an Alphonse de Lamartine* or a Hugo, showing an adolescent inability to discern between the qualities of two very different Romantic poets (letter of June 24, 1837); and the following year he elevated Hugo to the rank of such authors as Jean Racine, Pedro Calderón de la Barca, and Lope de Vega (letter of September 13, 1838). After meeting Hugo at the Pradier studio in 1843, he sent to his sister Caroline the following portrait of Hugo:

He looks like any other man, a bit ugly, a common enough face. He has wonderful teeth, a superb forehead . . . he is very polite. . . . I like very much the sound of his voice. . . . I liked being able to look closely at him . . . this man seated next to me on a little chair, fixing his eyes on his right hand which has written so many beautiful things. There was the man who made my heart thrill since the day I was born. (Letter of January 1843?)

After meeting Hugo in the Pradier studio, future impressions were filtered through Flaubert's relationship with Louise Colet whom he met in this same place of rendezvous for nineteenth-century Romantics. Because of her already important literary reputation, she could say almost anything with great authority. Flaubert shared her opinion that Hugo was the most important writer of contemporary times. Later, Hugo's exile, provoked by the Falloux Act,* was seen by Flaubert as a contemporary tragedy. Flaubert admired Hugo for protesting the action of Napoléon III and for going into voluntary exile, but the fact that other great French writers remained silent he considered a national disgrace.

Flood, The. This epic poem, consisting of three parts (chants-songs) for a total of 414 lines, was written in 1816 when Biblical themes, such as the flood and the last judgement, were very popular in France. For an adolescent of fourteen years, the poem is remarkable in its composition and its vivid imagery; it practically has the structure of the mature poet. The rhythm is slow, betraying the young poet's desire to give a formality to the Biblical text (Gen. 6–10) from which he departs only by instilling in Noah a short anger at God as he views the destruction wrought by the flood. Noah quickly repents and is pardoned by the Lord. Each section is preceded by a prose summary of what is to follow.

In Part 1, Noah reveals to his sons his apocalyptic dream foretelling the destruction of the earth by great fires, hurricanes, and the flooding of the entire surface of the earth. Mankind, with the exception of Noah and his family, is to be punished for its infidelity to God by their worshipping of idols. Noah will be chosen to repopulate the earth. On his orders the sons level an entire forest to build the ark.

In Part 2, God, seeing that the ark has been built, orders the Archangel Gabriel to start the flood. There follows a brief description of some of the animals brought aboard: the noble lion and the ferocious panther are both caged; while the dog, the roe-buck, and the fallow-deer, tamed and close to man, are allowed freedom of the ship. There are multiple descriptions of the victims of the flood and their efforts to escape in vain.

In Part 3, the ark comes to rest and the waves are returned to their former beds. Noah, viewing the destruction, temporarily accuses the heavens, but repents and is pardoned by God. In gratitude he sacrifices a white bull. God prophesizes that Noah will have many descendants who will populate Africa and Europe. While Noah himself will not have many more years on earth he will soon be in paradise with the Lord (in Jewish scriptures he is said to have lived 350 years after the flood and was 950 years old when he died). The poem concludes with Noah's reaction to these prophecies: *Soudain la voix se tut, l'on vit trembler la terre,/Et Noé plein d'effroi tomba sur la poussière* (Suddenly the voice grew silent, the earth was seen to shake,/ and Noah, filled with fright, fell into the dust).

Although it was written within the popular taste for Biblical subjects, the poem is in no way imitative, and it shows Hugo's individual style in the process of development.

For Some Things, Chance is Worthwhile. *See* A.Q.C.H.E.B.

Free Theatre. See Théâtre en liberté.

Frollo, Claude. Frollo, one of the most important characters in Hugo's *Notre-Dame de Paris* (1831), is a studious young seminarian who, after ordination, was assigned as canon to the cathedral. His generous heart toward his adopted son, and also toward the hunchbacked Quasimodo,*

was unfortunately overtaken by his passion for the gypsy Esmeralda.*
As a result of his guilty conscience, he orders, as prosecutor, her execution. For this, the enraged Quasimodo throws the abbé Frollo from
one of the towers of Notre-Dame. Hugo successfully caught the concu-
piscence of medieval celibacy in this novel where priests were caught
between their vows and their desires.

Funeral of Victor Hugo. Hugo died at 1:30 in the afternoon on May 22,
1885. Four years earlier most of the population of Paris had come to
greet him at his home, on the Avenue Victor Hugo, for his eightieth
birthday. Now Paris came to bury the greatest modern French poet. No
funeral of the nineteenth century, except that of Emile Zola,* could equal
the Romantic fervor of this event. For the critic Roger Shattuck (*The Banquet Years*), the death of Hugo signaled the end of the nineteenth century
and ushered in modernism. Photos, maintained mostly in the Hugo archives in Paris at the Place des Vosges* museum, show a gigantic cata-
falque placed under the Arc de Triomphe on the Champs-Elysées.
Representatives of most European countries came to the ceremony, and
newspapers around the globe mourned the passing of a modern genius.
Hundreds of thousands of people followed the funeral procession as it
moved down the avenue, crossed to the Left Bank, ascended the Boule-
vard Saint-Michel, and turned left into the rue Soufflot to place the casket
in the Panthéon, the former church of the patroness of Paris, Sainte Ge-
neviève which had been, off and on since 1771, a church and then a
secular memorial, depending upon the political turn of events in the
nineteenth century. Upon Hugo's death in 1885, the Panthéon became
the official burial place for France's great personages. In fact, one can
read over the portal, the inscription *Aux grands hommes, la patrie reconnaissante* (To the great men, a grateful country). With Hugo are also in-
terred Voltaire, Jean-Jacques Rousseau, Emile Zola, Victor Schoelcher,
and Léon-Michel Gambetta.

G

G: The Conventionist. In the introductory chapters of *Les Misérables*,*
Book One, *An Upright Man* (translation by Lee Fhanestock and Norman
MacAfee, New American Library, 1987), we witness an extraordinary
rendezvous between Bishop Myriel (*see* Bishop Bienvenu) and the dying
Conventionist, "G." Hugo's intent here is born of charity for those who
believe in God and salvation outside of the orthodox pattern of Catholicism. The conventionist and the bishop are equally saintly, but the
bishop who is working inside the Catholicism in which he was raised,
still bemoans the outrages committed by the French Revolution and the
Reign of Terror in 1793.

The conversation between the two men not only confronts superficial
conflicting ideologies, but acts as a confessional for the bishop. The
bishop, thinking of the excesses of the revolution, is very politely re-
minded of the excesses committed during the ancien régime.

The conventionist "G" is a believer in a way which many a straight-
minded orthodox person would find hard to comprehend. He knows of
God, and of his charity. From this conversation, the bishop learns and
accepts the pardon of the dying conventionist, who is neither truly a
revolutionary nor an atheist, just a man who did his duty as he saw it.

"G" who, on a superficial level, could be seen as an unbeliever, brings
to mind the sanctity of those who appear without belief, what Albert
Camus called the appeal to belief. Camus stated that there was only one
problem for the twentieth century: how to become a saint without believing in God—how to be holy without adhering to dogmatic systems.
This is exactly the stance of "G" which is finally understood by Bishop
Myriel.

It is for these reasons that the bishop seems to be having his confession
heard by the republican. It is for this reason, when asked his identity,

the bishop replies "Vermis sum" (I am a worm) and, as the chapter concludes, he only asks for the "blessing" of the dying "G."

Hugo, in creating the personage of Bishop Myriel, who protected Jean Valjean* in the episode of the stolen candlesticks, has hit upon a deep and intuitive sense of spirituality and the quest for God. Not all is dependent upon sacramental and liturgical structures; often the answers are found in the humanitarian concerns preached by Jesus to love one's neighbor as oneself. The dead "G" is heaven-bound, which leads Bishop Myriel into multiple reveries about the meaning of good and evil, especially as he ponders the events leading to the French Revolution. This has to be one of the most important of Hugo's texts in regard to spirituality.

Garibaldi, Giuseppe. Giuseppe Garibaldi (1807–1882) was an international leader of movements for independence in both the old and new worlds. He was born in Nice when it was French (from 1793 to 1814; again French by plebiscite in 1860) so it may be supposed that he was a French national which is important in understanding Hugo's relationship to this revolutionary whom he greatly admired and who Hugo defended after the invalidation of his election to the Bordeaux assembly of 1871 following the Franco-Prussian War. While Garibaldi might be considered a "general" of fortune, for his causes were never excessively radical, he can be seen as the prototype for such modern revolutionaries as Fidel Castro and Che Guevara. Garibaldi is one of the main authors of the push toward Italian unification. Early in his career he participated in a republican revolution in Piedmont for which he was exiled. While spending the years from 1836 to 1848 in South America, he participated in all sorts of guerilla operations in Brazil and Uruguay. However it was back in Italy that he participated in the *Risorgimento* (resurrection), first against the Austrians and then against the French defending the papal states. After Napoléon, Garibaldi represents a second generation of Romantic military leaders. He had a worldwide reputation as a rugged individualist determined to bring republican principles to the entire world. President Abraham Lincoln, in 1861, offered him a command in the Union troops fighting in the south, an offer he declined because of his opposition to slavery as opposed to Lincoln's early more moderate stance. He first came to French attention through the interest of Alexandre Dumas père (who was, himself, of black descent) who caused his image to flourish in France.

It is obvious that Hugo and Garibaldi had much in common in their personalities, rugged individualism, belief in democracy, republican principles, and desire for freedom for the people. A lively exchange of correspondence took place between them. Hugo looked forward to receiving him on the island of Guernsey.

Hugo wrote an ode in Garibaldi's honor after his defeat at Mentana in November 1867. In 1870 Garibaldi, with his own troops, called the *Chemises rouges* (red shirts), fought for the French. The following year he was elected to the National Assembly convened at Bordeaux which would ultimately lead to the formation of the Third Republic which had been proclaimed de facto on September 4, 1870. There, Hugo maintained long-range goals for the future, goals which, for the most part, he had espoused all of his life: abolition of the death penalty, reform of the judicial system, preparations for European unification, and free public education. Although Garibaldi was not an intellectual, he Romantically intuited these issues. When Garibaldi's election was declared invalid, Hugo, in turn, resigned from the assembly.

BIBLIOGRAPHY

Parris, John. *The Lion of Capreara*. 1962.
Smith, D. Mack. *Garibaldi: A Great Life in Brief*. New York: Knopf, 1956.

Gautier, Judith. Daughter of the flamboyant Romantic Théophile Gautier* (1811–1872), Judith Gautier (1845–1917) was in her own right a poet, novelist, and essayist. Her main interests were certainly more scholarly than those of her father. For the most part, she concentrated on a study of the Far East, particularly China, a reflection of the final stages of the phenomenon known as Orientalism,* in contrast with the fascination of the first Romantics with the Mideast. Her erudition enabled her to translate, rigorously, Chinese poetry, and her imagination manifested itself in her novels concerning the Far East, such as *Le Dragon impérial* (1868), which was received with enthusiasm by the intellectual French public. A work of 1875, *La Soeur du soleil* (Sister of the sun) was honored by the French Academy (*See* Académie Française and Victor Hugo). Turning erudition into art recalls a British equivalent of Judith Gautier, namely the scholar Mary Renault (1905–1983) who re-created in historical novels her studies of ancient Greek history and legend. In 1911 Judith Gautier was the first woman to be elected to the Goncourt Academy, which had a great interest in contemporary literature.

It was her intriguing relationship with Victor Hugo, however, that showed her independent spirit. Her *Mémoires* gives one the impression of a woman willing to be accepted as an equal in the world of men; she thus continues the tradition of Madame de Staël and George Sand* and anticipates the twentieth-century writer Colette. Judith Gautier would not be restrained by rules of marriage and a woman's proper place in the household. Her marriage to Catulle Mendès (1841–1909), who wrote Parnassian poetry, was quickly followed by a legal separation that led to speculations about her relationship with the aging Victor Hugo.

With the collapse of the Second Empire,* Hugo returned to Paris by train and was greeted by an immense crowd. Judith Gautier was there and led Hugo to a café across from the station. With her foot she blocked the crowd from entering the café. Hugo seemed delighted to be on the arm of such a beautiful admirer, and this admiration continued in a short poem Hugo sent to the young beauty who had had to decline a dinner invitation: "If you had come, beautiful one whom I adore/ I would have offered you a banquet without comparison/ I would have killed Pegasus and had him cooked/ So as to serve you a wing of this marvelous horse." Judith Gautier seems to have led the throng of female admirers which Hugo had during those last years. It appears more than likely that Hugo was actively courting Judith. In the company of her husband, she visited Hugo in Brussels to speak about her father and of the good old days of Romanticism. On July 12, 1872, he sent her a sonnet entitled *Ave, Déa, moriturus te salutat* (Hail goddess, death salutes you), which is more or less an admission of the incompatibility of old age and youth (a theme found in Hugo's early Romantic dramas such as *Hernani**), which is expressed in the final line of the second quatrain: *Puisque vous êtes belle et puisque je suis vieux* (Since you are beautiful and I am old). Hugo was then seventy; Judith but twenty-two. The situation does seem equivocal, and it certainly raised the suspicions and jealousy of Juliette Drouet who suspected that Judith was indeed her new rival.

Curious biographical critics have long speculated on the relationship between the two. Given Judith's passionate, admiring, and independent spirit, and Hugo's well-known womanizing, the speculations may have some truth behind them. This cannot, however, be proven.

On a higher level, Judith Gautier remains the link between the first days of Romanticism when her father participated as a mischief maker, shocking the classicists at the opening of *Hernani*, and the last days of Hugo's life when she was not just a source of flirtatious conduct, but also of a loving recall of the Romantic rebellion.

BIBLIOGRAPHY

Camacho, M. D. *Judith Gautier, sa vie et son oeuvre* (Judith Gautier, her life and work). Droz, 1939.
Gautier, Judith. *Le Collier des jours, souvenirs de ma vie* (The necklace of the days, memories of my life). Paris: Felix Juven, vol. 1, 1902; vol. 2, 1903; vol. 3, 1909.

Gautier, Théophile. Friend and faithful admirer of Hugo from the very first days of Romanticism, Gautier (1811–1872), who in his own right was a first-rate minor French poet and novelist, carried the banner of the new school of poetry if only by his flamboyant appearance at the premiere of *Hernani*,* which was shocking to the stodgy classicists ready to boo the new play. As movements changed, from Romanticism into Parnassian poetry,* Gautier seems to have followed the herd but that never bothered Hugo who found him always to be a sincere friend (unlike his relationship with Charles-Augustin Sainte-Beuve*).

Toward the end of his life, Gautier suffered from severe heart problems. Hugo wanted to take him to Guernsey for rest, but the trip would have proved impossible. He did arrange, however, in good French manner, for a financial subsidy from the government for the ailing poet.

Upon Gautier's death, Hugo sent an elegy to Judith Gautier,* his daughter, whose lines are considered among the most beautiful in the French language: "Friend, poet, spirit, you flee from our dark night./ You go out from our noise so as to enter into glory . . . /I greet you at the severe threshold of the tomb." Hugo, of course, was not far behind, dying just thirteen years later.

Gautier, in his own way, remains an important figure in French Romanticism. His poetry, especially during his Parnassian period, is sharply drawn like that of the painter he had always wanted to be. His *Symphonie en blanc majeur* (Symphony in major white) certainly was a prelude to what would be produced by the symbolist poets, especially Stéphane Mallarmé.* His novels, especially *Mlle de Maupin* (1835), reveal an extraordinary insight into human sexuality at a period when such would have been seen as inconceivable. He shared with Hugo an enormous love of Spain, which, in his case, was only of the imagination.

Théophile Gautier is a fine representative of Hugo's absolute and abiding loyalty to his friends, something Hugo offered even to his enemies, except Napoléon III.* There is no understanding of French Romanticism without some appreciation of the fraternal and literary relationship of the great poet Hugo with a lesser one, Théophile Gautier.

Gay, Delphine (Madame Emile de Girardin). Delphine Gay (1804–1855) was a minor poet and novelist of the French Romantic movement and also a chronicler of Paris during the reign of Louis-Philippe. As a young woman she contributed to *La Muse française*; as a chronicler, she was a gossip columnist who published under the name Charles de Launay in her husband's paper *La Presse*. These articles were subsequently published as *Lettres parisiennes* (4 vols., Paris: Michel Levy, 1857). One of Victor Hugo's closest friends, Madame de Girardin and Hugo met at the salon of Charles Nodier* in the Bibliothèque de l'Arsenal probably in 1824. The young woman was a stunning beauty; her blond good looks, combined with her intense Romantic feeling and literary interests, made her a stellar attraction at various Romantic literary gatherings, and she was universally referred to in Romantic circles as *La Muse française*.

Her relationship to Hugo is paramount for an understanding of his biography, due to her visit to Hugo's home, Marine Terrace, on Jersey, in September 1853. Hugo had already found her physically changed, due to the cancer that was to take her life two years later. Her visit, however, was welcomed by the poet in exile as a chance to recall old times together. But more important, she was welcomed for introducing the Hugo clan to spiritism* through the medium of the *tables tournantes* or moving tables, which purported to establish contact with the spirit world. Spiritism was all the rage in Paris at that time, and Delphine Gay offered to introduce this practice to the Hugos. Although at first skeptical, in spite of his own inclination to believe in the supernatural, the transmigration of souls, and the soul-life of inanimate objects (ideas that found expression in Hugo's mature poetry, especially in *Les Contemplations**), Hugo out of good will did participate in a séance in which the spirit of the dead Léopoldine Hugo* seems to have been made manifest. The family was converted to these procedures, and séances became a regular part of daily life in the Hugo household from September 1853 to October 1855, as reported by Hugo's daughter Adèle Hugo* in her journal (see the edition by Frances Vernor Guille, *Journal d'Adèle Hugo*, 3 vols., Paris: Minard, 1968, pp. 71 and 84).

Delphine Gay, then, aside from the abiding and loyal friendship she had for the poet, is directly responsible for introducing the spiritist quest of Léopoldine (and other personages, including Shakespeare) into the life of Victor Hugo. The haunting attempt to resurrect Léopoldine found in a major poem of *Les Contemplations; A celle qui est restée en France*, had its real-life equivalency in the table turnings held on Jersey starting in 1853.

Genealogies (Hugo family). The records here recorded do not include Victor Hugo whose life is summarized in the opening pages of this encyclopedia. For fuller details, consult the work of André Maurois, in either the French or English version, both of which are listed in the general bibliography.

JOSEPH LÉOPOLD SIGISBERT HUGO (1773–1828)

Victor Hugo's father was a general in the Napoleonic armies. General Hugo combined the "manly" virtues of the warrior with a sentimental Romanesque aspect; in personality, he was a Romantic before the Romantics. His marriage to Sophie Trébuchet was, to say the least, stormy. The Hugo children seem to have had ambivalent feelings about their father, but he must have received some measure of respect and affection from Hugo, who named his eldest daughter, Léopoldine, after him.

SOPHIE TRÉBUCHET HUGO (1772–1821)

Victor Hugo's mother married Joseph Hugo in a civil ceremony in Paris on November 15, 1797. Sophie displayed a fiery Romantic temperament. In spite of her lower Breton origins (Nantes) she was an energetic Voltairian and anticlerical. Her free spirit launched her into an amorous affair with General Victor Claude Alexandre Lahorie (1766–1812), a former close friend of her husband.

General Lahorie became involved in royalist intrigues through the influence of General Jean Victor Moreau (1783–1813), which rendered him suspect by the government. Sophie hid her lover in a house behind the gardens of the Feuillantines* property where she was living with her sons. This Byzantine and clandestine adventure came to a dramatic conclusion with the arrest and execution of Lahorie in 1812.

ADÈLE FOUCHER HUGO (1803–1868)

Victor and Adèle were almost childhood sweethearts since she first met her future husband in the Feuillantines gardens where she and her brother would come to play with the three Hugo boys, starting around 1809. A love correspondence beginning in their adolescence has been recorded in Hugo's *Lettres à la Fiancée*, 150 letters written from 1820 to the time of the marriage, which took place on October 12, 1822, in the Saint-Sulpice church in Paris. As is well known, the Hugo-Foucher marriage had its own form of subtle tensions reminiscent of those of Victor Hugo's parents.

Adèle, who was adored by her young husband as demonstrated by many of the early poems, was not attracted to the literary life of her husband, or perhaps she was somewhat apprehensive about his growing reputation. In any case, it was not long before liaisons upset the domestic tranquillity. Theirs was, all the same, a conjugal life that was never destroyed by divorce or even an alienation of affections. Adèle had a brief and flirtatious relationship with a family friend, the Romantic critic, poet, and novelist Charles-Augustin Sainte-Beuve,* and it was not long before Hugo, in a sense, almost took a second wife, Juliette Drouet, without of course abandoning Adèle. Hugo, with sexual appetites not unlike those of his father the general—for example, the scandal of Victor's affair with Léonie d'Aunet—continued throughout his life to have a strong and inordinate interest in women. This was suffered, usually in silence, by Adèle; but with less tolerance in the final years by Juliette Drouet.

These amorous, if not sexual, matters Madame Hugo chose to ignore in her biography of her husband (corrected by Charles Hugo, their son, and August Vacquerie) *Victor Hugo raconté par un témoin de sa vie*, published in 1863. This work reviews Hugo's life up to that time, based mainly on interviews with her husband and with anecdotes from her own point of view. Adèle Hugo's silence on these matters, as well as the discretion found in most of her life, given the openly and obvious erotic peregrinations of her husband, is a tribute to her dignity and sense of worth as the wife of the greatest French writer of the nineteenth century.

ABEL HUGO (1798–1855)

Victor Hugo's oldest brother, he married Julie Duvidal de Montferrier.*

EUGÈNE HUGO (1800–1837)

Eugène, the middle one of the three brothers, did not go completely mad the day after Victor Hugo's marriage to Adèle, but his schizophrenia may have been increased by jealousy.

VICTOR HUGO'S CHILDREN AND DESCENDANTS

Léopold Hugo: Born July 16, 1823, died the same year on October 9.

Léopoldine Hugo* (1824–1843): Drowned in the Seine near Villequier* with her husband Charles Vacquerie.*

Charles Hugo (1826–1871): Journalist and writer, died at Bordeaux where he had gone with his father to make preparations for the Third Republic. He married Alice Lehaene (1817–1908).

François-Victor (1828–1873): A loyal and liberal son of Hugo, he spent much time during the exile in the Channel Islands translating the works of Shakespeare which was indeed helpful to Victor Hugo's own evaluation of the English playwright.

Adèle Hugo* (1830–1915): Hugo's last child, who died insane. (*See also* Insanity.)

Alice Lehaene (1817–1908): Married Charles Hugo in 1865, by whom she had three children:

Georges I (1867–1868)

Georges II (1868–1925)

Jeanne (1869–1941)

Jean Hugo* (1894–1984): Son of Georges Hugo II and a painter, stage designer, and friend of Jean Cocteau,* he was important to French theatre immediately before World War II.

George, Mademoiselle. A celebrated French actress of the early nineteenth century, Mademoiselle George created quite a stir when she stubbornly refused to play opposite Juliette Drouet in Hugo's *Marie Tudor*,* which had its first performance on November 6, 1833. Mademoiselle George, a very temperamental artist (who was rumored to have been the mistress of Napoléon Bonaparte), felt it was beneath her dignity to be playing opposite Juliette Drouet. Hugo, blinded by his love for Juliette, was oblivious to her limitations as an actress. Thus, Drouet's short-comings were exacerbated by the direct and indirect insults hurled at her by Mademoiselle George and the director Harel. The play was poorly received, and Juliette Drouet was obliged to withdraw from it bringing to an abrupt close her theatrical career.

Mademoiselle George figures anecdotally in Hugo's *Choses vues*, vol. I, pp. 237–238 in an entry entitled *Théâtre, Mademoiselle George*, in which she complains about the fate and pecuniary difficulties of aging actresses.

Ghost, The. *See Revenant, Le.*

Gide, André. André Gide (1869–1951) was a French novelist and the author of an important anthology, *Anthologie de la poésie française* (Gallimard, 1949), in which he commented at length on Hugo's poetry. The question allegedly put to Gide: "Who is France's greatest poet?" received the response "*Hugo, hélas*" This remark has been overblown since it was first uttered. It may mean that in spite of a manifold overproduction, sometimes reducing the lyric impact by excessive length and, at other times, falling into a rhymed rhetoric filled with discursive elements, Gide remained strongly attracted by Hugo's poetry. This was probably also the position of the poet-critic, Paul Valéry.*

Gilliatt. Gilliatt, the main protagonist of Hugo's *Les Travailleurs de la mer*,* is a very complicated depiction made by Hugo of a Guernsey fisherman. Gilliatt, who lives with his mother in a *maison visionée*,* is on the outside of society, and he is seldom seen with other human beings. His relationship with persons of the opposite sex is ambivalent. He has the qualities of a voyeur since he spies on women bathing in the sea, but at the same time he is repulsed by the female form. All the same he has a silent and respectful admiration and love for Deruchette, the niece of Mess Lethierry. In a heroic effort lasting some months, he is able to salvage the principal parts of the *Durance*, the steamship which had made Mess Lethierry a comfortably rich man on its trips between Saint Malo and Guernsey, and which had been destroyed during a storm at sea. Because of this tenacity, he has made it possible for Mess Lethierry to rebuild his small empire; as recompense, Mess Lethierry would have him marry Miss Deruchette. Gilliatt, however, understands that Miss Deruchette is in love with the local Anglican pastor Ebenezer, and he arranges their elopement. As a wedding gift, he offers Miss Deruchette the trousseau his mother had prepared for his future bride, but there will be none since he has no intention of ever marrying. As the young married couple leaves on the *Cashmere* for London where Ebenezer's uncle's will is to be read, Gilliatt watches the departure of the ship. As it disappears, the high tide comes in, and in what can only be called a suicide, he allows his entire body to be engulfed by the water.

Watching ships disappear on the horizon must have been a favorite activity of Hugo during his exile. It arises here as a type motif, which also will be found in the sea novels of Pierre Loti, and it is utilized again in *L'Homme qui rit** when the abandoned boy Gwynplaine* watches the departure of the *Matutina* with its underworld passengers.

One of the most famous of the dramatic scenes in *Les Travailleurs de la mer* is Gilliatt's struggle with the octopus which has provoked much critical comment on Hugo's uncanny ability at creating a modern mythology of the sea.

God. *See Dieu.*

Grand-Mère, La. Hugo wrote this verse drama in 1865, and it was put into the collection entitled *Le Théâtre en liberté** (1886) one year after Hugo's death. The play is not difficult, but it is puzzling for people at the end of the twentieth century to understand the sexist attitudes of nineteenth-century males. Nineteenth-century society engaged in gender segregation, frequently assigning women to separate rooms at social functions; for example, the after-dinner smoking areas were reserved for males. George Sand,* a liberated woman for her time, who was an exception, frequented these exclusive male domains.

La Grand-Mère (The Grandmother) has as its theme the maternal evolution of a woman who is a poor mother, who perhaps rejects maternity, but turns into a tender and caring grandmother.

Great Britain and Victor Hugo. The reconciliation of opposing literary tendencies in modern France and England was due to the triumph of the Romantic movement, basically a northern idea accepted by such a "northern" Latin country as France with Hugo as the leader of the new literature. Hugo's literary fate in nineteenth- and twentieth-century England, Scotland, Wales, and the Channel Islands is both a personal and literary phenomenon which is better understood after a brief review of the social, literary, and geopolitical factors at play since the Norman invasion of England on October 14, 1066, when William the Conqueror defeated Harold II and effectively turned England into a Norman colony, or what is commonly called "The Normanization of England."

It is during the Plantagenet dynasty, founded by Henry II, (formerly known as the count of Anjou) that Norman England, in opposition to a small and weak France, developed a literature derived from the courtly tradition as well as from Celtic and Arthurian romances. The Plantagenets, who were to rule until 1485 when they were replaced by the Tudors, produced a very high literary tradition written for the most part in Anglo-Norman which was spoken on both sides of the Channel.

The first great French medieval woman writer, Marie de France, probably lived in England and wrote there, and it is speculated that she was the abbess of Shaftsbury. Since, at this time, most of the west coast of present day France was ruled by the Plantagenets, linguistic, literary, and cultural affinities existed. France, small and weak, did not count until the reign of Charles VII, at first aided by Joan of Arc, who succeeded in ejecting the English from French soil. It is at this point that we can speak of a budding French nationalism that will develop a literary philosophy that will go counter to that which was developing in England. It should be recalled, however, that for the twelfth-century renaissance there was no essential difference between England and Normandy.

French nationalism and its literary manifestation developed in the seventeenth century with the founding of the French Academy (*see* Académie Française and Victor Hugo) and the development of literary theatre, particularly for a theatre which claimed to be derived from classical Greek doctrine filtered through the Italian renaissance. France, aspiring to be the new Greece, supposedly modeled itself on Greek tragedy and comedy. England, like Spain, created high theatre out of indigenous national traditions, for example Shakespeare's use of the history of the English kings as material for his histories and tragedies. While the French maintained a classical theatre derived from Greek and Roman mythology, the English were able to make myth out of their own national history. Furthermore, French theatrical tradition disapproved of any display of violence of the scene, and there were linguistic and social conventions that could not be defied. It was thus that a group of English actors were driven out of Paris in the seventeenth century when they tried to produce *Othello* because the handkerchief, central to its plot, was considered a vulgar object and not to be viewed.

As classicism declined despite the halfhearted attempts made to renew it in the eighteenth century (Voltaire), new critical waves were being felt (such as André Chénier's* citing the values of German classical-romantic theatre; and above all the voice of Madame de Staël, whose two important critical dissertations *On Literature* (1800) and *On Germany* (1810) encouraged the French to abandon their narrow-minded classicism and to imitate Germany and England). On the heels of the pioneering work of Madame de Staël came Stendhal's* critical work *Racine and Shakespeare* (1823–1825), in which Stendhal chose William Shakespeare as the better of the two writers of tragedies and the playwright to be imitated by the moderns.

Shakespeare did indeed become a key player in Hugolian aesthetics. Hugo's son François-Victor translated the complete works of Shakespeare; his work was certainly an improvement over the poor Letourneur edition that had preceded it. Hugo's English was extremely limited and it was thus through the translations made by his son that he became truly acquainted with the Bard, with whom he had believed to have been in spiritist conversation during the table-turning activities that took place on the Channel Islands (*see* Spiritism). This led to the publication of Hugo's *William Shakespeare** in 1864.

The English could have been impressed beginning with the publication of *Les Orientales*,* poems of Mideastern inspiration. Some of these poems are preceded by citations in English from Shakespeare, others were to be found in later collections of Hugo's poetry.

The reaction to Hugo in England had its political as well as its literary side. The young Hugo was certainly perceived as a royalist which could only be pleasing to an English public who feared that it too might experience something similar to the French Revolution. As Hugo's liberalism developed, however, especially with his exile and his protest of the visit of Queen Victoria to Napoléon III* in Paris, there was a negative reaction. All the same, Hugo's works, from the very earliest years of the nineteenth century were published in England, read at least by the cultivated public, and commented on in critical reviews and short pieces in leading English literary journals.

A comprehensive and detailed analytical and statistical evaluation of Hugo's impact in England was made by Kenneth Ward Hooker: *The Fortunes of Victor Hugo in England*, first published in 1938 by Columbia University Press and reissued in 1966 by AMS Press in New York. Hooker's book is invaluable for those interested in a year-by-year account of Hugo's reception by English literati. The foundation of Hugo's reputation resided in the success of *Notre-Dame de Paris*.* Afterward, English criticism recognized Hugo's theatre, his lyric poetry, and his other novels, favorably acquiesced to his exile years in the Channel Islands.

Hugo's reception in England, as well as elsewhere in the Western world, established him as an international writer. Although Hooker's evaluations stop with 1902, the years of the twentieth century are not difficult to explain. Although Hugo's popularity with the general public is unknown, his works form a major part of the curriculum in French departments in the United Kingdom, and not just at Oxford and Cambridge. The red-brick universities of the north, such as Liverpool, Manchester, and Leeds, are well-known centers for the study of Romance literatures, and Hugo is a basic part of the curriculum in modern French studies. Furthermore, the English, like the Americans, have professional journals dedicated to French literature, and a perusal of their bibliographies indicates his importance. The European communities' Erasmus program for the exchange of Continental graduate students and professionals with England is another source that reveals the abiding presence of Hugo in English belles-lettres. The breakthrough for these "electric affinities" between the two warring countries, now and forever friends despite some grumblings over the European community, must be attributed to the Romantic movement. Romanticism brought England and France together. Hugo, as chief of the French Romantic school, has received on a biographical but also on a literary level a presence that has not always been positive but which still persists at the end of the twentieth century.

BIBLIOGRAPHY

Gosse, Edmund. *Life of Algernon Charles Swinburne.* London: Macmillan, 1917.
Gribble, Francis. *The Passions of the French Romantics.* London: Chapman, 1910.
Hooker, Kenneth Ward. *The Fortunes of Victor Hugo in England.* New York: Columbia University Press, 1938. Reprint. New York: AMS Press, 1966.
Marezials, Frank T. *Life of Victor Hugo.* London: Walter Scott, 1888.
Moraud, Marcel. *Le Romantisme français en Angleterre de 1814 à 1848. Contributions à l'étude des relations entre la France et l'Angleterre dans la première moitié du XIX siècle.* Paris: Henri Champion, 1933.
Nichol, J. Pringle. *Victor Hugo: A Sketch of His Life and Work.* London: Swan Sonnenschein, 1893.
"Oeuvres complètes de Victor Hugo." *Edinburgh Review* 196 (9 July 1902): 156–77.
Thomas, John Heywood. *L'Angleterre dans l'oeuvre de Victor Hugo.* Paris: Pierre André, 1934.

Gueux, Les. This verse play in four scenes, written in a fragmentary manner between 1872 and 1875, seems to be a cross between the Spanish picaresque tradition and the *esprit gaulois* (mocking spirit) found in medieval French literature, and also in the tongue of François Rabelais' Panurge. Simply put, *Les Gueux* are people who have decided not to live by society's conventions; they are marginal, but they are not alienated people. The best model of this in Hugo is Don Cesar de Bazin* of *Ruy Blas.** *Les Gueux* see through the pretexts of society and, unlike Ruy Blas himself, make no effort to reform it. Hugo's spirit of buffoonery herein anticipates the antics of the great actor Charlie Chaplin who in turn will announce the two tramps of Samuel Beckett's play *En attendant Godot* (Waiting for Godot).

Guttinguer, Ulric. Despite the Germanic sound of his name, Ulric Guttinguer (1785–1866) should be counted among the most fervent of French Romantics. His passionate engagement in the Romantic movement surpasses even Chateaubriand's. More a close friend of Charles-Augustin Sainte-Beuve* than of Hugo (see the Sainte-Beuve correspondence especially concerning Sainte-Beuve's courtly and partially unfulfilled

love for Hugo's wife Adèle), he is given a dedication in the fourth book
of *Odes et Ballades** (Ode 8, *L'Homme heureux*, 1822).

Guttinguer was a collaborator on the *Muse française* where he met
Hugo. He also frequented the salon of Charles Nodier* and produced
many Romantic pieces, prose and poetry, among which the most famous
is *Arthur*, an autobiographical novel of 1832 (1836) (see Saint-Beuve's
appreciation in *Portraits contemporains*, vol. 2), which recounts his conversion to Catholicism, albeit of the Romantic variety. This work was
considered important enough for the Abbé Brémond (1865–1933), an important critic of French religious thought and of hermetic poetry, to make
an edition of Guttinguer's *Arthur* in 1925. Guttinguer is important for
understanding the early days of French Romanticism, but it is only
through his friendship with Sainte-Beuve that Guttinguer became a minor side figure in the Hugo biography.

Gwynplaine. The protagonist of Hugo's novel *L'Homme qui rit,** he was
named the laughing man because his face had been disfigured in childhood by the *comprachicos,** at the command of Charles II. He is grotesque
in the same sense as an earlier Hugo creation, Quasimodo* of *Notre-Dame
de Paris*. Hugo has hit upon a most tragic phenomenon in Western history, namely the kidnapping and maiming of children either to serve as
peculiar pets in aristocratic households, or to be sold as circus freaks.
The latter is the fate of Gwynplaine, who is taken in by the good Ursus*
who runs a second-rate traveling vaudeville spectacular among his other
specialties. Gwynplaine is, in fact, the son of a peer of the United Kingdom. His father chose exile in Switzerland because of his loyalty to the
short-lived republic. King Charles II, seeking to prevent the heir from
taking his rightful place in his estate and in the House of Lords, has had
the child kidnapped and disfigured.

The story changes tempo when Ursus' group, heady with success, because of Gwynplaine and his eternal smile as a result of the disfigure-
ment, decides to go to London. Gwynplaine is temporarily restored to
his peerage, and he gives a rather socialist address to the House of Lords,
where he is not taken seriously because everyone thinks he is laughing
at what he is saying. Uncomfortable in that world, he returns to the
caravan, to the wolf Homo,* to Ursus, and to his beloved, the blind girl
Dea* whom he had saved from certain death in a deep snow blizzard
many years before.

Gwynplaine has an honest and simple heart which beats in harmony
with that of Dea. She does not need eyes to see Gwynplaine's soul; they
have a deep spiritual love. But, as in so many pieces of Romantic psychology, for reasons unknown, Dea dies aboard the ship which is taking
them to Holland, and Gwynplaine, in his despair at losing the one and
only person in this world who matters to him, follows her in death by

jumping off the ship. For Gwynplaine, as for Dea, following the example of Ursus and the wolf Homo, the simple life of *saltimbanques* had lyrical charms which could never be found in the high life of the English aristocracy to which he was called, and which he refused. In a sense, Gwynplaine has followed the example of his own father in refusing to compromise his principles to a corrupt system.

This novel has some of the qualities of *Les Misérables*,* in pitting lyrical poverty against hypocritical power. Hugo, in the personage of Gwynplaine, shows himself to be his usual defender of the people against the corruption of government and politics.

H

Habibrah. Habibrah, the obi or witch doctor in Hugo's novel *Bug-Jargal*,* is a hideously deformed dwarf who serves as a court jester on the plantation of Captain d'Auverney's* uncle, where he is treated like a pet. His deformity is not unlike those found in Hugo's later novel *L'Homme qui rit.** He is given special privileges, is allowed to sleep in the master's bedroom (on the floor), and receives tidbits from the master's table. At the time of the insurrection he is at first believed to have been killed with the master. This turns out not to be true, for he is discovered acting as the "chaplain" in the rebel army headed by Biassou.* It is there that he performs a parody of the Catholic Mass. As the action of the novel moves toward denouement, it is revealed that Habibrah has asked Biassou for permission to torture and then kill Captain d'Auverney. In a tense dialogue between the two men, the dwarf reveals his true feelings, boasts that he had killed his master, and now wishes to exterminate any remaining members of the family from whom he had suffered long years of abjection and humiliation. In a powerful physical struggle with the captain, Habibrah is thrown off the cliff and meets his death.

Some critics have compared this descent to that of Claude Frollo* in *Notre-Dame de Paris.** This seems dubious. Given his years of servitude during which he was mocked and ridiculed, his desire for revenge seems plausible, and it cannot be attributed solely to a spirit of malevolence.

Halte en Marchant. The concluding poem of *Aurore* of *Les Contemplations*,* a seventy-four-line narrative and visionary poem, is a serious conclusion to the lyrical poems with which Book 1 begins, suggesting that we shall yet encounter darker forces when we proceed out of the forest and into the remaining landscapes of the collection. *Halte en marchant* (Stopping along the way) is a pilgrim's progress, suggesting a new geographical or even photographic perspective on what Hugo is attempting to achieve through nineteenth-century verse form.

The narrative contains medieval and mystical elements in its description of the forest hovel where the poet and an unidentified friend seek refuge for the night. Indeed, its quick narrative is reminiscent of Chrétien de Troye's *Perceval*, the young seeker of truth who is unable to distinguish a knight's lavish tent from a forest cathedral.

The poetic narrative quickly jumps from a description in the imperfect past to an existential and somewhat chilling present; from a lyrical description of nature to the approach to a shelter, surrounded by herbs and weeds; and a statue of a saint, with the question turning in the head of the narrator, is this a religious temple or simply an inn?

The narrative continues in a startling linguistic manner with a hidden or silent, almost unknown dialogue between an "innkeeper" and the travelers: *Nous entrons. Qu'avez-vous?—Des oeufs frais, de l'eau fraîche* (We go in. What do you have? Fresh eggs, fresh water). This exchange is followed by a quick snapshot of a young girl fetching water (Greuze-like) from the well. The scene quickly shifts to the traveler composing himself in his room, where he discovers on the wall an engraving of the beating of Christ before his trial and crucifixion.

Part 2, which begins with the idea of Christ as a vagabond become God (*le vagabond flagellé devient Dieu*), goes on with a discursive allocution by the poet on Dante, Socrates, Milton, and Thomas More, among others.

Part 3, however, returns to the poetic intuitions of the nature scenes of the opening strophes, now complemented by the poet's interpretation of the copied engraving of the flagellated Christ. One of the sadistic soldiers who is beating Christ, in some sort of fury, pulls out locks of Christ's hair to take to Caiphus and, en route, discovers a frightening transformation: *Stupéfait, pâle, et comme en proie aux visions,/Frémissant!—il avait dans la main des rayons* (Aghast, pallid, as if victim to nightmares,/ shuddering—he had in his hand beams of light).

This final poem of *Aurore*, despite some discursive notes, remains fundamental to his poetic genius which knows how to combine the new Romantic lyrical narrative with a visionary conclusion, seemingly born out of a type of prepoetic, almost prosaic narrative of a trip through a forest with a stop for the night at a third-rate inn.

Han d'Islande. This novel of Hugo's youth was written between 1821 and 1823 when he was between nineteen and twenty-one years old. Published in February 1823, the novel contains three prefaces, the last dating from 1833 in which Hugo alerted the reader to its faults, attributing them to his lack of novelistic maturity. The center of the narrative, the intense and chaste love between Ordener and Ethel, is seen by those interested in imposing biography on fiction as a hint to Hugo's deep love for his future wife Adèle. The work, however, is not without merit; it contains elements that will be used by the mature novelist, and it has the same faults and virtues that we find in the adolescent works of the young Gustave Flaubert.*

This novel contains multiple characters and characterizations, too numerous to be delineated in this entry. The plot itself is also complicated, with allusions to Scandinavian mythology and folklore. Consequently, attention here will focus on the principal characters and the main events of the very long novel.

Ordener, the son of the viceroy, is in love with Ethel, the daughter of Schumacker, a former high minister in the king's government who is now in prison for life on charges of treason. Ethel shares his prison quarters. Spiagudry, a superstitious scholar and morgue keeper, accompanies Ordener on his quest to find and conquer the wicked Han d'Islande. There are two characters named Han d'Islande. The real one is a short man of monstrous inclination whose only companion is a white bear. This Han, an incarnation of evil, kills for the sake of killing, drinks the blood of his victims, and eats their flesh. It is he who, at the novel's conclusion, sets the prison on fire and is, himself, either consumed by it or, according to legend, disappears into the sky. A fake Han, a giant from the mountains, is stupid and without personality. He heads the revolt of the miners against the protectorate.

Ulrica d'Ahiefeld is the intended bride of Ordener, but he loves only Ethel. Finally, there is Nychol Orugix, the executioner, who dreams of being more than a provincial hangman. He executes his own brother, Musdoemon, the private secretary to the chancellor, who, under the name of Hacket, devised a plot to discredit Schumacker, making it appear that Schumacker was responsible for the revolt of the miners.

The narrative is centered on Ordener's love for Ethel, which leads him to seek a battle with the wicked Han d'Islande, a quest worthy of a medieval romance. This amorous plot is crisscrossed with the narrative of the revolt of the miners and their defeat and ultimate judgment in the courts. In the end, however, all turns out well: secret documents, which reveal Ordener's and Schumacker's innocence, are discovered. The wicked Musdoemon is punished; Ethel and Ordener, who had married in prison just hours before his scheduled execution, celebrate life: their union produces a new race (giving the work an epic quality), that of the counts of Danneskiold. By a gracious act of the king, the miners are pardoned and released from the tyranny of the protectorate.

The work, albeit that of a very young writer, has some essential Hugolian themes such as the metaphysical problem of evil, the idea of justice, and a consideration of revolution in the name of liberty. Evil is personified in the real Han d'Islande, and the revolt of the persecuted miners is Hugo's statement on liberty for all mankind.

The novel, which is in the tradition of the English *roman noir* (black novel), displays the atmosphere of haunted castles, ruins, and hidden passageways also found in the works of Ann Radcliffe (1764–1823) or Monk Lewis (1775–1818), both of whom put the Romantic Gothic novel in vogue in England and subsequently in France. Much is also indirectly derived, through Madame de Staël, from the foggy and melancholic ruin atmosphere of the pseudo-Ossian style of James MacPherson.

Hugo's habit of affixing a meditation from others' works at the head of each chapter (a process he will continue in *Notre-Dame de Paris**) is derived from Shakespeare, Lope de Vega, Pedro Calderón de la Barca, Sir Walter Scott, and old Spanish Romances.

Han d'Islande seeks a kind of absurd verisimilitude with frequent references to the *Edda*, the body of ancient Icelandic literature, and a curious French mode (the novel is set in the late seventeenth century) with the vogue in Scandinavia for the novels of Madeleine de Scudéry (1607–1701), the author of the *Clélie, histoire romaine* (1654–1661).

The Reformation had, of course, already occurred in Norway, but the atmosphere is heavily Catholic with emphasis on the crucifix (especially in the courtroom, anticipating an important poem on judicial misconduct in *Les Contemplations**) and the invocation of saints. The Lutheran pastors seem very Catholic.

As a final note, the love of Ordener and Ethel and the miners' revolt should be seen against the backdrop of the evil Han d'Islande, diabolic in intent, who gives the novel a Manichean aspect. This fits perfectly with the meditation by the major French Romantics (Alfred de Vigny's* *Eloa* poem of 1824; Alphonse de Lamartine's* *La Chute d'un ange* 1838) of the problem of evil and how to atone for it. Redemption does not seem possible in *Han d'Islande*, but Hugo, at length, meditates on the reconciliation of God and Satan, for example, in the long *Ce que dit la bouche d'ombre** poem of *Les Contemplations** and *La Fin de Satan*.*

Han d'Islande, therefore, despite its easily identified novelistic faults, is already posing deep moral problems and dilemmas which will, of course, be more fully developed in later works.

Han d'Islande (theatrical presentation). The first adaptation of Hugo's early Nordic novel *Han d'Islande* was made by the French Romantic-symbolist poet Gérard de Nerval (1808–1855). This novel seems an unlikely source of inspiration for the poet of *Chimères* and the novel *Aurélia* in which reality, fantasy, and dreamlike landscapes seem to fuse. All the same, Nerval is also known as a translator who rendered Goethe's *Faust* into French in 1828, just a year before completing his dramatic rendering of the Hugo novel. Nerval's text encountered all sorts of difficulties in his effort to reconcile classical notions of time, space, and action. Electing to focus on the unity of action, he reduced the time element of the novel to forty-eight hours occurring within nine scenic tableaux. He furthermore tried to render more comprehensible to a potential French audience the difficult Nordic names found in Hugo's novel. No Parisian producer in 1829, however, showed any interest in this adaptation, and it was never performed. In 1832 a small group of French authors, totally unknown today, undertook the rendering of Hugo's novel into a theatrical piece. The authors were Palmir, Octo, and Rameau (whose stage name was Francisque, and who played the role of Han). This musical melodrama was performed for the first time at the Théâtre d l'Ambigu in January 1832. It was presented infrequently until 1834 and has never been performed since.

Harel, Felix A. A government administrator, theatrical producer, biographer, and playwright, Felix Harel (1790–1846) is important in the life of Victor Hugo as the director of the Porte-Saint-Martin theatre where Hugo had both personal and professional interests.

Early in his life, Harel had a government career: first as a subprefect of Soissons in 1812, and then as head of the prefecture of Les Landes in southwestern France during Bonaparte's 100 days. It was only natural that he would be under police scrutiny (1815) during the Restoration, and, in fact, he was in exile in Brussels in 1816. It was then that Harel's theatrical career took off as he headed an itinerant group of actors wandering throughout the continent. Authorized in 1819 to return to France, he became director of the Odéon theatre in 1829, and shortly thereafter he headed the theatre of the Porte-Saint-Martin. Harel's love of the theatre is manifest in his *Dictionnaire théâtricale* (1824) and in two plays of 1843, *Le Succès*, a comedy in two acts produced at the Odéon, and *Les Grands et les petits*, a full-length comedy presented at the Théâtre-Français.

Harel's contacts with Victor Hugo started with the production of Hugo's play *Lucrèce Borgia** (1833). It was during the preparatory readings at the Saint-Martin that Hugo made the acquaintance of Juliette Drouet, who was assigned the minor role of Princess Negroni. Harel, pleased with the success of *Lucrèce*, needed another play from Hugo, and thus the same year *Marie Tudor** was presented. *Marie Tudor* had difficulties with the press even before production. It would seem that, even after the success of Romantic theatre, there were still some problems with what was deemed proper and improper on the French stage; in this case, having an executioner (on scene) raised questions about propriety. The real reason seems, however, to have had to do with the rivalry between the celebrated Mademoiselle George* (mistress of Harel), who was to play the Queen to Juliette Drouet's Jane (in the third act, the audience hissed and whistled at Juliette). Whether this was a planned revenge or simply a disapproval of what was seen as a bad play cannot be determined. Juliette withdrew for health reasons.

Harel thus was an agent through which two of Hugo's plays were produced, but he was also responsible for bringing together Hugo and the love of his life, Juliette Drouet.

Health of Victor Hugo. Unlike other members of his family who suffered from serious mental breakdowns (his brother Eugène and his daughter Adèle) or diseases (his son Charles, a victim of the cholera epidemic in 1832, died suddenly in Bordeaux in 1871 and his son François-Victor died from tuberculosis in 1873 at the age of forty-five), Hugo, who was born frail and was hardly expected to survive, lived for eighty-three years with very few sick days in his life. Although he had a voracious appetite, he drank very little wine. His sexual appetite seems to have been without limit. Aside from minor ailments of an ephemeral nature, colds and intestinal grippe for example, Hugo led a healthy and robust life which some have attributed to the genetic contribution of his father, General Léopold Hugo (*see* Genealogy).

Heard on the Mountain. *See Ce qu'on entend sur la montagne.*

Heaven and Hell. Heaven and Hell is the theatrical adaptation of the legend of Pécopin and Bauldour* found in letter twenty-one of Hugo's *Le Rhin** (1842). It was Hugo's wish to adapt this tale for the theatre. In collaboration with H. Lucas and E. Barre, this project dates back to 1842 itself. It was only in 1898 that Hugo followers became aware of the existence of this production through an article published about it in *Le Temps* by J. Claretie. This lyric play was accepted by the Ambigu Theatre in 1852 and performed there in 1853. At that time Hugo was already in exile in the Channel Islands, and his name appeared nowhere in the program.

The spectacle, mixing song and dance, was composed of five acts and twenty tableaux, and every possible use was made of theatrical machinery to achieve the effects of magic and hallucination.

As is usual in adaptations, there are multiple changes from the original text. For example, the enchanted forest seems more like a formal French garden than a forest in the Vosges mountains. The Middle Eastern scenes in Baghdad are now centered around Antioch with vague oral comments on the prophet Mohammed. The names are changed—Pécopin becoming the knight Gérard and Bauldour, curiously enough, Bertha (with its uncomplimentary allusions for the modern reader both to the big Bertha cannon and to the legendary mother of Charlemagne, Big-footed Bertha, queen of France).

While in the original legend Pécopin is without will or purpose in life, a wandering hunter with an idée fixe on hunting (not unlike the weekend football spectators in front of television sets in America), in the play he is given a reason for his knightly pilgrimage—to be worthy of Bertha by his deeds which will cause him to be annointed Count of the Rhine. The famous talisman of the legend is not given by an oriental princess, but now by the god Amour, who saves Gérard and his beloved.

Hernani. *Hernani* is the most important, historically, of the revolutionary Romantic rejection of a dying French theatrical tradition. There was no longer any general admiration for the dramaturgists of the generation of 1660 (Jean Racine) and their predecessors, such as Pierre Corneille, who seems in his own way to be a Romantic, *avant le lettre*. It signifies rather a tedium, even boredom with a neoclassic theatre that had outlived its time. This may be partly the reason for Hugo's enormous success with this play, which was derived from his and other Romantics' fascination with Spain as the departure point for the Middle East.

Hernani (1830) is somewhat similar to Corneille's religious drama *Polyeucte* (1643) in its insistent motif on the importance of honor. Corneille also had been attracted to Spain as evidenced by his theatrical rendition of *Le Cid* (1637), perhaps the most important "modern" of the French tragicomedies that pits passionate love against duty.

Such is the essential point of Hugo's *Hernani*. The hero, noble in origin, but outlawed because of his father's disloyalty or refusal to follow royal commands, deeply loves Doña Sol de Silva* who is sought not only by the king, soon to be named Holy Roman Emperor, but also by her uncle, the old and seemingly unscrupulous Don Ru Gomez de Silva.* Since Don Ruiz had given Hernani* house protection (a bit like church sanctuary), he demands from Hernani a ransom of death, which brings about the denouement, just after the nuptials of Doña Sol with her young lover. It catered to the new Romantic sensibility, seeking sensationalism, which is most likely the indication of a change in French sociology. Followers of the classic theatre of the seventeenth century, filled with admiration and imitation of Greek tragedy, found the plot and action of *Hernani* melodramatic and without sound psychological justification. The battle of the Romantics versus the classicists was fought in the theatre. The brilliant poetry of *Hernani* was sooner admired than its dramaturgy. *Hernani* is, from the point of view of theatricality, stunning. The new idea of scenery, historical moments, and histrionics puts the play in direct opposition to French classical theatre which was more of the mind than the body. The seventeenth century needed no scenery, only the spoken voice, usually in monologues given in front of an ill-defined palace or courtyard.

For these reasons, *Hernani* must be seen as an absolutely revolutionary piece of theatrical history.

Hernani. Hernani, the first and most important theatrical hero of French Romanticism (*Hernani*,* 1830), is the Romantic equivalent of Pierre Corneille's Cid (*Le Cid*, 1637); both heros are based in Spanish myths about honor, loyalty, and love. Hernani, although noble, is an outlaw, the victim of misunderstandings between royal central authority and noble rebellions, in a situation similar to the *Fronde* wars of seventeenth-century France against unification moves made by Jules Mazarin and then by Cardinal Richelieu. Hernani, as personage, embodies correctly the ideas of Spanish honor and machismo, something which Hugo either intuited or accepted from his own male authority. This personage of outlaw and prince (an idea Hugo had previously used with his slave-prince hero in *Bug-Jargal**) had to be high entertainment for the new Romantic public. It certainly is the equivalent, in superstar adulation, of Don Rodrigue in Corneille's *Le Cid*.

Hernani's qualities as hero, however, are basically enhanced by the high poetic quality of his speeches, a soaring Romantic poetry, which at times is contrasted with the more prosaic anxieties of the heroine Doña Sol.

When Doña Sol avows her desire to follow Hernani wherever and forever, Hugo's poetry reaches for a marriage of drama and verse. Act 1, scene 2 is representative of this dramatic union. Doña Sol's prose, *Je vous suivrai* (I shall follow you) is met by Hernani's poetry based on the motif of the verb *suivre* (to follow) in which a Romantic monologue projects the possibilities of exile for the two of them to mountainous hideouts, and then possible execution. This speech must be counted among the high points of French Romantic theatre.

Hernani (performances). This play is one of the most important of all the French Romantic dramas, and a brief survey of its production across the nineteenth century indicates a lingering and abiding taste for Romantic histrionics, in spite of the inroads of the newer tastes for realism and naturalism in both written form and the theatre.

*Hernani** had, in nineteenth-century terms, a record run of thirty-six performances between February 25 and June 22, 1830. It was frequently presented also in the 1840s, but was, naturally enough, forbidden during the reign of Napoléon III,* archenemy of Victor Hugo. Although it was perhaps reluctantly performed in 1867, it experienced its most important revival in 1877, thanks to the talent of Sarah Bernhardt* (thirty-three years old, in contrast with Anne Boutet (Mars,* the original ingenue, who played the part at the age of forty-one), and *Hernani* went through a spectacular run of 300 performances. It, of course, remains in the canon of the Comédie Française, along with the works of Jean Racine.

Hired Clappers. *See* Claque, La.

Homme qui rit, L'. One of the strangest yet most compelling of Hugo's novels, combining his old theory of the sublime and the grotesque as found in the *Préface de Cromwell, (see Cromwell, Preface to)* and in his Gothic novel *Notre-Dame de Paris,** *L'Homme qui rit* was finally published in 1869. This fantasy of Hugo was started and then abandoned in 1866. This was unusual for Hugo, who customarily brought all things literary to closure rapidly.

The narration is simple. The protagonist Gwynplaine,* in reality the son of a peer of Great Britain, has been disfigured by a group of *comprachicos** (child abductors and disfigurers) at the request of the king of England. The reasons seem somewhat obscure but appear to be based in Charles II's desire to usurp the lands of Lord Clancharlie (Gwynplaine's father), who has chosen voluntary exile in Switzerland because of his support for the doomed republic, and thus prevent Gwynplaine from any legal claims to succession. All of this is thwarted, however, because of a shipwreck of the *comprachicos* in which they confess their sins and, before drowning, send a bottle with documents proving that Gwynplaine is indeed a legitimate heir in England. The bottle with its contents, which has washed ashore, is convincing enough to establish Gwynplaine's rights.

As the narration begins, Gwynplaine has been abandoned by the *comprachicos*, left ashore on a cold, snowy day. He wanders across the moors and plains where he finds a dead woman holding her child, Dea,* whom he rescues. The boy and his infant charge arrive at the gypsy wagon of Ursus,* a traveling Bohemian, medicine man, and actor who takes them in. A new family, which also includes the tamed wolf Homo,* is thus formed. As time passes, the traveling group becomes famous because of Gwynplaine's deformity; he is an amusing freak in a sideshow. Ursus, whose financial situation is greatly improved by the phenomenon of Gwynplaine, is able to expand his business, hire additional personnel, and buy a new and better equipped house-wagon, the "Green Box." Dea, who is blind, and Gwynplaine form a close, if chaste, alliance. The traveling circus finally comes to London where it is a huge success, and it is there that Gwynplaine's true identity is revealed. He is taken to Windsor, outfitted in garments appropriate to his rank, and told to speak at the next session of the House of Lords. He does so in a revolutionary fashion worthy of his father. The essence of his speech is a cry against the social injustice found in eighteenth-century England. The other peers laugh at him thinking he is not serious because he always seems to be laughing himself. Unable to continue this charade, Gwynplaine abandons his peerage, leaving it to his brother, and returns to his wandering family which is to sail from England to Holland, for they have been ordered out of the country. Gwynplaine and Dea express their love for each other, but it is too late for Dea is dying (a typical unknown Romantic malady), and indeed she does die. Gwynplaine, fearing that there is no life without her, jumps off the ship in an act of suicide.*

This novel, with its expressionistic style (*see* Expressionism), recalling that found in *Les Travailleurs de la mer*,* is an excellent vehicle for Hugo to explore the question of individual and social injustice. Gwynplaine has been dealt a bad hand with his disfiguration, but beneath the exterior ugliness is found a beautiful and generous soul, not unlike that of Quasimodo* in *Notre-Dame de Paris*.* His deformity complements Dea's blindness; they both see only each other's souls. Furthermore, Hugo's extensive research in English political history uncovers a multitude of sins in the caste system in force there (the disfiguration commanded from on high to the lowest rogues on the bottom of the social scale reveals a society without conscience).

The simpler life, that of traveling comedians, is preferred both by the narrator and the inhabitants of the Green Box. In this regard, Hugo's novel is very much like the *Sans famille* (1878) of Hector Malot (1830–1907) with its emphasis, as in *L'Homme qui rit*, on abandonment, which is certainly the motif of this novel.

Homme qui rit, L' (theatrical adaptation). Hugo's novel, published in 1869 with its symbolic implications of the grotesque formation of nineteenth-century society, was adapted to the theatre in 1971 by Yves Gasc at the Halles de Baltard. Although the apparent laughter of Gwynplaine* is relegated to a minor role, the complaint against social injustice is felt all the same. It is Gwynplaine's love for Dea,* the blind girl, which may be the major cause of the protagonist's laughter: a laughter hiding tears along the lines of the Italian opera *I Pagliacci* of Ruggiero Leoncavallo, first performed in Milan, on May 21, 1892, or the *Fantasio* play of Alfred de Musset* (1833). In both the novel and its theatrical adaptation, the reader and viewer are confronted with the nineteenth-century concept of the sublime and grotesque first enunciated by Hugo in the *Préface de Cromwell (see Cromwell, Preface to)* and illustrated in the personage of Quasimodo* in *Notre-Dame de Paris*.*

L'Homme qui rit (The Man who laughs) continues, in a minor way, to fascinate a modern public. *L'Homme qui rit* was performed in Arlington, Virginia, in English in 1996 at Le Néon French-American Theatre. This rendering successfully blended the close-knit family of Ursus, Dea, and Gwynplaine, the traveling itinerants in the "Green Box," without ignoring the political realities underlining the message of both the novel and the play.

Homo. Homo is the domesticated wolf that belongs to Ursus,* the itinerant peddler of health cures and second-rate vaudeville acts in *L'Homme qui rit*.* Homo joins the ranks of the many thinking and sensitive animals* inhabiting the fiction of Victor Hugo. He is not only faithful but also very intuitive, demonstrating Hugo's own personal belief in the intelligence of all matter. It is because of Homo that the protagonist of this novel, Gwynplaine,* is able to find again his old friends of the caravan days, Ursus and his beloved Dea.* Like all animals, Homo cannot talk, but he knows his way around the human heart, and he knows how to take appropriate action, when necessary. It is because of Homo that Ursus must leave England because the mean-spirited Barkilphedro, the envious, as Hugo calls him, threatens to have the wolf killed as it is illegal to possess them in England. Homo has the qualities of Hugo's dogs such as Ponto* from *Les Contemplations** and Rask,* Bug-Jargal's* dog from the novel *Bug-Jargal*.*

Hugo, Adèle. Adèle Hugo (1830–1915) was the youngest of Victor Hugo's five children, the longest surviving, and the most curious and enigmatic because of her erratic behavior and her obsessive preoccupation with a man she believed to be first her fiancé and then her husband. She wandered to Canada and to the Caribbean in pursuit of him and was eventually incarcerated in mental institutions for the affluent.

The story of Adèle is one of the most bizarre in the history of modern French biographical literature. She may have been disturbed by the death of her sister, Léopoldine Hugo,* and remained a dedicated if distant observer of the household events, the famous visitors, and the brilliant intellectual and aesthetic discussions of her famous father and his guests, all of which have been recorded in her very long, and frequently cryptic diary *Journal de l'Exil* (Diary of the exile), which focuses primarily on life on the Channel Islands of Jersey and Guernsey (*see* Hugo, Adèle, *Le Journal d'*).

It was in 1856 (the year of the publication of *Les Contemplations**) that the first apparent signs of mental disorder were noticed. This may have been aggravated by the spiritism* and séances from 1853 to 1855 in the Hugo household, instigated by the Romantic poet Delphine Gay.* Her condition, that of schizophrenia (in a family already burdened with mental illness, specifically that of Hugo's brother Eugène), was aggravated by the unrequited love she bore for an English military officer, Albert Pinson,* whose original interest in Adèle may have been motivated by infatuation, perhaps by her position as the daughter of France's most famous writer, and perhaps also by her money. In any case, Pinson soon lost interest, and he was transferred to Halifax, Nova Scotia. Adèle arrived in Halifax in 1863, carrying with her her mother's jewelry, nine years after having met the English officer. She later followed Pinson to Barbados where her mental condition deteriorated further and she began to identify herself as Madame Pinson. Pinson left Barbados. Adèle was taken in by a kindly former slave, Madame Céline Alvarez Baa, who returned with her to France where she was placed in a comfortable mental asylum in which she died at the age of eighty-five.

Adèle Hugo's strange amorous odyssey not only sprang from a simple case of mental derangement but also from a quest for independence for women in a century that had placed them squarely in inferior roles (Adèle had refused several proposals of marriage before she met Pinson). Her position parallels, in many ways, that of Paul Claudel's* sister Camille, who was a fine sculptor and an intimate friend of Rodin, who also was finally confined to a mental institution.

Adèle's journals, ably edited by Frances Vernor Guille, are the main source of François Truffaut's 1974 film *The Story of Adèle H.*

BIBLIOGRAPHY

Dow, Leslie Smith. *Adèle Hugo, La Misérable.* Fredericton, N. B., Canada: Goose Lane Editions, 1993.

Guille, Frances Vernor. *Journal d'Adèle Hugo.* Paris: Minard. Vol. 11, 1852 (1968); vol. 2, 1853 (1971); vol. 3, 1854 (1984).

Gúillemin, Henri. *L'Engloutie: Adèle, fille de Victor Hugo, 1830–1915.* Paris: Editions du Seuil, 1985.

Truffaut, François, director. *The Story of Adèle H.* Film. Paris, 1975.

Hugo, Adèle, *Le Journal d'*. Adele Hugo's diary, also known as the *Diary of the Exile*, has been collected into three volumes (1852, 1853, 1854). This diary is important in its recordings of family activities on Jersey and Guernsey, especially in its almost maniacal scrupulosity in recording the slightest of details. In her introductory remarks to the diary, Frances Vernor Guille aptly notes this characteristic. She notes that Adèle retraces, almost by the hour, her trip with her mother from Paris through Villequier, Le Havre, and Southampton. Guille gives us a clear idea of Adèle's observations, often made in the form of dialogue and sometimes in coded language, but also recording who was present and who was not. She recorded such diverse items as the coup d'état of Napoléon III,* the Crimean War, a play being performed in Paris, an article from the *Illustrated London News*, Catholicism, the spiritist séances, and the United States of Europe. The trivial and the profound are all recorded, from observations on the family's dogs to discussions of the nature of good and evil (*Le Journal d'Adèle Hugo*, "Introduction et notes par Frances Vernor Guille," Paris: Minard, 1968, vol. 1: 22–33).

The history of the manuscript is in itself a fascinating piece of literary detective work. J. P. Morgan had acquired some pages of the diary between 1896 and 1905. In 1962 the same library acquired one hundred pages from the library of Marc Loliée of Paris, documents previously discovered by a chair repairman, found between the pages of a sixteenth-century Bible. The artisan sold them to a French diplomat, Jean Delalande, who in turn sold them to Loliée. Finally, a typewritten transcription of previously unknown pages of Adèle's diary, translated into English, were found in the Victor Hugo museum.

It was on the basis of these materials that Guille began her work, which led to the publication of three volumes brought out by the Minard publishing house in Paris (this information is derived from the meticulous scholarship of Leslie Smith Dow).

BIBLIOGRAPHY

Dow, Leslie Smith. *Adèle Hugo, la Misérable*. Fredericton, N. B., Canada: Goose Lane Editions, 1993.
Guille, Frances Vernor. *Le Journal d'Adèle Hugo*. Vol. 1, 1852 (1968); vol. 2, 1853 (1971); vol. 3, 1854 (1984). Paris: Lettres modernes.

Hugo, Jean. Jean Hugo (1894–1984), the great grandson of Victor Hugo, a primitive painter, was born in Paris in 1894, the son of Georges Hugo II, Victor Hugo's grandson. He was educated at Elizabeth College on Guernsey in the Channel Islands, while living in the Hugo property, Hauteville House. On Guernsey he learned English at an early age, and, like his great grandfather, he was proficient in literature and in classical languages (Greek and Latin), as well as Provençal and Catalan. In 1919 he married the painter Valentine Gross (1887–1968). After World War I he entered fully into the musical, literary, and artistic world of Paris, hobnobbing with Eric Satie, Georges Auric, Pablo Picasso, Paul Morand, Darius Milhaud, and above all Jean Cocteau.*

In 1921 he designed masks and costumes for Rolf de Maré's Swedish ballet production of Cocteau's *Les Mariés de la Tour Eiffel*. In 1938 he designed sets and costumes for the one-hundredth anniversary production of his great grandfather's play *Ruy Blas*.* It is well known that Victor Hugo himself was a very fine sketcher (*see* Drawings), and it can be assumed that Jean Hugo inherited his great grandfather's talent or had a predisposition to the world of art. Like his famous ancestor, he, for his generation, was one of the avant-garde. Jean Hugo was part of the revolution in theatre, poetry, music, and dance after World War I and thus seems to have rediscovered the artistic bent of Victor Hugo.

To describe Jean Hugo's work simply as primitive is too limiting. In some ways it reminds one of the world of the American painter Paul Cadmus (except that Hugo's group scenes are all veiled or semiveiled whereas Cadmus' work veers toward nudity) or the work of the Colombian painter Botero (without the obesity).

Jean Hugo has been included in the genealogy of this encyclopedia. He is also mentioned here because of the continuation of the aesthetic interests of his great grandfather.

BIBLIOGRAPHY

Art Gallery of Ontario. *Jean Hugo: La Nouvelle Revue Française.* Vol. 3 (Summer 1939): 167.
Maritain, Jacques. *Frontières de la poésie et autres essais.* Paris: Louis Rouart et fils, 1935, pp. 178, 220–21.
————. *Creative Intuition in Art and Poetry.* New York: Pantheon Books, 1953.
Wattenmaker, Richard J. *The Art of Jean Hugo.* Art Gallery of Toronto, May 19–June 27, 1973.

Hugo, Léopoldine. Léopoldine (1824–1843), Victor Hugo's older daughter, drowned in the Seine at Villequier on September 4, 1843. Her husband, Charles Vacquerie,* an excellent swimmer, would not abandon his new wife and they perished together. Hugo received this sad news (as reported in the journal of Juliette Drouet), while he was reading a newspaper in the Café de l'Europe in the village of Soubise, near Rochefort, on the Atlantic coast. This enormous tragedy, the loss of the preferred daughter, marked a great deal of the rest of Hugo's life. He lived long enough to bear with the many sufferings of his offspring, especially those of Adèle who spent most of her life insanely in love with an English military officer who did not return her affection.

The death of Léopoldine is pivotal in understanding Hugo's middle-class family values. Although a womanizer, he valued family, children, and grandchildren, and these thoughts echo across his volumes of poetry, beginning with *Lorsque l'Enfant paraît** (When the child comes into the room) and continuing through the final filial poems entitled *L'Art d'être grand-père* (The art of being a grandfather).

Léopoldine's death is the centerpiece for what can be considered Hugo's greatest poetic work, *Les Contemplations** (1856), especially Book Four, *Pauca meae*. The evocation of family and love of daughters, however, crosses the entire collection. Thematic representations of family values can be appreciated in the following entries in *Les Contemplations: A ma fille* (To my daughter) and *Mes deux filles* (My two daughters*) from Book one, *Aurore*. From *Pauca meae*, there is *Oh, je fus comme fou dans le premier moment* (O I was as if insane the first moment when I got this news) and the famous short lament *Demain dès l'aube** (Tomorrow at daybreak) on the father's visit to Léopoldine's grave, as well as the very long Romantic outpouring of insufferable grief in *A Villequier*. *Les Contemplations*, which mixes personal grief and political outrage, is dominated by the absence of the daughter. It ends appropriately with *A celle qui est restée en France* (To She who remained in France), the father's meditation from the Channel Islands on Léopoldine who is removed from him physically and geographically.

BIBLIOGRAPHY

Frey, John A. *Les Contemplations of Victor Hugo: The Ash Wednesday Liturgy*. Charlottesville: University Press of Virginia, 1988.
Nash, Suzanne. *Les Contemplations of Victor Hugo: An Allegory of the Creative Process*. Princeton, NJ: Princeton University Press, 1976.
Peyre, Henri. *Hugo*. University: University of Alabama Press, 1980.

Humanitarianism. Until the advent of Romanticism, the concept of humanitarianism would hardly have been comprehended or discussed. Corporal works of mercy, as they were then called, were strictly allied with spiritual endeavors; for example, the public testimony of Saint Francis de Salle (1567–1622) who, with Jeanne-Françoise de Chantal (1572–1641), founded the contemplative Order of the Visitation. But such works of mercy are better known through the works of Saint Vincent de Paul (1581–1660) whose concern for the poor, the imprisoned, and the homeless is still manifested in the twentieth century throughout the Western world. The word humanitarianism, in modern times must not be confused with the "humanism" of the sixteenth century, which simply described the Renaissance study of pagan antiquity and the advent of secular knowledge as opposed to the late scholasticism of the Middle Ages.

Hugo was part and parcel of what can be called the "humanitarian urge of the Romantics" and should be so noted. This means an atmosphere warmed by an optimism engendered by the positive side of the French Revolution of 1789, with a strong belief in moral, scientific, and humanitarian progress. This is the basic meaning of many of the utopian and progressive movements brought about during the Romantic period— those of Charles Fourier and Claude-Henri Saint-Simon in France. In France, Great Britain, and the United States, the novel became the instrument of social change. Hugo must be included among such novelists along with George Sand and Emile Zola; in England, Charles Dickens; in the United States, the transcendentalists Ralph Waldo Emerson and Nathaniel Hawthorne along with the social experiment of Brook Farm. Latter-day reformers in the United States would include Frank Norris (1870–1902), a naturalist novelist.

Hugo's generous and humanitarian impulses are easily gleaned from most of his poetry, in addition to the social impact of his novels, including *Le Dernier Jour d'un condamné** (The last day of a condemned man), *Notre-Dame de Paris,** and the celebrated *Les Misérables.** His attitudes in his own life were equally magnanimous. As a politician, he fought against slavery (*Bug-Jargal**) and capital punishment.* When the infamous Falloux Act* (still on the books in the French legal system) was discussed, he became the leader of those who wished to strengthen public and secular education in France. His noble defense of the American abolitionist John Brown* is another aspect of this nineteenth-century existentialist.

A concise appreciation of Hugo's social attitudes can be found in just a few short poems from the 1856 collection *Les Contemplations,** all of which show Hugo to be in step with the major concerns of the nineteenth century; for example, *Le Mendiant** (The beggar) from Book Five, *En Marche*. The beggar is, of course, the never-asking poor man, who should not be turned away for he may be Christ in disguise. Similar sentiments are expressed in *Croire, mais pas en nous* (Believe, but not in us) *Halte en marchant* (Stopping along the way), and *Les malheureux* (The unfortunate), all from *Les Contemplations*, which act as poetic corollaries to the more famous prose of *Les Misérables*.

BIBLIOGRAPHY

Frey, John A. *Les Contemplations of Victor Hugo: The Ash Wednesday Liturgy*. Charlottesville: University Press of Virginia, 1988.

Hus, Jan. Jan Hus (1372–1415) was the most important Czech religious reformer who anticipated the Lutheran reformation of 1517. He took a particularly strong stance against the sale of indulgences and was executed for his beliefs. Hugo, ever the defendant of the underdog, be it Hus, or John Brown* or Mr. Tapner, well understood the current of protest, one man against an unjust system, in this case the institution of the Church. In the case of John Brown, it was his abolitionist beliefs that brought him to the scaffold; for Mr. Tapner, it was a crime that required capital punishment* (his was the last hanging to take place on Guernsey) (*see* Tapner, the execution of Mr.).

Hugo's poetic eye focused on the symbolic individuals who actively or passively defied systems. His ardent opposition to the death penalty, for whatever reason, was made clear in poem fourteen of *La Pitié suprême** (The highest degree of compassion).

I

Impressionism. This school of painting started in France in about 1874 in opposition to official or academic painting. Its ancestors would be the Barbizon school, certain English landscape painters, and Eugene Boudin and Jongkind. The most famous impressionist painters in France were Claude Monet, Pierre-Auguste Renoir, Paul Cézanne (although demi-expressionist), Paul Gauguin, and Henri de Toulouse-Lautrec.

There is, however, a type of literary impressionism which technically can be seen as the syntax that holds off the subject until the last moment, much like viewing too closely an impressionistic painting where subject or meaning is effaced, but with distance, the whole becomes clearly a unity. This technique is common in the works of Gustave Flaubert.*

Hugo exhibits and incorporates many of the nineteenth-century artistic manifestations in spite of his squarely rooted Romanticism. While his syntax hardly appears "impressionistic" in the sense of Flaubert or Pierre Loti, he could properly be called a type of impressionist *avant la lettre*. A fine example would be the *Mazeppa* poem from the 1829 collection *Les Orientales*.* While Ivan Stepanovich Mazeppa* is tied naked, to the back of a wild stallion for a wild gallop across the steppes of Ukraine, his upturned head is on a roller-coaster ride across hundreds of kilometers that present a kaleidoscopic vision more impressionistic than expressionistic (*see* Expressionism). The *Mazeppa* poem has much in common with Arthur Rimbaud's *Bateau ivre* which participates in the impressionism of the symbolists (*see* Symbolism). Without wishing to stretch an argument too far, Hugo, by his genius and his longevity, as well as his prolific literary production, assumed most of the literary currents of the nineteenth century, including their transformations of painterly techniques and effects.

Inez de Castro. This melodrama, written by Hugo in 1818 or perhaps later, contains three acts and two interludes presented in song and dance. It was accepted by the Panorama-Dramatique, an avant-garde theatrical group of Romanticism, but forbidden by the official censor. Inez de Castro's tragic life has inspired several writers, including, in France, Henri de Montherlant (1896–1972) in his *La Reine morte* (The dead queen), of 1942.

Hugo's play departs radically from history. In reality Inez de Castro went to her death upon the orders of Don Pedro's father, King Alfonso IV. In Hugo's melodrama, the onus for the poisoning death of Inez is laid upon the queen; Alfonso is regarded in the play as *Alphonse le justicier* (Alphonso, lover of justice). After the death of Alphonso, after he is mortally wounded in a battle with the Moors at the gates of Lisbon, Pedro ascends the throne and takes vengeance on Inez's murderers.

The plot revolves about the queen's plan to marry Pedro to Constance (in fact, Pedro was already married to Constance when he fell in love with Inez). When it is discovered that Inez has borne two children to Pedro, a trial is called, for she has violated the law. The ambitious Justice of Peace Alpunar, acting as an agent of the queen, avoids holding the trial by administering a poisonous drug to the imprisoned Inez. Thus, despite a royal blessing on the marriage of Inez and Pedro, Inez dies in the arms of her husband and children. Pedro's coronation in the last act is to take place in the burial vaults of the Castro family. It is there that he plans to take his own life, but in the best tradition of both the *autos sacramentales* (sacramental plays) of Pedro Calderón de la Barca (1600–1681) and the romantic *Don Juan Tenorio* (1844) of José Zorilla (1817–1893) (in which the miraculous intervention of one of the women Don Juan had seduced ensures his salvation because he had at least once, amidst some seductions, loved truly), Hugo concludes his play with an apparition, that of the dead Inez who counsels Don Pedro not to commit suicide, but to live for their children and for his country while hoping for their eternal union after death.

The play itself, with the two interludes, especially the first after act 1 (followed by another entr'acte of less importance after act 2), is filled with song and dance, probably ballet, in an exotic rendering of the camp of the Moors. Furthermore, the arrival of the hunting party of the royal entourage (a disguise to cover their inquiry as to the whereabouts of the children of Inez and Pedro) recalls the tradition of nineteenth-century classical ballet in which the rich stop for refreshments at some humble bucolic inn or cottage and, while resting, are entertained by the peasants.

It is difficult to understand the censorship of this play to begin with, except to say that royalty is not portrayed in the best light, since the queen is evil. Any attack on royalty anywhere could be construed as a veiled attack on royalty at home.

This work of the young Hugo is important, as are other plays from his youth, in evaluating his evolution away from classical form. The first play of his youth, *Irtamène*,* was designed as a classical tragedy; *A.Q.C.H.E.B.*,* as a vaudeville; *Inez de Castro*, as a melodrama; and, finally, *Amy Robsart* (1822), the first example of the new form, *drame*.*

In Praise of Trees. See *Aux arbres*.

Insanity. Mental derangement for whatever cause, genetic or brought on by emotional trauma, is found in the Hugo family. The critic Agnes Mary Frances Robinson contends that Hugo himself was saved from madness only by the creative spirit in him. Writing poetry, dramas, and novels kept his mind on an even keel. Such was not the fate of Hugo's brother Eugène or his daughter Adèle, both of whom suffered mental breakdowns, brought on, it would seem, by unrequited love.

Eugène Hugo's problems seem to have been aggravated by Victor's marriage to Adèle Foucher (*see* Genealogies) on October 12, 1822. It became clear that Eugène was himself desperately in love with Adèle, and the marriage pushed him over the brink. At the wedding banquet and later at the dance held in the main hall of the War Ministry, Eugène's behavior was unusual, even bizarre. He was heard uttering incomprehensible fantasies. During the night Eugène was seized with total madness owing to his love for Adèle, of course, but also perhaps to a literary rivalry between the two brothers that went back to their adolescence. The intensity of Eugène's madness increased during the month following the marriage. Once he was found in his room, illuminated as for a wedding, with the furniture ripped to pieces by a sword. Eugène's father, General Léopold Hugo (*see* Genealogies), then residing at Blois, took his suffering son there hoping for a recovery. Such was not to be the case. When his condition worsened, he was placed in a psychiatric hospital at Charenton in 1823. He died there in 1837 never having recovered his reason.

Adèle Hugo,* the fifth child of Victor Hugo, was born on July 28, 1830. In some ways, she seemed always to be in the shadow of her sister Léopoldine Hugo,* whose tragic death in 1843 put a great shadow on the entire Hugo clan. She followed her father into exile on the Channel Island of Guernsey where she fell into nervous depressions frequently brought on partly by the isolation but also by a taciturn nature. In 1861 Adèle fancied herself engaged to an English lieutenant named Alfred Pinson.* It was with some relief that Pinson found himself transferred to Halifax, Nova Scotia, for he must have been disturbed by the romantic frenzy of Adèle's imaginary passion. Adèle, pursuing her love, followed him to Canada but he had already married someone else. Her behavior in Canada was at first seen simply as eccentric. She was in the habit of going out in the evening, dressed in men's clothing, a vogue she had perhaps picked up from George Sand.

Adèle's itinerary finally took her to Barbados in the Caribbean from which she was returned to France by a kindly, devout black woman. In 1872 she was placed in a clinic at Saint-Mandé. Adèle Hugo died in April 1915 at the age of eighty-five, never having recovered her reason. Her Romantic pathology, confusing reality and imagination, is somewhat reminiscent of Gustave Flaubert's* psychological portrait of Emma Bovary in his 1856 novel *Madame Bovary*.

In her more lucid moments, Adèle, always a great letter writer and journal keeper, wrote a *Journal de l'exil* (*see* Hugo, Adèle, *Le Journal de*), which is filled with important quotidian details of life in the Hugo family during the exile.

BIBLIOGRAPHY

Dow, Leslie Smith. *Adèle Hugo, La Misérable*. Fredericton, N.B., Canada: Goose Lane Editions, 1993.
Gourevitch, Michel, and Danielle Gourevitch. "La folie d' Eugene Hugo." In Victor Hugo, *Correspondance familiale et ecrits intimes*. Vol. 2. 1828–1839. Paris: Robert Laffont, 1991.
Robinson, Agnes Mary Frances. *Victor Hugo*. Port Washington, N.Y.: Kennikat Press, 1972.

Ionesco, Eugène. In the intellectual tradition of many of his countrymen, Romanian dramatist Eugène Ionesco (1912–1994) emigrated to France where he became one of the new avant-garde playwrights at the same time as Samuel Beckett (of Irish origin) and Jean Genet. These three playwrights did not have much in common except their revolutionary theatrical talent. Through the performance of his play *La Cantatrice chauve* (The bald soprano) (1950), which is still playing in Paris without interruption at the Théâtre de la Huchette, Ionesco introduced the concept of the "theatre of the absurd," as it was called by Martin Esslin in the book of the same title.

Ionesco's interest in absurdity goes back to the mocking spirit of his youth when he wrote what he called an ironic biography of Victor Hugo seeking, in the spirit of a young iconoclast, to devalorize Hugo from his reputation as the greatest French writer of the nineteenth century. For the young Ionesco, influenced by academic critics hostile to Hugo, the poet was the embodiment of bourgeois mediocrity, not worthy of the glory France had bestowed upon him. All this is made quite clear in his parodistic and fanciful pseudo-biography of the French poet, in its English translation, *Hugoliad, or, The Grotesque and Tragic Life of Victor Hugo* (1982).

BIBLIOGRAPHY

Ionesco, Eugène. *Hugoliad, or, The Grotesque and Tragic Life of Victor Hugo*. Grove Press, 1987.
Esslin, Martin. *The Theatre of the Absurd*. Garden City, N.Y.: Doubleday, 1961.

I Paid the Fisherman. See *Je payai le pêcheur*.

I Picked this Flower for you from the Hill. See *J'ai cuelli cette fleur pour toi sur la colline*.

Irtamène. This tragedy in five acts, written in 1816 when Hugo was fourteen years old, follows the format of French classical tragedy. Although Hugo was steeped in the theatre of Jean Racine, this first play is more in the manner of Pierre Corneille with its emphasis on *devoir* (duty), honor, and loyalty. The verse is astounding for a boy of fourteen. Yet the play, hardly a tragedy in the Greek or classical sense, since only the villain is slain, violates the classic unity of place, and it has some of the elements of melodramatic decor (the concealed door leading to the prison cell of Irtamène, for example). Irtamène's rigorous attention to duty and loyalty to the deposed King Zobéir recalls in its firmness the resoluteness of Corneille's fanatical hero in *Polyeucte* (1641). The propensity of the hero Irtamène and his wife Phalérie to tears is, of course, a violation of classical *bienséance* (propriety), and it could possibly be derived from the popular *comédie larmoyante* (weeping theatre), a mixed genre between tragedy and comedy designed to bring the audience to tears. This genre, popularized by Nivelle de la Chaussée (1692–1754), could have influenced the young Hugo; on the other hand, incursions into pure classical form were becoming common enough in the years preceding *Hernani*.*

The plot is simple. Irtamène is willing to die in order to restore Zobéir to the throne of Egypt. The enemy is Actor, the fearful, tyrannical governor of Egypt. Actor is finally overthrown by Zobéir in a mad dash to the execution scene of Irtamène, which gives the populace enough courage to overturn the evil tyrant.

Biographically, the play seems to reflect Hugo's fervent royalist convictions, learned at his mother's knee.

The play contains an interesting poetic motif built around the verb *suivre* (to follow)—follow Irtamène even to death, for such is the intention of Irtamène's wife Phalérie. Repeated at intervals across the play, it must be the source for the *suivre* motif of Doña Sol de Silva addressed to Hernani* in *Hernani*. What saves a juvenile and somewhat naive work by a young boy from total failure is the poetry that surges forth. Victor

Hugo's poetic genius is manifest in his early verse writings. Poetry will save most of Romantic drama from a frequent negative criticism engendered by its too original and modern psychology, its power of subversion, and lack of consideration for classical verisimilitude.

J

J'ai cueilli cette fleur pour toi sur la colline. Hugo's twenty-eight-line
love lyric, poem twenty-four from Book Five of *Les Contemplations*,* addressed to Juliette Drouet, built from the romantic idea of picking a
flower for the beloved, transcends any purely romantic exaltation in nature (William Wordsworth's *Daffodils* for example), for it incorporates in
the 1850s what shall be experienced in the love lyrics of Charles Baude-
laire* as found in *Les Fleurs du mal* in 1856, the same year *Les Contemplations* was published. As *J'ai cueilli cette fleur pour toi sur la colline* (I picked
this flower for you on the hill) concludes with the narrator's contemplation of the fragile flower, picked from a rock on a cliff above the English
Channel (at Bouley Bay on Jersey and not on Sark as stated in the publication), dark forces intervene between the flower/poem and the beloved. The beloved is now seen as someone fragile, dependent on many
human factors—love holding on in spite of many obstacles including the
depression of exile, with France only a few short kilometers away.

The poem, in perfectly balanced alexandrines, contains many elements
of surprise, the most important of which is the passage of time as marked
by the poet in line six: *Je voyais* (I was seeing). The *pauvre fleur* (poor
flower) seems to have little life left in it, much as the day seems to disappear into a dark night announcing the *gouffre* (the abyss). Hugo's
thought, rendered in Romantic form, looks thematically but not formally
like two very hermetic sonnets of Stéphane Mallarmé.* The first, *Victorieusement fui le suicide beau*, also entwines lover and nature in which a
brilliant sunset is recorded (quatrain 1), not unlike the majestic and romantic sunset of this poem: *Un grand arc de triomphe éclatant et vermeil,/
A l'endroit où s'était englouti le soleil* (A bursting and blood-red arch of
triumph/at the spot where the sun was drowned [immolated]).

Hugo's poem also has some thematic kinship with Mallarmé's *A La*

Nue accablante tu sonnet. The poem reiterates, amidst the destruction of the brilliant sunset and the onset of the night, a love that persists, like little dots of light in the hollows of the hills.

Apart from its innate lyrical beauty, this work is a clear example of the complexity of Romantic thought as found in Victor Hugo's mind, although it did not, of course, ever cultivate the syntactical equivalents found first in the works of Baudelaire, and then in the sonnets of Mallarmé.

Janin, Jules. Jules Janin (1804–1874), a novelist and drama critic for the *Journal des Débats* starting in 1836, wrote a six-volume *Histoire de la littérature dramatique*, which was published between 1853 and 1858. Janin, the romantic, was naturally sympathetic to the new theatre, especially to that of Victor Hugo to whom volumes 3 and 4 of his monumental work are given over entirely to Hugo's dramaturgy. Hugo was delighted with the praise heaped upon him and thanked Janin by letter (December 26, 1854) and honored the critic with a poem (8) in Book Five, *En marche*, of *Les Contemplations: A Jules J*. This poem illustrates how adept Hugo is at taking reality and transforming it into a work of art. Janin had gone to see Hugo during the first stages of the exile in Brussels, where he found him asleep on the floor (see Pierre Albouy's interpretation and transcription of Janin's meeting with Hugo, a fine example of Romantic camaraderie, *Hugo, oeuvres poétiques*, vol. 3, pp. 1574–75). What Janin describes in his notebooks, which were published in volumes 3 and 4 of his *Histoire de la littérature dramatique*, is aesthetically rendered as high poetic *vers de circonstance* (circumstantial verse). Thus the opening strophe restates poetically what Janin had reported: *Je dormais en effet, et tu me réveillas./Je te criai: 'Salut' et tu me dis: Hélas/ Et cet instant fut doux, et nous nous embrassâmes;/Nous mêlâmes tes pleurs, mon sourire et nos âmes.* (I was truly sleeping, and you woke me up/I cried out to you 'Greetings' and you said 'Alas'/ And that moment was sweet, we embraced/We mixed your tears, my smile, and our souls). These lines certainly represent high Romantic friendship, something Hugo deeply treasured. The poem, written at Marine Terrace on Jersey (Channel Islands), concludes with Hugo's expressions of gratitude to Janin for his kind and generous words in the *Histoire de la littérature dramatique*. Janin is united to Hugo by his deep respect for the intents of Romanticism, and by their common opposition to tyranny. Jules Janin was elected to the French Academy in 1870.

BIBLIOGRAPHY

Janin, Jules. *Histoire de la littérature dramatique*. Vols. 3 and 4. Paris: Michel Lévy, 1853–1854.

Javert. Javert, a police detective in Hugo's novel *Les Misérables** (1862), relentlessly pursues the hero Jean Valjean,* who after spending nineteen years in penal servitude in Toulon, was released and required to carry the yellow passport of convicted felons. Since Jean Valjean takes on many identities as his moral character, as well as his business skills, develop, Javert is in a position to arrest him at will, and he pursues Valjean ceaselessly in self-righteousness, similar to the perversion of justice in Charles Dickens's *Bleak House* (1853). Toward the novel's conclusion, Javert, whose life has been saved by Jean Valjean, glimpses what the moral life is all about (so contrary to his habitual literal mode of following the letter and not the spirit of the law). Finally he comes to understand that there can be two duties to be recognized: duty to the law; the other duty, above it, to the individual conscience. When he is unable to reconcile these contradictory emotions within himself, he commits suicide. Suicide is also marked in the final scene of *Hernani** in which Don Ruy Gomez de Silva,* after enforcing a rigid code of honor, provokes the double suicide of Hernani* and Doña Sol de Silva.* Upon their deaths, he realizes in an epiphany come too late that he was wrong in trying, as an old man, to marry his niece Doña Sol, and he also was wrong in demanding, in the name of a superficial code of honor, the death of Hernani. Seeing himself damned, he too commits suicide.

Javert is the antithesis of Jean Valjean. Valjean, a former criminal for misdeeds too minor to justify imprisonment, develops along the road to sanctity and he dies peacefully, echoing the fabled death of Saint Joseph. Jean Valjean is seen on the road to salvation and even sainthood; Javert, in his despair, cannot hope for any paradisical afterlife.

Jeanne était au pain sec dans le cabinet noir. This sentimental and formerly very well-known work, is poem six from Part Six of *L'Art d'être grand-père** (The art of being a grandfather), which deals primarily with the aging poet's doting on his two grandchildren, Georges and Jeanne.

Jeanne était au pain sec (Jeanne was put on dry bread in the dark pantry) is in the best tradition of Hugo's poetry of children and childhood, and it has the same exaltation and beatitude found in a very early Hugo poem, *Lorsque l'enfant paraît* (When the child comes into the room), written in May 1830 and published in 1831 in *Les Feuilles d'automne*.*

Jeanne était au pain sec presents a familiar scene in which Jeanne is being punished for some misdemeanor. There seems to be a cast of characters: Jeanne, her grandfather Victor Hugo, and perhaps the scolding mother. Despite admonitions not to visit the "outlaw," the grandfather does so and takes a pot of jam to the little girl. The rest of the family is indignant at this amelioration of Jeanne's punishment—the family being recorded by the poet as *ceux . . . de ma cité* (Those . . . of my city). The social order has been upset, the child will go on doing as she pleases, and nothing will stop her. In such a situation, the grandfather has no choice but to confess his sin, and he is willing himself to be put on a dry bread regime.

Jeanne does promise that she will stop picking her nose, among other misdeeds, and she has the last word: If grandfather is to be punished, then: *Eh bien, moi, je t'irai porter des confitures* (In that case, I shall bring you some jam).

This type of domestic poetry did not exist in France before Victor Hugo.

There are some critics, notably Jean Massin, who would see higher metaphysical implications in the poem. The grandfather, like God, the all-pardoning one, could lead to speculations about Satan's pardon by God. Other critics, like Arnaud Laster and Anne Ubersfeld, interpret the fable as a very subtle manner of asking amnesty for the people condemned because of their support of the commune of Paris.

Jeanne was on a Dry Bread Diet in the Small Dark Room. *See Jeanne était au pain sec dans le cabinet noir.*

Jeannie. Jeannie is the heroine of the narrative poem *Les pauvres gens* (Poor people) from the first series of *La Légende des siècles*.* Hugo, through his characterization of the poor fisherman's wife, is capable of presenting the feminine psychology of a woman on whom too much responsibility has been placed, but who accepts all the same the burdens of maternity (she has five children). She defies her husband and risks a beating in order to rescue the two children of her neighbor, a widow, whom she has found dead in her hovel. It would appear from the depiction of the husband-fisherman that the beating never took place, or would, but it is a thought in the back of her mind, an intuition felt by many women in the nineteenth century.

Jeannie perhaps deserves more than this short cameo appearance in an important poem. She represents the maritime woman: one concerned about the safe return of her husband, fiancé, brother, or father. In this way, she is a narrational issue from Hugo's celebrated ocean poem *Oceano nox** (The ocean at night), which speaks to the perils of the sea.

Je me penchai. This short poem, of only twenty-two lines, is Hugo at his best. His escatalogical vision remains based in physical assumptions of the placings of heaven, purgatory, and hell. In *Je me penchai* (I bent over), the poet-narrator is gazing down into a hole, some sort of cavern or cave, in which are encased many of the most evil persons to have inhabited earth. This abyss, which he qualifies as *patibulaire* (pertaining to the gallows), is a central symbol of evil confined and punished. The least offender seems to be Satan himself (about to become a newly redeemed hero in *Ce que dit la bouche d'ombre** of *Les Contemplations.**

This poem is important for three reasons: its brevity, which is unusual for Hugo; its meditation on the concept of evil; and its imagery of a pit, a hole, a cavern, a place of incarceration which is almost a redundant metaphor in Hugo's poetics.

The poem is number 23 in the complementary series of *La Légende des siècles**; it is undated but appears to be from around 1875.

Je payai le pêcheur qui passa son chemin. This very short poem of eighteen lines, poem twenty-two from Book Five of *Les Contemplations,** taken from a quotidian story, about the purchase of a crab from a fisherman (I paid the fisherman who passed on his way) is a deep meditation by the poet on the relationship between good and evil, and beauty and ugliness, and the place in creation of all God's works, small and large (for this sea creature, if larger, could be a hydra, if smaller, a wood louse), meaningful or seemingly meaningless in the order of existence. The small scene is not unlike a seascape painted by Eugène Boudin. Not much happens; the purchase is made. The fisherman disappears over the horizon, behind a dune perhaps. The crab struggles to be free and bites the poet who then throws it back into the sea.

Out of this ordinary scene from any seaside village, Hugo has constructed a work of high symbolism* which cannot be reduced to an allegorical or logical interpretation. The real Hugo is bitten by a crustacean and this sets his mind to pondering the place of this rather ugly creature in God's plan. Such a meditation leads to the generous act of forgiving and liberating the creature. The mysterious fisherman, who arrived and then left, seems to have been sent to give Hugo this idea. Trying to make the image any more precise than this could only weaken its symbolic effect.

The religious tone is clearly stated in the poet's reference to the ocean seen now as a baptismal font for the sun, both acting as sacramentals of redemption and life.

Jeux Floraux. This famous poetry academy of Toulouse, restored through the efforts of Clémence Isaure, was an outlet more accessible than the French Academy's annual poetic competitions for aspiring poets, and Hugo did indeed participate.

The Jeux Floraux has an ancient history. Founded originally in Rome in about 238 B.C., it was continued in Toulouse in 1323 by a group of troubadours. Reorganized in the sixteenth century, its name was changed to the Académie des Jeux Floraux in the seventeenth century during the reign of Louis XIV. It was suppressed in 1790, but it was reestablished in 1806 and is still in existence.

At a very early age, Hugo had much success with this academy. He submitted his *Odes sur les Vierges de Verdun*, who were martyrs of the

French Revolution because they had participated in an evening dance with Prussians, and a poem on an assigned topic, *Le Rétablissement de la statue de Henri IV* for which he was honored, despite his young age.

His reception by this academy, as well as the annual prize of the Institute in Paris, indicates the debut of Victor Hugo's acceptance into the world of official and conservative poetic competition.

Joanny. This French actor (1775–1849) was as renowned as Anne Boutet Mars,* opposite whom he played in Victor Hugo's *Hernani** (1830), in the role of the lecherous Don Ruy Gomez de Silva* who lusts after his young niece, Doña Sol de Silva,* despite his moral principles of honor, in the sense given to that word in Golden Age Spanish theatre. Mademoiselle Mars was forty-one when she played the role of Doña Sol; Joanny was fifty-five (more befitting his own age in that role).

Joanny's diary is filled with minute documentation on the difficulties encountered during the rehearsals for *Hernani*, as well as his deep intuitions into the nature of the new Romantic drama. The eminent French dramatic critic Maurice Descotes, who has written on the major French dramatists Jean Racine, Molière, Pierre-Augustin Beaumarchais, and Pierre Marivaux, has also done extensive documentation not only on *Hernani*, but also on Victor Hugo in general, and has done a critical edition of Joanny's memoirs.

BIBLIOGRAPHY

Descotes, Maurice. *Victor Hugo et Waterloo.* Paris: Lettres modernes, 1984.

L

Lamartine, Alphonse de. Traditionally viewed as the first Romantic with the publication of his *Méditations poétiques* (1820) with its celebrated elegy *Le Lac*, Lamartine (1790–1869), senior to Victor Hugo by twelve years, is his opposite in poetic energy and intent, but they were allied through their common and increasingly liberal convictions as the century moved forward.

Politically speaking, they had much in common. Lamartine's involvement in the revolution of 1848, for he had helped in the downfall of Louis-Philippe, gave pause to a middle-aged Hugo caught between his old conservative alliances and his budding liberalism. Lamartine, who participated in the new Regency, almost became a president of the Second Republic. The victory of Louis Napoléon Bonaparte,* however, put an end to his political career and returned him to his traditional Burgundian passivity.

In poetry, these two men differ radically. Lamartine appears from the beginning as a flaccid, almost too passive Romantic. He is lacking in the energy which he does not admire, for example, in the poetry of Lord Byron* (see his poem *To Lord Byron*). Lamartine's timidity in aesthetics, contrasted with his political engagement in the events of 1848, is not only manifested in his poetry but also in his general life attitudes. For example, he had counseled Hugo after having read the 1826 edition of the *Odes et Ballades** to avoid "originality" which most would assume to be the very characteristic of the new Romantic movement. (*See* André Maurois, citing Gustave Simon, "Lamartine et Victor Hugo," *Revue de Paris* [April 15, 1904], p. 683; Maurois, *Olympio, ou, la vie de Victor Hugo* [Paris: Hachette, 1954], p. 138.)

Lamartine and Hugo are both Romantic poets, but certainly not of the same ilk. It is partially a generational gap; Lamartine was still attached to the eighteenth century and also to his rich, aristocratic, and Catholic background in Mâcon in Burgundy. Hugo is too energetic for him. Hugo was a very decisive poet, thinker, and politician. Lamartine seems for a short period during the events of 1848, to have been a poet trying to be an existential mover. Political and literary events overwhelmed this first of the Romantic writers. His Romantic idealism was crushed by the events of his time. Dying in 1869, he seemed to be far from modern poetry. Today he is remembered mainly for his brief political emergence in the revolution of 1848 and as the author of the famous *Elvire* elegy, *The Lake*.

Lamennais, Félicité de. Félicité de Lamennais (1782–1854) represents an attempt made by sincere liberal Catholics to marry the principles of the French Revolution to Christian belief. The abbé Lamennais can be regarded as the leader of a fervent Romantic Catholicism, along with Lacordaire (1812–1861), a Dominican preacher often referred to as the Bossuet of the Romantic era, and Charles, comte de Montalembert (1810–1870). In 1830 the liberal Catholics formed a political party and a journal, *L'Avenir*, which had as its subtitle *Dieu et la liberté* (God and liberty). Lamennais' attempts to ally Catholicism with revolutionary commitments to liberty led to papal condemnation, first in the encyclical *Mirari vos* (1832) and again in the encyclical *Singulari nos* (1834). Lamennais' spectacular transformation from conservative believer to radical socialist in spirit, if not in name, parallels that of Victor Hugo with whom Lamennais was on close personal terms while he was assigned to the church of Saint Sulpice in Paris. In the end, Lamennais left Catholicism, as did Victor Hugo whose faith was initially more akin to his youthful conservative and royalist leanings. Lamennais is important in understanding the trajectory of the French Romantics who ultimately are obliged in conscience to leave the conservative and, by nineteenth-century standards, reactionary Catholicism of an insular Vatican.

Lamennais was in close contact with Hugo in those early years, as can be seen in Lamennais' correspondence. His journal, *L'Avenir*, published excerpts from Hugo's *Notre-Dame de Paris*.* On a very personal note, it was Lamennais who helped arrange the religious marriage of Hugo to Adèle Foucher, which took place at Saint Sulpice on October 12, 1822. This marriage in the church would have been almost impossible for the simple reason that there was no record of Victor Hugo's ever having been baptized. This obstacle was overcome by Hugo's father who declared that Victor had been baptized in Italy (which is most unlikely given the Voltairian opinions of Hugo's mother). Assured of this so-called baptism, Lamennais supplied the necessary certificate of baptism, and the religious ceremony was thus assured.

The correspondence of Lamennais, especially the letters found in volumes 5 and 6 of the Le Guillou edition, reveals a close personal relationship. A letter to Charles-Augustin Sainte-Beuve* from Rome, on February 25, sends affectionate greetings to "Victor." Other letters in which Hugo is referred to only as Victor attest to this affection. A letter of December 4, 1832, however, to Montalembert raises concerns, justifiably, that Hugo's faith was diminishing: "Victor Hugo . . . is daily becoming more intractable and alien to religion," which is somewhat ironic since that will indeed be the very path that the abbé Lamennais himself would follow. It is also the case for many other young Romantics, such as Alphonse de Lamartine,* who at first were part of the Romantic Catholic revival but who rolled along with the century in distancing themselves from formal religion.

Lamennais then is important as a corollary to a new kind of Romantic spirituality which places emphasis on the gospel of the here and now and of the idea of the liberty of the people. This message was anathema to the Rome of the nineteenth century. Consequently, to understand Hugo's own spiritual odyssey, we must see it in the light of the spiritual anguish of the 1820s and 1830s, the attempt at synthesis of Christian belief with democratic and egalitarian principles.

BIBLIOGRAPHY

Lamennais, Félicité de. *Correspondances.* 8 vols. Edited by Louis le Guillou. Paris: A. Colin, 1971–1981. See especially vols. 5 and 6.
——. *Words of a Believer* (1834). *Paroles d'un croyant.* Edition of Yves le Hir. Paris: A. Colin, 1949.
Le Guillou, Louis. *L'Evolution religieuse de Lammenais.* Paris: Desclée de Brouwer, 1989.
Milner, Max. *Le Romantisme 1 (1820–1843).* Paris: Arthaud, 1973. See especially pages 183–86 on the modernism of Lamennais' political and religious beliefs.

Last Day of a Condemned Man. See *Dernier Jour d'un condamné, Le.*

Latin America and Victor Hugo. Since the time of independence movements, Latin American intellectuals have looked to France for political and literary inspiration. With a certain time lag, French writers of the Romantic, Parnassian (*see* Parnassian poetry), and Symbolist (*see* Symbolism and Victor Hugo) periods have had great influence, especially in Mexico, Peru, Argentina, and Venezuela.

The most important evidence of Hugo's influence in Latin America comes from Mexico's most important literary giant, Alfonso Reyes (1889–1959), whose contributions to the understanding of all literature (but mainly European) is recognized by all scholars of literature. Reyes' interest in French literature was extraordinary. He was able to penetrate the most difficult French texts, the hermetic poetry of Stéphane Mallarmé* (his major work in this regard was *Mallarmé entre nosotros* (Mallarmé amongst us). Still, although he deeply appreciated the most advanced nineteenth-century French poetry, Reyes understood the profundity of Hugo's poetry, and within his completed works are found three interesting articles on Hugo: one on Hugo's fascination with the abyss (referring to the claustrophobia* of the French poet); another on Hugo's experiences with spiritism* while he was living on the Channel Islands; and a third about Hugo's possible literary affinity with the Italian writer Gabriele D'Annunzio (1863–1938), with whom Reyes discovered intellectual relationships, even though he came later in time.

Reyes remains the best example of Latin American appreciation of French literature, and especially of Hugo and other poets of the nineteenth century. As other entries in this encyclopedia demonstrate, such appreciation is evidence of Hugo's universality.

The Laughing Man. *See Homme qui rit, L'.*

Leaning Over. *See Je me penchai.*

Légende des siècles, La. Begun in 1859, with additional poems added in 1877 and 1883, *La Légende des siècles* (The legend of the centuries), a dense philosophical and quasi-metaphysical collection, is considered by some to be one of Hugo's best poetic efforts. Others would disagree, seeing in it too much narrative discourse and explanatory material, lessening the poetic effect which is to be found, for example, in *Les Contemplations.**

There is no doubt that the collection contains some memorable Hugo pieces, such as *Le Sacre de la femme*, a tribute to femininity incarnate in the first woman, the mythical Eve, which while interesting in its speculations on mankind's primitive history as found in the book of Genesis, would just as easily be understood without the historic setting, for it is a typical Hugolian tribute to the female human being, her mind, body, and soul. Other Biblically oriented poems are *La Conscience,** a truly symbolic recounting of Cain's murder of his brother Abel, the first recorded murder in Jewish history; and the lovely and lyrical *Booz endormi*, a recounting, almost symbolical, of the conjugal union of the ancient Booz with Ruth, from which will spring the house of David, through Jesse's lineage, leading to Jesus Christ. Hugo's reworking of epic materials from Spain and France, from the *Cantar del mio Cid* and from *La Chanson de Roland*, are worthy of attention as they demonstrate the interest of the Romantics in medieval national history. *Le Satyr*, the opening poem of the section on the sixteenth century and the Renaissance, is certainly unhistorical recounting in visionary fashion the creation and dominance of man within the universe. Out of chaos is born Pan who informs the gods, especially Jupiter, to bend knee in front of this new creation: the human race. Other poems that caught the mind's eye of nineteenth-century readers of poetry are *La Rose de l'Infante** with its strong stance against the totalitarianism of Phillip II of Spain; a whole series of poems entitled *Le Groupe des Idylles*, which pay homage to poets having celebrated love. The list, which includes Orpheus, King Solomon, Aristophanes, Virgil, Dante, Petrarch, Pierre de Ronsard, William Shakespeare, Voltaire, Denis Diderot, Pierre-Augustin Beaumarchais, and André Chénier,* is eclectic, revealing Hugo's personal predilections as he scans the past. Perhaps the most touching of all the poems in this collection is *Les Pauvres Gens*,* which speaks not at all of history, but of Hugo's abiding humanitarian if sentimental concern for the plight of the poor.

In composing *La Légende des siècles*, Hugo does not intend to write history. He aspired to be a historian in a book like *Histoire d'un crime* (about the coup d'état of Louis Napoléon Bonaparte), but not in his novels (*Notre-Dame de Paris**), nor in his dramas (*Hernani*,* *Ruy Blas*,* *Les Burgraves*,* *Marie Tudor**), even if they have historical dimensions. He uses history freely here and there, picking up some knowledge, either from his school days or from his haphazard readings, provoked by the moment and the place. For example, there is no doubt that the Channel Islands exile put him in direct contact with the role of the English in history, stimulating his curiosity and then his imagination, which turned history into poetry or fiction.

La Légende des siècles' historical outline is sketchy and murky and chose what he alone wished to emphasize. The chapter on the Renaissance is a case in point. While his argument would seem to lead to a consideration of the secular and humanistic nature of the sixteenth century, the poems instead concentrate on its iniquities: Spanish totalitarianism, the Inquisition, and the conquest of the New World. It is apparent to even the most lay reader of history that Hugo's poetic "method" ignores or forgets certain great historical moments. In his chronology of the sixteenth century, it would seem to most people appropriate to consider the most essential phenomenon of that time, namely the Protestant Reformation, yet there is no mention of Martin Luther, John Calvin, John Knox, or any other of the great reformers. Equally ignored are the wars of religion which almost destroyed France in the sixteenth century and were resolved only by the stoic resignation of Henry IV to become a Catholic to bring peace to that country. Hugo's *La Légende des siècles* is selective and subjective, and frequently this makes many of the entries in this collection unexpected or surprising.

Some poems leap beyond history into apocalyptic visions of the end of the world, such as *La Trompette du jugement* (The trumpet of Judgment Day), which show that Hugo, in spite of his rejection of Christian dogma, was firmly entrenched psychologically in nineteenth-century Christian eschatological visions of the meaning of history. In fact, Hugo's concluding poems are manifest proof of his almost eccentric theology.

La Légende des siècles has been preferred by many critics of the nineteenth century, including Baudelaire. *Les Contemplations*, Hugo's incursion into history, must not be compared with the serious nineteenth-century historiography as seen, for example, in the work of Fustel de Coulanges or Michelet, in France, or the earlier English historian Edward Gibbon, author of *The History of the Decline and Fall of the Roman Empire* (1776–1788).

Historians in both France and England in the pre-Romantic and Romantic periods were able to make significant speculations and meditations on the meaning of events, particularly in the Western world, because of their solid, daily scholarly activity. Hugo, on the other hand, appears somewhat dilettante, picking here and there in many a volume and choosing those items that appealed to his mind and imagination. *La Légende des siècles* can still be considered, as a whole, among his great aesthetic achievements.

Leroux, Pierre. In a pre-Marxist Europe, Pierre Leroux (1797–1871) played an important role in the development of Hugo's social consciousness, as he did even more successfully with the novelist George Sand.* It is incorrect, however, to think that Hugo was without a social conscience from the very beginning of his writing career as witness his very early condemnation of capital punishment* in *Le Dernier Jour d'un condamné** in 1828. Like Hugo, Pierre Leroux was in exile during the Second Empire,* mainly in London where Hugo did not want to go, perhaps because of his limited knowledge of English. Leroux did visit Hugo on Jersey, however, where it would seem that there were spirited conversations on the nature of literature's goal, with Leroux pushing for the social *engagement* of the writer. Leroux certainly, like Félicité de Lamennais,* had a great influence on Hugo's thought, and it should be conceded that the seed of social activism in the young Hugo was nurtured by the ideas of the Romantic humanitarians. Hugo's own socialist beliefs seem to have resisted the confusion found in the thought of the Romantics in which they either made parodies of Catholicism or duplicated it, starting their own "socialist" religions, all of which was suspect to a Hugo whose own spirituality resisted systems. Leroux was part of the original pack of the followers of Claude-Henri Saint-Simon (1760–1825) who preached a new religion of science, not unlike that of Auguste Comte (1798–1857), the founder of the new sociology and religion of positivism. Saint-Simon's works parody Catholicism with such titles as *Le Catéchisme des industriels* (1823) or *Le Nouveau Christianisme* (1825). Although Leroux ultimately went his own way, breaking away from the *Globe*, the vehicle of Saint-Simonism, he all the same maintained in his writings, such as *L'Encyclopédie nouvelle* (1836–1843) and *La Revue indépendante* (1841–1848), the same religious fervor, filled with deistic thought, that is found in most of the Romantic humanitarians as they sought to fill a void left from the shell of Catholicism after the French Revolution. George Sand's early sentimental novel *Lélia* (1833) was filled with the vocabulary of a new Romantic religion which only needed the push of Leroux's ideas to develop the socialist thought of her later works. The new dogmatism, based on the old one, caused Hugo to distance himself from most of the socialist Romantics, but these ideas were in the air, and certainly they were partially responsible for the deepening of Hugo's social thought as found in *Les Misérables*,* in contrast with art for art's sake found in Gustave Flaubert's* *Madame Bovary*.

Lettres à la fiancée, Les. Hugo's love letters to Adèle Foucher number about one hundred and fifty. They were kept by Madame Hugo and left to her children. These engagement letters cover the period from January 1820 to October 1822, the month of their marriage at Saint-Sulpice church in Paris. The style and posture is uniquely Hugolian. The letters are at one and the same time passionate, idealistic, sentimental, and naive, stressing the necessity for the lovers to remain chaste and pure in preparation for their union. In one letter, March 4, 1820, Hugo complains to Adèle that he caught sight of her crossing a street with her dress raised a bit too high.

Hugo's concept of love, be it for Adèle or later for Juliette Drouet, mixes, in true Romantic fashion, carnality and spirituality; it stresses love between souls but also the physical side of love. These letters and many poems to follow, for example, *Puisque j'ai mis ma lèvre à ta coupe encore pleine** (Since my lips have touched your still full cup) from *Les Chants du crépuscule*,* 1835, represent a type of marriage between heaven and earth, body and soul. This is a French Romantic variation on what is found in the poetry of the Spanish mystics, John of the Cross and Teresa of Avila, and what will be expressed in the love poetry of the Brownings in England.

Light and Shadows. *See Rayons et les ombres, Les.*

Lise. What few facts we have about Lise are related in the standard Hugo biographies. Victor Hugo first encountered this young girl or her model, who was between fifteen and sixteen years old, in 1811 (Hugo was only nine), when Madame Hugo and her children lodged in a building close to where Lise lived in Bayonne, on the border, while en route to Spain. Lise found the young boy interesting, and she treated him with affection. In his travel document *Alpes et Pyrénées* Hugo describes his return to Bayonne in 1843, with multiple memories of Lise. He recalls Lise, who was blonde and svelte, who had a Virgilian profile . . . a beautiful neck, an adorable purity, a little hand, a white arm, a reddish elbow, normal enough for her age (*Elle était blanche et svelte . . . un profil virgilien. . . . Elle avait le cou admirablement attaché et d'une pureté adorable, la main petite, le bras blanc et le coude un peu rouge, ce qui tenait à son âge*, pp. 373–74). This passage is either Romantic adornment of the past or a testimony to an extraordinarily sensual memory on Hugo's part.

Since Hugo's older brothers often went off on their own, he was frequently alone. It was then that Lise would say: *Viens, qu je te lise quelque chose* (Come, let me read you something). *Elle me lisait je ne sais plus quel livre ouvert sur ses genoux. Nous avions au-dessus de nos têtes un ciel éclatant et un beau soleil qui pénétrait de lumière les tilleuls et changeait les feuilles vertes en feuilles d'or. . . . Pendant qu'elle lisait, je n'écoutais pas le sens des paroles, j'écoutais le son de sa voix* (She would read to me, I don't know what, from a book open on her knees. We had overhead a dazzling sky, and a beautiful sun which penetrated with its light the linden trees, changing the leaves from green to gold. . . . While she would read, I was not paying any attention to the sense of the words, I was listening to the sound of her voice, p. 374). This is a rather impressionistic remembrance of things swelling up, in a Proustian manner, from a distant past. Hugo is rivaled only by Gustave Flaubert* and, of course, Marcel Proust in his ability to remember idyllic Romantic moments in the past. It reminds one of Flaubert's evocations of Madame Elisa Schesinger coming from swimming at Trouville, passing the young, golden-haired Flaubert, with water dripping from her bathing outfit.

Lise is accorded poem eleven in Book 1, *Aurore*, of *Les Contemplations*.* Entitled simply *Lise*, it is one of the most touching of all of Hugo's love lyrics; here is the innocence and purity of first love. *Elle m'aimait, Je l'aimais. Nous étions/Deux purs enfants, deux parfums, deux rayons* (She loved me, I loved her. We were/two pure children, two perfumes, two rays of light). The last strophe is framed with a nostalgic regret for a past lost forever: *Jeunes amours, si vite épanouies,/Vous êtes l'aube et le matin du coeur* (Young loves, so quickly bloom,/You are the dawn and the morning of the heart).

The brief innocent interlude spent with Lise in Bayonne is significant if a true picture of Hugo's sentimental adventures is to be comprehended. It is the first step in love, to be followed by the passion for his future wife, the intense passion then for Juliette Drouet, and the countless affairs, some of long duration, others ephemeral in nature, which will complete the amorous cycle of the poet.

Littérature et philosophies mêlées. First published in 1834, based on both previously published and unedited brief notes, the work in its entirety figures in the *Complete Works* in the standard edition published by the French National Printing Office (Imprimerie nationale). In brief, the two-volume set contains literary, philosophical, political, and historical entries. For the most part, it proceeds chronologically. A long and somewhat rambling preface explaining the nature of the work pairs the entries with Hugo's own literary production. Thus the Journal of 1819 is coupled with Hugo's writing of an early novel *Han d'Islande*,* while the journal of a revolutionary of 1830 dates from the time of *Notre-Dame de Paris*.* The preface is written in the antithetical style used by Hugo from the very beginning of his literary career, especially in the prefaces to his historical meditations on the theatre (the preface to *Ruy Blas** is part of a meditation on the meaning of history), and which he continued to use in his mature texts. This contrastive style is succinctly stated in the preface concerning the meanings of the eighteenth century, and it is an appropriate introduction to the essays found in the second part of the work on Voltaire and the Comte de Mirabeau. The articles on these two men are themselves a contrast in length; that on Voltaire is very short, whereas the one on Mirabeau is approximately fifty-seven pages long. The preface, however, gives a long sentence résumé for what is to follow: *Voltaire, en effet, c'est le dix-huitième siècle système; Mirabeau, c'est le dix-huitième siècle action* (Voltaire is the eighteenth-century system; Mirabeau is the eighteenth century in action).

The work contains twenty-four entries, some of which are very brief (one page in one instance); others are minimal paragraph entries, journal notes, and jottings. Some articles concern persons almost entirely ignored by readers of the twentieth century, for example, the poet Dovalle, killed at the age of twenty; or the Swiss Ymbert Galloix.

The entries for 1830, with the exception of the one on Dovalle, which comes much later in the volume (thus violating the established chronology) are arranged by the months of the year (with the exception of a final undated entry) starting in August and ending in March.

Aside from the important historical essays on Voltaire and Mirabeau, mention should be made, under the rubric of 1823–1824, of the perceptive essay on Félicité de Lamennais'* *Essay on Indifference in Matters of Religion*, probably born of Hugo's initial friendship with this priest at Saint Sulpice at the time of Hugo's marriage. Lamennais and Hugo marched hand in hand in the evolution of their thought. The essay is important in understanding Lamennais as the leader of an increasingly liberal, if not left-wing, Romantic French Catholicism. Another essay, attesting to the importance of Sir Walter Scott (on *Quentin Durward*) in France in the 1820s, presents another angle on Scott's role in the development of the French historical novel. A third essay of this time period concerns the death of Lord Byron* in 1824, written in a touching, lyrical style. Both the Scott and Byron essays demonstrate the enormous influence on Romantic poetry and novels in France by two giants of British Romanticism.

The eclectic nature of this collection in general fulfills the promises made in the preface, with perhaps the exception of "philosophy" but then the word is being used broadly, encompassing politics, history, and even theology.

The reader is referred to the apt description of this work, its sources in contemporary periodicals, and to antecedents as found in the short and concise entry found in Philippe Van Tieghem, *Dictionnaire de Victor Hugo* (Paris: Librairie Larousse, 1985), p. 145.

Lorsque l'enfant paraît. *Lorsque l'enfant paraît* (when the child comes into the room), from *Les Feuilles d'automne*,* was written in May 1830 and published in 1831. It has exactly the same lyrical form as *L'Enfant* from *Les Orientales** of 1829 (six line strophes broken with half lines at three and six). This nine-part poem fusing the bourgeois but intellectual Hugo household with the sobering presence of childhood, amid too serious adult discussions, was endearing to nineteenth-century readers who found in the presence of young children a respite from grappling with intellectual, political, and moral questions.

Containing some difficult syntactical constructions, it lyrically transforms age, corruption, intellectuality, and aesthetics by the simple appearance, in a room of serious adults, of a little child, probably one of the Hugo girls. It does this through verbal permutations, partly through rhythmic grammatical manipulations of the subjective mode, and through a modern and Romantic "preciosity" (*que novembre/Fasse autour d'un grand feu vacillant dans la chambre/Les chaises se toucher* (That November causes the chairs in the room to touch one another around a big flaming fire).

The apparition of the child into the circle of adults calms old and wrinkled foreheads; it makes the conversation about country, God, poetry, and the soul seem a bit silly. The young Victor Hugo, paterfamilias, writing this poem, already knows the sorrows of adulthood and its responsibilities. He closes, therefore, with a prayer that there should never be a summer without bright red flowers, a cage without birds, a hive without bees, or a home without children (*De jamais voir, Seigneur, l'été sans fleurs vermeilles,/La cage sans oiseaux, la ruche sans abeilles,/La maison sans enfants*).

Loves of a Poet. This curious collection of odds and ends from the writings of Hugo was published in 1919 by the celebrated French politician Louis Barthou (1862–1934), and it was reprinted and integrated into the edition of Hugo's works commonly referred to as the edition of the National Press, or Imprimerie nationale, in 1935 and 1941. The Imprimerie nationale inserted the items selected by Bartou into their interpretation of *Toute la lyre* (The whole lyre) and *La Dernière Gerbe* (The last wreath). This eclectic selection probably informs us more about the personal tastes of Louis Barthou than about Hugo. It contains items dedicated to Juliette Drouet; an early piece from the *Conservateur Littéraire*, a royalist organ of Hugo's youth; the novel *Han d'Islande**; the *Odes et Ballades** (which seems somewhat ambitious, considering the number of editions and additions made by the young Hugo in the 1820s); assorted other items; *Les Orientales**, published by Hugo in 1829; and two of his prose dramas, *Lucrèce Borgia** and *Angelo, tyran de Padoue*.*

Without wishing to take serious critical aim at such a great statesman as Louis Barthou, the modern scholar of Hugo can only remain amazed, if not baffled, by his curious collection of Hugoalia. The most famous plays (*Hernani** and *Ruy Blas**) and the most important collections of poetry (*Les Châtiments** and *Les Contemplations**) are singularly absent. The collection, then, does not merit the attention of any Hugo scholar or lay person interested in his work. Barthou was quite old when he put this anthology together. Perhaps it was requested by the publisher, or it was, for him, a memory of texts by Hugo that he had enjoyed in his younger years.

Lucrèce Borgia. This prose drama in three acts, dating from 1832, was originally called *Le Souper de Ferrare*, most aptly, since it was at the dinner of the Princess Negroni that the hero, Gennaro, and his friends were all fatally poisoned by Lucrèce in revenge for her humiliation at their hands during a soirée held in Venice (act 1) at the Palace Barbarigo. The play was received with critical accolade in the press and by Hugo's Romantic followers.

It is reasonable to classify *Lucrèce Borgia* as influenced by melodrama if only because of the startling and rapid turn of events. At the beginning of the play, Lucrèce laments her sinful past and seeks purification and atonement. When she encounters Gennaro, she kisses him on the forehead, but at this point there is no indication that she is indeed his mother. Thus the current of maternal instinct, hinted at by Hugo in the preface and sustained by some historical critics, plays second fiddle to an intrigue of poisonings and murders, reinforced by exaggerated depictions of Lucrèce's past, including adultery, incest, and poisonings. History, however, does not support the perverse sexuality of Lucrezia Borgia attributed to her in this play.

As the scene shifts to Ferrare (the two sites make more sense than the artificial division of the play into parts with acts as subdivisions), the action moves rapidly: someone (Gennaro) effaced the B on the noble inscription outside the palace, changing Borgia to Orgia (orgy). Lucrèce,

demanding vengeance approaches her husband who already has the cul-
prit. She is forced to administer the poisoned wine but because she has
the antidote with her, she saves the life of Gennaro and plans for his
escape. He stays on, however, and with his companions he takes part in
the feast of Princess Negroni. (This role was given at the Porte-Saint-
Martin theatre to Juliette Drouet. It was during these readings and rehearsals that the famous liaison between Hugo and Juliette Drouet
developed.) After the entire crowd has been poisoned at the banquet,
Lucrèce arrives with a group of monks and coffins; the first for their
religious confessions, the second for their burials. A final scene between
Lucrèce and Gennaro exposes their blood relationship, but not until Gennaro stabs her does she reveal that she is his mother: *Ah! . . . tu m'as
tuée!—Gennaro! je suis ta mère* (Ah! you have killed me! Gennaro! I am
your mother).

The in-depth psychology of maternity advocated by Hugo, and which
he contrasts with the paternal love of Triboulet* in *Le Roi s'amuse,** is
undermined by attention to sensational detail. If there is any point it is
that of "bad blood" in the sense to be elaborated upon by Emile Zola*
and the other naturalists at the end of the nineteenth century. Frequently
performed, the play has inspired the libretto of an opera by Donizetti.

M

Magnitudo parvi. Poem thirty, the last one, of Book Three, *Les Luttes et les rêves* (Struggles and dreams), *magnitudo parvi* is the longest, most important poem in *Les Contemplations** to decipher what appears to be a natural illumination, or natural mysticism, on the part of the poet. The title, roughly The greatness of things small in English, encapsulates Hugo's message of faith, hope, and charity learned during a beach stroll at twilight with his daughter. (The composition of this opus covers, according to René Journet and Guy Robert, a long period of time, not just for redaction, but also for clarification of thought; therefore, the earliest dating would be 1840, then 1846, and finally 1855, a period of fifteen years.)

The poem is divided into four sections, with no apparent consistency in versification, although its alterations create pyrotechnical delights. These correspond to the discoveries of the poet in the night sky, which lead him to a synthesis on the meaning of creation and life, not to be resolved as a problem in the materialistic sense, but as mystery that can be grasped only by the intuition. Thus the poem, according to some major critics, enters into the land of symbolic landscapes, the meaning of which is only hinted at, but which when stated discursively comes out to the affirmation of the importance of all life, and the equalization of all creation. Gone are all categorizations of assigning superior and inferior positions to the world, the universe, and the cosmos.

It can be said that, with one deft stroke, Hugo succeeded in destroying the materialistic and cynical position of Voltaire on extra-planetary life, compared with life on earth (his *Micromégas*, 1752), which intends to put man in his proper, if inferior, place in creation. This also transcends the sentimental pantheism of Jean-Jacques Rousseau, who, despite his great prose style found in such beautiful pieces of eighteenth-century French literature as *Les Rêveries du promeneur solitaire* (1776–1778), remains fixated on the God in nature, but whose sensibilities approach Hugo's in the sixth *Promenade* of this work.

Hugo, the modern metaphysical astronomer, goes beyond Rousseau. His meditation of the stars led him to startling conclusions that resolved the problems of good and evil and man's final place in God's creation. Thus it could be said that this poem, found right in the center of *Les Contemplations*, seems to resolve questions raised later by Hugo, especially in the concluding poem, *Ce que dit la bouche d'ombre.** It does not work very well, however, in resolving the drowning death of his daughter Léopoldine Hugo,* which is a submotif of the collection (see the second to last poem, *A celle qui est restée en France* (To she who remained in France).

Magnitudo parvi is important also because it introduces the reader to the multitract personality of the poet. *Les Contemplations*, a title that implies mysticism, also contains other aspects: political poems; love poems, addressed especially to Juliette Drouet; a whole book dedicated to Léopoldine, *Pauca meae*; and a good deal of erotic poetry (the reader is referred to such poems as *Lise*, *La Coccinelle* [Ladybird], and *Elle était déchaussée, elle était decoiffée* [She was shoeless, her hair undone]), especially the famous eighteenth-century darkness poem *La fête chez Thérèse* (Thérèsa's garden party), which ends on a bittersweet and melancholic note, hinting dissatisfaction with sexual desire and fulfillment—a type of indirect literary disgust, a feeling of coitus aborted. It is less difficult at the end of the twentieth century to understand what, at first glance, could be interpreted as contradictory urges in Hugo. The answer is found in the fact that Hugo was able to integrate love, and even eroticism, into his whole personality without negating the mystical bent. This is in line with some of the most advanced current theological speculations.

Some critics can see in *Magnitudo parvi* the high spiritual symbolism found, for example, in the poetry of the Victorian priest-poet Gerard Manley Hopkins (1844–1889). On the other hand, Hugo's natural mysticism probably had its point of departure in his nature contemplations, not unlike those of the English writer and critic C. S. Lewis, who, in a remarkable review of his early life *Surprised by Joy: The Shape of My Early Life*, revealed something about transcendency, which he calls *Joy* (a word familiar to the Provençal courtly poets, and probably also the equivalent of *Ecstasy* in the vocabulary of the Western mystics), a communion with the spirit life first discovered in nature, but then going beyond this. For Lewis, however, there could be no reconciliation, as there is in the work of Hugo, with the flesh and the spirit.

In this poem of 161 strophes, Hugo's thought makes temporal and spatial manipulations. Although he reviews the scientific and philosophical discoveries of Thomas Hobbes and John Locke, it is clear that the poet is seeking a person, a personal God (?), a person in the highest Jungian sense. It should not be forgotten that Hugo, especially in his anthropomorphic verses, gives the reader the impact of God and Lucifer as persons, not as abstract concepts.

The poet will be like the shepherds, the singular solitary ones making the night watch with their sheep and, by implication, the shepherds who see the star leading to Bethlehem where the God-man is to be born (thus Jesus becomes the great equalizer between heaven and earth, taking on all aspects of the human personality while nevertheless retaining his divinity).

The commentaries of Pierre Albouy in his introduction to the Pléiade edition of *Les Contemplations* are essential to gain an understanding of this poem. First, that contemplation of astronomical spectacles, the bridge between the possible and the real, has been broached. Man, plunged into the cosmos, recovers his dignity and greatness (for Christian theologians, this might mean recovering the full measure of the psyche before the fall as recorded in Genesis of the Jewish scriptures). Albouy concludes that the poem gives meaning to life by affirming an afterlife, not through magic as in the case of the occult (beliefs held by the Irish poet William Butler Yeats), but through the redemptive act of Christ which opened the gates of heaven to a fallen humanity. As a result, mankind is on a par with the rest of creation. Thus *Magnitudo parvi* is replete with the spiritual longing of all creation. The trees are "religious" in nature. For mankind—by turning to prayer, by maintaining an abiding faith, and by perpetually examining man's persecution of his fellow man—redemption will be at hand. These are, of course, simply critical commentaries that are not so easy to prove. Behind the text, however, seems to be implied another text borrowed from the Christian system abandoned by Hugo, but apparently his disavowal left intact the psychology of Christianity which is fused in this poem with the contemplation of the night sky. It brings the shepherds and wise men of the Incarnation to the beaches of the Channel Islands where a modern poet ponders things contemporary and final.

Magnitudo parvi is a very long poem that disproves what critics would in general call the defects of the overextended lyric. This is metaphysical poetry at its best. It would be impossible to do a strophe-by-strophe textual analysis here; however, two strophes should be underscored. The first is the opening strophe of Part 1, in which the poet walks along the beach with his daughter. The scene is homey, especially in capturing the silence of the child who seems most aware that something tremendous is about to take place: *Le jour mourait; j'étais près des mers, sur la grève/Je tenais par la main ma fille, enfant qui rêve,/Jeune esprit qui se taît!/La terre, s'inclinant comme un vaisseau qui sombre,/En tournant dans l'espace allait plongeant dans l'ombre/La pale nuit montait* (Day was dying, I was near the sea, on the beach/I held the hand of my little girl, child who dreams/ Young spirit which remains quiet/The earth, tilting like a ship which is sinking/while turning in space was plunging into shadow/Pale night was rising). This last verse is almost like the raising of a curtain on the long metaphysical drama that is to follow.

Second, Hugo's virtuosity in this drama produces an astonishing poetic effect: *Quel Zorobabel formidable/Quel Dédale vertigineux, Cieux! a bâti dans l'insondable/Tout ce noir chaos lumineux?* (What formidable Zorobabel/What a dizzy Daedalus, Heaven has built in the unfathomable/All this luminous black chaos.) These lines have somewhat, *avant la lettre*, the ring and energy of the music of Richard Wagner.

Magnitudo parvi may be considered as one of the best of Hugo's poems because it gives adhesion and clarification to his religious thought, which is frequently inaccessible because of the intrusion of other aspects of his poetic genius.

BIBLIOGRAPHY

Barrère, Jean-Bertrand. *La Fantaisie de Victor Hugo*. Paris: José Corti, 1949, 1950.
Frey, John A. *Les Contemplations of Victor Hugo: The Ash Wednesday Liturgy*. Charlottesville: University Press of Virginia, 1988.
Hugo, Victor. *Oeuvres poétiques, Les Châtiments, Les Contemplations*. Edited and annotated by Pierre Albouy. Paris: Gallimard, Bibliothèque de la Pléaide, 1967.
Lewis, C. S. *Surprised by Joy: The Shape of My Early Life*. New York: Harcourt, Brace, 1955.
Nash, Suzanne. *Les Contemplations of Victor Hugo: An Allegory of the Creative Process*. Princeton, N.J.: Princeton University Press, 1976.

Mailbox. *See Boîte aux lettres.*

Maison visionée. The word *maison visionée* (visionary house), a peculiar usage made by Hugo in his novel about Guernsey, does not exist in standard contemporary French. It seems to be a subdialectical form of Anglo-Norman as originally spoken at the time of the Norman conquest, and well corrupted by the nineteenth-century setting of his novel *Les Travailleurs de la Mer*.* Such houses are described as barricaded hovels, sometimes without windows, at least on the side facing the sea. They are perceived in local superstition as the sites of witchcraft, sorcery, and devil worship. At one point, in referring to such places, the narrator states, "The Devil comes there during the night." These dead houses are not rare in the Channel Islands. It is strange that the protagonist Gilliatt,* a man of infinite goodness and physical and moral strength, would live in such a place. Hugo is probably just contrasting local superstition with some specific architectural traits of Guernsey homes.

BIBLIOGRAPHY

Hillsdon, Sonia. *Jersey: Witches, Ghosts, and Traditions*. Norwich, England: Jarold Colour Publications, 1984.
Hugo, Victor. *Les Travailleurs de la Mer*. Annotated by Jacques Seebacher and Yves Gohin. Paris: Gallimard, 1992.

Mallarmé, Stéphane. Stéphane Mallarmé (1842–1898), who, with Arthur Rimbaud and Paul Valéry, was among the greatest of the post-Romantic symbolist poets, admired throughout his personal and critical life the poetry of Victor Hugo. If the admiration is sometimes qualified, as it was with Gustave Flaubert,* by the overt middle-class tone of some of Hugo's early writings, such as *La Prière pour tous* in *Les Feuilles d'automne** (1831), an ambivalency toward a revered literary hero, Mallarmé's judgment of Hugo remained firmly committed to regarding him not just as the greatest of the nineteenth-century poets, but as the most important of poets—if only because of the haunting lyrics that hang in the hearts of latter-day Romantics such as Mallarmé.

Mallarmé, like all writers in the second half of the nineteenth century, left Romanticism behind, but perhaps with a bit of nostalgia. The young Mallarmé, who had received a classical education, found here and there in Hugo's verse deep symbolic approaches to poetry and its intimations of immortality as expressed by the American transcendentalist Ralph Waldo Emerson.

On the day of Victor Hugo's funeral, Mallarmé remembered a legendary, if improbable, visit to Hugo in exile in Brussels where Hugo baptized the very young, if not naive poet, *Mon cher poète impressionniste* (My dear young impressionist poet), which certainly accords Hugo credit for seizing what may have been going on in literature after Romanticism (as recorded by Henri Mondor, *Vie de Mallarmé*, p. 459). Stéphane Mallarmé did not participate at the funeral, which was surrounded by poets whose names are hardly remembered today, such as Jean Aicard. Mallarmé, instead, stayed at his table, leafing through *La Légende des siècles*,* a copy of which he had purchased in 1861, and pondered Hugo's description of him as an impressionist poet.

In the summer of 1880 Mallarmé went canoeing with a friend, Léopold Dauphin, on the Seine, near his summer home at Valvins. It was late summer (September), just after the death of Mallarmé's son Anatole. As the two men paddled their canoe, pipes in mouths, looking a bit like a Claude Monet painting, Mallarmé looked at the setting sun and said to Dauphin: "Do you know what is the greatest line in Victor Hugo?": *Le soleil s'est couché ce soir dans les nuées* (The sun set tonight in the clouds).

This is, of course, a proof of Mallarmé's recognition that Victor Hugo understood the symbolic nature of poetry, without formally being called a symbolist (*see* Symbolism). Any reading of Mallarmé's sonnet *Victorieusement fui le suicide beau* (Victoriously fled the beautiful suicide) leads one to see that this Monet-like poem has taken as its source of inspiration the Hugo text.

In part two of Mallarmé's *Variations sur un sujet*, subtitled *Crise de vers* (written over a long period 1886–1892–1896), we find a very short segment in the prose, written for the *National Observer*, of eighteen lines dedicated to his deep appreciation of Hugo, almost a latent thought on the meaning of Hugo's death, written in Mallarmé's typical hermetic style, with verbal (in the sense of verb) insistence on Hugo's and poetry's immortality (pp. 360–361).

BIBLIOGRAPHY

Mallarmé, Stéphane. *Oeuvres complètes*. Edited by Henri Mondor and G. Jean-Aubry. Paris: Gallimard, 1989.

Mangeront-ils? This two-act play in verse form was written during the first four months of 1867 and later incorporated into Hugo's *Théâtre en liberté*.* *Mangeront-ils?* (Will they eat?) is the longest and most important of the collection, and it has had successful stagings in the twentieth century. It is also heard on French radio and seen on French television. The play is best known for the personage of Airolo,* called by the French a *gueux*, a word that incorporates the idea of a clown or tramp who lives marginally, but not alienated, in society.

There is a long tradition for this type of mocking character which dates back to medieval French theatre and literature. It is an anti-establishment type that probably provoked the outrage igniting the French Revolution and the frequent street demonstrations and strikes for which even contemporary France is well known, a spirit found only occasionally in the more reserved psychology of the English and the Americans. Hugo, himself a kind of revolutionary, approved and applauded such free spirits.

Manuscripts. Most of the manuscripts of Victor Hugo are housed, according to his will, in the Bibliothèque Nationale, in Paris, although some are found in the Hugo archives at no. 6 Place des Vosges; others are in private collections. Hugo's final codicil, dated August 31, 1881, three years and nine months before his death, clearly states his desire to leave all of his materials to the national library: *Je donne tous mes manuscrits et tout ce qui serait trouvé écrit ou dessiné par moi à la Bibliothèque Nationale de Paris, qui sera un jour la Bibliothèque des Etats-Unis d'Europe* (I leave all my manuscripts and whatever else written or drawn by me which may be found, to the National Library of Paris, which someday will be the Library of the United States of Europe).

Hugo obviously, even in his most Utopian moments, dreaming of a unified Europe, still regarded France as the leader of that unification movement, an attitude that might surprise some who, at the end of the twentieth century, may see that as Germany's role.

The catalogue numbering of the Hugo materials published by the Bibliothèque Nationale can be found on pages 87 to 95 in *Répertoire des manuscrits littéraires français*, compiled by Anne Herschberg-Pierrot (Paris: La Bibliothèque, 1985).

Manuscripts, posthumous works. Hugo manuscripts, those known about and considered lost, continue to turn up mainly in France but also around the globe. Additionally, unknown poems, fragments, and letters surface from time to time. It is therefore almost impossible to compile a complete list of Hugo's writings, although it can be safely stated that the corpus of his work is intact and printed.

At the time of his death, enough materials remained extant to form a solid twenty volumes. These materials have since been published and studied critically: *La Fin de Satan** (1886); *Théâtre en liberté** (1888); *Choses vues** (1887); *Toute la lyre* (1889–1893); *Dieu** (1891); *En voyage—Alpes et Pyrénées; France et Belgique: Voyages et excursions* (1891–1894); *Amy Robsart and Les Jumeaux; Correspondance, 1815–1892* (1896); *Lettres à la fiancée: Postscriptum de ma vie* (1901); and *Dernière Gerbe* (1902).

Mariage de Roland, Le. This important medieval re-creation from the imagination of Hugo was published for the first time in the *Revue des Deux Mondes* on September 1, 1859. The poem is found in the first series of *La Légende des siècles** (1859) in section 10 which contains five poems under the rubric of *Le cycle héroïque chrétien*. Hugo got the idea for the *Petites epopées* (Little epic poems) from an article published in the *Journal du Dimanche* on November 1, 1846, written by the medievalist Achille Jubinal.

The poem demonstrates the medieval renaissance brought about by the Romantics; for example, Alfred de Vigny's* poem *Le Cor* concerns the disastrous defeat of Roland at Roncevaux (Roncesvalles) in the kingdom of Navarre in Spain where Charlemagne's rear guard was attacked in 788, and during which Count Roland was obstinate and filled with pride and determination. Because he refused to blow his horn for help he and the rest of his group, including Olivier, perished at the hands of the Saracens. De Vigny's poem is faithful in spirit to the original epic.

How faithful Hugo's *Le Mariage de Roland* is is difficult to determine. It is certainly far removed from the studies of France's two most famous Romance philologists of the nineteenth century, Gaston Paris (1839–1903) and Joseph Bédier (1864–1938). Although both scholars were primarily interested in rooting out the origins of the *Chanson de Roland*, their interests were not limited to it. In fact, Bédier published, in 1922, a critical edition of the *Roland*. It can be concluded, as Jacques Truchet states in his notes to his Gallimard edition of *La Légende des siècles*, that Hugo's poem is derived from the Jubinal article.

The poem has peculiarities that make it a rather unique interpretation of chivalrous manners as described by Madame de Staël in her critical writings. A sword fight, more like an ardent gentlemen's duel, between Olivier and Roland takes place on an island in the Rhone river. In the third strophe, the ancestors of Olivier, described as *buveurs de vins* (wine drinkers) rout the Normans seen as *buveurs de cidre* (cider drinkers: an aside to Normandy as the country of apple trees, cider, and Calvados). Roland, nephew of the king of France, is depicted with his magical sword Durandal. After he disarms Olivier, he politely tells him to get another sword. This is followed by an amusing line: *Tu feras apporté a boire en même temps,/Car j'ai soif* (And bring us something to drink because I am thirsty). Olivier returns and pours a goblet of wine for Roland, and then the battle recommences. It is at this point that Roland announces that he is worn out and needs to rest, to which Olivier accedes. After a repose, the battle is rejoined for four days and nights. This time Roland's sword is lost in the Rhone. Roland uproots an oak tree, and Olivier an elm with which they continue to fight. The denouement is rapid: Olivier tells Roland that they can continue to fight like lions and panthers, but to what avail. It is better that they become friends. Olivier proposes that Roland marry his sister Aude, and the two drink to celebrate but also because they are very hot. The poem concludes with *C'est ainsi que Roland épousa la belle Aude.*

The poem obviously, in its deliberate "naiveté," strays far from the heroism of the original epic. It appears more like an athletic contest that we might find in any football or soccer game played in the twentieth century, where the stress is on the idea of macho, healthy and wholesome young men, enjoying the game. The duel is a game. This, however, does not capture the spirit of *La Chanson de Roland* which relates that, upon hearing of the death of Roland, the beautiful Aude collapsed and died in France. The original epic insinuates the collapse of a founding dynasty (which could have been possible with the marriage of Roland and Aude). For those familiar with the original, Hugo's little epic is not much more than an amusing and at times startling interpretation of medieval heroes.

Marie Tudor. This prose drama in three acts, of which the third is in two parts, was poorly received by the critics, and the downfall of the premiere may have had something to do with the rivalry between the seasoned actress Mademoiselle George,* in the role of the queen, and Juliette Drouet as Jane. The third act was roundly denounced by catcalls and whistles, and Juliette Drouet withdrew from the cast, ostensibly for reasons of health.

The political history of the Tudors, with the exception of some references to a possible ascendancy of Elizabeth I in act 3, is not the main subject of this play which concentrates instead on the amorous intrigues of the queen and of Jane, raised as an orphan child by Gilbert, a commoner. The queen has a paramour, a devious Italian or Spaniard of dubious origin, Fabiano Fabiani, who has succeeded in seducing Jane. Through an involved intrigue, Fabiano is brought up on charges of regicide, when his true crime actually is his infidelity to the queen. Gilbert, who is brought into the plot, accuses Fabiano of lèse-majesté. In the final scenes, the people of London are incited to demand Fabiano's head, and a frantic effort is made by the queen and Jane to save both Fabiano and Gilbert. Through a ploy, Fabiano is executed, but Gilbert is spared.

The play contains what may appear as a touch of contemporary antisemitism in the role of a Jewish entrepreneur who is murdered by Fabiano (this man had papers attesting to Jane's noble heritage as the child of Lord Talbot). But the worst insults come from the villain of the play (Fabiano) and thus are condemned. Likewise the play, by modern standards, may seem sexist in its depiction of the queen as fickle, if not hysterical, not knowing what she wants to do for or against her lover, Fabiano; and Jane learns late to love her former protector, Gilbert. But there are extenuating circumstances which excuse them and mainly the latter, who is young and has been perfidiously seduced.

In fact, the play partly reflects the sentimental crisis Hugo had just lived through because of his wife's infidelity and the outcome offered by Juliette Drouet's love.

Marine Terrace, Island of Jersey. Marine Terrace was Hugo's first home on the Channel Islands following the exile, after a short period in Brussels, and later in Guernsey. Hugo lived at Marine Terrace from 1852 through 1855, a short distance away from the capital of Saint Helier, but close to the sea (which was important to Hugo who regarded the Channel waters as his own separation from France). It was an unfortunate inclusion in a protest letter of French exiles, concerning the visit of Queen Victoria to Napoléon III,* that caused his expulsion from Jersey and resettlement on Guernsey. The idiosyncrasies of Channel Island laws, which have been trust territories of the British crown since the Norman conquest of 1066, may make it difficult for readers to understand Hugo's island hopping.

Marine Terrace, for those interested in Victor Hugo today, is above all remembered for the famous spiritist séances (*see* Spiritism) inaugurated

by Hugo's friend, the French Romantic poet and novelist Delphine Gay*
during her long visit to the poet. Whereas the spiritist séances occupy
most of Hugo's biographers, for indeed he wanted to contact his dead
daughter Léopoldine Hugo,* the marriage of grief and vindictive feelings
toward Napoléon III gave prominence to his most important satirical
volume of poetry, *Les Châtiments*, written for the most part on Jersey and
published in 1853. Hugo, ordered out of Jersey, moved to Guernsey on
October 31, 1855.

BIBLIOGRAPHY

Hazard, Paul. *Avec Victor Hugo en exil*. Paris: Les Belles Lettres, 1931.
Seregent, Jean. *Description of Victor Hugo's House in Guernsey and Historical Notes*.
        Guernsey Press, 1985.

Marion de Lorme. This verse drama, composed by Hugo in 1828, was
not performed until 1831, after the July revolution, because of official
censorship. Originally it was entitled *Un duel sous Richelieu*, which is a
more apt title if the play is viewed from the perspective of Richelieu's
implementation of the ban against dueling. It is the violation of this
stricture that leads to the trial and execution of the protagonist, Didier,
and of the marquis de Saverny. The new title stresses the theme of the
redemption of the fallen woman through true love. Such is the case of
Marion de Lorme, played by the great actress Marie Dorval. After a life
of debauchery, the heroine seeks redemption in the Loire valley, away
from the temptations of Paris. There, with her new love Didier, she undergoes a spiritual transformation. Her past, however, does not leave
her alone, and Didier finds it hard to forgive her for an act she engaged
in to save Didier's life by giving herself to M. de Laffemas who in turn
guarantees an escape route which Didier surmised. Hugo had originally
denied Marion any pardon from Didier in the 1829 version, but friends
pressured him into the Romantic scene of forgiveness found in the final
version of 1831.

    Thus the play intertwines internal French political policy with the Ro-
mantic theme of redemption of the fallen woman through true love, anticipating the 1848 novel *La Dame aux camélias* of Alexandre Dumas *fils*
(1824–1895), which was turned into a play in 1852 known in English as
Camille, which became the libretto source for Giuseppe Verdi's *La Traviata* (1853).

    Two aspects of this drama need to be stressed: first, the absolute love
of Marion for her lover Didier, using as a leitmotif the *suivre* (to follow)
motif which will be paramount in the early part of *Hernani;** and second,
Didier's Romantic fascination with fate and death. On the surface, this
is a desire to maintain his moral integrity. On another level, however, it
appears as Romantic posturing, a Romantic penchant for things final.

Romantic heroes and heroines seem to look forward to death and to love life beyond the grave.

Hugo's troubles with the censors probably had something to do with the character of Louis XIII, who is depicted as a weak monarch under the control of the cardinal, hardly a role model for the monarch Charles X. The censors particularly objected to act 4, in which the king seems to be unable to make up his mind about whether to pardon the duelers.

In general, it can be said that the play is partly dependent upon absolute psychological stances throughout the action: Marion's undying love; Didier's death wish; the king's jester, L'Angely, who proves in act 4 that he is nobody's fool; and finally the condemned nobleman, the marquis de Saverny, who remains unconcerned about his imminent execution, sleeping through his last hours, in contrast with the Romantic meditations on the meanings of love and death of Didier.

While far less famous and less performed than *Hernani* and *Ruy Blas*, it is worth becoming acquainted with and, by the circumstances of its production one may get some idea of the problems Victor Hugo faced with official censorship, a problem that endured for art in France throughout the nineteenth century.

Marius. Marius is a principal character in Hugo's novel *Les Misérables*. He moves, as the narrator recounts, from ultraconservatism to the left. In some ways, he seems to represent Hugo's own political evolution. (See also Cosette and Valjean, Jean.)

Mars, Anne Boutet. Anne Boutet Mars (1779–1847) was perhaps one of the most famous actresses of the Comédie Française during the Romantic period of theatrical revival provoked in no small part by Alexandre Dumas, and then Victor Hugo. In spite of being forty-one, she played the ingenue Doña Sol de Silva* in Hugo's *Hernani**—who was supposed to be only seventeen—her reputation certainly helped the new Romantic theatre to succeed in opposition to a dying classical tradition. Nineteenth-century audiences apparently had less problems with age or weight (for example, the soprano who inaugurated Giuseppe Verdi's *La Traviata*), but today there are also exceptions to the need for dramatic verisimilitude when the actress or singer has superior talents.

Mazeppa, Ivan Stepanovich. This historical and legendary figure, a Cossack hetman, less by his wartime life and more by the legends about him, apparently derived from Voltaire's *History of Charles XII* (1731), inspired Lord Byron* in England to write *Mazeppa, a Poem* (1819) and Victor Hugo in France to author the famous *Mazeppa* poem found in *Les Orientales** (1829).

Historically, Mazeppa (1644–1709) is a confusing personality, complex in his reasoning and in his alliances. While certainly to be admired as a Ukrainian patriot, his misadventures hint at a soldier of fortune aspect in his personality. A few facts show a dazzling display of alliances and misalliances. After entering the service of Pyotr Doroshenko, hetman of the Ukraine west of the Dnepr River, Mazeppa quit Doroshenko and joined his rival Ivan Samolovich. In some ways he appears responsible for the prolonged war engagements among the Turks, Poles, Russians, and diverse Cossack groups who were all vying for control of Ukraine.

In 1687 Mazeppa succeeded Samolovich as hetman and took part in the campaign of Prince Vasily Golitsyn, chief of foreign affairs during the regency of Sophia Alekseyevna (1682–1689), in the war against the Crimean Tartars. Golitsyn was exiled when Peter I, the Great, overthrew Sophia Alekseyevna, but Mazeppa managed to stay in favor with the tsar, thus retaining his powerful position in the Ukraine. Mazeppa, however, soon became disillusioned with Peter, fearing that Peter was using the Cossacks in extraordinary military duties, but also for his perception of the persecution of civilian Ukrainians. At the beginning of the great Northern War (1700), Mazeppa entered into secret negotiations with Charles XII of Sweden and his Polish allies, and he planned, dependent on a Swedish victory, to make the Ukraine part of a federation with Poland, with Sweden guaranteeing Ukrainian rights and privileges within the confederation. Charles led his forces into the Ukraine in 1708, and Mazeppa joined his Cossack forces with the Swedes, who were finally defeated by the Russians at Poltava in June 1709. Mazeppa fled with Charles into Turkish-controlled Moldavia where he died.

It is the legendary Mazeppa, however, that fascinated the French and English Romantics, especially Byron and Hugo as respective leaders of the English and French schools of Romanticism. Equally important are the paintings inspired by this legend, notably those of Louis Boulanger and Horace Vernet of the Romantic school, and subsequent works by Chasseriau and Devilly. The legend is derived from an anecdote in Voltaire's *History of Charles XII*: Mazeppa is tied naked to the back of a wild horse and forced to gallop across the steppes of Ukraine. Rescued by the Cossacks, more dead than alive, Mazeppa joined their itinerant lifestyle, and because of his courage, was elected their leader.

Two paintings by Vernet on the theme of Mazeppa's ride (now in the Avignon museum), inspired by the poem of Lord Byron, display a main characteristic of Byron, the idea of Romantic heroism and energy.

Hugo's poem *Mazeppa*, one of the major pieces in *Les Orientales*, was inspired by the painting of Louis Boulanger (Rouen museum), which competed, as did the Vernet painting, in the salon of 1827. Hugo's poem, dedicated to Boulanger, shows the influence of painting on poetry. The poem can be divided easily into two parts. The first part describes the unbridled run of the horse across the plains of Russia. It is witness to

Hugo's virtuosity, the genius of a Romantic poet manifest not only in rupturing classical versification, but also in introducing techniques that can only be called Romantic impressionism. The wounded Mazeppa, with his eyes wide open, views the passing landscape and the heavens. It is truly an impressionistic kaleidoscope, a Romantic subjective appraisal of nature which, in some ways, announces the impressionistic art at the end of the century. The second part of the poem is seen as an allegory of the creative process. It is poetic genius which Hugo wishes to impart to the ride of Mazeppa. While being carried away by a fiery, impetuous, and spirited horse, the man of genius hears howling about him the hounds of envy: *Il court, il vole, il tombe/Et se relève roi* (He races, he flies, he falls/And rises again king).

The Mazeppa legends continued across the century, notably in painting, for example, that of Chasseriau exhibited in the salon of 1853, entitled *A Cossack Daughter Finds Mazeppa Unconscious, Dead with Fatigue, on a Wild Horse*, and another Mazeppa by Devilly which was exhibited in the salon of 1870.

BIBLIOGRAPHY

Hatzfeld, Helmut. *Literature through Art: A New Approach to French Literature.* Chapel Hill: University of North Carolina Press, 1952.

Mendiant, Le. *Le Mendiant* (The beggar) is found in Book Five, *En Marche*, poem nine, of *Les Contemplations.** Its title belies its contents, for the poor old man of the poem never begs or asks; it is the narrator who brings him in out of the cold, wintery day and offers him food and warmth.

The poem could be considered religious in its tone. At the same time, it is the expression of Hugo's concern with social injustice, the plight and the needs of the poor; in this case, that of the elderly impoverished.

Religious or Romantic humanitarianism, *Le Mendiant* has spiritual dimensions, recalling the beatitudes (Blessed are the poor, for they shall see God). It has French literary antecedents in the medieval lives of the saints, the story of Christopher the Christ-bearer, and the legend recounted by Gustave Flaubert* of Saint-Julien l'Hospitalier. The poem is based on a firm belief that the poor must not be turned away.

The scene, a dramatic one, looks somewhat like a medieval miniature of a winter day, recalling the seasonal landscapes of Pieter Brueghel, the Elder (circa 1525/30–1569). From his comfortable room, the narrator sees a poor man in the street, amidst the ending activities of a cold day, donkeys coming back from the market, carrying peasants sitting on the pack-saddles. He brings the old man in out of the cold, but he is not identified by name, only allegorically as *Le pauvre* (the poor man).

As in other miracle poems of Hugo (*Halte en marchant** or *Booz endormi**), the sanctity of the old man is illuminated through the transformation of his ragged, worm-eaten coat. As the coat hangs before the warm hearth to dry, the poet sees, on one level, simply the firelight shining through its holes. Yet this piece of ragged realism turns into Romantic lyrical symbolism, for to the poet the coat is the firmament through which he sees a star-filled sky: *Et je regardais, sourd à ce que nous disions/Sa bure où je voyais des constellations* (And I kept looking, oblivious to what we were saying/at his coat where I saw constellations). This miracle has taken place because the poor man is holy (perhaps poverty and sanctity are linked in Hugo's thought); he is *plein de prières* (filled with prayers).

Mes deux filles. *See My Two Daughters.*

Meurice, François Paul. Meurice (1818/20–1905), a loyal and fervent friend and admirer of Victor Hugo, was an eager participant in all causes espoused by the poet. First should be mentioned Meurice's journalistic endeavors in behalf of Hugo's opinions. In 1848 he served as editor in chief of *L'Evenement*, which Hugo's sons and Auguste Vacquerie* had founded; and in 1869, with the same team, Meurice started the radical journal *Rappel*, which had frequent run-ins with the government.

It was Meurice entered into the Hugo entourage through his friend, Auguste Vacquerie, the brother of Charles Vacquerie* who married Hugo's older daughter, Léopoldine Hugo.* Meurice was the confidant and the intermediary between France and the Channel Islands during Hugo's exile, and in the end he served as the executor of Hugo's estate.

It is for these things, and not for his dramatic or novelistic efforts, that Meurice is mainly remembered. His penchant was for historical drama, such as his *Benvenuto Cellini* (1852). His *Falstaff* (1842) is according to Shakespeare as is his variation on *Hamlet* (1847). His *Antigone* (1844) is derived from Sophocles. Naturally enough, he turned to Hugo for inspiration, and between 1878 and 1881 there appeared three adaptations: of *Les Misérables,** *Notre-Dame de Paris,** and *Quatrevingt-treize.** Like Auguste Vacquerie and Louis Boulanger, Paul Meurice is best remembered as a faithful devotee of Victor Hugo.

Misérables, Les. Published in 1862, Hugo's novel derives from the utilitarian and social concerns of the Romantics, not unlike the concerns of the transcendentalist movement in New England in the early nineteenth century. Its essential point is human suffering, partly caused by a social system that would send a person to prison for stealing a loaf of bread. At the same time, however, it underlines a spirituality that might not be apparent to readers who did not understand Hugo's own spirituality which had developed in a manner divorced from the established church.

Jean Valjean,* the novel's protagonist, after spending years as a prisoner in Toulon, undergoes a spiritual transformation provoked in part, after stealing silver candlesticks, by the generosity of the good bishop of Digne and finally because his conscience bothers him from his last sin, stealing a coin from a poor, young chimney sweep.

In Hugo's world there is always a struggle between good and evil, which sometimes erupts as a physical confrontation, an idea that he pondered all his life.

Jean Valjean is not just cleansed of a minor infraction, stealing a loaf of bread, but he goes on to become a benevolent mayor, and then he moves on to Paris where he and the little Cosette* hide from the inspector Javert,* a detective who pursues the former convict to satisfy his implacable sense of law and order. Javert, after an existential encounter with his own conscience, commits suicide in the Seine, thus fulfilling the "Judas" character of the Christian gospels.

Hugo's long novel is in the tradition of the great Russian moralist novelists of the nineteenth century, Tolstoy, for example, who reflect on human suffering and seek to understand its causes. This meditation of Hugo certainly is related to his important poem *La Conscience,** which concerns the killing of Cain by his brother Abel, the first recorded fratricide, perhaps the beginning of mankind's fall after the expulsion from Eden.

The novel speaks painfully of the seduction of Fantine,* mother of Cosette, Fantine's death, Cosette's Cinderella existence with the immoral Thénardier family,* and Cosette's rescue by Jean Valjean.

The novel concludes with the encounter of Cosette with Marius* during her daily walks in the Luxembourg gardens, the marriage of the young couple, followed, after a last painful proof which Jean Valjean imposes on himself, by his serene death.

Les Misérables can, with its social and spiritual conscience, be considered one of the greatest messages not just to the nineteenth-century reader, but also to an audience of the twentieth century trained to measure it, negatively, against the detached novel of Gustave Flaubert,* as found in *Madame Bovary*.

Misérables, Les (musical play). The phenomenon of this modern musical, dating back to its first French production on September 18, 1980, is mind-boggling as it continues to be produced all over the world and, in its own way, attests to what can be called the universality of Victor Hugo's genius. The story of its genesis in France and its English mutations is fascinating and complicated. It began in Paris with the collaboration of composer Claude-Michel Schönberg and lyricist Alain Boublil, and its artistic journey has continued with the English language version produced in 1985 by Cameron Mackintosh.

The French lyricist and the French composer discovered their mutual interest in serious musical comedy while viewing British and American musicals such as *Jesus Christ Superstar*. Having also seen the revival of *Oliver* in London, Schönberg and Boublil thought it might be possible to create a modern musical out of French history. Their first effort, *La Revolution française*, which became a best-selling record, had a long run at the Palais des Sports. It then occurred to them that if the English-speaking world could make a musical drama out of the work of Charles Dickens, there was no reason why Hugo's great epic *Les Misérables** could not also become a musical drama. It should be remembered that, throughout the nineteenth century, many of Hugo's novels had been thus transposed, mainly *Notre-Dame de Paris** and *Les Misérables*. After much soul-searching and many delays, the French version was put together, and it opened in September at the Palais des Sports, a venue celebrated for such spectacular productions as *Nijinsky, clown de Dieu* by Maurice Béjart.

It occurred to Cameron Mackintosh, however, that the French script would require massive modification in order to be comprehensible to an English or American audience. The fact that almost every French person was familiar at least with the main story line of the Jean Valjean* legend made it easy to adapt the story musically for a French audience. However, the same could not be said for a public on the other side of the English Channel. Furthermore, the English team felt that the French version was nothing more than a series of vignettes or tableaux from the novel. The English version, therefore, entailed a considerable amount of writing, following the Hugo text very closely from the very first episode of Jean Valjean's stealing of Bishop Bienvenue's silver candlesticks—an episode that is missing from the original French musical version.

The first English version was performed on October 8, 1985, at the Barbican Theatre in London. Although there were a few minor negative criticisms, the play received favorable acclaim in the major newspapers of London, New York, and Washington, D.C. After that, "*Les Mis*" seems to have taken off on its own. A list of opening nights for 1985 includes the Barbican and then, in December, it opened at the Palace Theatre in London. On December 27, 1980, the musical opened at the Kennedy Center in Washington, D.C. In 1987 it opened at the Broadway Theatre, New York; Imperial Theatre, Tokyo; Camerri Theatre, Tel Aviv; Rock Theatre, Szeged, Hungary; Theatre Royal, Sydney; Shubert Theatre, Boston; National Theatre of Iceland, Reykjavík. In 1988 it opened at the Chunichi Theatre, Nagoya; Umeda-Koma Theatre, Osaka; Shubert Theatre, Los Angeles; Raimund Theatre, Vienna; and Forest Theatre, Philadelphia. 1988 also saw touring companies going to Tampa, Miami, Orlando, and St. Petersburg, Florida; Kansas City and St. Louis, Missouri; Columbus and Cincinnati, Ohio; Grand Rapids and East Lansing, Michigan; Bloomington, Indiana; Louisville, Kentucky; and Nashville, Tennessee, to name a few of the cities covered during this American tour. In 1989 *Les Mis* played at the Royal Alexander Theatre, Toronto, and also at the Princess Theatre in Melbourne, Australia. In 1990 productions were being prepared in Mexico City, Paris (for 1991), and Amsterdam (1991). Under discussion were productions in Barcelona; Buenos Aires, Dublin, East Berlin, Hamburg, Moscow, Munich, Odense, Prague, Rio de Janeiro, Rome, São Paulo, and Sofia.

Probably it has never happened in the past, nor will it probably ever happen again in the future, that a single musical opera was able to take the entire planet by storm. As of 1997 *Les Mis* is still running in major cities of the world. This might have delighted Victor Hugo. *Les Misérables*, which many suggest is the best French novel of the nineteenth century, surpassing such canonical favorites as *Madame Bovary* of Gustave Flaubert,* *The Red and the Black* of Stendhal,* and *Germinal* of Emile Zola,* obviously has had a universal appeal. In the English-speaking world, beginning students of the French language were frequently taught the episode of the bishop's candlesticks. This episode is, of course, a pivotal moment in the novel—it is the source of Jean Valjean's redemption—and it is for this reason that the English producers decided to include that episode as a prologue.

It is not easy to explain why Victor Hugo's work adapts so well to the theatre; probably it is for the same reasons that Dickens' works adapt so successfully. This has something to do with the social consciousness of these two humanitarian novelists. In part, also, it is because of Hugo's dramatic dialogue in novelistic form and his ability, and that of his adapters to the theatre, to raise what on the surface appear to be stereotypical types to deep human characterizations embodying good and evil, pride, patience, and suffering. While such abstract concepts act as motifs in both the novel and the musical, the characters transcend the abstractions, making the moral choices involved as attributes of the human personalities involved. All of this is sustained, of course, through a musical score that reiterates what is taking place in the narrative.

A complete analysis of the genesis of the musical, the persons behind its creation, and the problems involved in its production is found in *The Complete Book of Les Misérables* by Edward Behr (New York; Arcade Publishing, Little, Brown and Company, 1989).

Misérables, Les (theatrical adaptations). Curiously enough, short theatrical pieces, derived from various parts of the humanitarian novel of 1862, were performed in Italy. A full theatrical adaptation was planned almost immediately upon publication of the novel, and a complete transposition was ready for production in Brussels (French censorship would not allow its production in France) on January 3, 1863, at the Galeries Saint Hugert theatre. The text and all aspects of direction and production

were in the hands of Victor Hugo's son Charles and François Paul Meurice* who had received positive advice from the author. This adaptation
has been the standard one performed for a long time. It was again performed in 1878 at the Porte-Saint-Martin theatre, with Hugo in the audience, who was totally satisfied with the performance. It was performed
again in 1889.

Montreuil-sur-Mer. The industrial revolution brought prosperity to this
city and to the region. Later, much against his will, Jean Valjean* is
named mayor of the town, a secular leadership equivalent to that of his
spiritual mentor the good Bishop Myriel (Bienvenue) of the candlestick
story.

Hugo's intuitive perception of spiritual reformation must have led him
to choose the name Madeleine, after the famous Mary Madeleine (or
Magdalene), wrongly accused in Christian iconography of being a reformed prostitute. In any case, Jean Valjean is reformed.

It should also be noted that Jean Valjean seems, almost like his creator
Victor Hugo, to be a great walker or traveler. As is narrated in the opening chapters of *Les Misérables*,* Jean, released from prison in Toulon,
walks all the way, via Grasse, to Digne, a distance of over 100 kilometers.
In this episode at Montreuil he is now on the other tip of the French
hexagon. Hugo may be suggesting some relationship between geography
and redemption along the lines suggested by Charles Dickens in his
novel *Bleak House*.

Mort du Duc de Berry, La. Taken from the first book of *Odes et Ballades*,*
those written between 1818 and 1822, this long poem in four parts dates
from February 1820. Charles Ferdinand de Bourbon, duc de Berry (1778–
1820) was assassinated by Louis Pierre Louvel (1783–1820) who had
hoped, by this act, to extinguish the Bourbon dynasty. Louvel was executed in the same year. It is reported that this ode had a great emotional
impact on the aging Louis XVIII (1755–1824), who was moved to tears
by part of the ninth strophe: *Monarque en cheveux blancs, hâte-toi, le temps
presse;/Un Bourbon va rentrer au sein de ses aieux;/Viens, accours vers ce fils,
l'espoir de ta vieillesse/Car ta main doit fermer ses yeux* (O white-haired monarch, hurry, time urges you on/ A Bourbon is going to return to the
breast [Biblical echo] of his ancestors/Come, run toward this son, the
hope of your old age/For your hand must close his eyes).

Hugo opens his conservative patriotic ode with an apt quote from
Friedrich von Schiller: "Murder, by a violent hand, breaks the most holy
of ties; Death has just taken a young man in the flower of youth, and
misfortune approaches like a clever enemy in the midst of our festive
days."

Part 1 contains only one strophe, built on antitheses between happy life activities and the intruder, Death. *L'hymne des saturnales/Sert de pré-lude au chant des morts* (The saturnalian rites serve only as a prelude to the chants for the dead). Part 2 contains eleven strophes filled with ele-gaic lament directed toward the city of Paris, anticipating a similar de-vice used by the twentieth-century English poet Wystan Hugh Auden (1907–1973) who, in a state of profound personal grief, composed a poem asking that all human activity cease: Stop the clocks, don't let the dogs bark, cancel airplane flights. Hugo asks all of Paris to cease the activities of the City of Light, to stop dancing; instead, the Parisians should carry funeral torches. The following strophes address the grief of the family of the duke: a saddened father, brother, sister, and his wife. The poet then speaks directly to the dead nobleman about the monster Anarchy which might profit from this assassination, followed by Hugo's personal intercession to Louis XVIII. The last strophe imagines the funeral cortège on its way to Saint-Denis basilica where all the kings and queens of France were buried until its desecration by the fanaticism of the French Revolution.

Part 3 is more historical in nature, with references to the Condé branch of the house of Bourbon. In a curious approach to the widow, the poet suggests that better days will come, and the apocalyptic monsters of the Bible (the enemies of the Bourbon restoration) will be destroyed. The ode concludes with a reference to a woman crushing the head of the Serpent, meaning Mary, the mother of Jesus, in her salvational role. Here Hugo is applying the Biblical passage to an ephemeral, historic event that did not change history, at least not until the revolution of 1830.

Hugo frequently took this type of poetic license. In fact, in some ways, as it abolishes traditional concepts of time and space, it anticipates sim-ilar poetic pyrotechnics that would be practiced by some of the French and Belgian symbolist poets (Max Elskamp, 1862–1931). While the poem, on its surface, seems perfunctory, a close analysis would indicate pro-found figurative modifications of a historical event.

Muse française, La. A short-lived (1823–1824), highly influential literary magazine, *La Muse française* disseminated many theories of the Romantic movement and published the works of the new Romantic generation, among them the young Victor Hugo and Alfred de Vigny.

Music and Victor Hugo. Being a great lyric and epic poet, Hugo could only be inclined toward music since its muse Euterpe is not too far dis-tant from Polymnia (Polyhymnia), the muse of sacred poetry. Hugo's appreciation of the high value of music is expressed on both the aesthetic and personal levels, especially in the poems of *Les Contemplations** ded-icated to Louise Bertin (*see* Bertin family). The poem *Ecrit sur la plinthe d'un bas-relief antique* (Written on the plinthe of an old bas-relief), from

Book Three, *Les Luttes et les rêves* (Struggles and Dreams), of *Les Contemplations*, brings forth an impressionistic kaleidoscope of many possible sounds, all of which lead to music, for *La musique est dans tout. Un hymne sort du monde* (Music is in everything. A hymn comes forth from the earth).

Another poem, also dedicated to the composer Louise Bertin, recalls the happy days spent in the past at Les Roches, the summer property of the Bertin family, with homey, sentimental scenes in the manner of the painter Jean-Baptiste Greuze—snapshots which include homage to Louise Bertin's musical talent: *O vous l'âme profonde! o vous la sainte lyre!* (O you most profound soul! O you the holy lyre incarnate).

It was with enthusiasm that Hugo agreed to write the libretto for Louise Bertin's operatic renderings of *Notre-Dame de Paris*,* entitled *La Esmeralda (see* Esmeralda). Although it was a failure, the libretto proved Hugo's adherence to friendship and to music. Furthermore it is well known that many of Hugo's texts were readily seized for operatic production, notably Giuseppe Verdi's *Rigoletto* (1851) and his *Ernani* (1844), which were derived from the most famous and revolutionary of Hugo's dramas.

It would be impossible to list all of the musical compositions inspired by the work of Hugo, for they continue to be produced. The reader is directed to the splendid article and compilations of Arnaud Laster in the centenary publication of Hugo's death, *La Gloire de Victor Hugo*. Among the most important composers inspired by Hugo was Hector Berlioz, above all by *Les Orientales** and *Le Dernier Jour d'un condamné** for the *Symphonie fantastique*. Franz Liszt, who enjoyed about fifty years of friendship with Hugo, was inspired by such works. Laster has even found traces of Hugo in the works of Richard Wagner, and for the twentieth century he cites Maurice Ravel and Sergey Rachmaninoff. Laster's article includes an alphabetical listing of 198 composers who have been musically inspired by Hugo's work, whether it is poetry, drama, or novel. In addition to those already mentioned, attention should be given to the work of Georges Auric, who composed the music for the 1956 film *Notre-Dame de Paris*; Aldred Bruneau, musical collaborator of Emile Zola* for his lyrical drama based on *Angelo, tyran de Padoue*; Léo Delibes for the musical accompaniment to *Le Roi s'amuse* in 1882; Arthur Honegger for the musical background of the film *Les Misérables* of 1934; Jules Massenet for a musical background to *Notre-Dame de Paris*, 1879; and Jean Wiener, music for the film *L'Homme qui rit* for French television, 1962. These listings are only samplings of Laster's exhaustive list; musicologists and serious students of music should carefully study Laster's article and listings.

BIBLIOGRAPHY

"Histoire de la musique." In *Encyclopédie de la Pléiade*. Paris: NRF, 1977.
Laster, Arnaud. "Berlioz et Victor Hugo." *Romantisme* 12 (1976). Paris.
———. *La Gloire de Victor Hugo*. Paris: Editions de la Réunion des Musées nationaux, 1985, pp. 633–57.
Saint-Saëns, Camille. *École buissonnière, notes et souvenirs*. n.d.
Verdi, Giuseppe. *Autobiographie à travers la correspondance*, n.d.

Musset, Alfred de. Alfred de Musset (1810–1857), the so-called spoiled child of French Romanticism, was not much appreciated by Hugo, and the feeling was mutual on Musset's part. Hugo shares the only condemnation made by French symbolist poet Arthur Rimbaud of the Romantic poets, all of whom he found worthy with the exception of Musset. Hugo, who once referred to Musset as "Miss Byron" (Maurois, p. 468), perhaps a reference to his delicate features and blond hair, found him inferior to Alphonse de Lamartine.* Musset, on the other hand, had next to no appreciation of Lamartine, and he was not exactly ecstatic about Hugo's *Hernani*,* which he found too rhetorical. Although Musset sometimes has been considered the least of the French Romantic poets (Lamartine, Hugo, Alfred de Vigny,* Musset), he retains the reputation of having been the best of the Romantic playwrights, especially with his *Lorenzaccio*, which is the best French equivalent of the desired Shakespearean model. It did not take Musset long to become disillusioned with the Romantic movement, which his father recognized in a letter of 1830 in which Musset commented on his growing suspicions of where the Romantic movement was heading. The young man was going through a process of being "dehugotized" (*Correspondance de Victor de Musset avec M. de Cayrol, critique de L'Universel*).

The relationships among the Romantics should be seen within human rivalries of a new and truly revolutionary movement called Romanticism. Hugo's dislike of various aspects of Musset are not deeply considered; Musset's reactions to Hugo should be seen as the natural revolt of the youngest of the Romantics against the leader of the tribe.

My Two Daughters. This poem, from Book One, *Aurore* (Dawn), of *Les Contemplations* of 1856, opens, avowedly by the poet, with concern and love for his daughters. This third poem of *Aurore* is a ten-line ecstatic portrait made by a proud father of his two daughters, the elder, Léopoldine Hugo,* the younger Adèle Hugo,* sitting on the doorstep in the late twilight. It demonstrates Victor Hugo's abiding love of family and children which carried on into his old age when he wrote about his remaining family, his grandchildren, in *L'Art d'être grand-père** (The art of being a grandfather).

Aesthetically, the poem looks like a cross between a nineteenth-century painting, a Claude Monet, a James Whistler, or, more specifically, a Mary Cassatt or a Pierre-Auguste Renoir, in its appreciation of the lyrical beauty of innocent childhood surrounded by nature. The children are silent in this poem-painting, as are the white butterflies transformed from the white carnations hovering over the two girls.

Structurally, the poem, as is often the case with Hugo, anticipates procedures to be developed later in the nineteenth century in Parnassian poetry* and in the poetry of the school of symbolism.*

Myriel, Bishop. *See* Bienvenu, Bishop.

N

Napoléon I, Napoléon-Bonaparte. Victor Hugo was, like Alexandre Dumas, the son of one of Napoléon's generals, whose career remained attached mostly to Spain. His mother, on the other hand, was a fervent royalist, and in his first works he celebrated the regime his mother supported.

In 1827, however, an incident occurred in the Austrian embassy in which French generals were announced by their names (Mortier, Soult, Oudinot, MacDonald) rather than their titles of Ducs de Trévise, de Dalmatie, de Reggio, and de Tarente, all Austrian territories. The incident made Hugo return to his paternal roots and write the *Ode à la colonne* (Vendôme) in which he stressed that Napoléon's era had left an indelible mark on Europe. The poem is included in *Odes et Ballades** (1828) which also contains *A mon Père*; here Hugo recalled the campaign of Spain in which his father behaved as a hero. In another poem, *Sur Lord Byron, à propos de sa mort*, Hugo insisted that one can no more write like Voltaire when one lived in the century of Napoléon.

In *Les Orientales** (1829), the poem *Bounaberdi* (Bonaparte's name in the Arabic tradition) shows how Arabs remembered Napoléon, and *Lui* shows how much the new generations were obsessed by his memory: his shadow was even more impressive in retrospect, given the consecration that his tragic fate conferred on him: *Toujours Napoléon, éblouissant et sombre, /Sur le seuil de ce siècle est debout* (Always Napoléon, both dazzling and somber,/ Is standing at the threshold of this century).

After *Les Orientales*, Hugo, inspired by the paintings of Raffet et Charlet and the Songs of Béranger which openly celebrated Napoléon's cult, joined the new generation which called itself "Jeune France" and dreamed of Napoléon without having lived under his boot. Although it had been born under the blessing of the throne and the altar, French

Romanticism was led by Hugo toward a more leftist position, under the aegis of Napoléon. In the *Feuilles d'automne** (1831, Autumn Leaves), Napoléon's figure formed the background of his youthful memories: *Ce siècle avait deux ans, C'est une chose grande, Souvenir d'enfance* (This century was two years old, It's a great thing, a Memory of childhood), all celebrate the Empire as a new era.

After the Revolution of 1830 and the establishment of the Orleans dynasty, Hugo's first real political stand about Napoléon took place after his play *Le Roi s'amuse** (1832) (the inspiration for Verdi's *Rigoletto*) was censured. He publicly declared that he preferred the open grand despotism of Napoléon to the hypocritical tyranny which was characteristic of the new bourgeois regime of Louis-Philippe.

In *Les Chants du crépuscule** (1835), Hugo showed in *Napoléon II* the Emperor crying in the middle of battle while remembering his son. A second *Ode à la colonne* was inspired by General Lamarque's petition to have the ashes of Napoléon returned to France and buried under the colonne Vendôme, that remembrance of Napoleonic glories. The riots and barricade that form one of the central episodes of *Les Misérables* were, in fact, incidents provoked by General Lamarque's own burial.

In *Les Voix intérieures** (1837), Hugo celebrated the completion of the Arc de Triomphe under Louis-Philippe, but he also expressed his sorrow that the name of his father had been omitted from the list of generals inscribed on the monument (*A L'Arc de Triomphe de l'Etoile*).

In 1840, the return of Napoléon's ashes under Louis-Philippe was a popular triumph, celebrated by Hugo in *Le Retour de l'Empereur (Les Rayons et les ombres,* 1840). Napoléon was presented as "une âme grande et bonne" (a great and good soul), "un proscrit magnanime et serein" (a magnanimous and serene exile), and the French people cheered him with sacred emotion.

When the Revolution of 1848 erupted, Hugo was material in the establishment of the Second Republic but realized too late the ambitions of Louis-Napoléon (*see* Napoléon III), the nephew of Napoléon I, who was elected president of the Republic. In 1851, after the coup which established the Second Empire, Hugo became an exile. The image of Napoléon I evolved again and from that point on, Hugo used it only to contrast the image of the great emperor with that of Napoléon III in *Napoléon le petit*, a poem from his collection *Les Châtiments** (1853). In *L'Expiation*, a poem of 7,000 lines from the same collection, Hugo proclaimed that, for his own coup of the 18 Brumaire and his betrayal of the First French Republic, Napoléon I suffered four successive punishments: his retreat from Russia, his defeat at Waterloo, his martyrdom on Saint-Helena, *and* his being succeeded by Napoléon III. In fact, Hugo did not renounce completely his admiration for Napoléon but turned it into a tool to humiliate Napoléon le petit. Hugo was pained to realize that his powerful vision of the First Empire had perhaps been instrumental in the coming of the Second Empire. For him, this worked as a sort of psychoanalytical rejection; from then on, the Empire was remembered only for the evocation of its glorious but vain slaughters.

In spite of the amnesty of 1859, Hugo remained in Guernsey (*Et s'il n'en reste qu'un je serai celui là!*) and published *La Légende des siècles* (Le cimetière d'Eylau*, 1859) and *Les Misérables* (1862), in which the entire First Book of the second part takes place on the plain of Waterloo, where Marius' father was saved by Thénardier. In this long section, the memory of Napoléon remains only in the harsh reality of the battlefield as it was visited by the narrator himself.

Hugo returned to France in 1870, having become the most popular French icon, but never mentioning Napoléon again.

Napoléon III. Louis-Napoléon (1808–1873), the nephew of the great emperor, had always considered his family to be the rightful heirs to the French throne, and in that quest he attempted a coup in 1836, failed, and was expelled to the United States. A second coup failed in 1840. He was to be jailed, but he escaped to Great Britain where, ironically after the collapse of the Second Empire* in 1870, he would be obliged to spend the rest of his life. After the collapse of the bourgeois monarchy of Louis-Philippe, he won election to the presidency of France, and at first was greeted warmly by liberal thinkers, among them Victor Hugo, who thought they saw in him the implementation of progressive economic and social policies. Napoléon III, however, rapidly evolved into a rightist if benevolent position. The passage of the famous Falloux Act,* which gave special subsidies to private schools, especially the resurgent Catholic schools, was the last straw for Victor Hugo who felt betrayed by the erstwhile liberal. He became for the liberals (Hugo) and the socialists (Pierre Leroux*) the symbol of authoritarianism. Hugo regarded the whole period of the Second Empire as a personal insult, and he refused to return to France when offered amnesty.

Whether or not Napoléon III was the tyrant depicted in the poetry of Hugo and the novels of Emile Zola* is a moot point. Historians are divided; some take Hugo's position, and others see him as a benevolent dictator with progressive ideas to strengthen France economically and technically (for example, the rebuilding of the Right Bank of Paris under the supervision of Baron Georges-Eugène Haussmann), but poor geopolitical decisions which finally led to France's defeat during the Franco-Prussian War. The historical question of the true nature of Napoléon III may never be resolved. He seems to have been a complex, nervous individual who lived in the shadow of his famous uncle. Thus to Hugo, and to Zola, he appeared crafty, furtive, aloof, and uncaring for France—in short, a usurper.

Ninety-three. See *Quatrevingt-treize.*

Nodier, Charles. While regarded today as a minor literary figure of the nineteenth century, Charles Nodier (1780–1844) remains important as an early animator of the Romantic movement. As librarian at the Bibliothèque de l'Arsenal, he held the first Romantic gatherings, starting in 1824, where most of the young Turks, including Victor Hugo, met on a regular basis to discuss the new trends in literature as opposed to the moribund classical tradition. Nodier's own writings are often considered sensational, if not juvenile, but they seem to anticipate the early works of the adolescent Gustave Flaubert.* Without Nodier, however, Hugo would not have had a safe haven to discuss the new ideas spreading across Paris, until, of course, once established, Hugo could hold his own gatherings which, by then, replaced the fervent literary activity of the Bibliothèque de l'Arsenal.

Notre-Dame de Paris. Although the young Victor Hugo had already published much poetry and two rather naive novels, his great success came with *Notre-Dame de Paris* in 1831, which was equaled only by his 1867 *Les Misérables,** considered by some, in spite of its Romanticism, to be the best novel of the nineteenth century. Hugo's humanitarian concerns are evident from his earliest years. Although, on its surface, this novel seems to be a simple Gothic tale, its underlying message is a struggle for goodness and the hope that evil might disappear from the world. Hugo's charity persists despite his revulsion to organized nineteenth-century religion. This fine work, however, centers on Catholicism as embodied in the most important Gothic structure in France. The tale of the scholastic Claude Frollo,* his nephew a student, Esmeralda,* and Quasimodo* remains a Manichean struggle which Hugo, despite his irreligious background, seemed to intuit. Hugo had a sense of the meaning of architecture, hence the structure of this novel, as did Honoré de Balzac* and later Paul Valéry.* It remains one of the most important documents of French Romanticism.

Notre-Dame de Paris **(theatrical adaptations).** Of all of Hugo's novels, *Notre-Dame de Paris,** because of its many "dramatic" scenes or tableaux, such as the festival of the fools, the dangerous scene in the Court of the Miracles for the playwright Pierre Gringoire, and the possibility of crowd scenes in front of the cathedral (anticipating, like Emile Zola,* the collective unanimism of twentieth-century writer Jules Romains, 1885–1972), lends itself most easily to dramatic presentation. Hugo himself was obviously interested in staging this novel since he wrote the libretto for the Esmeralda opera with music composed by his dear friend Louise Bertin (*see* Bertin family).

The first adaptation, made by the actor Dubois, was performed at the Théâtre du Temple on June 1, 1832, just sixteen months after the publication of the novel in two volumes. There was a rather parodic presentation of parts of the novel at the Théâtre Saint-Antoine in 1836 under the title *La Cour des miracles*. This representation did not do justice to Hugo's text; in fact, it seems to have deformed it.

A one-man monologue, entitled *Quasimodo* and written by Alfred Goy, focuses on the plight of Quasimodo* as a human misunderstood and threatened by society. Speaking in perfect alexandrine verses, Quasimodo seems representative of the Romantic outcast, along the lines of Alfred de Musset's* *Fantasio*. These attempts are all almost abortive compared with the work accomplished by Hugo's brother-in-law Paul Foucher in collaboration with a man named Goubaud. Thus, on March 16, 1850, nineteen years after the publication of the novel, the drama *Notre-Dame de Paris*, in five acts with fifteen tableaux, with music by Arthus, was presented at the l'Ambigu-Comique theatre. With the exception of Louis XI, all the personages of the novel are found in this representation. It seems to have been a very successful presentation; according to Théophile Gautier,* *"Tout le côté pittoresque du livre a été transporté au théâtre avec un art merveilleux"* (The entire picturesque aspect of the book has been transported to the theatre with a marvelous art). Gautier's remark, while probably true, should be considered in the context of his exuberant enthusiasm for the new Romantic theatre starting with his Bohemian presence at the premiere of *Hernani*.* The novel is totally respected in this adaptation, the chapters are transformed into tableaux, and the main line of the narrative is faithfully followed. Only Hugo's denouement is radically changed in this production.

In 1879 François Paul Meurice* rearranged the 1850 adaptation and reinstated Hugo's denouement. This time the play was still presented in five acts but with only twelve tableaux. While some literary and dramatic critics might object to the dramaturgical changes, it has to be admitted that the art of the novel is not that of the theatre; each is bound by its own aesthetic integrity. Some novelists and even some playwrights object to either the theatrical transpositions or to the optics of the director and production manager (Jean Genet is a good example of this in the twentieth century). Hugo appeared satisfied, perhaps out of his own ego, with almost any production that brought his work to a larger public. He seems to have been as benign as the twentieth-century playwright Eugène Ionesco* in matters of stage detail. He certainly had to be happy with the 1850 production of his brother-in-law and the 1879 work of his close friend Paul Meurice.

O

Oceano nox. This poem, from *Les Rayons et les ombres** (1840), while partially eclipsed by the more famous *Tristesse d'Olympio** from the same collection, is a nocturnal meditation of the sea which proves that Victor Hugo is absolutely in union with the Romantic sentiment invading England and, above all, Germany. *Oceano nox* (Ocean at night) has the feeling of Caspar David Friedrich's painting of the *Monk at the Sea* and seems to anticipate Gustave Courbet's painting of a premodern, estival scene at Palavas-les Flots, near Montpellier; both paintings record the wonder and amazement at the majesty and mystery of great bodies of water, as does this poem and, for example, Charles Baudelaire's* *L'Homme et la mer*.

This short work starts off appropriately with a temporal consideration. Betrothed women, wives, and widows await the return of men or victims of adventures on the sea. It then moves quickly, in typical Hugolian manner, to an explication of what is seen by the poet who looks at the movement of the waves, the ebb and the tide, but above all, sees the ocean at night. The conclusion is that humans will never understand the sea; in their infirmity, they are but sands upon a nature which remains ever there.

This poem is more tolerant of the human condition than, for example, *Ce qu'on entend sur la montagne*,* a mitigation derived from knowledge of the perils of the sea felt in maritime villages.

Odes et Ballades. The six prefaces to *Odes et Ballades* give us clues as to young Hugo's thinking and its evolution in these first volumes of poetry. At the time of the first collection of *Odes et poésies diverses* of 1822, when Hugo was twenty, we see the stance, with his brother Abel, of militant conservatives allied to the monarchy and to Catholicism. Hugo announced in the 1823 preface a new concept of the ode which will replace the fake colors of pagan mythology with Christian theology. This seems all the more bizarre since Hugo was never baptized as a Christian. It points out, however, how much Hugo is under the influence of both Chateaubriand and of Madame de Staël and of her concepts of Christianity and chivalry, tentatively outlined in *De la littérature* (On literature) of 1800 and amplified in *De l'Allemagne* (On Germany) in 1810. The preface of 1823 also indirectly criticizes atheism and anarchy (as opposed to monarchy?).

The preface of 1824, to the original edition of the *Nouvelles Odes*, brings up, in spite of his denial of it, a discussion of the differences between classicism and Romanticism. Again, Hugo is basing himself in the writings of Madame de Staël, defending the new literature as embedded in the monarchy and religion. Thus he has given a correct interpretation of Madame de Staël's thoughts on these issues.

The preface of 1826 stresses Nature as the poet's only model, and new interpretations of the meaning of ballad are again based on his readings of Madame de Staël, as well as inspiration derived from the epic poems of the pseudo-Ossian James Macpherson and readings in Sir Walter Scott and Goethe.

The preface of 1828 is indeed a conservative interpretation of what is found in the *Préface de Cromwell* (*See Cromwell, Preface to*), with the slogan *La liberté dans l'ordre, la liberté dans l'art* (Liberty in order, liberty in art) which, along with the *Cromwell* preface, indicates Hugo's complete conversion to Romanticism. It should be noted, however, that the nature of this Romanticism will evolve. Slowly it will be released from conservative, monarchical traditions in favor of total liberty in art and politics. Thus, the preface to the Hetzel-Lecou edition of 1853 speaks of changes in attitudes—for Hugo, from royalist to democrat. This last preface admits that the *Odes et Ballades* were the works of a child and an adolescent. The man now knows better, and the fact that the preface is written from his exile is testimony to Hugo's conversion to the liberal camp.

Olympio. Hugo used this fictive name to project his own personality, and usually its amorous side, into his poetry, especially in *Les Voix intérieures** and *Les Rayons et les ombres*.* It is best associated with the romantic liaison with Juliette Drouet as expressed in *Tristesse d'Olympio* (Olympio's sadness) found in *Les Rayons et les ombres*. While it has been suggested that this name could indicate the classical calm which is found in both the heart and mind of those who rise above human agitations, this could hardly be the case in this poem or elsewhere in the emotional lyrics of Hugo. It may have something to do, however, with superiority, suggesting Olympus, dwelling place of the gods.

The name has been considered important enough that Hugo's standard biographer André Maurois so entitled his biography of the writer. In France, fiction and reality intertwine more easily than in other countries. A good example is the legal transformation of the town of Illiers outside Chartres to the hyphenated name Illiers-Combray because Marcel Proust so named his fictive town based on the real Illiers in his *Remembrance of Things Past*.

Orientales, Les. Published in 1829, this work was an immediate success, for Hugo had capitalized upon the vogue of the Orient, what is now called Orientalism,* which was a major aspect of both English and French Romanticism. The collection is divided into thematic parts by which we would number the poems at forty-one; a closer scrutiny, given the nature of Hugo's divisions, would make the total a more likely sixty-two. Most of the poems were written in 1827 and 1828.

Thematically, the poems fit into easily defined categories. There are Biblical echoes, especially the poetic recounting of the destruction of Sodom and Gomorrah, the tower of Babel, the voyeuristic *Sara la baigneuse** (Sara at her bath, number 19), which recalls Alfred de Vigny's* *Suzanna and the Elders* of 1822. Both poems express male romantic ogling. There are Near-Eastern scenes, descriptions of nomads, with depictions of lascivious nude dances: *Les vierges aux seins d'ébène* (Virgins with ebony breasts); *Les hommes, les femmes nues/Se baignaient au gouffre amer* (Men, naked women/bathe in the bitter gulf) (*Le Feu du ciel*, part three). There are descriptions of Egypt, the pyramids, the sphinx, and the Nile and descriptions of harems and intimations of sexual perversions and exotic practices behind the doors of the seraglio.

A major part of the collection is devoted to the Greek wars of independence from Turkey, which had solicited sympathy and aid from several French and English poets, especially Lord Byron,* and from the French government. Major poems in this category are devoted to the Greek hero Kanaris (or Canaris, 1790–1877), a Greek politician and admiral who distinguished himself during the wars of independence. Hugo seems to be a roving Romantic journalist as we read of the fall of Nissolonghi (1825–1826), the city in which Lord Byron died in 1824, and a poem on Navarin, the Greek port where in 1827 French, British, and Russian naval forces decisively defeated the Turkish-Egyptian flotilla. Separated at some distance in the collection is the famous poem of these wars, *L'Enfant,** in which a blue-eyed, blond Greek boy, whom the poet-narrator seeks to comfort, asks only for ammunition to continue the struggle against the massacre of the inhabitants by the Turks in 1822.

The exchanges of cultures, east and west, are noted in many of the poems (Christians made slaves; beautiful Christian maidens brought into captivity). Finally, the scene shifts to Russia with Hugo's poetic interpretation of the myth of Ivan Stepanovich Mazeppa,* the famous Cos-

190   Orientales, Les

sack hetman who, in legend, was tied naked to the back of a stallion which was sent galloping across the steppes of the Ukraine. For Hugo, this was the symbol of genius, but the Mazeppa legend equally interested painters and the English poet Byron.

Finally, without any apparent connection to the themes of *Les Orientales*, Hugo presents his famous poem *Lui*, in praise of Napoléon Bonaparte. Aside from its intrinsic poetic grandeur, the poem is a high point in demonstrating Hugo's evolution away from his anti-Napoléon stance of his royalist days to a position of admiration. It should be added that this admiration will, in later poems, such as *L'Expiation*,* be mitigated by certain historical reservations.

The poems of *Les Orientales* certainly form part of what is called Romantic sensationalism, that is, the shock value: decapitated heads talking, bodies in sacks thrown into the sea from the seraglio, or the Greek boy seeking arms to avenge his people.

It has been said that Parnassian poetry's* movement of objective and descriptive poetry can find its roots in this collection, and this seems to be a proper evaluation. Hugo's power of description had no antecedents at the time, although it must be acknowledged that French Romantic prose, especially that of Chateaubriand, had already developed this technique. This is a question of what is called *faire voir* in French, meaning a seen landscape or figure as opposed to a felt landscape, as in the writings of Jean-Jacques Rousseau. Hugo's descriptions of Near-Eastern cities, of elephants and camels, make him a Leconte de Lisle (head of the Parnassian school of poetry) *avant la lettre*. In fact, it could be speculated that Leconte de Lisle might have found much inspiration in the animal descriptions of *Les Orientales: Et sur les cailloux blancs les écailles crier/Sous le ventre des crocodiles* (And on the white pebbles the scales (of fish) cry out/Under the belly of the crocodiles); *Comme une peau de tigre, au couchant s'allongeait/Le Nil jaune, tâcheté d'îles* (Like a tiger skin, at sunset the Nile/The yellow Nile stretches out/spotted with islands). Poem seven of *Le Feu du ciel*, with its description of two Oriental cities, looks very much like the precise, geometric description of Carthage in the first chapter of Gustave Flaubert's* historical novel of the Punic wars, *Salammbô* (1862).

The painter Eugène Delacroix (1798–1863) found inspiration in Mid-Eastern scenes, and Hugo's poems are a literary transformation of those paintings.

It can be said that, with these poems, Hugo had liberated himself from the classical tinge that covered most, but not all, of the various editions of the *Odes et ballades** of the 1820s. He was on the road to being his own unique master with his own particular structure and style. The revolutionary innovations in both poetic measure and rhyme (a true feat of verbal acrobatics, especially in *Les Djinns** and *Sara la baigneuse*) will be just the beginning of Hugo's mastery of modern poetic form, and will make him the most important poetic innovator of the nineteenth century in France. *Les Orientales* represents the true unlocking of the poetic genius of Hugo.

The two prefaces to *Les Orientales*, January and February 1829, have little bearing on the collection itself. They are especially sarcastic in their treatment of literary critics. The essential idea, also found in the *Préface de Cromwell (see Cromwell, Preface to)*, is that art must have total liberty. In stressing a moral relativism, Hugo informs his readers that art has neither good nor bad subjects, just good and bad poets.

Orientalism. This basically post-enlightenment phenomenon is associated primarily with British and French Romanticism, but also with the imperialistic incursions into the Middle East made by Napoléon's armies and colonization by both the British and the French. Fascination with the Orient is noticed in almost all the major French writers of the nineteenth century. On the one hand, it is the confrontation of two cultures; and on the other, it is an attempt by the Europeans either to impose Western culture on the East or to assess mores and manners in North Africa and Egypt. The vision of the Orient of the writers and painters, a pure product of their minds, had little to do with reality. The English novelist E. M. Forster observed this clash of cultures and hidden hostilities in his famous novel *A Passage to India* (1924). For the first half of the nineteenth century, there is both learned and creative interest in the Middle East. Toward the end of the century, with writers like Pierre Loti, the emphasis will shift to the Far East.

The scholarly endeavors started as early as 1793, as a special *École publique des langues orientales* whose purpose was to teach Arabic, Turkish, and Persian. There quickly developed in the early years of the nineteenth century Orientalists in Paris. One of the most famous was Ernest Renan (1823–1892) whose philological interests in ancient languages partly contributed to his alienation from the Catholicism of his youth. Some of his works, such as *Histoire générale et systèmes comparés des langues sémitiques* (General history and comparative system of semitic languages, 1855) or his *Essai sur l'origine du langue* (Essay on the origin of language, 1858), are keys to a scholarly assessment of the Near East. Renan was the most famous; as the century moved along, scholarship in this area grew by leaps and bounds.

The Romantic writers, however, used the Middle East for different purposes. First, it was used to develop descriptive art, to bring to the French, who had never been across the Mediterranean, some idea of the local color and the exotic geography of the Middle East. This started with Chateaubriand who traveled through Greece, Constantinople, Palestine, and North Africa in preparation for *Itinéraire de Paris à Jérusalem*

(Itinerary from Paris to Jerusalem). After Chateaubriand, the best land-scapist among the writers was Gustave Flaubert* who made the trip to the Orient in the company of Maxime du Camp. Flaubert has left a rich legacy of descriptive materials of the Middle East, and it was there that he honed his visual literary powers. Flaubert had other reasons for going to the Middle East, however, for he was in search of the exotic Oriental woman who haunted his romantic imagination. Upon finding her, he could not bear the crush of cruel reality which did not measure up to his dreams. All the same, the Orient furnished him with the fragrance of the East, especially in the depiction of the heroine of his novel, *Sal-ammbô* (1862). Imagined Near Eastern colors are found in the poetry of Alfred de Vigny,* especially in two poems, *Moïse* (Moses) and *Le Mont des Oliviers* (The Mount of Olives). The Westerner, as voyeur of the Oriental woman, is presented in Théophile Gautier's* *Le Roman de la momie* (The novel of the mummy, 1858). It was left to the late Romantic Pierre Loti (1850–1923) to exploit, in a novelistic manner, both the Near and the Far East. Thus *Azivadé* (1879) is set in Turkey, *Le Roman d'un Spahi* (1881) in Africa, *Jérusalem* (1898) in the Holy Land, *Vers Ispahan* (1904) in Persia, *Madame Chrysanthème* (1887) in Japan, and *Pékin* in China.

It is in the above context that we can place Hugo's participation in the *oriental* mode of the nineteenth century. His very early collection of Oriental poems, *Les Orientales** (1829), is an important contribution to the illusions and fantasies of the French Romantics about the Middle East which they were about to conquer and colonize.

BIBLIOGRAPHY

Said, Edward W. *Orientalism*. New York: Pantheon Books, 1978.

P

Pape, Le. See Pope, The.

Paris. Paris was a political, historic, literary, and aesthetic experience for Victor Hugo, perhaps on the surface less apparent than the Paris found in the *Scenes of Parisian Life* in the novels of Honoré de Balzac,* or in the Parisian meditations found in Charles Baudelaire's* *Les Fleurs du mal* (The Flowers of Evil). It is there, however, in Hugo's work from its first manifestation in his novel *Notre-Dame de Paris** of 1831, and also in its complement, *Les Misérables* (1862). Even without specific topological mention, Paris, especially when confronted with the political and social problems of the nineteenth century, is also present across Hugo's poetry.

Viewed from exile, while writing *Les Misérables* on the Channel Island of Guernsey, Hugo's poetic and visionary imagination had to re-create a Paris he had not seen in many years, just as in *Notre-Dame de Paris* he had to re-create a Paris of the late fifteenth century (1482), first by documentation, then by mounting the towers of the cathedral and conjuring up Paris' Gothic past.

Here, in the sense of the historical novel, he seems to have outdone Sir Walter Scott, both visually (with his solid architectural documentation and synthesis) and psychologically, in his attempt to penetrate the morals and manners of late medieval Paris. Thus, while this popular novel may be evaluated as a work of his youth (Hugo was only thirty when it was published), it has the correct documentation and psychology usually attributed to the practical end of the historical novel in the nineteenth century, namely Flaubert's *Salammbô* (1862), published the same year as *Les Misérables*.

Paris in the thought and work of Hugo properly begins with Book Three, "A Bird's Eye View of Paris" in *Notre-Dame de Paris*, which, when considered with the first chapter on Gothic architecture, successfully interrupts the novel's narrative flow (the dance of Esmeralda,* Quasimodo's* crowning as Pope of the Fools, and Pierre Gringroie's capture and redemption in the Court of Miracles).

The chapter, a view of Paris from the towers of Notre-Dame, combines history, architecture, and certainly poetry in its abundant figurative language. It could also be considered impressionistic in the same sense as Hugo's *Mazeppa* poem from *Les Orientales*.* Paris, viewed from the towers of Notre-Dame, could be considered a nineteenth-century equivalent of any naive view of New York City from either the Empire State Building or the World Trade Center. Any view from such a height is impressionistic and dazzling. Hugo's perspective was to give the reader a sense of Paris as seen from on high.

By following the opening pages of this novel scrupulously, we gain an eclectic fusion of history, poetry, politics, and architecture. Hugo blends the history of Paris (Lutetia) through the Paris of the ramparts of Philip-Augustus. His theme is that Paris cannot be contained by its walls and towers; the city, in a gigantic Gargantuan manner, "Burst its four belts of wall, like a growing child splitting last year's clothes."

The text continues to trace late medieval Paris like a Michelin green guide, frequently contrasting the medieval plan with that of the nineteenth century.

For Victor Hugo, Paris is divided into three parts: the city, the town, and the university, accompanied by poetic subdivisions and additional digressions on student rights and their noisiness within the confines of their forty-two colleges.

Concluding pages return to Hugo's speculations on Parisian architecture, with historical observation and poetic exaltation. Paris is "a full grown forest of spires, bell-turrets, chimneys, weathercocks, winding stairs, lanterns," a kaleidoscope of impressions by which a young Romantic novelist, enamored of the Middle Ages, makes that Paris live again for the modern reader.

These pages also ridicule Paris of the nineteenth century, a city too often torn down, effaced, and destroyed for the Romantic imagination of the young Hugo. Nineteenth-century Paris is not made of stones (endurance), but of plaster. Hugo did not know about plastic. For Hugo, the new church of Sainte-Geneviève is the "finest sponge cake" ever made of stone; the Palace of the Légion d'Honneur is a "distinguished slice of *pâtisserie*"; the towers of Saint-Sulpice are "two huge clarinets."

This is the medieval Parisian nostalgia of the first generation of French Romantics. What remains of the past for Hugo, atop Notre-Dame is, in the manner of Chateaubriand, the symphony of the bells from the towers of the churches of Paris—stone flutes three hundred feet high that turn the city into an orchestra.

This medieval symphony of bells, still heard in the nineteenth century, however, could turn into a "storm," the tocsin (bell of alarm) of revolution, an idea Hugo well understood as he meditated on the events of nineteenth-century France. Neither the Paris of Balzac nor the Paris of Baudelaire, Paris remains a political matter, encased within the Romantic medievalism of his important Gothic novel, which will change in mood during his exile, and after his return to a more modern city which he could only have imagined. The aging Hugo enjoyed riding the new omnibus around town, satisfied with his role as a venerable leader of the Third Republic. The final vision of Hugo is of his triumphal funeral procession which, proceeding from the Arc de Triomphe to the Panthéon, closed his Parisian days.

Parnassian poetry. Poetry in the nineteenth century in France, in traditional literary history, is divided into three distinct movements: Romantic, Parnassian, and symbolist. Such a neat demarcation belies the truth, however, for the movements overlap, and each one contains elements of the other. Victor Hugo, as the main Romantic poet, cannot be confined to the beginning years of Romanticism. His poetry crosses the entire century, but aside from that chronological fact, Parnassian and symbolic intent, even if unconscious, can be discerned in his work.

Parnassian poetry in general corresponds to realism in prose. It is generally seen as a reaction to the overt emotionalism of the Romantics, seeking instead to rival the plastic arts through impersonal descriptions and the recounting of historical periods through an impersonality that hides the personality of the poet. It did not always succeed in this regard. Its main practitioners were Leconte de Lisle (1818–1894), Sully Prudhomme (1839–1907), Théophile Gautier* (1811–1872)—a fervent Romantic with a painter's soul—and the symbolists Paul Verlaine (1844–1896) and Stéphane Mallarmé* (1842–1898), who can be considered originally as Parnassians, having all published in the Lemerre (editor) series of *Le Parnasse contemporain* (1866, 1869, and 1877).

Hugo had much in common with these poets, first by their rigorous attention to the formal aspects of poetry—Hugo was a pastmaster at this—but also by the evocative powers of his descriptive poetry, mainly found, despite a certain Romantic sensationalism, in the 1829 collection *Les Orientales.** Hugo's descriptive powers were not limited to that collection. He was capable of making the objective description across his entire oeuvre, and in this his poetry sometimes rivals the prose of Gustave Flaubert* (1821–1880). Many critics see *Les Orientales* as the precursor to the entire Parnassian movement. Parnassianism, therefore, should not be viewed as diametrically opposed to Romantic poetry; it was an extension of what was incipient in Romanticism.

Pasteurs et troupeaux. *Pasteurs et troupeaux* (Shepherds and flocks), poem twenty-three of Book Five, *En Marche*, of *Les Contemplations,** was dedicated to Louise Colet, his correspondent and mail delivery service in Normandy. This poem, one of Hugo's most lyrical expressions since the events of the exile and Léopoldine Hugo's* death, captures the imagination of all lovers of poetry, and indeed it shows the greatness of Hugo's poetic insights. A forty-six-line pastoral with its contrasting images of the Corbiere lighthouse on Jersey, this poem is a tribute to Hugo's contemplative seizing of the inner workings between the heart and the outside forces that could disturb it. Such seem to be the antithetical images found in this work.

Shepherds and Flocks illustrates the dangers near and around a peaceful nature, an Eden not to be disturbed by political or geological events. The stagnant or quiet pond of Part One of the poem seems safe enough, even though it makes Pascalian waves for a passing ant; nevertheless, the ocean, filled with unknown dangers, is unfortunately just over the horizon. The poem makes two parallel constructions which focus on the young girl tending her sheep and goats, without hearing the fearsome shepherd, the great shepherd, *pâtre promontoire* (the sea-cliff shepherd) roaring at his ocean flock. He alone knows the meaning of the sea wind which scatters *La laine des moutons sinistres de la mer* (the mysterious wool of the sheep of the sea): actually enormous puffs of foam from the crashing waves.

Patriotism. Hugo was a patriot, albeit with a new twist, fashioned from the events of the French Revolution and the phenomenon of Napoléon Bonaparte.*

The patriotic poems of *Les Châtiments*,* an invective against what he saw as the rape of France by Napoléon III,* can also be counterpointed with the viewpoints expressed in his revolutionary novel *Les Misérables** (1862). This is evidenced above all in the evolution of the political thought of the character Marius,* a corollary to the street urchin Gavroche, the radical child, the new France about to be born out of the winds of revolution. Hugo's own patriotic and even socialist stance finds its fictional representation in the serious turnabout of Marius in Book Sixteen, chapter 6 of *Les Misérables*—his own conversion from the royalist position of 1814 to that of a liberal, if not a revolutionary.

Like Hugo, Marius is able to look beyond the personal defects of Napoléon to glimpse his prophetic and symbolic role as the messenger of a new France, a new nationalism indeed born of 1789, which Bonaparte spread to the rest of Europe, precipitating and abetting German and Italian unification. Hugo, as narrator, sums up Marius' new ideology: "Where he had formerly seen the fall of the monarchy, he now saw the rise of France . . . what had been the setting was now the rising of the sun" (*Les Misérables*, p. 634).

The political conversion of Hugo (Marius) is not unlike the recognition by the good bishop of Digne, Myriel, that the remarks of the old Conventioner "G"* (Book One, chapter 10,) on the excesses of the ancien régime which find their purgation or expiation in the retributions of the revolution.

Hugo is a new patriot, and his work represents a new model as much in contrast with the old regime as classicism and Romanticism.

Pauvres gens, Les. From the first series of *La Légende des siècles,** *Les pauvres gens* (Poor people) enjoyed enormous popularity in its day and with reason, for, again, it showed Hugo's enormous charity and compassion for the oppressed of the earth. Dating from 1854, it was obviously written during the Channel Islands exile, which partially explains the hallucinatory attraction of the ocean for Hugo.

Victor Hugo will remain one of the most difficult of French writers to understand. He seems torn between many mediums or genres to be a poet, a novelist, a playwright. In this poem, divided into ten narrative sections, there is poetry, but there is also a story, the story of poor people. While it may appear to some modern readers to be overly sentimental (Hugo, like the other Romantics, is frequently that), it all the same concentrates on the problem of poverty, an issue that finds redress in both French and English literature of the nineteenth century.

The narrative sequence is simple. Jeannie, the heroine, is married to a fisherman. They have five children, but next to nothing to live on. He has gone to sea, and she worries about her husband's fate. The little details found within the poem suggest that this could have been a short story; for example, the narrator's camera focusing on the fish soup she is preparing: *Surveillant l'âtre où bout la soupe de poisson* (keeping an eye on the hearth where the fish soup is cooking). She dreams about her husband while he, at sea, thinks about her: a vision of conjugal love surviving amidst their poverty.

Part Four is important in presenting a motif found elsewhere in Hugo's maritime works, namely the fear of the chaos of the ocean. Both the sea and the coastal landscape are presented in an expressionistic manner (*see* Expressionism), quite similar to what will be found in *Les Travailleurs de la mer** and *L'Homme qui rit.**

Worried, the wife leaves the house and passes by the hovel of a neighbor, a poor widow with two children. She knocks at the door but receives no response; the poet notes that the door *s'ouvrit d'elle-même* (the door opened itself), a sign perhaps of divine intervention. Finding the widow dead, Jeannie takes the two infants to her own home. The husband returns, without any catch. Learning that they now have seven instead of five children, he accepts this responsibility with the ease of only the truly poor.

This poetic narrative reinforces Hugo's overwhelming concern with the plight of the poor. Once a week on Guernsey, he offered a splendid meal to the poor children of the island. Lack of the fundamentals of living inundates his work, especially in *Les Misérables*.* A similar sentiment is expressed in the poem *Le Mendiant** (The beggar) from *Les Contemplations** (Book Five, poem nine), in which the poet-narrator brings a poor old man suffering from cold and hunger into his room, and then discovers that the beggar might be Christ in disguise or, more simply put, poverty as a sign of high spirituality. A similar sentiment is found in a sonnet of Charles Baudelaire,* *La Mort des pauvres* (The death of the poor) from *Les Fleurs du mal*, in which he, perhaps the most effete poet of nineteenth-century France (equaled only by Oscar Wilde in England), recognizes the relationship among virtue, sanctity, and poverty.

Les pauvres gens belongs to a section of *La Légende des siècles* called *Maintenant* (Nowadays), perhaps proving that the nineteenth century's humanitarianism is situated in the poor people.

Pavie, Victor. This provincial Romantic, through an initial and very positive review of Hugo's *Odes et Ballades** in a local journal in Angers, caught the attention of Hugo, who wrote to thank him. Thus began a correspondence which led to an intimate friendship when the two met in 1827. It was through Pavie that Hugo met the sculptor David d'Angers.*

Pavie can be considered among a group of fervent young admirers of the new direction Hugo was giving to French letters. For him, Hugo could do no wrong; consequently, we see him writing panegyrics about *Les Orientales*.* He was also a fervent defender of *Hernani** with which Romanticism was to triumph.

Pavie quickly penetrated the Parisian circle of Romanticism, finding himself included in the Hugo circle. He also developed a correspondence and friendship with Charles-Augustin Sainte-Beuve* whom he even advised, without success, to reconcile himself with the Hugos.

BIBLIOGRAPHY

Pavie, Théodore. *Victor Pavie, sa jeunesse, ses relations littéraires*. Anger, France: P. Lachese et Dolbeau, 1887.

Peace conference in Lausanne. Between September 13 and 18, 1869, a peace conference was held in Lausanne, Switzerland, to which Hugo was invited and at which he became one of the main directors. His visit there coincided with the crumbling of the Second Empire* which became apparent in his address to the congress. The nervous Napoléon III,* now proclaiming himself a liberal, had again offered amnesty to Hugo, who rejected it with a barb from his play *Cromwell**: *Allez, je vous fais grâce. Et de quel droit tyran?* (Come on now, I pardon you. And by what authority, tyrant?). If Hugo's tone at the conference was especially belligerent, it was because he knew what was happening in France, and he knew that Napoléon III's hour was drawing to a close. His main theme, however, which again proves how prophetic he could be, was his reference to the United States of Europe, a political theme that ran throughout the exile and thereafter. Hugo dreamed of a Europe united, and in typical nineteenth-century, anticlerical fashion, this Europe would be freed from the domination of the papacy.

Pécopin and Bauldour, The legend of. The legend of Pécopin and Bauldour is one of the more interesting aspects of Victor Hugo's so-called letters to a friend describing his Rhine Valley trip. There were two trips: one in 1838 with Juliette Drouet, and another in 1840 (*Le Rhin,** 1842). In letter twenty-one, the legend of Pécopin and Bauldour is found. Many of the legends found in *Le Rhin* certainly were derived from Hugo's scanning of German sources, such as Schreiber's *Le Rhin et la Forêt Noire* (The Rhine and the Black Forest) and other available German sources concerning popular and oral traditions.

While the legend of Pécopin and Bauldour may indeed be an authentic German tale, it reflects, all the same, in both style and orientation the hand of Hugo. He obviously did not invent the legend, but he did embellish it.

The fact that Germany inherited the courtly materials of Provence either directly or through their presence in northern France, as well as the Celtic materials which were fused with the Provençal courtly love tradition, may explain what appear to be purely French materials in this legend. This must be in part the inheritance from the minnesinger, the German poet-musicians of the twelfth and thirteenth century whose materials may have drifted downward to form part of the popular tradition. Much of the material found in the legend of Pécopin and Bauldour certainly echoes back to the twelfth-century tradition of the *merveilleux* (the marvelous, the fantastic), as found in the poem-novels of Chrétien de Troyes and the lays of Marie de France, as well as the popular *romans d'aventures* (adventure novels), all dating from the twelfth century. The *romans d'aventure* is represented in France by the Byzantine tale *Aucassin et Nicolette*, an early thirteenth-century *chantefable*. In fact, it is to this French tale that the legend of Pécopin and Bauldour most closely adheres.

In *Aucassin et Nicolette*, the lovers, one Christian and the other a converted Muslim, are imprisoned, manage to escape, and, after many adventures including a shipwreck, finally are reunited. The source, as in another French legend of that time, *Floire et Blancheflor*, finds its source in Moorish and Greco-Byzantine materials.

The happy ending, however, of *Aucassin et Nicolette* is unfortunately missing from this Germanic tale. While the German legend bears the mark of complementary psychological balancings and strict stylistic symmetries (as found, for example in the nineteenth-century play of Alfred de Musset,* *On ne badine pas avec l'amour*, 1834), the German legend ends on a pitiful and fantastic note. The opening paragraph of letter twenty-one sets the tone of harmonies and complementarities: *Le beau Pécopin aimait la belle Bauldour, et la belle Bauldour aimait le beau Pécopin* (Handsome Pécopin loved beautiful Bauldour, and beautiful Bauldour loved handsome Pécopin); that is, beauty attracts beauty.

So the legend starts, but there are multiple complications. Pécopin's love of the hunt vies with his love for Bauldour and ultimately brings to an end what should have been a beautiful romance. Pécopin embarks on a series of adventures beginning with an encounter with talking trees and birds. After becoming a good friend to a prince, he accepts the position of envoy to Dijon in Burgundy, where his favor there sends him as envoy to Paris, then to Spain, and finally to Baghdad.

There he is befriended by a beautiful harem lady who hands him a talisman against death and old age, and he survives a push from a tower by the sultan and many an adventure with the devil (perhaps the most important Germanic element in this legend) who goes about collecting souls in his sack, even seeking the help of some saints who are strolling by the Red Sea. Pécopin becomes, indeed, not a knight errant, but, as Hugo calls him in chapter 8 (one of nineteen long chapters), the "wandering Christian," which brings to mind the novel of Eugène Sue (1804–1857), *The Wandering Jew*, published in 1844–1845, two years after the publication of Hugo's *Le Rhin*.

Pécopin's final adventure in the forest of lost steps is the longest and most fantastic. A midnight hunt is arranged by an old chevalier (the devil in disguise) who promises to return Pécopin to Bauldour after this five-year absence. An eerie scene, filled with goblins, dwarves, and a chilling atmosphere, leads to a banquet of the dead (and of those not yet born whose portraits all the same adorn the walls of the castle), all of whom disappear with the morning light. When he returns to Bauldour's castle, he finds an old woman, over one hundred years old, who turns out to be the waiting Bauldour. More time had passed than Pécopin had realized. In horror, he runs from the castle and strips off his finery. He loses his talisman in the water, and immediately he becomes an old man, close to death.

While Hugo called this his *conte bleu* or fairy tale, it obviously contains elements that would not be found within the French tradition, in spite of Hugo's own personal touch to the telling. While filled with the fantastic, it has no character depth whatever; in fact, Pécopin at times appears to be a simpleton. French fairy tales up to the present have psychological qualities, for example, those found in the stories of Maurice Maeterlinck (1862–1949), such as *The Blue Bird* (1908), or even Emile Zola's* sentimental novel *Le Rêve*, placed within the midst of the twenty naturalistic volumes of his *Rougon-Macquart* series.

This legend seems to have struck a chord in Hugo's heart, or at least it stimulated his pensive considerations of the Germanic character, and it did lead, with his approval, to a theatrical representation entitled *Le Ciel et l'enfer* (Heaven and hell*).

Periodicals, Romantic and classicist. To understand Victor Hugo's role in the formation and definition of Romanticism, it is necessary to review the role of literary and political journals of the 1820s.

To the modern mind, a presupposition would be that the Romantic movement and Hugo represented from the outset a modern and liberal point of view in politics and literature. Hugo of the 1820s was still in a period of intellectual evolution, his mind firmly set in traditional royalist and Catholic views, and his model was Chateaubriand (1768–1848); he aspired to be his literary disciple. The liberal viewpoint was represented by those who still had their mind-set in the eighteenth century. Only the end of the 1820s would resolve the question of Romanticism's modernity. It is then that the old eighteenth-century liberals, adhering to a moribund classicism, would have to relent to the new Romanticism as signaled in the triumph of Hugo's *Hernani** in 1830.

LE CONSERVATEUR

Founded in 1818 by Chateaubriand and others, *Le Conservateur* was the organ of the ultraroyalist party, ruefully trying to restore a prerevolutionary France, without, however, any association with the deism or pantheism of the eighteenth century. Chateaubriand's desire was clear, the establishment of a royalist and Catholic France. This point of view represented the young Hugo for about ten years.

LA MINERVE FRANÇAISE

This classical, liberal periodical was replaced by *La Minerve Littéraire*, and then by *Abeille*. This periodical is important in understanding the political nature of early Romanticism pitting Victor Hugo and the new royalists and conservatives, as Romantics, against the liberal classic heir of the eighteenth century.

LE CONSERVATEUR LITTÉRAIRE

Founded by Hugo and his brothers, this ultraconservative periodical was fashioned as a continuation of Chateaubriand's *Le Conservateur*.

Hugo, who was seventeen at the time, provided most of the articles, under pseudonyms; in a period of sixteen months, about 120 articles and 22 poems. His virtuosity can be compared only with that of Arthur Rimbaud at the end of the nineteenth century. Hugo controlled both Greek and Latin, had a good acquaintance with foreign literatures, and demonstrated an almost total disrespect for the eighteenth century (later to be repudiated), especially for Voltaire.

LA MUSE FRANÇAISE*

This review, the successor to *Le Conservateur Littéraire*, was founded in 1823 by Hugo, Sonnet, Emile Deschamps, Alfred de Vigny,* etc. It lasted until 1824 and published poems and articles by Hugo about Walter Scott and Byron.

BIBLIOGRAPHY

Hatin, Louis Eugène. *Bibliographie historique et critique de la presse périodique française*. Paris: Firmin-Didot frères, fils et cie, 1866.
Romantisme: Textes des petits romantiques/pamphlets/études. Geneva, Switzerland: Slatkine Reprints, 1973.

Phoebus de Chateaupers. This important, if minor personage in *Notre-Dame de Paris** is engaged to Fleur-de-lys. At the same time, he has an adventure with Esmeralda,* which leads to an encounter with the obsessed priest Claude Frollo,* who stabs him. Phoebus, captain of the archers, seems to cross class lines, as often happens in amorous inclinations. In the novel, he regains his health, forgets Esmeralda, and marries Fleur-de-lys. In the libretto of *La Esmeralda,* before expiring, he comes to the defense of Esmeralda and makes accusations against Frollo.

Pierrot. Pierrot is the slave name of the African prince Bug-Jargal,* hero of Hugo's novel *Bug-Jargal** of 1826.

Pinson, Albert. Adèle Hugo, daughter of Adèle and Victor Hugo, met this English military officer in 1854, and she met him again during her father's exile on the Channel Island of Guernsey. Already of a highly nervous disposition and inclined to severe depressions, Adèle became convinced that she was first engaged, and then married, to Pinson. Her obsession with this English officer led her to follow him to Canada, and then to the Caribbean. He was indeed a man stalked. While he had at first indicated some sentimental interest in Adèle, he had other things on his mind, including his military career and his own wife. His rejection or indifference certainly contributed to Adèle's mental derangement.

Pitié suprême, La. The title of this long epic and philosophical poem, *La Pitié suprême*, almost defies translation into English. It concerns, however, Hugo's deep and abiding virtue concerning all types of human persecution. Hugo was strongly opposed, from his earliest years, to capital punishment,* for whatever reason. Evident in such an early text as *Le Dernier Jour d'un condamné*,* it is fittingly expressed in *La Pitié suprême*, composed in 1857 but published twenty-one years later in 1878. Hugo had a way of pulling old documents out of his literary closet, for reasons unknown, perhaps financial. All the same, *La Pitié suprême* is high evidence of Hugo's enormous compassion for his fellow man. While Hugo remains a riddle to those inclined to make either-or judgments, this work, combined with *Les Misérables*,* among other aesthetic documents, attests to the total Hugo: a man of enormous sensuality, sexuality, and spirituality. Poem fourteen of this collection, on the martyrdom of the reformer Jan Hus,* is noteworthy in Hugo's visionary meditation on the tragic mistakes found in human history.

Place de Grève. Since 1830 the Place de Grève has been the site of the Hôtel de Ville, the city hall of Paris, and most Parisians have not forgotten that it was once a place of horrible executions, especially as recounted in Hugo's text *Le Dernier Jour d'un condamné*.* The beheadings that took place there perversely excited the crowd of people who gathered to witness them (this type of scene is typical of modern French literature, starting with Romanticism, which accentuates a taste for blood and gore). As recounted by Hugo, the executions were frequently, if not always, very cruel. The preface of the *Last Day of a Condemned Man* underlines this fact as Hugo recounts the abortive beheading of a criminal whose head is not totally severed, but who walks about with his head hanging half off; several repeats of the same operation were required to complete the beheading. Hugo witnessed executions, and it was from his youth that his obstinate opposition to capital punishment* stemmed. The Place de Grève also figures prominently in *Notre-Dame de Paris*.* With the revolution of 1830 the Place de Grève was transformed into a symbol of liberty. By 1854 Georges-Eugène Haussmann, the architect of modern Paris, quadrupled the space in front of the city hall. Thus disappeared from the sight of Parisians the place where the horrors had occurred for so long. Gavroche, the street urchin of *Les Misérables*, with his mocking spirit, refers to this place of executions as the best spectacle in Paris: *Pas de fête qui vaille la Grève* (Nothing like the Grève area for a good time).

Place des Vosges. Hugo's home at no. 6 Place des Vosges, in the Marais district of Paris from 1832 to 1848, was designated in 1902, the year of the centenary celebration of Victor Hugo's birth,* to become a museum and center of research. Today it is an important archival center and museum where visitors can view the Hugo apartments and furnishings. The residence is filled with portraits and mementos of Hugo and his family. The library, dedicated to scholars working on Victor Hugo, is a sizeable and well-maintained center for research and documentation. It and Hauteville House on the island of Guernsey were left to the city of Paris. The museum in Hugo's house opened in 1903, thanks to the generous donations made by Hugo's friend and executor, François Paul Meurice.* Hauteville House, at no. 38 Hauteville Street, is also a museum.

Since 1903 there have been eight directors or superintendents of these two establishments. Thanks to the work of Professor Henri Cazavmayou, we have a complete list of the curators of Place des Vosges and Hauteville House:

1903–1912: Louis Koch and codirector Eugène Planès

1912–1914: Eugène Planès

1914–1932: Raymond Escholier (perhaps into 1933; one of the pioneer biographers of Hugo, see: *La Vie Glorieuse de Victor Hugo*, Paris, 1928)

1934–1942: Paul Souchon

1942–1960: Jean Sergent

1960–1979: Martine Ecalle

1980–1995: Henri Cazavmayou

1996–   : Danielle Molinari

The work at both houses is no easy sinecure. It involves frequent trips to the Channel Islands for negotiations and discussions with the bailiff of Guernsey, for, although the property is legally possessed by the municipality of Paris, it is, all the same, located within the United Kingdom with the very special legal status of the Channel Islands which, while under British control and protection, have their own legal prerogatives. In Paris the work is even more considerable. In addition to the maintenance of the museum living quarters of the Hugo family, there is also a large library of primary and secondary materials requiring the presence of a full-time librarian and secretarial help. Number 6 Place des Vosges, in the fourth *arrondissement* of Paris, is directly under the control of the municipal director of Parisian cultural affairs.

Poems, early (Found in private collections). Not all of Hugo's poetry can be found in published form, in his *cahiers*, or in his manuscripts in his possession. It is for this reason that Pierre Albouy published, in the Pléiade edition of 1964, eight poems under the rubric *Pièces ne figurant pas dans les trois cahiers*. The source is the scholar Canon Venzac. Of the poems, five were unedited (see Venzac, *Origines religieuses de Victor Hugo*). Albouy's critical edition includes six poems which had already been published. The poem dedicated to Madame La Générale Lucotte was published in *La Revue hebdomadaire* on February 14, 1914, by Louis Barthou with the title, *Victor Hugo à douze ans*. The second poem, untitled, is from the collection of Pierre Duché, an homage to a certain wise gentleman of Clermont. The third piece is from the archives of the marquis de Montferrier (descendant of Julie Duvidal de Montferrier,* who married Hugo's brother Abel). The poem honors a royalist hero whose identity can only be guessed. The fourth poem, *Sur Glycère*, which is eight lines long, was found at the end of the manuscript of the comic opera *A quelque chose hasard est bon* (For something chance is good), dating from 1817. It was published in the edition of the Imprimerie nationale in its sixth volume of Hugo's theatre in 1934. The sixth poem, *Dialogue entre le drapeau et la girouette* (Dialogue between the flag and the weathervane) was published for the first time in the 1964 Pléiade edition of Albouy. It is an interesting conceit: the weathervane speaks of the messages brought to it by the wind, a wind which the flag regrets for it has been torn apart by it. The poem puts in opposition classical antiquity and the Bourbon fleur-de-lys. The seventh poem is a fragment of the young Hugo's tribute to the general of royalist sympathies, who was allied with General Lahorie, the friend and lover of Hugo's mother. This fragment, which was first published in the catalogue of the library of Louis Barthou, dates from either 1820 or 1821. The final poem is *A Gaspard de Pons*. De Pons was a friend of Alfred de Vigny,* who introduced him to Hugo. The poem dates from 1820.

This rapid survey indicates that these poems, found in diverse collections and published in various works over a period of time, reflect Hugo's early royalist sympathies and his desire to ennoble his friends to posterity. They were all published after Hugo's death.

Poésie pure. *Poésie pure*, or pure poetry, a concept usually associated with symbolism,* a movement at the end of the nineteenth century in France, is manifest chiefly in the work of Paul Verlaine (impressionistic symbolism), Arthur Rimbaud, Stéphane Mallarmé, and Paul Valéry. Its chief literary exponent was Henri Bremond (1865–1933) whose revolutionary work *La Poésie pure* (Pure poetry) of 1926 instigated an enormous literary debate between those who believed in a rational basis beneath each poem—with the formula, *pensée* (thought) and then *idée* (idea)—as opposed to *idée* followed by *pensée*. That is, the poem could be returned to the world of rational discourse through the interpretation of the critic, usually defined by the French term *explication de texte* (textual explanation).

The idea of pure poetry could be considered rare except in the case of the highly hermetic (recondite) poems of Rimbaud and Mallarmé. Even Valéry seems, at times, in great poems like *Le Cimetière marin* (Cemetery by the sea), to mix rational discursive, almost Cartesian elements, with lines of pure poetry which cannot be reduced to discursive significance.

Pure poetry means ridding poetic language of, or abolishing, discursive elements that relate back to rational discourse, making the words have other than communicative meaning—that is to say, a prose statement on which action can be taken, for example: "Go to the store and buy five pounds of potatoes" or "The class will begin promptly at three o'clock."

The abbé Bremond would maintain that a proper reading of a poem does not demand from the reader a seizing of the poem's sense in terms of its *langue* (tongue): *pour lire un poème comme il faut, je veux dire poétiquement, il ne suffit pas, et, d'ailleurs, il n'est pas toujours nécessaire d'en saisir le sens* (to properly read a poem, I mean poetically, it is insufficient and hardly ever necessary to get its rational submeaning) (*Poésie pure*, 1926, 18). For Bremond, pure poetry means *poésie/musique* (poetry / music), not *poésie/raison* (poetry / reason). That is the poem can be apprehended rather than comprehended.

By citing examples from the ancient classical writers, then from the writers of seventeenth-century France, and on to the poetic production of the nineteenth century, Bremond made a convincing case. For example, taking a famous line from Jean Racine's *Phèdre* (1677), wherein Phèdre is described as *la fille de Minos et de Pasiphaë*, Bremond (p. 336) refutes the argument of those in favor of rational interpretation who say that the line is meaningless to those who do not know who Phèdre's parents were. The line wins out by its pure musicality; it is an abstraction that does not rely upon reason. In addition, it could be added that, unlike Racine, who knew his Greek mythology inside out, the seventeenth-century audience did not have this knowledge, but all the same they reacted to the line, moved by its sonority.

Bremond offers a striking example from Hugo—*L'Ombre était nuptiale, auguste et solennelle* (The shadow was nuptial, majestic and solemn, p. 54)—to affirm that poetry is an idiom separated from all others: *où les mots, à travers leurs sens usuels, révèlent un sens nouveau, inédit, supérieur, surnaturel et nécessaire* (In which the words, across their usual meaning, reveal a new meaning, unedited, superior, supernatural and necessary).

Not all critics would agree with Bremond's enthusiastic defense of pure poetry. His case, however, remains reasonable, and it should be considered in relationship to the development of Romantic symbolism, especially in Hugo's poetry. More modern critics follow in the path established by the abbé Bremond, among them Alfred Glauser, Helmut Hatzfeld, and Wylie Sypher.

Glauser sees deep pure poetry in process in the idea of *gouffre* (abyss), a motif that crosses many of Hugo's poems: "With Hugo you have to pass through step by step the trip to the abyss [not unlike a trip through a Dantean purgatory or hell], frightening! cavern after cavern! obscure beehive of evil, crime and remorse." *Gouffre* becomes a symbolic whole from which all discursiveness has been eliminated, making of the poem a highly symbolic or pure poetry structure (Glauser, 1957, 55–56). Glauser affirms that the quest of the dead Léopoldine Hugo* gives birth to a similar process. (Jean Gaudon's work on *Les Contemplations** would not be in total agreement; he regards the Léopoldine motif as a starting point.) Glauser writes that the tomb is not in the church yard at Villequier, but in the father's chest. Thus the quest of Léopoldine is the means of arriving at great poetry:

When we listen to Hugo talking with the abyss, throwing himself into it, weeping for his daughter, looking everywhere for her, sobbing on his fate as an outlaw [meaning alienation from normal paternal affectivity] we can say that it is the poet [and not the father] who has intensified the suffering, these sentiments out of which come high sonorous poetic lines. (Glauser, 129–130)

Helmut Hatzfeld, in his *Literature through Art*, notes similar pure poetry aspects in Hugo's poems, including *La Conscience*,* based on the text of Gen. 4:13–24, in which the eye of God is the leitmotif, piercing all of Cain's hideouts and accusing him relentlessly of having killed his brother Abel (Hatzfeld, 1952, 149), and *Saison de semailles* in which the old sower, as twilight turns into night, is turned into a sower *sub specie aeternitatis* (Hatzfeld, 156).

Wylie Sypher has noticed similar trends in the nineteenth century in which Romanticism, led by Hugo, tried to turn itself into high pure poetry.

A close reading of Hugo's poetry by any sensitive reader could add multiple examples, such as the *Mazeppa* poem from *Les Orientales*,* which certainly anticipates the symbolic processes of Rimbaud; *Booz endormi** from *La Légende des siècles*,* a motif that traces the founding of the tree of David and leads to the birth of Christ; or simply the opening and closing *Pegasus* poems of *Les Chansons des rues et des bois*.*

BIBLIOGRAPHY

Bremond, Henri. *La poésie pure*. Paris: Grasset, 1926.
Glauser, Alfred. *Hugo et la Poésie pure*. Geneva, Switzerland: Droz, 1957.
Hatzfeld, Helmut. *Literature through Art*. Chapel Hill: University of North Carolina Press, 1952.
Sypher, Wylie. *Rococo to Cubism in Art and Literature*. New York: Random House, 1960.

Poetry, nineteenth century. When measuring Victor Hugo's poetry against the principal poetic movements of the nineteenth century in

France, namely Romantic, Parnassian, and symbolist, it is not difficult to understand how, despite the obvious faults in an overly productive literary life, Hugo remains the greatest of modern French poets.

Hugo is seen within the general cadre of the Romantics: first, Alphonse de Lamartine,* then Hugo's fellow poet Alfred de Vigny,* and finally the so-called spoiled child of French Romanticism, Alfred de Musset.* Hugo supersedes these well-known Romantics by the scope of his work and by his growing control of metrics.

After the great success of his *Méditations poétiques* and other elegies, Lamartine lapsed into long, somewhat tedious poetic and prose works, leaving behind his early, if passive, interest in man's fate (his attraction and repulsion to the work of Lord Byron*) and his Romantic religiosity, to become involved in political issues to the extent of entering the presidential elections of 1848 against Napoléon III.* Alfred de Vigny's limited poetic career, narrow in outlook and limited in productivity, came to a halt perhaps due to illness and concern for the hypochondria of his English wife, Lydia Bunbury. Musset has been aptly called a poetaster, whose high emotionalism overwhelmed his ability to master his verse form. Musset is the only Romantic poet given no esteem by the symbolist Arthur Rimbaud. Across the Romantic years, only Hugo demonstrates evolutionary thought and mastery of form, the latter perhaps a result of his classical education.

Yet, within the corpus of Hugo's poetic production, one which spans the century, we see the seeds of all the poetic propensities of the nineteenth century. It is with good reason that some critics regard Hugo's *Les Orientales** (1829) as the rockbed of the Parnassian movement despite its Romantic sensationalism and political fervor (the Greek wars of independence against Turkey). This collection shows Hugo to have been a master of poetic form, with rich rhymes anticipating the impressionistic symbolism of Paul Verlaine (see *Sara la baigneuse**), or with a verbal virtuosity anticipating the cubist efforts of Guillaume Apollinaire at the beginning of the twentieth century (see *Les Djinns,** a poem whose very form resembles a whirlwind, with the visual aspect of a tornado; this poem of fifteen strophes goes from two-syllable verse, to three, four, five, six, eight, ten, then with decreasing syllable count back to the original two, creating the form of a twister).

At the same time, samples of Hugo's poetry across the century show penchants for symbolism, as will be found in the poetry of Rimbaud and Stéphane Mallarmé.* The famous *Mazeppa* poem from *Les Orientales* is an example; its kaleidoscopic, impressionistic interpretation of the ride across the steppes of Russia of the hetman bound naked to the back of a wild stallion certainly anticipates Rimbaud's *Bateau ivre*. Without knowing it, Hugo, in some manner unknown to the conscious Romantic mentality, announced the symbolism of the late 1880s and 1890s. He sounded the depths sought by Rimbaud and Mallarmé, and many astute pieces of Hugolian criticism recognize this. This is especially clear in the poetry of exile, even in the satirical pieces of *Les Châtiments,** and also in the deeply meditative poems of *Les Contemplations** (see the Verlainian *La Fête chez Thérèse,** *Le Rouet d'Omphale Eglogue, La Statue, Magnitudo parvi;** Je payai le pêcheur qui passa son chemin,** Pasteurs et troupeaux,** O Strophe du poëte, autrefois, dans les fleurs*). Yet, what is observed in the latter collections, is present in the earlier ones. Thus, poem thirty-six, *La Statue,* of *Les Rayons et les ombres** (1840) seems Mallarméan in intent if not in form; while Ode eight of Book Four, *Odes et ballades**, with its ennui motif, anticipates Charles Baudelaire's* *Je suis comme le roi d'un pays pluvieux.*

The greatness of Victor Hugo resides in his ability not to be restricted by the neat divisions of a simplistic literary history. It is incorrect, for example, to see in Mallarmé a progression away from lyricism (*Brise marine*) to the highly symbolic sonnet sequences of his maturity. The lyric mode is inherent even in the symbolic. The same may be said of Victor Hugo. Deep metaphysical poetics do not preclude the lyric spirit. Poetry sings at many levels. It is for this reason that Hugo, indeed, incorporated the evident poetic trends of the nineteenth century which are too easily divided into chronological developments called Romantic, Parnassian, and symbolist.

Political life of Hugo. It is a recognizable aspect of Victor Hugo's life, as the most important writer of France in the nineteenth century, that he not only led a revolution in poetry, drama, and the new novelistic genre of sociological humanitarianism (*Les Misérables** and even the earlier *Notre-Dame de Paris**), but that he was also a public figure, both in literature and in politics. He thus fulfilled the existential promise of Jean-Paul Sartre* that the artist must be dedicated to the national commonweal. In this, he was engaged both literarily and politically, a trait that seems to characterize many French writers; Emile Zola* is an outstanding nineteenth-century example, and Sartre himself in the twentieth century. This sets Hugo apart from the nonpolitical stance of the eminent writer Gustave Flaubert,* who refused to become involved in politics, as has Alain Robbe-Grillet in the twentieth century, who writes in the objective and disinterested style of the so-called new novel (*nouveau roman*).

Hugo was an ambitious person; he wanted to be part of the nineteenth-century Parisian scene. To that end, he pursued election to the prestigious French Academy (*see* Académie Française and Victor Hugo), to which he finally won election in 1841. He actively pursued a political career and served as a member of the Chamber of Peers in 1845 and 1848. The declaration of the Second Republic saw him as a deputy for Paris in the Constituent Assembly, and then in the legislative house. His increasingly liberal views led him at first to support Louis-Napoléon (*see* Napoléon III) whom he saw as a leader with progressive views; he was quickly disenchanted by the supporting of the pope against the Italian republicans and by the passage of the Falloux Act* (still on the books in France), which gave state subsidies to private, mainly Catholic, educational systems.

With the coup d'état of December 1851, he first fled to Brussels, and then to the Channel Islands of Jersey and Guernsey, where he remained in defiant exile until the overthrow of the Second Empire* after the Franco-Prussian War. He returned to Paris, in 1870, where he was met at the train station by Judith Gautier,* the daughter of the eminent admirer of Hugo, Théophile Gautier,* himself one of the most important of the *Jeune France* (Young France) movement of early Romanticism. The relationship with the young Judith seems equivocal if one reads between the lines of the standard biographies. She seems to have been part of his perpetual "womanizing" endeavors.

The period of exile gave Hugo a lot of time to meditate, as well as bitterly reflect, on the reasons for it. In this vein, Hugo published several important works critical of Napoléon III: *Napoléon le petit* and *Histoire d'un crime* (The story of a crime), a minute and scrupulous recording of the new Bonaparte's usurpation of power. (Similar sentiments are found in Zola's twenty-volume study of the Second Empire, *Les Rougon-Macquart*.)

The proclamation of the Third Republic returned Hugo to the National Assembly, but after the suppression of the Paris commune, with which he was liberally sympathetic, he was again back in exile in Brussels, thus continuing the tradition of political protest dating back to Voltaire, and continuing in the twentieth century with the left wing and Left Bank radical politics of Jean-Paul Sartre and Simone de Beauvoir.

It should be recalled that, at this time, Hugo was an old man by nineteenth-century standards, and his whole life had been beset by personal tragedies. His last days were marked by the deaths of his sons Charles, in 1871, and François-Victor, in 1873. His ever-faithful companion Juliette Drouet died in 1883.

In his final years, Hugo withdrew from public life and turned inward to the hearth bestowed upon him by his grandchildren, Jeanne and Georges, who became the subjects of his final lyrical output, *L'Art d'être grand-père** (The art of being a grandfather), in 1877.

Victor Hugo, like Zola and Sartre, was heir to the antiestablishment tradition of Voltaire. He was honest till the end in his commitment for the French principles of Liberty, Equality, and Fraternity. While perhaps best remembered as the greatest and most prolific of the French writers of the nineteenth century, his political involvement is an abiding aspect of his personality.

Ponto. Ponto was Victor Hugo's frequent companion on his walks on the island of Jersey, and he is the subject of a poem with this title in Book Five, *En Marche*, of *Les Contemplations*.* Although the dog did not belong to Hugo, he showed up from time to time to accompany him. What is striking in this poem is the poet's meditation on crimes recorded across history. For the poet, the dog Ponto has made the better choice: better to be an animal than a vile human being. Hugo well understood that animals* follow their nature entirely and are incapable of sin or misdeeds, despite a tendency in puppyhood to mischievousness: *Le chien, c'est la vertu/Qui, ne pouvant se faire homme, s'est faite bête./Et Ponto me regarde avec son oeil honnête* (The dog is virtue/which unable to be man, becomes an animal/And Ponto looks at me with his honest eye).

August Vacquerie* gave some details about Ponto, a black Spaniel, which led to a discussion of the privileged position of animals in relationship to God. Vacquerie went on to explain that dogs, through their courage, devotion, and intelligence are superior to humankind. While this may seem anthropomorphic or even sentimental to the modern reader, it is important in understanding Hugo's theosophy. He believed in the immortality of all life. In respect to animals, he is more akin to the theology of the Franciscan Duns Scotus, than to that of the Dominican Thomas Aquinas who reserved immortality for human beings. Pierre Albouy indicated, in his notes to *Les Contemplations*, that one year before he wrote this poem, Hugo had denounced the decadence of Roman morality and had exalted the virtues of the lion of Androcles in *La Légende des siècles*.* Hugo may have believed in communication with him during the experiments in spiritism* conducted on Jersey. He concluded not only that animals have souls, but also that God allows himself to be perceived by them. Herein lies the importance of the Ponto poem and related poems on animal life in Hugo's poetry.

BIBLIOGRAPHY

Victor Hugo, Oeuvres poétiques. Vol. 2, *Les Châtiments, Les Contemplations*. Edited and annotated by Pierre Albouy. Paris Gallimard, 1967.

Pope, The. Hugo's anti-papacy statement, in poetic form, was published in 1878. It is conciliatory in intent, trying to find a model for a spiritual leader whom he did not see anywhere in evidence in Rome. He proposes a model of the ideal pope, somewhat along the lines of the benign Bishop Myriel in *Les Misérables*. Such a spiritual father would be the opposite of the dogmatic types who dominated nineteenth-century Catholicism, a true father to the poor, a humble defender of humanity.

Hugo's poem should be evaluated in terms of the tensions between Rome and the rest of Europe in the nineteenth century. The rise of Italian nationalism, personally embodied for Hugo in his friend Guiseppe Garibaldi,* perhaps the most important leader of the Italian struggles for unification, was opposed, of course, by the papacy which wished to maintain its control over Rome. The first Vatican council (1869–1870) may have also been in his thoughts, especially with its extraordinary definition of papal infallibility, an insult not only to other Christian communities, but also even to skeptics who might have hoped for more from Rome.

It is coincidental, perhaps even providential, that the very year of Hugo's anti-Vatican poem was, in fact, the year of the installation of Pope Leo XIII (1878–1903) who might have embodied, through his social teachings (*Rerum novarum*, 1891), the humanistic principles Hugo sought in such a man as Bishop Myriel. It is possible that Hugo's 1862 text could have been prophetic or at least convincing to reform-minded Catholics of that time. Hugo's concern about the humanistic mission of the church was shared by many Romantic writers, including Father Lacordaire; Jules Michelet, the Romantic historian, and, above all, Félicité de Lamennais,* the priest who brought Hugo back to Catholicism. Lamennais, however, after unsuccessfully trying to marry Catholicism with social progress, abandoned the faith, and even at his death refused its last rites. Such was the turbulence of orthodoxy in the nineteenth century.

Leo XIII would have been a good role model for the church that Hugo sought, as would have been Pope John XXIII whose short reign ushered in breezes of social and liturgical reform that are still being experienced today. Hugo would have been pleased with both of these pioneering pontiffs. It is to be regretted that he seems to have said nothing about Leo XIII. The poem was published just two months after the elevation of perhaps the first modern pope, whose concern for justice and pity certainly coincided with that of Hugo, especially as clarified in the personage of Bishop Myriel of *Les Misérables*.

Pradier, Claire. Claire Pradier (1826–1846) was the daughter of Juliette Drouet and the then famous sculptor Jean-Jacques (called James) Pradier (1792–1852) at whose studio many writers of the Romantic generation met. Juliette was the model of the statue Strasbourg which can be found on the Place de la Concorde in Paris and Claire died at the age of twenty, soon after Léopoldine Hugo,* the daughter of Victor Hugo, died by drowning. In a sense, Hugo became Claire Pradier's father figure; he saw to her education, upbringing, and affairs, which were ignored by the sculptor who had become too important in official society to be concerned about his child. Hugo, at great personal risk of dishonor, given his illicit and well-known relationships with women other than his wife, was all the same the principal mourner at Claire's interment in the cemetery of Saint-Mandé. His own personal grief over the death of Léopoldine was only augmented by young Claire's demise, Juliette's only child.

This sorrow received great Romantic elegiac expression in poem eight of Book Six of *Les Contemplations** (*Au bord de l'infini*), dedicated to Claire.

This poem expresses typical nineteenth-century confusion about things eschatalogical, such as turning dead children, especially little girls, into flying angels who look down upon earth where those who remain continue to engage in their physical embraces. Despite its length (forty-two verses composed of four lines) and its rhetorical appeal to nineteenth-century propriety, the poem is a homily, funeral oration. Nonetheless, heartfelt grief similar to that found in Hugo's greater and shorter poems, such as *Demain, dès l'aube*,* does break through. The elegy dedicated to Juliette Drouet's child has practically the same substance as the well-known *A Villequier** (forty verses), in which the father hopes for some sort of resurrection of dead children. Victor Hugo's eclectic theology is derived from grief and not from books, and the lyrical spirit of this work was meant to comfort Juliette Drouet, and himself. Leaving aside nineteenth-century platitudes, no reader can fail to be moved by such lines as *Quoi donc! la vôtre suit la mienne!* (What now, yours also, follows mine), its opening line, mingled with Hugo's abiding joy at looking at the pure innocence that he finds in the mien of children.

Préface de Cromwell, La. See *Cromwell, Preface to*.

Puisque j'ai mis ma levre à ta coupe encore pleine. This five-strophe poem, included in *Les Chants du crépuscule* (1835), written at 12:30 A.M. on January 1, 1885, is a passionate love note to Hugo's mistress Juliette Drouet. *Puisque j'ai mis ma levre à ta coupe encore plein* (Since my lips touched your still full cup) adroitly combines elements of spiritual and physical love, as understood by both of them, neither of whom share the bad Catholic conscience of Charles Baudelaire* with his bifurcation of mankind into two distinct entities: one spiritual and the other carnal, which is his idea of *homo duplex* as expressed in *Les Fleurs du mal* (The flowers of evil). Hugo's love poem supports fundamental psychologies found, not only in his poetry, but also in his prose, his commentaries to Juliette, and also in her own recorded beliefs on what love should be about. The physical-spiritual union expressed in *Puisque j'ai mis ma levre* can be seen as a French equivalent of what the Browning couple express in nineteenth-century English poetry.

The poem is a Romantic syllogism, with an affirmation opening the first three verses, *puisque* (since or because) with the *ergo* (therefore) response to time in the two concluding verses, that nothing can destroy a love that will remain eternal. Hugo used a similar linguistic formula in the poignant *A Villequier** (*Les Contemplations**) but for reasons leading not to happiness but sorrow (the death of Léopoldine Hugo*).

Critics who have noticed the less-than-spiritual intent of the poem's vocabulary have concluded that the so-called spiritual nature of the love is but a veil for highly charged sexual innuendo. While this may be so, for Hugo's physical appetites were not minimal, it would be incorrect to minimize the importance that he and Juliette Drouet gave to deep psychological commitments of persons who have pledged themselves to each other, despite the many falls from grace recorded across the Hugo biography.

This poem was written just about two years after the beginning of Hugo's liaison with Juliette. Hugo had first glimpsed her at a ball in 1832 and was immediately struck by her beauty, but he did not dare to speak to her. The first meeting took place during readings for Hugo's play *Lucrèce Borgia** and continued during rehearsals until the play was performed at the Théâtre Port-Saint-Martin in 1835. Juliette played the very small role of Princess Negroni. It was not long before they became lovers.

Biographical documentation indicates that Juliette Drouet was ready for something more than an endless succession of lovers interested only in her body. As for Hugo, given the end of passionate conjugality with his wife Adèle, he too was ready for an intense and abiding passion. When Juliette's lover, Alphonse Karr, suggested some initiations into more nuanced sexual practices, she wrote to him the following: "It seems to me that my soul has desires just as does my body, even a thousand times more ardent. . . . You give me pleasures followed by exhaustion and shame. My dream, on the other hand, is a calm and harmonious happiness. Hear me well for I am too proud to lie; I will leave you, I shall abandon you, the earth and life itself if I find a man who can caress my soul as you like to caress my body" (Escholier, 1953, 137–38).

Likewise, an entry made at a later date by Hugo in Juliette's diary reflects the spiritual resurrection this new love was giving to the poet—prose which, in many ways, seems to paraphrase parts of the poem: "The day your eyes met mine for the first time, a ray of light went from your heart into mine much like dawn glistening over a ruin" (Maurois, 1956, 172). In the poem we read, *Ta bouche sur ma bouche et tes yeux sur mes yeux* (Your mouth on my mouth and your eyes on my eyes) and *Puisque j'ai vu briller sur ma tête ravie/Un rayon de ton astre* (Because I saw shining on my enraptured head/a beam from your star), an emotional affirmation that fixes itself semantically in the aesthetics of the poem.

Victor Hugo is hardly Manichean, nor is Drouet. Hugo wants to marry the physical and the spiritual, heaven and earth, as later, romantically, he will want to redeem supreme evil, absolve Satan, and undo the fall (see *Ce que dit la bouche d'ombre* at the conclusion of *Les Contemplations*).

BIBLIOGRAPHY

Escholier, Raymond. *Un Amant de génie: Victor Hugo*. Paris: Fayard, 1953.
Maurois, André. *Olympio: The Life of Victor Hugo*. Translated by Gerard Hopkins. New York: Harper and Brothers, 1956.

Q

Quasimodo. In the liturgical calendar, Quasimodo literally refers to the first Sunday after Easter. In Hugo's novel *Notre-Dame de Paris*,* Quasimodo is the name of the mute and deformed adopted son of the sensual priest Claude Frollo* whom Quasimodo obeys without hesitation. As the bellringer of the cathedral he has visual insights into medieval Paris, and a sensitivity that only a Romantic writer such as Hugo could give to an extraordinary combination of the sublime and the grotesque. Intuiting Frollo's betrayal of Esmeralda,* he throws the apostate priest from one of the towers of Notre-Dame. In a popular American film, the *Hunchback of Notre-Dame*, the film reproduced the intent of Hugo's first, most famous novel. The character's name is a spiritual insight by Hugo who had some sense of the benign hidden under deformity.

Quatrevingt-treize. Quatrevingt-treize (Ninety-three), the last novel published by Victor Hugo, was written in 1872–1873 and published in 1874. The title suggests that the novel concerns the Reign of Terror (September 5, 1793–July 27, 1794) as it is found in Charles Dickens's *A Tale of Two Cities* (1859) or in Anatole France's *Les Dieux ont soif* (The Thirst of the Gods, 1912); however, it concentrates instead on the counterrevolution or the civil war in the Vendée, undertaken by those forces loyal to throne and church. While the action, description, and portraits permit the work to be classified as a historical novel in the tradition of Sir Walter Scott, the heavy ideological sentiments of the characters and the narrator (Hugo) would also allow this work to be considered a philosophical and psychological interpretation of the French Revolution, the work of the Convention, and the Reign of Terror.

  The three main characters, turned into symbolic representations, are the vehicles by which contrasting points of view on the revolution are expounded. The portrait of Cimourdain, the ex-priest and now the representative of the committee on public safety in the Vendée (portrait of Cimourdain, Part Two, chapter 2), is a concise drawing of a benevolent but implacable intellectual revolutionary whose sense of the justice and mission of the revolution is absolute. A contrary but equally absolutistic perspective is that of the novel's antihero, the marquis de Lantenac, defender of the rights of the monarchy, of tradition, and the heroic ancestry of the Breton nobles. In between these two is found the vicomte de Gauvain, a republican but also the grandnephew of Lantenac, who represents the human and idealistic revolution—what Hugo himself reads into its events.

Hugo's position is not ambivalent, but he does have reservations about revolutionary excesses. Thus the Convention that sent Louis XVI to the guillotine (executed June 21, 1795) and caused the arrest of about 300,000 people and the execution of 17,000 had, for Hugo, a positive aspect. Of the 11,210 decrees of the Convention, only one-third had political goals; the other two-thirds were humanitarian and progressive in nature. For Hugo, the "wind" of the Convention was coming from the mouths of the people; he also saw it as providential, being inspired by God. So viewed, Hugo's historical meditation seems to be stressing the purgative necessity of the revolution. There is a sense of a spiritual and historical inevitability, perhaps akin to the forces unleashed by the Protestant Reformation of the sixteenth century.

Hugo's attitude, however, is less judgmental and certainly more poetic than that of Thomas Carlyle in his *The French Revolution* whose three volumes, *The Bastille*, *The Constitution*, and *The Guillotine*, cover the events in France from 1774 through 1795. Carlyle saw in the French Revolution the judgment of God upon the monarchy and nobility. Hugo would concede this, but less vociferously. His views on capital punishment* put him in opposition to the guillotine, viewed here (Part Three, chapter 6), as in many of Hugo's poems, as a vicious instrument of destruction. Hugo's attitude is that of his young hero Gauvain.

Gauvain, after freeing his great uncle the marquis de Lantenac from his prison cell, takes his place and goes forth to receive his own death warrant delivered by his tutor and spiritual father, Cimourdain. His last words, *Vive la République* (Long live the Republic), may be recalled by the final words of the hero of Herman Melville's *Billy Budd* (1924), "God bless Captain Vere!" In both cases, what is being expressed is death with honor for innocent and pure spirits. *Quatrevingt-treize* is a novel that places honor above all other sentiments. It is the world of Romantic absolutism, whether it is of the classic variety, found in the theatre of Pierre Corneille (*Le Cid*, 1636; *Polyeucte*, 1641), or in the works of Hugo, many of whose protagonists work out their destinies based on absolute standards of conduct and morality (*Hernani*,* 1830), ignoring or even defying common sense, practicality, or reasonability.

The entire novel is framed by the story of Michelle Flechard whose children are held hostage by the royalists. An act of generosity on the part of the marquis de Lantenac, which saves the lives of the three children from the burning *La Tourgue*, ensures his imprisonment until he is released by the vicomte de Gauvain (a decision based on Gauvain's Romantic ruminations on the meanings of family, ancestry, royalty, and revolution, in Part Three, chapter 2, "Gauvain pensif").

Among the novel's peregrinations should be mentioned the meeting in the cabaret on the rue du Paon (Book Two, chapters 1 and 2) of Jean-Paul Marat, Robespierre, and Georges-Jacques Danton, a structure that recalls that in *Ruy Blas** (act 2, scenes 1 and 2) of 1838, with Cimourdain of *Quatrevingt-treize* duplicating the intervention of Ruy Blas in the Council of Ministers. Both scenes stress political motives and objectives.

The novel, therefore, plays back and forth between Paris and Brittany, with most of the narrative focusing on the royalist insurrection. Paris in *Quatrevingt-treize* serves as the backdrop and catalyst for the action in the Vendée, with the added substratum of Gothic novel details (hidden escape passages through moving walls, underground hiding spaces) and local color elements concerning nature and the character of the peasants, above all their superstitions. The novel neatly places Hugo in the liberal camp. He approved of the events of the revolution and, to a lesser degree, the supposedly preordained happenings of the Reign of Terror.

Quatrevingt-treize (theatrical adaptation). Hugo's 1874 novel of the events of 1793 (the Reign of Terror, in which most of the action does not take place in Paris) was prepared for the theatre by Hugo's friend François Paul Meurice* and performed on December 24, 1881, with Hugo present in the audience. What is particularly striking about this adaptation is Meurice's fidelity to Hugo's novelistic text. The play, divided into four acts and twelve tableaux that are identical with certain chapters of the novel, relies heavily on Hugo's original dialogues or on his narrative sequences.

Reaction to the play depended upon political leanings. Thus the conservatives disliked its reminders of the events of 1793; the Third Republic found in it a confirmation of its liberal principles, albeit bourgeois in nature.

While most of the roles, those of Cimourdain, Lantenac, Gauvain, and Radoub remain faithful to the original novel, several new personages, including Jean Mathier, Bapaume, and Dorothée, were added.

The play continues to have success in the twentieth century. André-Léonard Antoine (1858–1943), inventor of the new French realism at the end of the nineteenth century, formed a touring group in 1914, but the play was suppressed by official censorship. In 1921 A. Capellani directed a film based on the novel, and in 1935 H. Cain wrote an opera with music by C. Silver. There was a popular presentation in 1959 in the Indre department; in 1962 a television adaptation was made by C. Santelli and A. Boudet; and another performance was mounted in Brittany at the Chateau de Fougères, directed by M. Philippe, in 1979.

Of all Hugo's novels that were adapted to the theatre, *Quatrevingt-treize** has been almost as successful as the adaptations of *Notre-Dame de Paris** and *Les Misérables*.

R

Rabbe, Alphonse. Alphonse Rabbe, the French critic and historian (1786–1829), was a great friend of Victor Hugo especially in their common defense of liberal politics. Rabbe died on December 29, 1829, from an overdose of laudanum (a derivative of opium) which he was applying as a poultice to his face to counteract the effects of syphilis, which had horribly deformed him. His suffering partially explains his misanthropy and his isolation from society (much like that of Rémy de Gourmont who was disfigured by lupus).

Rabbe was extremely erudite as demonstrated in his *Résumé de l'histoire d'Espagne* which Pierre Albouy wryly remarks could hardly be called a résumé since it is 512 pages long (*Victor Hugo, Oeuvres poétiques*, vol. 1, *Avant l'exil 1802–1851*, Edition de la Pléiade, Paris, Gallimard, 1964, p. 1449). Rabbe's best-known work *L'Album d'un pessimiste* (1835, re-edited in 1924 by Jules Marsan in the *Bibliothèque romantique*), was preceded in the 1835 edition by the poem that is found in *Les Chants du crépuscule,** poem seventeen, *A Alphonse Rabbe*. In the tradition of *Les Chants*, the poem is excessively long and digressive (122 lines), but all the same contains a touching couplet at its beginning, used again as a concluding refrain: *Hélas! que fais-tu donc, ô Rabbe, ô mon ami,/ Sévère historien dans la tombe endormi* (Alas, what are you doing now, o Rabbe, my friend,/Severe historian asleep in the tomb).

Rachel, Elisa Félix. One of the greatest French actresses of the nineteenth century, Rachel (1820–1858) is best known for her interpretations, during her short life, of French classical roles in the plays of Pierre Corneille and Jean Racine. She did, however, do contemporary works of Alexandre Dumas *père*, Alfred de Musset,* and Victor Hugo, and she seems to have incited, somewhat, the jealousy of Juliette Drouet.

Rask. Rask, Bug-Jargal's* dog in Hugo's novel *Bug-Jargal,** is a *dogue*, or mastiff. When Bug-Jargal rescues Captain d'Auverney's* fiancée from certain death at the hands of the rebelling slaves, the dog carries the youngest child of Marie's decimated family to safety. He proves to be a mirror image of his master, instinctively knowing what to do to save the day. He can be considered the humanitarian equivalent of Hugo's meta-physical dog Ponto* found in a poem in *Les Contemplations.** After the death of Bug-Jargal, Rask goes to France with Captain d'Auverney and dies with him in battle.

Rayons et les ombres, Les. Volume 4, the last of the volumes of the July Monarchy, is considered by some critics to be Hugo's best lyrical work before the exile. Others might argue that the collection continues in the same vein as the previous ones, with some notable changes in emphasis. The collection is longer than the other three preceding ones, forty-four entries.

The preface to *Les Rayons et les ombres* (Light and shadows), of 1840, is within the tradition of Hugo's dialectical argumentation. Among its many theses are the role of the poet as the defender of liberty, conse-quently the political role of the engaged poet. It contains an argument on the nature of theatre, the novel, and poetry. The spirit of man is reduced to three elements: namely, *savoir*, to know; *penser*, to think; and *rêver*, to dream. *Tout est là* (Everything is found therein).

A thematic review of the collection reveals no major shift in Hugo's scale, but there is a change of emphasis. The political poems, more nu-merous, stress the relationship between poet and society. A theme first encountered in the first book of the *Odes et Ballades** is reintroduced with vigor. In *Fonction du poète* (poem one), the poet takes responsibility for reacting and judging political acts. He cannot run away from contem-porary problems because he prepares the way to a future of progress, and in his function, he must condemn those who abuse the social struc-ture with no interest in the commonweal. Poem two, a specific illustra-tion of the poet's moral responsibility, speaks to the censorship of his play *Marion de Lorme.** The scene painted therein, Hugo's interview with King Charles X (including a description of the room in which Hugo was received), seems more appropriate for a prose essay (in the tradition of Alfred de Vigny's* *Servitude et grandeur militaire*, 1835). Poem three, com-prising four lines, is a typical Hugo statement against capital punish-ment.* At least six of the poems can be classified exclusively as political in nature. Other themes, such as Hugo's affection and sympathy for the honest poor—expressed in poem four, *Regard jeté dans une mansarde* (A glance into an attic window), can be seen as a proletarian lyric in the age where atelier production will soon be ushering in the Industrial Rev-olution. There are also six poems to Juliette Drouet, as well as the usual apostrophe of nature, nine in number, and a bittersweet recall of child-hood in all its forms, especially his own in the Feuillantines* garden.

There are new emphases, however. Man's fallen nature is stressed in poem ten. While man, in the manner of Charles Baudelaire,* looks ide-alistically toward the sky, he is all the same bogged down in snake-filled mud. The theme of man's imprisonment or confinement, which will run across *Les Contemplations*,* is presented in a haunting manner in *Puits de l'Inde! tombeaux* (poem thirteen). The idea of vaults, wells, dampness, hollowness, grottoes, crypts, and tombs will be more fully developed in *Pleurs dans la nuit* of *Les Contemplations*.

The most important development, thematically, however, is that of Hugo's religious thought. Two antithetical tendencies are noted: first, Hugo's desire to believe, almost in an orthodox sense; and second, his inability to do so and his move toward rebellion and revolt. Hugo is plainly on the road to developing his own metaphysics. These are per-haps the most important poems of the collection as Hugo seeks a balance in all serious matters. The concluding poem *Sagesse* relies upon Louise Bertin's (*see* Bertin family) common sense to guide the poet away from extremes. Poems twenty-five, *Que la musique date du seizième siècle* (That music dates from the sixteenth century), and twenty-six, *La Statue*, show a new profundity in the nature of the aesthetic experience, the first an-ticipating Baudelaire; the second, with its image of the faun as the statue yet to be called to life, anticipating Stéphane Mallarmé. The boundaries between dream and reality are becoming clearer to the reader yet more blurred to Hugo.

The collection contains some of the most popular of Hugo's poems, among which should be mentioned *Caeruleum mare* (poem forty); *Oceano nox** (forty-two), which stresses the perils of the sea, sentimental perhaps to all save those who lived in nineteenth-century fishermen's villages; and *Tristesse d'Olympio*,* Hugo's search for relics of love in the Vallée de Bièvre.* This poem is in the tradition of the souvenir poems so popular with Romanticism, namely *Le Lac* of Alphonse de Lamartine* and *Sou-venir* of Alfred de Musset.* Hugo's poem differs significantly from that of Lamartine in its specific physical details, which make of the liaison with Juliette Drouet one of an adulterous nature. Lamartine's experience with Madame Charles may have been the same, but the neoclassic lan-guage of Lamartine keeps his poem within the Petrarchian tradition. Fur-thermore, *Tristesse d'Olympio* is so long, thirty-eight strophes in all, that school editions have frequently expunged whole sections, mainly phil-osophic, from their texts, with no apparent damage to the integrity of the work. This perhaps confirms the feeling that Hugo would have done well to temper his lyrical impulse. Finally, while we can read *Les Rayons et les ombres* within the context of the three previous volumes, we must all the same note evolutionary processes, especially in the areas of political engagement and religious fervor. Control of metrics also seems to be announcing the poet of exile.

Religion and Victor Hugo. Victor Hugo came out of an eighteenth-century tradition of disbelief or indifference to orthodoxy. It would seem that he had never been baptized, and whatever flirtation he had with French Roman Catholicism, especially under the influence of Félicité de Lamennais* and Charles-Forbes-René, Comte de Montalambert, was not of long duration. He had hoped, as did many of the early Romantics, that there could be a marriage between the Church and the liberal march toward progress. In this he was sorely disappointed, and as time passed he moved more and more into a profound meditation on the nature of man's spiritual quest in which he elaborated a personal theology, sometimes hard to comprehend, and which is best expressed in the concluding poem of *Les Contemplations*: *Ce que dit la bouche d'ombre.**

Hugo's spiritism* was derived from grief over the drowning death of his daughter Léopoldine Hugo,* and it led to the holding of séances at his home in exile on the island of Jersey. Nevertheless, vestiges of a Catholic cultural heritage remained in his poetry and novels, and in his letters. Hugo may be considered the cultural Catholic, as Joseph Ernest Renan would later in the century describe the exodus from the Church by the Romantics. His position and that of the other young Romantics, a generation called *La Jeune France*, is aptly described by Charles-Augustin Sainte-Beuve*: "In France we shall remain Catholic long after stopping to be Christians." Hugo combined, in what may seem to be a very modern manner, eroticism and belief in the afterlife. He was a sort of Manichean; he saw a duel between good and evil in this world, and in the one out of sight. He prayed constantly, had enormous charity toward the poor and the suffering, and left a great sum of money to the poor upon his death. He epitomizes the nineteenth-century drift away from established religion, a trend that continued until the Catholic revival first seen in France in the writings of the poet Charles Baudelaire,* and in England with the work of the Irish poet Oscar Wilde, as well as that of Cardinal Newman.

Religions et religion. This long-winded philosophical, theological, and historical poem (fifteen hundred lines), started in 1870 and finished in 1880, was published in 1880, five years before Hugo's death. The religious question seems to have become more acute for Hugo as he approached the end of his life, and he became more vitriolic in his opposition to institutional religions. This certainly went beyond normal French anticlericalism; it betrays an exasperation with simplistic dogmatic modes which, for Hugo, derail man's quest of the absolute. This certainly must have been true for the Gallican church of the nineteenth century with its emphasis on devotionalism, its quasi-superstitious practices, a church filled with threats of eternal damnation. Hugo does not believe in a theology of damnation as can be seen in his redemptive poem *Ce que dit la bouche d'ombre** from *Les Contemplations*,* in which Satan and Jesus Christ walk hand in hand to the throne of the Godhead, or in the complementary poem *La Fin de Satan*,* published after the poet's death, in 1886. Both works deny the Manichean principle of an eternal opposition between good and evil. The Romantics redeemed Lucifer, starting first with Alfred de Vigny's* best theological narrative poem *Eloa* (1824). The influence of de Vigny on Hugo's religious speculations is apparent. They were close friends. In fact, de Vigny was Hugo's best man at Hugo's marriage to Adèle Foucher in the church of Saint Sulpice in 1822.

Most of *Religions et Religion* is dedicated to a well-deserved denunciation of the contradictory notions and frequent repressions brought about through religious systems. There follows a brief consideration of agnosticism and atheism, both of which are rejected by the poet who concludes with an absolute affirmation of the existence of God, which is perhaps best perceived by observing God's creation: humankind, animals, and nature. Firm belief in God's existence is thus divorced in Hugo's thinking from organized religious systems. It cannot be called deistic, in the sense of Voltaire's cynical thought on such matters, but it is certainly allied to the pantheism found in the writings of Jean-Jacques Rousseau, especially in his *Rêveries du promeneur solitaire* (Reveries of a solitary wanderer, 1781–1788) and in the *Profession de foi du vicaire savoyard* (Profession of faith of a Savoyard vicar), derived from his *Emile* (1762).

Hugo's thoughts in this poetic treatise, although published during the twilight of French Romanticism, reflect the same basic natural Romantic idea of religion, derived from Rousseau certainly, and reflected in many Romantic works such as Alfred de Musset's* *Confessions of a Child of the Century*, or even in the work of the arch-Catholic Chateaubriand, who marries Catholicism and pantheism in his short and exotic novels of the New World, *Atala* and *René*.

Research on Hugo. In Paris there is an avid monthly meeting of Hugo scholars, formally known as the *Groupe interuniversitaire de travail sur Victor Hugo* (Interuniversity research group on Victor Hugo), which now meets at Jussieu, on the campus of the University of Paris 7 (also called the University Denis Diderot). This monthly meeting, which began in 1969, was founded by the eminent Hugo scholar and editor of the Pléiade editions, Pierre Albouy, who was then a professor of French literature at the Sorbonne.

After Albouy retired, he was succeeded as head of the *Groupe Hugo* by Professor Jacques Seebacher, who, after the student uprisings of 1968, preferred to establish himself at the University of Paris 7. Upon Seebacher's retirement, Professor Guy Rosa became the new head of the group.

The Parisian Hugo scholars, of diverse political opinions, have formalized their activities to a certain degree and could be considered the equivalent of an academy, albeit a minor one. It is through their efforts that there has been a coordination of biographical and bibliographical activity, especially at the newly created branches of the University of Paris. Furthermore, they have been responsible for establishing the Bouquins edition of the works of Hugo, which takes its rightful place next to formal editions which can be found in the Bibliography of this encyclopedia.

Revenant, Le. In its day, *Le Revenant* (The ghost), (Book Three, poem twenty-three, *Les Luttes et les rêves* of *Les Contemplations**), was one of the most popular poems from this collection. It is not from the highest levels of verse. All the same, it claims our attention for three good reasons.

First, it continues Hugo's exploitation of the poem as narrative, vying in some ways with the novel. In this case, it is the question of a young couple's delight in watching their young boy grow up, walk, start to talk at age three, but then to die from croup, a common childhood malady in the nineteenth century—a realistic detail in the midst of a sentimental Romantic poem.

Second, the poem explores the idea of metempsychosis (reincarnation), which ranks with other medical and spiritual fancies rampant in the nineteenth century, such as phrenology (Honoré de Balzac*), spontaneous combustion (Charles Dickens and Emile Zola*), and medium contacts with the nether world (Hugo). The realism of the young couple's successful procreation of a second child is turned into a Romantic mysticism in which the newborn whispers to the mother: *C'est moi. Ne le dis pas* (It's me, don't tell anyone). The dead child is thus reborn in a delayed transmigration of souls.

Third, in spite of what may be considered bad theology or pseudoscience, the poem poignantly reflects the reality of infant mortality in the nineteenth century, and any evaluation of it should be mitigated by a pondering of the medical problems, such as cholera and croup, that plagued the progressive nineteenth century.

Rhin, Le. *Le Rhin* (The Rhine) is a collection of travel documents, written on site by Hugo, in the form of letters to his family. Hugo had made a first trip in 1838 with Juliette Drouet to eastern France; another in 1839, again with Juliette, first to Strasbourg and then to Switzerland. A final trip was made in 1840, and the impressions and letters from these trips form the voluminous volumes called *Le Rhin*, published in 1845. Some readers may find it boring, but it is not far from the quality of Gustave Flaubert's* *Par les Champs et par les grèves* (Through fields and beaches), describing a walking trip Flaubert made with his friend Maxime du Camp, in which each wrote alternating chapters, in 1847, while traveling along the Loire and the coast of Brittany.

Le Rhin is noteworthy for two reasons: first, it shows Hugo's attachment to and fascination with Germany, which has something to do with his own northern genealogy, and second, his desire to see Germany and France as sister states, complementing each other and wedded to the meanderings of the Rhine river which is the central organizing principle of a rather boring personal journal. *The Rhine* is filled with observations, mainly of the architecture of cathedrals, but also with anecdotes that clearly reveal that Hugo had more of a sense of humor than we ordinarily expect from the French Romantic writers. In classic Romantic fashion, like Madame de Staël, he is fascinated by ruins, by the contrasts of old places destroyed, and their modern ugly counterparts, a sentiment also expressed by Flaubert in his first *Sentimental Education* (1845).

The itinerary sometimes looks like a dry Fodor or Michelin guide to interesting spots in eastern France, Switzerland, and Germany. Hugo's visit to Aix-la-Chapelle, modern day Aaachen, near the Belgian and Dutch borders, acknowledges in a curt and dry manner the origins there of Charlemagne, without capturing the spirit of the opening lines in assonance of Charles' long siege of the Saracens in Spain, and his longing to return to Aix-la-Chapelle. Surprisingly, Hugo as a Romantic did not pick up on this obvious theme.

Against this Romantic complaint against the destruction of the past is found, however, the love that Hugo had for walking through unknown territories. This he does, with some degree of success, anticipating the gypsy itinerary of Arthur Rimbaud as found in his charming poem *Ma Bohème*. Hugo was always a walker and this becomes a behavioral personality trait found in his biography as well as in his fiction.

His visit to Worms could have concentrated more on the presence of Martin Luther. The work's long "conclusion" is typical of Hugo's attempts at syntheses, not unlike that found in the prefaces to his historical dramas (*Hernani,** *Ruy Blas,** or *Les Burgraves**). It has the form of a historical lecture given by a professor of modern European history.

Hugo's Romantic spirit appears in a minor key in this work. The reader senses his strong affinity for the relationship between France and Germany, France being, as he implies but does not state, the most Germanic of the Latin countries. He sees the Rhine River as a flowing liquid of reconciliation and harmony, anticipating the European union which is just beginning at the end of the twentieth century, under the leadership of Germany, with a positive if half-hearted response from her Gallic neighbor.

Roi s'amuse, Le. *Le Roi s'amuse* (The king has a good time), of 1832, is perhaps better known for Giuseppe Verdi's opera *Rigoletto* (1851), which was derived from the Hugo verse drama. *Le Roi s'amuse* in brief is the story of the ugly Triboulet,* the court jester to Francis I, who finds out that his virgin daughter Blanche* has been sexually assaulted by Francis I; she is just one among his countless amorous conquests (Blanche is hardly sixteen years old).

Seeking revenge, Triboulet engages the services of a hired killer, Saltabadil, to murder Francis who is in the act of seducing Saltabadil's sister Maguelonne. Maguelonne, like Blanche, finds such fine qualities in Francis that she pleads with her brother not to kill the sleeping Francis but to substitute anyone who might knock at their door. In this case, it is Blanche, who, disobeying her father's orders and dressed in male attire, has left town to return to the decrepit inn where Francis awaits his next conquest. Blanche, who accepts martyrdom for the love of this unworthy king, seems blinded by an unreasonable love that persists in spite of all contrary evidence. Blanche is, of course, murdered, and she dies in the arms of her distraught father.

It is not difficult to understand why the play met with the opposition of the royal censors. Francis I, considered one of the great kings of the French Renaissance, is depicted as a cheap philanderer (as are most of the members of his entourage including the Renaissance poet Clément Marot), without any sense of conscience, a man consistently living within the bounds of moral turpitude. The play was performed once at the Théâtre-Français on November 22, 1832; it was suspended the following day, then totally forbidden. Hugo's preface of November 30, 1832, speaks not of the play's significance, but rather addresses the question of censorship. The historical references of the play are relevant if not always accurate. The reference to the king's sister Marguerite de Navarre, who would like to fill the king's court with scholars, is a fine Renaissance contrast with the frivolity and lewdness of the court. Much dialogue is spent in scintillating erotic conversation among the courtiers, as they engage in efforts to seduce other men's wives. The portrait of Francis I seems false, or at least onesided, for Francis did indeed have his own genius in political and religious matters. It is Triboulet, the ugly buffoon, who appears to be the only person with a conscience. A devoted father, he is certainly able to articulate his feelings, unlike Quasimodo* of *Notre-Dame de Paris*.* Triboulet's monologues are soul searching and soul wrenching. He is indeed the avenging angel whose plans for justice are denied. This is perhaps caused by the cavalier attitudes of most of the personages, including the hired killer Saltabadil. Against the king's sexist portrayal of women considered as objects to be used by men, the young Blanche first appears like a victim but finally escapes from the father's law, Triboulet seeing the king as crime, himself as punishment: *Il s'appelle le crime, et moi, le châtiment!* (His name is crime, mine punishment).

The play probably is indicative of a growing impatience with all monarchies on the part of Hugo as he evolved away from royalism toward liberalism. *Le Roi s'amuse* can be seen, as can *Hernani* and *Ruy Blas*, as historical meditations on the role of royalty in society.

Romancero du Cid, Le. *The Romance of Le Cid,* composed in July 1856, containing 182 strophes, four lines each abab, for a total of 728 lines, is of interest to us as part of the Romantic movement's resuscitation of the romance of the Middle Ages. What Hugo had done by extending *La Chanson de Roland* in *La Légende des siècles,** he also did, in the same collection, with the famous Spanish epic *El Cantar de mio Cid* (The song of the Cid). His text seems to be based neither in the original epic, born either in the middle of the twelfth century or early thirteenth, nor in the drama of Guillen de Castro (1569–1637). It seems, like Hugo's *Roland*, to be born entirely from the imagination of the poet. Hugo's contribution to the legend of the Cid will not elevate that personage to the rank of myth, as is the case with the *Don Juan* motifs in Spain and France, but it does add an interesting Romantic wrinkle to the texts preceding it.

The fundamental thesis, as well as antithesis, in this long poem is the antagonism between the king of Castille, Sanchez, and the Cid. It is conceivable that the poem could be a disguised attack on Napoléon III,* but that cannot be proven. Two ideas come forth in this work. The first is the struggle between the central authority of the king, who seeks a unified Spain, and the rights of the landed nobility—somewhat akin to states' rights versus federal rights in the United States. In France, a similar struggle, called the Fronde wars, which started in about 1648, was an uprising against Cardinal Mazarin. Second, the poet pits the honor and loyalty of the noble Cid against a cowardly, mean-spirited king. The poem is divided into sixteen parts.

In Part 1, the Cid welcomes the king into his household, and not very politely: *Roi, soyez le mal venu* (King, you are not welcome). This part, entitled *L'Entrée du roi* (The king's entrance) stresses the above-mentioned tension between powerful nobles and central authority, an authority which will not be achieved fully before 1492 when Spanish unity was assured by the union of Castille and Aragon, and the expulsion of the Moors and Jews.

Part 2, *Souvenirs de Chimène*, seems to continue Pierre Corneille's drama, for now Chimène and the Cid are married, a possibility left open at the end of the seventeenth-century play. The Chimène theme is picked up again in Part 13, *Le Cid fidèle* (The faithful Cid), in which we are treated to a Greuze-like homespun scene—Chimène repairing the Cid's clothing put into relief by reference to the Cid's loyalty to the weak king: *Chimène recoud ma robe/Mais non pas ma loyauté* (Chimène resews my robe/but not my loyalty).

The structure of this mini-epic stresses that the Cid is at the end of his life, evaluating all he has done for the king, the conquests he has made, and his dilemma, caused by his Spanish honor, to remain loyal to a king whom he cannot respect. Although the poem seems to be a long list of grievances against the king, the various sections could be seen as types of introspections or musings about a life honorably lived for dishonorable persons.

Thus the titles of the parts inflict judgment and shame on the king who is seen by the Cid as the jealous king (3); the ungrateful king (4); the defiant king (5); the abject king (6); the double-dealing king (7); and the thief king (8); for Sanchez has imposed exorbitant taxes and has also appropriated the lands of the nobles. This section contains a very interesting turn of language, for the Cid ponders whether the king is *pendable* (hangable, or deserving of hanging). The suffix calls to mind in French the expression *L'eau potable* (drinkable water). The description of the king continues: in part 9, the ruffian king, by his actions, should not be considered Spanish; (10), the cowardly king, a man who would not dare to visit sacred shrines of true fallen heroes, such as Roland at Roncevaux; (11), the mocking king; (12), the mean king, now called a pygmy leader who is guilty of murders, executions, and the killing of women and children.

The remaining four parts touch on the high character of the Cid (13), his quality as an honest nobleman (*caballero cristiano* in the French sense of *honnêteté*), a man who lives, far from the corruption of the court, the simple life of a country gentleman. In conclusion, Part 15 states that the king is the king, a person filled with fear and anxiety, and, in 16, that the Cid is the Cid, a man better than the king. All that counts is high Spanish honor. The Cid, old now, will finish his days, without fear, and without being a leader of revolution, even against a corrupt king.

This is not one of Hugo's greatest poems, but it is important in understanding another aspect of Hugo's medievalism: his interest in epic materials (much like that of the American Romantic Henry Wadsworth Longfellow who studied the French and Spanish epics in great detail), which he embellished through his powerful Romantic imagination.

Romanticism and Victor Hugo. Romanticism ushered in what can properly be called modern literature. According to some literary critics, it is indigenous to the literature of northern countries; such was the idea of Madame de Staël (1766–1817) in her general commentary *De la Littérature*

(1800) in which she related literary development in terms of a country's political and sociological atmosphere. In this work she pleaded for a free French society as the only means for French literature to progress and develop. More important was her *De l'Allemagne* (On Germany), written in 1810 and published in 1813. This work introduced the French cultivated public to German style Romanticism, and to the works of Johann Wolfgang von Goethe, Friedrich von Schiller, Gotthold Lessing, and Friedrich von Schlegel. She concludes in Book Two, chapter 2, entitled *Le classique et le romantique*, that French poetry—in contrast to that of Torquato Tasso in Italy, Pedro Calderón de la Barca in Spain, Luiz Vaz de Camoëns in Portugal, and William Shakespeare in England—is restricted to a small aristocratic class; in these other countries, where literary expression is found in the national spirit, their works are read by all classes.

This is both an appeal to nationalism, a main characteristic of Romanticism (and thus it will be in France under the impact of the French Revolution and the Napoleonic wars), and a not too subtle attack on French classicism which she implies is moribund. In the same chapter, Madame de Staël praises those literatures that hark back to national origins, to medieval literature, Romances of chivalry, and courtly love. For her, Romantic literature alone is capable of being perfected because it is rooted in the very soil of the individual country. This is opposed to French classicism which she sees as a servile imitation of classical (and pagan) antiquity. Entering into the famous seventeenth-century quarrel concerning Christian literature, in which classic doctrine forbade the fictional use of Christian Truths, Madame de Staël opts for an art based on the tenets of Christianity. As a theorist and precursor of French Romanticism, she will be joined in this crusade by Chateaubriand (1766–1848) who makes similar claims in his preface to *René* (1802) and in his monumental *Le Génie du Christianisme* (The Genius of Christianity, 1802). Through Madame de Staël and Benjamin Constant (1767–1830), German models are introduced to the French—Constant stressing the importance of German dramatic art. These three figures then are the precursors to what will later be known as the French Romantic movement; they cannot be ignored in any appraisal of Romanticism in France.

Romanticism usually is defined in terms of its opposition to classicism, specifically to the unified stylistic group of writers of the famous generation of 1660; Jean Racine (1639–1699), François de La Rochefoucauld (1613–1680), Molière (1622–1673), and Blaise Pascal (1623–1662). While lyrical poetry was essentially banished from French classicism, as well as any medieval form that was considered uncivilized and barbarian, the real triumph of classicism was to be found in its theatre, in the tragedies of Racine and the comedies of Molière. The meaning of French classicism is found in Nicolas Boileau-Despréaux's (1636–1711) *Art poétique* (1674) which is considered to be the codification of classic doctrine. Romanticism, especially as it will be embodied in the poetry and theatre of Victor Hugo, is the complete opposite of the classic ideal. Classicism, through a process of imitation, assimilated classical antiquity and shunned Christianity as a source of poetic inspiration. This is clearly enunciated in the positions taken in the famous quarrel of the ancients and moderns, which raged during the last years of the reign of Louis XIV. The question was hypothetical, asking whether contemporary literature could surpass the literature of the ancients. Those on the side of the ancients, Boileau, for example, who was the leader of the defenders of the ancients, regarded French literature as capable of equaling but not of surpassing ancient literature. The moderns, on the other hand, felt that since the moderns knew more than the ancients, progress would be on their side and it would be possible to surpass them. This quarrel continued throughout the eighteenth century which sustained a classicism that had outlived the zeitgeist that had originally formed it. The quarrel came to its true end with the triumph of Hugo's play *Hernani** (1830), which signaled the defeat of classicism by the new Romantic generation.

Other aspects of the classic spirit would be denied by the Romantics. Nature, as understood by the Romantics, had been denied by the classic generation. Classicism was basically a metropolitan art or the art of the Court—where nature exists, it is controlled by man. Thus the manicured gardens of Versailles serve as a prime example of classical nature; this is a nature controlled by the principles of architecture. Romantic nature, on the other hand, is wild, untamed. It is in the writings of Jean-Jacques Rousseau (1712–1778) that we see the very first description of this Romantic nature and, apparently also, the first use of the word *romantique*, originally a French term denoting novels of chivalry and courtly romance of the twelfth century, which returns etymologically to France from Germany and England. In the fifth of Rousseau's *Les rêveries du promeneur solitaire* (The reveries of a solitary wanderer), we find the following description of a newly appreciated natural landscape coupled with the first definition of Romanticism: *Les rives du lac de Bienne son plus sauvages et romantiques que celles du lac de Genève, parce que les rochers et les bois y bordent l'eau de plus près; mais elles ne sont pas moins riantes* (The shores of Lake Bienne are wilder and more Romantic than those of Lake Geneva because the rocks and woods are closer to the water; but that doesn't mean they are less joyful).

Other characteristics of classicism, which would be rejected by the Romantics, with Hugo leading the way, are the three classical unities of time, place, and action. Partially inherited from Aristotle as filtered across Italian Renaissance criticism, the unities had the effect of rejecting particular historical moments, seeking instead an action which, in a sense, is timeless (mythological) and placeless (usually in front of a palace), with one single action. The effect was to produce a depth psychology which is lacking in French Romantic drama, as classic writers sought the universal man. Furthermore, classicism rejected any vocabulary that might be considered vulgar, or shocking, in the name of the so-called *bienséance* (propriety). Certain words were considered ill-advised, such as *les yeux* (eyes), perhaps too physical in tone, for which could be substituted *le miroir de l'âme* (the mirror of the soul). This of course led to excesses which were parodied by Molière in his play *Les Précieuses ridicules* (1659), in which the proponents of "preciosity" are ridiculed. This attitude explains why English thespians were driven off the stage in Paris during the seventeenth century while attempting to perform *Othello*, in which the action is dependent upon the fatal handkerchief. Apart from being a vulgar object (in French it is *mouchoir*, having to do with chasing flies away), it violated the French classical sense of having no action on the stage—no murders, duels, or lovemaking. Actors kept their distance and declaimed their alexandrines much in the manner of operatic arias.

French classicism sought the universal man and relegated the individual to historical importance: *Le moi est haïssable* (The self is hateable). It sought the ideal man, *l'honnête homme*, derived from the spirit of the *cortegiano*, developed by Baldassare Castiglione (1478–1529) in his *Il Libro del cortegiano* (The book of the Courtier), written in 1513–1518 and published in 1528, which describes aristocratic manners during the Italian Renaissance, but also expressed in Spain in the concept of the *caballero cristiano* (Christian knight).

In seventeenth-century classical France, sentiment was locked in by reason and duty (the theatre of Pierre Corneille); passions unleashed were deadly, fatal. The classical spirit attempted to marry what is called *l'esprit de géométrie* (the spirit of geometry) with *l'esprit de finesse* (the spirit of subtlety), or reason and intuition, or in Jungian terms, the *animus* and the *anima*. Pascal said it best when he wrote; *Le coeur a ses raisons que la raison ne connaît point (Les Pensées #477,* The heart has its reasons which reason does not know at all).

The Romantic revolution, foreseen by Rousseau, Madame de Staël and Chateaubriand, was slow to triumph, but it had done so by 1830 thanks to the prolific poetic production of Victor Hugo, to his theatre, and to his evolution away from royalist and conservative positions toward liberalism. Hugo embodies Romanticism in France, and although its characteristics can be found in the other Romantic writers, none could equal his practice of the new art.

For the Romantics, on the other hand, the individual takes precedence over any universal man. They wanted to see man in his historical context, which of course led to the development of the Romantic historical novel first seen in the work of Sir Walter Scott (1771–1832), who had an enormous influence on the French Romantics who imitated his anachronistic novels (time, costume, and local color correct with, unfortunately, a modern psychology attached). Prosper Merimée, Alexandre Dumas *père*, Alfred de Vigny,* and of course Hugo excelled in this new form. Hugo, in his famous *Préface de Cromwell* (*see Cromwell, Preface to*), proclaimed liberty in art, which meant the abolition of the three unities, and led to dramas encompassing many time periods, many places, and multiple actions. This liberty also led to an assault on classic versification, a prime example being the use of enjambement* in the first scene of *Hernani*.

Hugo's art became the antithesis of classicism. He introduced forms that had been banished from classical poetry, such as the ballad. The ego of the Romantic hero is evident throughout his theatre; the new art was subjective by nature, highly sensational, emotional, and even sentimental. Both Romantic poetry and theatre stressed local color and regional manners, and they thrived on the exotic and the historic. In fact, historicism must be seen as a major facet of the Romantic movement. Although it did not totally reject classical mythology, it was reworked in a Romantic mode; and new myths were added, such as that of Napoléon, who became a major subject of Romantic literature and painting.

Early Romanticism initiated a neoclassic concept of antiquity, which was more apparent in the work of Romantic painters, such as Pierre Paul Prud'hon (1758–1823), or in the work of Jacques-Louis David (1748–1825). It is also apparent in the earlier stages of Romantic poetry, such as that of André Chénier* (1762–1794) who tried to marry classicism and Romanticism, with his famous phrase: *Sur des pensers nouveaux faisons des vers antiques* (Let us create on old lines of poetry new ideas). Alphonse de Lamartine* (1790–1869), considered the first of the Romantic poets, could also be classified as a neoclassicist because of his restrained vocabulary and classical sensibilities, especially in his most famous poem *Le Lac* (The lake).

The main spirit of the new literature, however, is lyric, and Romanticism signaled the return of the lyric spirit, crushed by classicism, to a France in need of this type of individual song.

THE BATTLE FOR ROMANTICISM

Naturally enough, the Romantic polemic was fought on the terrain of the theatre if only because classicism's most important genre was found in tragedy, tragicomedy, and comedy. Romantic theatre is dependent upon coincidence and fate (for example, the arrival of the masque [Don Ruy Gomez de Silva*] in the final act of *Hernani*, in which the wedding of Hernani* and Doña Sol de Silva* is being celebrated). Seeking fulfillment of the promised oath, he offers Hernani a choice of death; Hernani chooses poison, and both he and Doña Sol commit suicide. The dramaturgy of Alfred de Musset* (1810–1858), the youngest member of Hugo's literary meetings (considered the worst of the French Romantic poets by the symbolist Arthur Rimbaud), is generally accepted with his fine analysis of love, including *Fantasio*, 1833; *On ne badine pas avec l'amour* (You don't play around with love), 1834; and his extraordinary play in the manner of Shakespeare, *Lorenzaccio* (1834), an in-depth analysis of the psychology of assassination at the time of the Medicis.

The battle of Romanticism in the French theatre continued for almost thirty years until the success of *Hernani*. A fine example of pre-Romanticism is the work of Népomucène Lemercier (1771–1840) who felt the urge, after writing in the classical manner, to innovate. In *Pinto* (1800), a historical comedy written in prose, he mingled tragic and comic elements, something Hugo would later advocate in the *Cromwell* preface: *Tout ce qui est dans la nature est dans l'art* (All that is in nature is in art). The battle of Romanticism, however, was not confined to the theatre; it was extended to politics.

POLITICAL ASPECTS OF ROMANTICISM

Early Romanticism can be easily divided into liberal and conservative camps; the liberals were led by Stendhal* (1783–1842), the conservatives, by Hugo. It was, however, Hugo's rapid evolution in the 1820s from royalist and conservative into liberal that made him head of the Romantic school in France. As he became radical in aesthetics, he exhibited the same tendencies in his political and philosophical beliefs.

Stendhal and Hugo represented rival factions. Stendhal considered himself a liberal and a modern (although a close scrutiny of his work would reveal him to be more a man of the eighteenth than the nineteenth century). He had defined Romanticism as that literature that is pleasing to contemporaries.

Stendhal had a distaste for poetry, for simile, metaphor, or any sort of figurative language. He prided himself on his attempts to write in the style of the civil code of Napoléon, a dry Senecan type using declarative simplicity as opposed to the more Ciceronian melodies to be found first in Chateaubriand and then in Hugo. A reading of his novel *Le Rouge et le noir* (The Red and the Black, 1831) makes this point clear. Where figuration exists it is found only in contemporary jargon, that is, out of the contemporary *langage* (language) of the everyday Frenchman. He also resisted any kind of descriptive art, which made him an oddball in the Romantic movement. Unlike Honoré de Balzac (1799–1850), who spent pages describing persons and objects in great detail, Stendhal was content with the briefest of all possible statements. The conclusion of chapter 8 of *Le Rouge et le noir* offers the Stendhalian antidote to the descriptive verbosity of Balzac. Julien's hand has accidentally brushed against that of Mme de Renal which was resting on *le dos d'une de ces chaises de bois peint que l'on place dans les jardins* (the back of one of those painted wooden chairs that people put in their gardens). Stendhal's lack of description would please neither Balzac nor Hugo.

It is somewhat ironic that Stendhal wanted to be a playwright like Molière, but it never happened. The closest he came to the theatre was his famous *Racine et Shakespeare* (1825), in which he opted for the English bard as the model for contemporary theatre. Here, he and Hugo were in agreement. His psychological penetration and the character analyses found in his novels, however, were a prose replay of the metonymical psychology of the classic generation of 1660.

HUGO BECOMES THE LEADER OF THE ROMANTIC SCHOOL

Hugo's ascendancy was first noticed in the literary salons of Charles Nodier* (1780–1844) held at the Bibliothèque de l'Arsenal and later, as Hugo's literary productivity came more and more to the notice of Paris, at his own literary meetings. The focal point was both poetic and political. By moving to a leftist position in politics, Hugo succeeded in outplaying Stendhal, but this was only a life posture equivalency of what he had already announced in his poetry. The poetry and theatre were liberal before the man.

More important is that Hugo, unlike Stendhal, insisted upon the primacy of poetry as the centerpiece of the Romantic movement, for poetry unto itself, and poetry as an integral part of most of his theatre (although he also wrote prose plays). It is the poetry that is mostly celebrated in Hugo's dramas. The mixture of the "grotesque" and "sublime" in *Hernani* is still astonishing. Scene 2 of act 1 has an interplay of soaring Romantic love poetry from the lips of Hernani to Doña Sol's concern about the fact that Hernani is soaking wet from a rainstorm: Hernani: *Doña Sol! Ah! c'est vous que je vois/Enfin! et cette voix qui parle est votre voix! Pourquoi le sort mit-il mes jours si loin de vôtre?/J'ai tant besoin de vous pour oublier les autres!* (Doña Sol! Ah! It is you that I see/Finally! and this voice which speaks is your voice!/Why has fate put my days so far from yours?/I so need you in order to forget the others). Doña Sol: *Jesus! votre manteau ruisselle! il pleut donc bien?* (Jesus! your coat is dripping wet! Is it really raining?).

Such encounters of prose and poetry surely produced apoplexy among the classicists present at the premiere, but it also brought cheers from the young French Romantics, especially Théophile Gautier,* who was dressed in an outlandish costume for this dramatic encounter between the two sides. Injuries in the audience were reported.

Romanticism's second area of success was in the form of the historical novel. Hugo early on wrote a fine and successful one, *Notre-Dame de*

*Paris,** set in Paris of the Middle Ages. It is Hugo's poetic genius, however, that gave the necessary boost to the Romantic movement, in poetry,
theatre, and the novel. Ultimately, the battleground of Romanticism
proved to be its least interesting aspect. The ground shifted to lyric poetry of countless varieties; for Hugo, it was a poetry of family, conjugal
love, and love of children; satirical poetry; Biblical poetry; philosophical
poetry; exotic poetry; love poetry; political poetry; and historical poetry.

The failure of Hugo's *Les Burgraves** in 1843 did not put an end to his
theatrical output, but it changed it radically, leaving behind the early
Romantic models.

What Hugo practiced was also accomplished by other major Romantic
writers—de Vigny, de Musset, and Lamartine, to mention a few. They
were the satellites who revolved around Hugo, who was not just the
head of the French Romantic school, but also the prime producer of
Romantic literature, achieved through a constancy and discipline, and a
dedication to the art of writing.

BIBLIOGRAPHY

Pascal, Blaise. *Les Pensées*, in *Oeuvres complètes*, edited and annotated by Jacques
    Chevalier. Paris: Bibliothèque de la Pléiade, Editions Gallimard, 1954,
    p. 1221.

Rose de L'Infante, La. From the first series of *La Légende des siècles,** La
Rose de L'Infante (Rose of the Infanta), whose manuscript is dated May
23, 1859, is one of the best known and loved poems depicting mankind's
history. Its Spanish motif continues what Hugo had already accomplished in this collection with the poems centering on the epic deeds of
the Cid, and it is also important in understanding the Spanish aspect of
Hugo's meditations as found in two of his most important plays, *Hernani** and *Ruy Blas.**

The narrative is rather long, but it is structured in a very strict manner,
which makes it a symbolic statement on power gone out of control, in
this case, the maneuvers of Philip II. The poem is startling in its construct, starting with a charming if melancholic view of the Infanta Maria,
who was born in 1580 from the union of Anne of Austria and Philip II.
The child unfortunately died at the age of three (not five as Hugo says
in the poem), and this premature death symbolizes for the poet, the
eventual collapse of the Spanish empire, so carefully built by Philip and
Charles V, which came to an end with the fateful events of 1492—the
discovery of America and the expulsion of the Jews and Moors from the
peninsula. Some historians have argued that 1492 leads directly to 1898,
which is the date of the end of Spain's worldwide empire.

The poem is framed by a typical Hugo drawing of a little girl, in all
the freshness of life, holding a rose in her hand. It is not unlike the

ecstatic poems Hugo wrote about his own daughters, such as *Lorsque l'enfant paraît** (When the child comes into the room) or *Mes deux filles** (My two daughters*).

This idyllic scene, however, is interrupted by a strongly negative portrait of Philip II, who is depicted as a dogmatic and evil dictator bent on controlling the world. His defeat, however, is in the wreckage of the Spanish armada, destroyed as much by nature's elements as by the English. The poem concludes with a sorrowful image of the infanta, whose rose petals are blown away by a wind, into a basin of water. She has nothing left in her hand but the thorn of the rose. This startling conclusion symbolically meshes the destruction of the armada with the impending death of the infanta, and the ultimate decline of Spain. The basin of water seems angry; the water is black, and filled with waves. The rose seems to have become a flotilla, the tragedy of the Spanish armada. The guardian of the princess remarks that all on earth belongs to sovereigns, except the wind.

This marriage of innocence and political and military corruption elevates Hugo to the level of a symbolist poet (*see* Symbolism). His historical meditation on the meaning of the geopolitics of Philip II has become a motif for which a word-for-word prose equivalent is virtually impossible. The predominant imagery of the little princess and her rose, and the pensive and melancholy Philip form a deep symbolic antitheses which makes this poem one of the masterpieces of *La Légende des siècles*.

Ruy Blas. *Ruy Blas* is probably the most important of Hugo's Romantic dramas, differing essentially from *Hernani** in that *Hernani* has less comic relief, a motive of the theatre that Hugo had announced some ten years earlier. The play concerns the rapid rise of a lackey, Ruy Blas, who loves the Queen of Spain, who is bored out of her mind by a husband who is always hunting (a bit like the last days of Louis XVI) but is controlled by strict Spanish baroque rules of etiquette. Ruy Blas is put into a high position by Don Salluste who has been exiled for flagrant délit with a damsel of the Spanish court. Ruy Blas not only loves the queen, but he loves Spain, and when he assumes political power, he confronts those nobles who have no respect for the king, and less for the queen.

The second scene of act 2 reveals the arrival of Ruy Blas, who has overheard the seditious discussions of the nobles about how they can divide the kingdom among themselves (perhaps an echo to the Fronde wars in France), and in one of Hugo's most famous lines simply says, *Bon appétit, messieurs!*

An important aspect of this play is the possibility of the people to save their country, part of Hugo's meditation of the difference between the common man and the mob. It was for these reasons that Hugo could see benefit in the French Revolution, in spite of its excesses.

Ruy Blas may appear superior to *Hernani*, first because of the ten years of maturation taking place in Hugo, but also because its motivations are more easily accepted. Some consider *Ruy Blas* to be Hugo's best play. It certainly is the closest to any French equivalency of Shakespeare, and it can be rivaled only by Alfred de Musset's* *Lorenzaccio*.

S

Sainte-Beuve, Charles-Augustin. Perhaps the most important and influential critic of French literature of the nineteenth century, Sainte-Beuve (1804–1869) was also a poet and novelist. He introduced the type of positive criticism that followed him, practiced by Vincent de Brunetière and Emile Faguet, in spite of their conservative and Catholic disclaimers.

Sainte-Beuve was an enthusiastic adherent of the Romantic movement, and he was a friend of Victor and Adèle Hugo. His early articles on Hugo's *Odes et ballades** certainly helped to establish Hugo's reputation as titular head of the French Romantic school. His affair with Madame Hugo, starting with secretive meetings in 1832, caused his banishment from the Hugo household. By 1834, Hugo, perplexed, had severed all relationship with Sainte-Beuve. Sainte-Beuve's liaison with Adèle Hugo is recounted in his novel *Volupté* (1834). Sainte-Beuve followed all the directions of the nineteenth century; he rolled with the times, and he was a forerunner of the positivist criticism that was to come.

BIBLIOGRAPHY

Antoine, Gerald. *Sainte-Beuve: Vie, poésies et pensées de Joseph Delorme.* 1957.
Billy, André. *Sainte-Beuve, sa vie et son temps.* 1952.
Sainte-Beuve, Charles-Augustin. *Premiers lundis.* Reprint. 1874–1875. Paris: Gallimard, 1956. Contains criticism of Hugo's *Odes et ballades and Cromwell* and includes a literary biographical essay on Hugo.

Sand, George (Aurore Dudevant). George Sand (1804–1876) was one of the most prolific novelists of nineteenth-century France. She first shared the intensity of outraged Romanticism fed by a felt, but not totally understood, early feminism, and moved on to socialist concerns in her novels, and finally made rustic presentations of her native Nohant where she became a benevolent aristocratic onlooker of peasant life.

Sand's ideological bents would, it would seem, have pushed her at least slightly into the direction of Hugo's works against capital punishment* and against social injustice, the great message of *Les Misérables*. Yet, her penchant was for her great friend Gustave Flaubert,* an intimacy in friendship which could hardly be shared by the divergencies in their views of the conception of the novel.

In reading Sand's letters, it becomes clear that she did not like Hugo's early works very much. There are strong negative feelings about Hugo's theatre; *Hernani** did not seem to please her, nor did *Ruy Blas*.* This play, performed in 1838, perhaps seen by Sand, gave her the following negative impression: "Out of curiosity I have read *Ruy Blas*. What a stupid play, how absurd, how platitudinous, how silly! . . . Maybe we are finally finished with Hugo?" (Sand, 1964, vol. 4, 617).

George Sand's attitude became much friendlier during Hugo's exile. She admired the poet as one of the greatest. He celebrated the "great woman" of the nineteenth century.

BIBLIOGRAPHY

Sand, George. *George Sand, Correspondance*, vol. 4, *May 1837–March 1840*. Reprint. Paris: Garnier Frères, 1964.

Sara la baigneuse. *Sara la baigneuse* (Sara at her bath), poem nineteen of *Les Orientales*, 1829, is typical of Hugo's erotic streak, which is found across his entire poetic output, an eroticism partially lewd in its thought, but not entirely, a sexuality less veiled than that usually found in the French Romantics. The poem, possibly an echo to a similar work by Alfred de Vigny* concerning Suzanne and the elders, bears more resemblance to the Biblical recounting of David's ogling the naked Bathsheba coming from her bath.

This poem, with its wanton invitation to the reader (strophe 5) to await the lascivious scene of the unclothed Sara, forms part of French masculine romantic fetish about the hidden and mysterious charms of the Oriental woman (cf Gustave Flaubert's* *Salammbô*, 1862). An equivalent voyeurism is found in three remarkable works of Théophile Gautier* (1811–1872): his novel *Mademoiselle de Maupin* (1835), in which questions of male and female gender are explored; the much later *Le Roman de la momie* (1858), which concerns the unraveling of a female mummy by an archaeologist and his assistant who is interested in her body more than in science. Gautier's not very well veiled eroticism, also exemplified in his poem on abstract aesthetics, *Symphonie en blanc majeur*, especially in its concluding stanza, wherein the poet seeks to transform abstract whiteness into the flesh-colored body of a real woman, is certainly akin to what we find in the major Romantic writers, namely a sensuality that wishes to be stated only indirectly. In Hugo's poem, the message is direct.

The poem, however, is a success because of its orchestration. Each strophe is composed of six lines with the rhyme scheme of aabccb with lines 2 and 5 creating a metrical unit of three syllables each. Here the intense musicality of Victor Hugo (*indolence/balance; demeure/heure; non-chatante/lente*, for example) anticipates what will be called for by Paul Verlaine (1844–1896) in his *Art poétique* poem of 1874: *De la musique avant toute chose* (Music above everything). Hugo anticipates what Verlaine will be practicing in his verse, and therefore he may be considered a forerunner of musical impressionism. Hugo's poem of 1828, if not identified by author, could easily be attributed to Verlaine.

Sartre, Jean-Paul. Jean-Paul Sartre (1905–1980) founded the French philosophical and literary movement of existentialism after World War II. It would appear impossible that the exponent of *littérature engagée* (engaged literature) could admire any Romantic writer, but such is the case, if only minimally, with Sartre. He went through the usual French formation of reading even in the early twentieth century, the now classical (Romantic) writers, such as Hugo, and in fact had an unusual liking for *Hernani,** a text condemned by the realist Honoré de Balzac.* Sartre's behavioral interest in Hugo may also be derived from the delusional conduct of his grandfather Charles Schweitzer who sometimes thought he was Victor Hugo (see Sartre's *The Words*, 14–15).

If Sartre approved of Hugo it was because his reading of *Les Misérables* led him to consider it as a document of engaged literature in spite of Hugo's own bourgeois formation. It is within the commentaries of Sartre's *Qu'est-ce que la littérature* (What is literature, Paris: Gallimard, 1948) that Hugo is made an exception to Sartre's doctrinaire review of all of French literature from the Middle Ages to the present time. With the single exception of Victor Hugo, Sartre found all French writers between 1848 and 1914 to be writing only for their own personal ends.

Sartre had concentrated on "engagement" in Hugo's work, and this certainly must point to the social outrage expressed by Victor Hugo in such an early work as *Le Dernier Jour d'un condamné* and in the later *Les Misérables*.

Satan's End. See *Fin de Satan, La.*

Satyre, Le. This poem, from the first series of *La Légende des siècles*, manuscript dated from March 1859, is considered by some critics to be the most important poem in the first issue of this collection. It is both ambiguous and paradoxical, especially if considered in the light of

nineteenth-century "faun" poetry, which culminates in the great eclogue
of Stéphane Mallarmé's* *The Afternoon of a Faun*, which celebrates, in the
tradition of Virgil, the bucolic dreams of woods and nymphs and human
sexuality. Hugo's very long poem seems to dwell less on sexuality than
on creation, and on domination of humankind over its own fall from
grace. The poem is Manichean within the tradition that Hugo's theology
had already established in such long works as the conclusion to *Les Contemplations,** *Ce que dit la bouche d'ombre,** the oracle dolmen from Rozel
Bay on the island of Jersey.

It certainly is included in most lists of the great poems of *La Légende
des siècles*, such as *Booz endormi,** *La Conscience,** *La Rose de l'Infante,** and
*Les Pauvres Gens.** Its theme is that of the evolution of man, the spirit or
soul that emerges, almost autonomously, without quickening, from outside itself, out of matter. The faun represents mankind in an enigmatic
manner, for this faun is lewd, monstrous, genial, heroic, a bit of earth
become man which puts the gods of Olympus in their place.

The poem is divided into four long parts preceded by a prologue. At
first glance, it would appear that the faun is in the tradition of Virgil or
that to be soon established by Mallarmé. The great difference, however,
is that this satyr, Promethean in nature, is found inhabiting Mount Olympus, much to the consternation of the gods. Shocking to the deities, he
is regarded, as the etymology would suggest, as a kind of sex maniac.
This should be read in Hugo not as sexually obsessed, but as procreative.

The narrator's obsession with the gods of Mount Olympus is in direct
contrast with the spirit of creation, represented in a very abstract manner,
which recalls the creative canvasses of the American painter Augustus
Tack. In fact, the gods, named by Hugo, seem a bit absurd and earth-
bound, with their zodiac equivalencies on the great astrological wheel.

This satyr seems more like an Orpheus in his ability to create life for
both trees and animals. While appearing half-asleep, his eyes watch the
chaos about him. Out of this chaos is created a soul, that of man. The
satyr seems almost Christ-like in his ability to understand suffering and
evil and to create, out of this chaos, a world of unity and harmony built
by man alone, without the help of the gods. Out of disorder is created
a new order, human in nature, upon which all creation is formed and
dependent. The satyr, in startling imagery, creates from his own body
forests, animals, and new humans.

From this panic cry is born the world of human beings, not dependent
on any force outside itself. The poem concludes with the orphic cry of
the satyr, who announces that he is Pan and that Jupiter and the other
gods should bend their knee, for mankind shall not be beholden to them.

The poem should be considered within the general theosophy of Hugo,
which is independent of most known metaphysical systems. It is often

contradictory and difficult to follow, but it is saved from seminary instruction or consideration by its soaring poetry.

Second Empire. Napoléon III,* who had been elected president of the Second Republic on December 10, 1848, very quickly moved, especially after the worker rebellions of 1848, into the direction of absolute control of France. He accomplished this by the coup d'état of December 2, 1852, in which he, Louis-Napoléon Bonaparte, proclaimed the Second Empire (1852–1870), which was to govern France until the debacle at Sedan in 1870.

The intellectual reaction to what seemed to be a true usurpation of power led to the exile of many of France's brightest minds, notably its greatest poet, Victor Hugo. Hugo's bitter satirical attacks hurled at the emperor from the Channel Islands are found in his poetic collection, *Les Châtiments*. After the fact, Emile Zola* traced the history of the Second Empire in his twenty-volume work *Les Rougon-Macquart*. Zola's attitude is less personal than Hugo's, but it also gives a negative impression of the empire, especially in the volumes entitled *La Curée: Son excellence Eugène Rougon* and *La Débâcle*.

Sexuality and Victor Hugo. Sexuality in nineteenth-century France and Victorian England is a most complex issue, more so than even today when there are more advanced psychological explanations to interpret it. The situation in the nineteenth century is particularly complicated when it concerns such writers as Hugo, Charles Baudelaire,* Arthur Rimbaud, Paul Verlaine, Stéphane Mallarmé,* and many others.

It would be facile and incorrect to assign to Hugo's psyche the role of lecher or womanizer. His spirit was not perverted. His sexuality in some way must have fitted in with his general cosmography. It had something to do with Hugo's refusal to separate the physical and the spiritual, or the spiritual and the erotic. This was not uncommon in the nineteenth century, and it can be measured to some degree in the poetry of Elizabeth Barrett Browning (1806–1861) and her husband, Robert Browning (1812–1889).

Hugo's position is in direct contrast with that of Baudelaire (1821–1867) whose love poems in *Les Fleurs du mal* (The Flowers of Evil) (1857) fit under a recognized category of *homo duplex* (the divided man), which enables some critics, such as Martin Turnell, to divide Baudelaire's love lyrics into the erotic strictly separated from the more spiritual. Thus the poems inspired by his mistress Jeanne Duval stress the temptations of the flesh, and the downward thrust toward hell, while a more spiritual note is sounded in those poems dedicated to Madame de Sabatier, who remains a spiritual muse for the poet.

Hugo may be closer to the truth embedded in Western religious thought, especially as found in the mysticism of Saint John of the Cross (1542–1591) and Saint Teresa of Avila (1515–1582). Christian mysticism is theologically defined as bridal mysticism—the union between Christ (the male element) and the Church or the individual soul (female element). The very liturgy of the Roman and Anglican churches on Holy Saturday, anticipating Easter which is considered the day of the conception of the church, is explicit in sexual implications as the Pascal candle is plunged into the baptismal font, the Christian symbolism of new life—the candle representing the spiritual penis, the font, the spiritual vagina.

John of the Cross himself speaks of the erotic sentiments associated with his ascension of the mystical ladder, especially in *Llama de amor viva* (The living flame of love). Saint Teresa of Avila expresses similar erotic-spiritual sentiments in her poetry, with her intense desire for union with Christ, expressed in such poems as *Que muero porque no muero* (I die because I do not die) and in her spiritual odyssey *The Interior Castle* (1577–1588). Gian Bernini's (1598–1680) statue in Rome, entitled *The Ecstasy of Santa Theresa*, has provoked much aesthetic argument, for it seems to hint at a fusion of sexuality and spirituality.

It is possible that we find something similar in Hugo's life and work, although it would be less defined and would be more eclectic than what is apparent in the strict orthodoxy of the Spanish mystics. Hugo's spirituality is not Christian, nor was he, probably never having been baptized. It certainly, though difficult at this moment to define, is related to the concept of the creative process, and is akin to what Auguste Rodin (1840–1917), the French sculptor, speculated on as he tried to capture, in his famous statues, the creative genius of the novelist Honoré de Balzac* (1799–1850). The final castings of the Balzac bust (one each in Paris, Washington, and Philadelphia) contain nothing explicitly sexual. Yet the *maquettes* (clay models) used in preparation for the finished statue are startling in their sexuality; they plainly exhibit Balzac with a full erection, relating the creative urge with the creative process found in the male seed. This may be akin to what is found in the personality of Victor Hugo whose creative spirit, especially in his poetry, is capable of fathoming the complete human, flesh and spirit, erotic and spiritual.

The evolution of Hugo's sexuality is not difficult to follow, at least in his biography. *Les Lettres à la fiancée** were written to Adèle during their engagement period from January 1820 to October 1822, the month of their marriage at St. Sulpice in Paris. These letters, passionate, idealistic, sentimental, and naive, stress above all the need for the young lovers to remain chaste and pure in preparation for their marriage, a type of amorous retreat, of nuptial preparation. One letter of March 4, 1820, complains to Adèle that he caught sight of her crossing a street with her dress raised a bit too high. The marriage, which produced five children in a short period of time, broke down for several reasons. Adèle seemed physically worn out from Hugo's incessant sexual needs. In addition, she was attracted to the courtly attention afforded her by the family friend Charles-Augustin Sainte-Beuve,* which culminated in a short-lived affaire.

It was, however, the liaison with Juliette Drouet, that complicated Hugo's amorous life. Hugo met Juliette, a second-rate actress, known more for her beauty than her talent, on January 2, 1833, when she tried out for one of his plays, *Lucrèce Borgia*,* at the theatre of the Porte-Saint-Martin. She was assigned the minor role of the Princess Negroni. This was the beginning of a major revolution in the lives of both Hugo and the actress, for their love blossomed and continued for the rest of their lives. It could be said that he had two wives; indeed, upon the death of Adèle Hugo, Juliette took her place as the mistress of the household. Everyone, including Madame Hugo, was aware of this affaire. During the exile, Juliette was set up in a house not far from Hauteville House on the island of Guernsey.

Hugo, however, was incapable of faithfulness to either his wife or Juliette. Throughout his life he engaged in a series of affaires, the most famous of which was with Léonie d'Aunet.* In later years, he had a liaison with Marie-Zelia Blanche* (simply called Blanche*), who subsequently became Madame Emile Rochereuil.

A member of the lower aristocracy, Hugo made the acquaintance of Léonie through a mutual friend, Frotunée Hamelin, and an adulterous liaison soon followed. Unfortunately for the lovers, Léonie's husband made a formal complaint to the police, and the two were found in flagrante delicto. Adultery was a very serious crime in the nineteenth century, and Léonie was arrested and sent to the Saint-Lazare prison. Hugo, recently named a peer of France, claimed immunity and, in such a sexist society, was allowed to go free. The scandal, however, was played up in some of the Parisian newspapers. Hugo confessed all to his wife. Léonie later tried to get Hugo to leave Juliette and, in a vindictive mood, sent to Juliette, in 1851, all the love letters she had received from the poet. Juliette was shocked to learn that this affaire dated back to 1844. In a move, which can only be interpreted as one of enormous sexual tolerance, she devised a plan by which there would be a period of four months in which Hugo could see his wife, Juliette, and Léonie. Following this period, he would be obliged to choose between her and Léonie. Juliette won out in the end.

A second major affaire was conducted with a woman simply known as Blanche. Hired by Juliette Drouet to be a linen maid at Hauteville House, Blanche was Hugo's last passionate affaire. She attached herself obsessively to him, much as his daughter Adèle Hugo* did to the English lieutenant Alfred Pinson.* An affaire quickly blossomed, and when it was discovered by Juliette, Blanche was sent back to Paris. Hugo quickly followed and set Blanche up in an apartment. Juliette, in a fit of jealousy, had Hugo followed, and suspected an affaire with another woman. She decided to leave Hugo and went to Brussels. Hugo, in despair, found her and she agreed to return home. The affaire was over, but Blanche continued to stalk the Hugo residence and send him letters (which were intercepted by Hugo's household and never reached him).

These two are outstanding examples of Hugo's intense sexuality. In between were the countless brief encounters with scores of other women of all ages, including the black woman who brought the insane Adèle back to France from the Caribbean.

Hugo's sexual escapades continued almost to the end of his life. His biography is reinforced by his poetry. A poem written for Blanche, entitled *En Grèce* in *La Légende des siècles,** dated July 12, 1873, contains three lines that demonstrate that Hugo was affirming not just the coexistence of the spirit and the flesh, but their intimate union: *Car l'hostie et l'hymen, et l'autel et l'alcove/ont chacun un rayon sacré du même jour/ La prière est la soeur tremblante de l'amour* (For the Eucharistic host and hymen, and the altar and the bedroom/each has the sacred ray of the same day/Prayer is the trembling sister of love).

Hugo's poetry is filled with an idealistic mixture of the erotic and the spiritual. To what degree this is related to the Spanish mystical experience is very difficult to assess. Some poems, such as *Tristesse d'Olympio** openly hint at sexuality. *Puisque j'ai mis ma lèvre à ta coupe encore pleine** would be considered by some as bordering on the pornographic. The satyr poem from *La Légende des siècles* mingles notions of genius, creativity, and love together.

It is for these reasons that we can see in Hugo a great lyric poet of women and love, a man not afraid to touch the boundaries of the erotic, but almost always with a spiritual statement attached. Hugo's tentative experimentation in erotic aesthetic poetics were continued by Mallarmé (1842–1898) with his *L'Après midi d'un faune* (1876), which was enhanced by the music of Claude Debussy (1862–1918) with his *Prélude à l'après midi d'un faune* (1894). Did the faun simply dream of these nymphs which the poem announces in its opening line as one of creation: *Ces nymphes je les veux parpétuer* (I would perpetuate these nymphs). This is but a development of that which was already incipient in the love lyrics of Victor Hugo.

Silva, Don Ruy Gomez de. This character is the lecherous villain of Hugo's *Hernani** (1830) for at least four reasons. This old man is intent upon marrying his niece, which would seem to be a violation of a normal genetic code (in spite of possible royal dispensations). Furthermore, he uses his prerogative, based on the Spanish code of honor, to demand, in the final act, the death of Hernani, *the hero, just moments after the latter's marriage to Doña Sol de Silva*, the sought-after heroine. After the double suicide of the young lovers, he himself commits suicide, shouting that he is damned, which according to Catholic tradition of that time, was probably true. The fourth reason for calling him a villain is his betrayal of trust. He is a grandee of Spain, with high civic and moral responsibility. This he seems to ignore, out of what seems to be a deep sexual lust, never made explicit in the play, for Doña Sol.

The tensions in this character derive from his high sense of honor and responsibility, which seem to be in conflict with his base sensuality, something that is not explained by Hugo, but is implicit in the text. As a man of honor he kept his word in protecting Hernani from imprisonment by the king, but for that, he exacted Hernani's death in the final scene of the play.

If Hugo's interpretation of Spanish culture were correct, it would be suspected that there was a double standard at work in Hispanic society. This is not the case. It is more likely that Don Ruy's moral turpitude was necessary for Hugo's dramatic construct.

Silva, Doña Sol de. Doña Sol is the heroine of Hugo's great Romantic theatrical triumph, *Hernani** (1830). Doña Sol is pursued by three men: by her true love Hernani,* by the king of Spain, Don Carlos,* and by her lecherous uncle, Don Ruy Gomez de Silva,* who is determined to marry her in spite of his old age, without considering the possibilities of a probable incestuous close blood relationship. Doña Sol's role in this Romantic drama is almost in the background, as the audience rivets its attention on the motivations of Hernani, the outlawed nobleman, on King Carlos, about to be named Holy Roman Emperor, and the uncle, Don Ruy Gomez de Silva.

Doña Sol does arise to the existential moment in the final scene where she threatens her uncle and finally chooses to commit suicide with Hernani, her spouse—a type of Romantic heroism.

Soumet, Alexandre. Soumet (1788–1845) was a French dramatist who, although respected by the young Romantics, became an applauded renewer of French classical tragedy during the mid-1820s. Hugo had met him in 1819, and in 1822 Soumet proposed to Hugo that they collaborate on a play derived from Sir Walter Scott's *Kenilworth*. The collaboration, however, did not work. After reading what Hugo had written, Soumet expressed his disapproval. Hugo, reluctantly it appears, finally finished the play himself and called it *Amy Robsart.** He also came to the conclusion that progress in the theatre would not be made by dramatizing the novels of Sir Walter Scott.

Spain and Victor Hugo. For almost the entire Romantic generation, especially for writers like Théophile Gautier* and Prosper Merimée (perhaps best remembered outside of France as the author of *Carmen*, turned into an opera by Georges Bizet), Spain was the center of their fascination with the Middle East, which is usually referred to as Orientalism.*

Hugo himself was no exception. As a child he had been taken to the Iberian Peninsula by his mother because his father, General Léopold Hugo, was serving in the Napoleonic forces stationed there. Hugo's poetry is filled, especially *La Légende des siècles*, with both biographical and literary echoes to the Spain of his childhood, and to the Spain of his literary intellect.

Here, however, it should be noted that Hugo has had an ongoing reputation in Spain, equal to that in the United Kingdom, the United States, South America, and even in the Far East. A recent sampling of catalogue entries in the National Library in Madrid proves that Hugo remains one of the most respected foreign writers. A quick check there of Hugo entries also demonstrates his modernity for modern Spanish intellectual society. Almost all of his writings have received new translations. An anthology of his poetry was published in Barcelona in 1987. Even his first novel, *Bug-Jargal*,* was reissued in 1989. The list of new editions continues ad infinitum: *Choses vues*,* 1990; *Notre-Dame de Paris*,* 1987; *Cromwell*,* 1979; and *Han d'Islande*,* 1995.

It is startling and somewhat amazing to see the extent to which Victor Hugo enjoys almost universal admiration. Other authors die, and their work is forgotten. Hugo, a true giant, continues to enjoy worldwide acclaim. Spain, France's neighbor and, at times in the past, its enemy, obviously pays homage through these translations of Hugo's poetry, theatre, and novels.

Spiritism. Victor Hugo's belief in the spirit world, the material life of this world, and the hidden world of the spirit, including the dead, is basic to his theological thinking, and part of his adherence to the universality and harmony of all existence. He had a profound belief in the existence of God and in the afterlife, but this is a belief divorced from any systematic religious system (*see Religions et religion*).

It is evident across his entire work that Hugo gave spiritual substance not just to man, but to animals, even to inert matter, such as rocks and stones; each, he felt, had differing degrees of consciousness.

There is no doubt that the drowning death of his daughter Léopoldine Hugo* in 1843 stimulated Hugo's desire to come in contact with the "other" world. Consequently, after the arrival of Delphine Gay* on Jersey, on September 6, 1853, a series of séances ensued introduced by Gay. Such séances were in great vogue during the first half of the nineteenth century. These became almost daily activities at the Hugo home, lasting through July 1855.

Hugo's son Charles seemed the most adept at calling forth the spirits

as the Hugo group sat around the three-legged table, passing the necessary "fluids" from one hand to another. Hugo would then pose questions to the table. Certain knocks would indicate the presence not only
of Léopoldine but also a striking assortment of Biblical and historical
personages, including Moses, Jesus Christ, and William Shakespeare. It
has been noted that most of the recorded words from these spirits bore
Hugo's linguistic and syntactical style. Even more striking were the ap-
paritions of abstract concepts, such as Idea or Shadow of the Tomb,
which were indicative of Victor or Charles Hugo's obsession with the
questions of what an afterlife could be all about. Some of the recorded
messages seem, if not obscene, then at least erotic, which may have again
something to do with Hugo's concept of the continuity of all aspects of
human life, even after death. Hugo, along with other early French and
English Romantic writers, does not seem to have been overtly aware of
how they were mixing spirituality and sexuality (*see* Sexuality and Victor
Hugo), an idea that is just now gaining theological importance at the
end of the twentieth century, but now with serious theological speculation.

It can probably be affirmed, especially on the basis of the love poems
found in *Les Contemplations*,* that Hugo believed that the love between
man and woman would be more intense and fulfilling in the spirit life
than it was here on earth—not unlike those sentiments found in the
poetry of Elizabeth Barrett Browning (1806–1861) and her husband Robert Browning (1812–1889). While at first glance such mixtures of the spiritual and physical might seem outrageous to the religiously inclined,
they have, all the same, a basis in Christian mystical theology as expressed in the writings of two sixteenth-century Spanish mystical poets:
Saint Teresa of Avila, and Saint John of the Cross.

Hugo's spiritism was an ephemeral experience which did not lead to
a total rejection of any rationalistic explanation of existence. Romanticism
reestablished spiritual values, but in a most unorthodox manner. The
spiritualism of the Romantics is evident not just in the table maneuvers
on the Channel Islands, but also in many of Hugo's religious and philosophical poems (and also in some of his love lyrics), which are aesthetic
translations of his quest for the absolute.

BIBLIOGRAPHY

Simon, G. *Les Tables tournantes de Jersey*. Paris, 1923.
Grillet, Charles. *Victor Hugo spirite*. Paris, 1929.

Stendhal (pseud. Henri Beyle). Stendhal (1783–1842) ranks with Hugo,
Honoré de Balzac,* Gustave Flaubert,* and Emile Zola* as one of the
inventors of the nineteenth-century French novel. His best-known work,
Le Rouge et le noir (1831), fits neatly within the tradition of the French

psychological novel, reflecting back to Madame de Lafayette's *La Prin-cesse de Clèves* (1678) while anticipating the analyses of love in the work of Marcel Proust's *A la Recherche du temps perdu* (Remembrance of things past), 1913–1928. Among Stendhal's small but important works can be found the *Charterhouse of Parma* (1839) and several other novels beginning with *Armance* (1827). His lifelong passion for Italy, and for music and painting, is revealed in his aesthetic studies on Joseph Haydn and Wolf-gang Amadeus Mozart; his history of Italian painting; and his travel documentary, *Rome, Naples and Florence.*

It is only in retrospect that we attach Stendhal's life to Hugo's as Ro-manticism began to be fashioned in the 1820s. Three elements need ex-planation: the cult of Napoléon; political Romanticism, and Romantic aesthetics.

Fascination, if not intellectual and emotional intoxication with the presence and impact of Napoléon Bonaparte on the first generation of French Romantics (born from the chaos of the French Revolution), is apparent in all the Romantic writers. For Stendhal, it was an unequivocal admiration derived perhaps from his service in the Napoleonic armies. Hugo, himself the son of a general, remained ambivalent toward the emperor. His early royalist and Catholic convictions, revealed in *Le Con-servateur Littéraire* (as opposed to a more liberal approach at the end of the 1820s evidenced in the periodical *Le Globe*), allowed him to write derisive opposition poetry, such as *Bonaparte*. All the same, admiration for Napoléon is found from practically the very start with such poems as *Lui* (Him). It could be that Hugo was trying to assess the impact of Napoléon on the Romantic generation. Hugo's latter day liberalism re-flects somewhat an eighteenth-century attitude, as does Stendhal's, in works like *Ô drapeau de Wagram, ô pays de Voltaire*, a nostalgic look at eighteenth-century liberalism that will inform the life of the mature Hugo. His faith in Napoléon was reinforced by his vitriolic protest against Napoléon III,* seen as the usurper of a greater Romantic glory. This is best expressed in the satirical poetry of *Les Châtiments* (1853), especially in the long poem *L'Expiation.**

Stendhal, more a man of the eighteenth century, if only by his dates, represents political Romanticism of the left, a liberal interpretation of the ramifications of the revolution and the advent of Bonaparte. Hugo's gradual conversion to liberalism and ultimately a type of Romantic so-cialism, made him the undisputed head of the Young France Romantics. Stendhal moved into the background not so much because of political or artistic defeat, as perhaps because of age. Stendhal's path was that of the modern novel, Hugo's that of modern poetry.

The decisive area of confrontation is within Romantic aesthetics. Sten-dhal, who had had dramaturgical ambitions (to be the new Molière) and who wrote an important document on the art of the theatre, *Racine and*

Shakespeare (1825), finally opted for the novel. His dramatic theory, however, seeking to replace classical French, mythologically based tragedy with the Shakespearean model of the history of the English kings (the marriage of history with myth), found its success with Victor Hugo, whose play *Hernani** (1830) was but the first in a series of historically based *drame*,* the new form that replaced classical tragedy. *Hernani*, which pitted the young Romantics against the die-hard classicists, established Hugo squarely as the head of the French Romantic movement.

A more important area, however, seems to be the question of literary language. Stendhal rejected poetry and figurative language. In his novels he tried to eliminate simile and metaphor as irrelevant to the modern age. This he called the style of the Civil Code of Napoléon. Hugo sensed something different, namely the marriage of prose and poetry as can be evaluated in the very opening scene of *Hernani*. It was poetry that won out through Hugo for French Romanticism, and although Hugo remains one of France's greatest playwrights and novelists, it was his sense of poetry that dominated even those two genres. This seems to have been Stendhal's fundamental misunderstanding of the new age of which he was a significant part, but he was more firmly planted than Hugo in the eighteenth century.

Stopping along the way. *See Halte en marchant.*

Story of the centuries, The. *See Légende des siècles, La.*

Suicide. Suicide was a major preoccupation and motif of European Romanticism. The most famous and perhaps most influential example is Johann Wolfgang on Goethe's *Die Leiden des jungen Werthers* (The sorrows of young Werther, 1774), in which the hero, despondent over his unrequited love for the married Lotte, shoots himself to end his amorous longing. Goethe's text had an enormous influence all over Europe; many young Romantics emulated the poses and postures of this early Romantic hero. Following the example of Goethe, the majority of, but not all, Romantic suicides seem to have been provoked by love situations which were in some manner or other compromised. The hero of Etienne Pivert de Senancour's early Romantic novel *Oberman* (1804) contemplates suicide less out of frustrated love and more out of a serious disillusionment with reality, a type of *mal du siècle* (century illness) not unlike the ennui felt by Chateaubriand's hero René from his novel *René* (1805). Oberman lives the life of a hermit in the Swiss Alps, away from a society whose false values he cannot abide, demonstrating the influence of Jean-Jacques Rousseau. A major section of this actionless novel is filled with Oberman's mental review of suicide as related in Western literature and biography.

Preparing the ground for Hugo's treatment of the subject is Chateaubriand's brief novel *Atala, ou les amours de deux sauvages dans le désert* (1804), in which the heroine, Atala, poisons herself in order to remain a virgin, despite her passionate love for the Indian Chactas.

Chateaubriand's Catholic theology presumed that Atala must remain a virgin to fulfill a promise made to her dying mother that she would remain pure, to spare her mother from eternal damnation. Alfred de Vigny's* Romantic drama *Chatterton* (1835) depicts the death of the poet Thomas Chatterton, who killed himself, partly because of his love for the married Kitty Bell, but also because he decided that the utilitarian society in which he lived had no place for a poet. This typical nineteenth-century quarrel focused on two opposing camps—materialistic utilitarianism versus art for the sake of art.

Three important Romantic suicides should be cited from the work of Victor Hugo. His play *Hernani** (1830) revolves about the passionate love of the bandit outlaw, who is truly a nobleman, for Doña Sol de Silva, a love that is reciprocated and leads to marriage. This love was opposed, however, by Doña Sol's uncle Don Ruy Gomez de Silva,* who intended, in spite of his old age and his blood relationship to her, to marry the young and beautiful girl. Having exacted a promise from Hernani* to put his life into his hands, Don Ruy arrives at the marriage nuptials and demands Hernani's life. Out of the code of honor, he is obliged to take poison. Doña Sol, determined not to live without her new husband, also takes poison, and they both die, somewhat in the manner of Romeo and Juliet. Don Ruy, realizing the extent of his evil ways, considers himself damned and kills himself.

Hernani, which ended the old quarrel between the ancients and the moderns in French dramatic theory—classical decorum forbade any violent action on the stage—brought forth the new Romantic theory of drama, in which killings and suicide were par for the course. Two related novels, *Les Travailleurs de la mer** and *L'Homme qui rit,** also include suicides brought on through the love question. Gilliatt,* hero of *Les Travailleurs de la mer*, commits suicide when he watches his beloved Deruchette depart with her new husband, an Anglican clergyman, for England. Seeing no reason to continue living, he allows the rising tide to engulf him. Similarly, Gwynplaine,* the deformed hero of *L'Homme qui rit*, is finally reunited, aboard a ship bound for Holland, with his beloved, the blind girl Dea.* But Dea dies, of unknown causes, and Gwynplaine, without a moment's hesitation, jumps off the ship and drowns, so as to be reunited in death with his beloved.

It can be seen that suicide in Hugo's work follows typical Romantic conventions, no more original than those found in Goethe, Senancour, Chateaubriand, or de Vigny.

Swinburne, Algernon Charles. One of the most important figures of literary England in the nineteenth century, Swinburne (1837–1909) was greatly attracted to French culture in general, and to French literature for which he had a deep admiration. As a critic he is known for his works on William Shakespeare (1880) and Ben Jonson (1889), as well as his very important study of Victor Hugo (1886).

As a student at Eton, the young Swinburne had won, as a literary prize, a beautiful edition of Hugo's *Notre-Dame de Paris*,* with illustrations by Tony Johannot. His passionate attachment to Hugo's writings and political views made him an ardent enemy of Napoléon III,* certainly an adverse position in the England of Queen Victoria. Aside from his devotion to Hugo, Swinburne in general was a Francophile; he was attracted to the poetry of Charles Baudelaire* and to the art-for-the-sake-of-art movement which had been in vogue in France since the time of Théophile Gautier* and the Parnassian poets,* a sentiment which the more utilitarian Victor Hugo might have found hard to understand.

Swinburne is a fine example, on the literary level, of a general English appreciation of Hugo in the nineteenth century, in spite of a general British cultural aversion to things French.

Symbolism and Victor Hugo. The symbolism of the Romantic painters and poets should not be confused with the symbolism at the end of the nineteenth century in France. Although the end result was basically the same, the procedures were radically different. On the surface, Romantic poetry gives the impression of being discursive and removed from the hermetic realms of *poésie pure*,* poetry as experienced by Arthur Rimbaud, Stéphane Mallarmé,* Paul Verlaine and Paul Valéry.* To put the symbolic thrust of the nineteenth century in some perspective, it is necessary to review briefly what was accomplished by the later symbolist poets (it should be remembered that there was never any unified poetic school of symbolism).

Charles Baudelaire* can be regarded as the true precursor of the symbolist movement in France. His poetry encompasses most of the tendencies of the century—Romantic poetry, Parnassian poetry,* symbolist poetry. Before Baudelaire, there was the work of the Romantic poet Gérard de Nerval (1808–1855) who may be considered a precursor of Baudelaire (1821–1867) and who, as a poet, anticipated the work of not just the symbolists but also the surrealists of the early twentieth century.

Baudelaire's symbolism is apparent in numerous poems in *Les Fleurs du mal* (The flowers of evil) (1857). Thematic in nature, the collection is often spoiled by the poet's eager willingness to explicate his poetry. Thus, in an early poem, *L'Albatros*, this graceful bird of the skies is taken prisoner by sailors on a ship and ridiculed. One senses here the abasement of something majestic and free, a high symbolism equivalent to that found in the twelfth-century poet Marie de France in her *lais*, especially the famous *Laustic* which has been interpreted by Leo Spitzer as the symbolic destruction of Joy. This poem could well have done without its concluding strophe in which the poet reduced the image to its discursive meaning: *Le poéte est semblable au prince des nuées/Qui hante la tempête et se rit de l'archer; Exilé sur le sol au milieu des huées/Ses ailes de géant l'empechent de marcher* (The poet is like this prince of the skies/who haunts the tempest and laughs at the archer,/exiled on the ground amidst the jeering/His giant wings keep him from walking).

Baudelaire's usual method can be called one of the permutations of an initial image. This is evident in such poems as *La Chevelure* (Head of hair) or *La Cloche fêlée* (The Cracked Bell). *La Cloche fêlée* recounts a winter evening in which the poet listens to the church bells from his room. Starting with a comparison of a vigorous and healthy bell, compared to an old soldier keeping guard duty in his tent, the poet compares himself to a broken bell and, in the second tercet, he changes the healthy guard duty to a scene of military carnage: *Semble le râle épais d'un blessé qu'on oublie/Au bord d'un lac de sang, sous un grand tas de morts/Et qui meurt, sans bouger, dans d'immenses efforts* (Seems the thick death rattle of a wounded and forgotten person/At the edge of a lake of blood, under a big pile of dead/And who dies, without budging, in immense efforts). It is in this manner that the poem proceeds from an observable prepoetic tonality (hearing the church bells) to an introspection on the poet's own moral position, visualized in the horror scene of the final strophe. This can be seen as the usual procedure of Baudelaire in symbolism, but there are other examples such as *Les Phares* (Beacons) in which he uses no point of departure outside the poem itself. It becomes, as Mallarmé would later state, a long metaphor. Baudelaire's symbolism is summarized in a kind of *art poétique* in the sonnet *Correspondances* which emphasizes the presence of a hidden reality in the universe. Baudelaire may be considered the link to Victor Hugo.

Verlaine's symbolism, impressionistic in nature, stresses the musicality of poetry. His poem *Art poétique* states that poetry is music above all else, and rhetoric should have its neck broken.

Rimbaud's symbolism could aptly be described as a symbolism of discovery, of a world to be uncovered underneath apparent forms. This is best illustrated in such poems as *Bateau ivre* (The drunken boat) or the very long *Une Saison en enfer* (A season in hell). His position, in general, is quite distinct from that of Mallarmé, who believed that poetry is born from the nothingness of existence (except for his exception *Prose pour des esseintes*, which speaks in the Rimbaudian sense of a voyage to a mysterious island of pure poetry that dazzles pure reason, and which in the long run becomes intolerable to the mind). That is, poetry is akin to the world before its creation. Out of the darkness is born the ephemeral and fleeting poetic creation.

Valéry, at first a fervent disciple of Mallarmé, abandoned poetry for almost a generation while he devoted himself to the study of mathematics. After he returned to poetry, we find in his work a mixture of symbolist Platonism with Aristotelian logic. Valéry's symbolism in a sense attempts, as did the seventeenth century, to create a cohabitation for reason and intuition, for the *esprit de géométrie* and the *esprit de finesse* (the spirit of geometry and the spirit of intuition).

Basically, Victor Hugo's symbolism did not make use of the techniques of the symbolists described above. A case could be made, however, that here and there in his poetry symbolism is effected by what Hugo leaves unsaid.

On a very basic level, certain poems come immediately to mind—first the famous *Mazeppa* poem of *Les Orientales*,* in which the ride of Ivan Stepanovich Mazeppa,* tied naked to the back of a vigorous stallion, presents an impressionistic kaleidoscope as the horse carries its captive rider across the Ukraine. It would not lack plausibility to see this poem of Hugo as a precursor to Rimbaud's *Bateau ivre*. The *Mazeppa* poem has been interpreted as the symbolic representation of genius, perhaps that of the poet himself.

The framing poems of Hugo's *Les Chansons des rues et des bois** also are written in a symbolic manner, meaning that it is hard to put a singular, one-to-one meaning on the poetic lines. The introductory poem, entitled *Le Cheval* (The horse), in thirty-six strophes, each of four lines, also seems to represent genius. This horse, Pegasus, is derived from the symbolism of Greek mythology, a winged horse born of the blood of the Medusa. Similarly symbolic is the concluding poem of *Les Chansons des rues et des bois, Au Cheval* (To the horse) whose symbolism is minimized by its excessive length (divided into nine parts, for a total of fifty-seven strophes, four lines each, for a total of two hundred and twenty-eight lines). Yet the poem is indicative of a deep meaning to be found in the ride of this horse, a horse which finds light in the darkness (as does the poet): *Faisant subitement tout voir/Malgré l'ombre, malgré les voiles,/Envoie à ce fatal ciel noir/Une éclaboussure d'étoiles* (Suddenly making everything clear/In spite of the shadow, in spite of the veils/Sends to this fatal black sky/a splash of stars). This is surely a symbolic presentation of the poet as a *voyant*, to use Rimbaud's word. In these "horse" poems, derived from the classics, we have in Hugo a Romantic version of what Rimbaud will call *le dérèglement progressif des sens* (the progressive disordering of the senses), or the abolition of any discursive ordering or perception of the universe.

In a very penetrating study of French Romantic symbolism (painters and poets), Helmut Hatzfeld uses Victor Hugo as the outstanding example of the symbolist thrust during the Romantic period. Starting with the famous *La Conscience** poem from *La Légende des siècles*, we see Cain pursued by the eye of God, a masonic symbol that adorns the American one dollar bill. Hugo turns Genesis 4:13–24 into a leitmotif of God's eye penetrating all of Cain's hideouts. It has an effect similar to that of the short stories of Edgar Allan Poe, such as the *Tell-Tale Heart* (it should be remembered that Poe was the favorite writer of the French symbolists who saw in both his prose and poetry their proper origins). Cain cannot sleep, and he wanders for thirty days and nights with his family. He finally builds a fortress and nails to its entrance: *Défense à Dieu d'entrer* (God is forbidden to enter). Hatzfeld concluded, "Hugo's clever solution of a symbolic Crime pursued by Divine Justice is exclusively poetic, the effectiveness of which consists in the geometric gradation of the conscience motif from *moderato* to *fortissimo*, stongly dependent on successive scenes in progression" (Hatzfeld, 1952, 150).

Hatzfeld also did a symbolic reading of Hugo's *Saison de semailles* (Season of planting).

> Hugo's apocalyptic approach penetrates still more profoundly. The sower is an old man, so he belongs to the evening that surrounds him. The sowing symbolizes the provisions the passing generation is making for the coming one, on the immense plain of the clan and even of mankind. This peasant is a conscious link in the chain of being. He throws the seed far, and his gesture, too, appears immense in the twilight between day and night, life and death, seeming to reach up to the stars. This makes him appear really a sower *sub specie aeternitatis*. (156)

The same could be said for Hugo's *Booz endormi** from *La Légende des siècles*. Boaz's dream is a symbolic prophecy of the founding of the house of David, from which Christ will issue.

These are but a few examples of the high symbolism that is found throughout Hugo's work. His immense productivity allowed him to reach many levels, discursive at times, most often lyrical and very often symbolic. As has been demonstrated in other entries in this encyclopedia, Hugo is at one and the same time a Romantic (*see* Romanticism and Victor Hugo), a Parnassian, and a symbolist even in the sense in which the term was used at the end of the century.

Simplified literary history did not recognize Hugo's symbolism, whose forms often were born from both Biblical and secular history and from Greek mythology. In other words, the symbolic depths of Hugo may have been properly understood only since the time of the later symbolists themselves. Such a traditional literary history, given to facile classifications, would assign to Alfred de Vigny* the role of the Romantic symbolist. This, as so interpreted, is not true. Alfred de Vigny wrote allegories that are susceptible to one-on-one interpretations. This is found in such poems as *La Mort du loup* (The death of the wolf), *Moïses* (Moses), *Le Mont des Oliviers* (The Mount of Olives); and *La Bouteille à la mer* (The bottle in the sea). Each poem suggests stoic resignation to man's fate, the destiny of the superior man, the despair of the human Christ, and the idea of progress. If there is a symbolism in de Vigny's poetry, it can be found perhaps in his landscapes which seem to carry the symbolic message better than the allegorical interpretations that he usually adds as a conclusion to his poems.

This is seldom the path of Victor Hugo. His genius incorporated all of the new poetic tendencies of the nineteenth century. His creativity well fits definitions of the poetic imagination as found in the theories of Samuel Taylor Coleridge and the German Romantic-classicist Goethe.

BIBLIOGRAPHY

Hatzfeld, Helmut. "Errors and Assets of Symbolism." In *Literature through Art: A New Approach to French Literature*. Chapel Hill: University of North Carolina Press, 1952.

T

Tapner, the execution of Mr. In 1854 a certain Mr. Tapner, a convicted murderer, was hanged on the island of Guernsey. Victor Hugo, consistently the enemy of capital punishment* (*Le Dernier Jour d'un condamné**) wrote a long letter of protest to the British foreign secretary Lord Palmerston (1784–1865). Although it had perhaps been written in vain, it did ensure that Mr. Tapner would be the last person to be executed on Guernsey and certainly, if indirectly, contributed to the abolition of capital punishment in the United Kingdom in the twentieth century.

The atrocity of execution, as seen by Hugo, is best translated, however, through his poetry rather than by a letter of protest. *La Nature* (Book Three, poem twenty-nine of *Les Contemplations**) further develops Hugo's sacramental concept of trees as the noble and aristocratic dwellers in God's creation. This poem speaks of the relationship, in the form of dialogue, between the tree and the good woodcutter, spelling out an ideal relationship that should be enacted harmoniously on earth. Trees are willing to do many things for mankind—warm the hearth, become rafters for a lodging, become part of a plough to till the earth—but never to be made into a gallows: *Ne venez pas, trainant des cordes et des chaines,/ Vous chercher un complice au milieu des grands chênes!/Ne faites pas servir à vos crimes, vivants,/L'arbre mystérieux à qui parlent les vents* (Do not come toward us dragging your cords and chains/looking for an accomplice amidst the great oaks/Do not try to make us serve your crimes,/the mysterious tree to whom speaks the wind).

La Nature, incorporating Hugo's social protest against execution, is but one of the many poems that illustrate his meditation of nature, and specifically of the role of trees in mankind's story.

Taylor, Isidore Severin, Baron. Baron Taylor (1789–1879) was a patron of all the arts and a loyal supporter of Hugo's efforts to reform French theatre. Taylor, born in Brussels of English parents, served in the French army with his great friend, Alfred de Vigny.* He had a passionate love for literature, and he was a frequent visitor to the salon of Charles Nodier* at the Bibliothèque de l'Arsenal. Taylor, who was given the title of baron by Charles X in 1825, soon found himself in official capacities with the French dramatic administration having been appointed royal commissioner of the Comédie-Française.

Baron Taylor took a lively interest in Hugo's career as a dramatist. It was 1826 and Hugo, after immersing himself in a thorough documentation effort for his play *Cromwell,* was invited to lunch with the actor Talma. It was unofficially agreed that he would star in the production of this play, but he died later that year. Taylor later asked Hugo for a reading of *Marion de Lorme.** The great success of *Hernani** capped the triumph of Romantic theatre and enraged the classicist critic Guillaume Viennet, who saw in Taylor the defender of Hugo and the destroyer of French theatre: "Under the mysterious patronage of Baron Taylor who has been formally made part of this confusion by the minister Corbière, with the purpose of destroying French theatre."

Hugo lost sight of his old friend and did not see him again until 1872 at the burial of Charles de Chilly, director of the Odéon theatre. Taylor was then in his eighties. After serving in an official capacity in the national theatre, Taylor was appointed inspector of fine arts which led to the publication of his *Voyages pittoresques et romantiques dans l'ancienne France.* He should be remembered as an enthusiastic defender of the arts while in service of successive French administrations that did not share his optimism for the future of the arts.

Testament, Hugo's last will and. Hugo's last will and testament comes from three documents: the first dated September 23, 1875; the second, August 31, 1881; and a final codicil, August 2, 1883. The first will acknowledged his dependency on the labors of three friends—François Paul Meurice,* Auguste Vacquerie,* and Ernest Lefevre—to whom he entrusted the proper deposition of his manuscripts. In a touching remark on one of his unfinished works, *Ocean,* which the writer put into the category of "fragments and diverse ideas," he stated that all of it was written during his exile, and it was his desire to return to the sea that which he had received from her. This literary attestation coincided remarkably with the very dominant theme of the ocean, which, while obviously attached to the island exile, began as early as the poem *Oceano nox,** written when Hugo had his first glimpse of the Atlantic.

The day after the reading of the will, the three executors made a public acknowledgment of their humble recognition of the honor bestowed on them by the aging writer. In true Romantic and filial manner, they accepted the charge, but refused the monetary gain offered them by Hugo.

Hugo's second will offers philosophical premises and a high degree of spiritual humility. In it, the poet states that only three things matter: God, the soul, and responsibility. He then bequeathed all of his manuscripts to the National Library. He also left sufficient funds for the maintenance of his daughter Adèle Hugo,* who was confined with mental illness to a rest home outside of Paris, and annual trust funds for his grandchildren. It is in this will that he emphatically refused any religious service upon his death; instead, he asked only for a prayer from everyone.

The codicil of August 2, 1883, is in line with Hugo's abiding concern for the dispossessed of the earth. He left the sum of fifty thousand francs (the equivalent then of $50,000) to the poor, and in the spirit of poverty he asked to be buried in a pauper's casket. He ended by affirming his belief in God.

That Terrible Year. *See Année terrible, L'.*

Théâtre en liberté. Théâtre en liberté (Free theatre) refers to the dramatic works written by Hugo during his exile which he never published. It is a general classification made by his editors. While these plays are less known by the general reader of Hugo, they elucidate many aspects of Hugo's varied fantasies. This collection includes, with dates of composition, the following: *La Forêt mouillée* (The damp forest, 1854), perhaps better rendered in English as the swamp; *La Grand-Mère* (The grandmother, 1865); and *Mangeront-ils?* (Will they eat?, 1867), the longest play in this edition, especially important for the role of Aïrolo,* a sort of tramp-clown anticipating the twentieth-century motion-picture work of Charlie Chaplin, and from which Samuel Beckett derived *Waiting for Godot.* Of all the plays in this collection, the latter frequently has been presented in French theatres as well as on radio and television.

Hugo had also intended to include other dramatic pieces in this volume, such as his *Torquemada,* but the 1886 posthumous publication included only the entries mentioned above. Other very important plays written during the exile have been published either inside a poetic collection (*Welf* in *La Légende des siècles,* 1877; *Les Deux Trouvailles de Gallus* in *Les Quatre Vents de l'esprit,* 1881); or separately (*Torquemada,* 1882; and, posthumously, *Mille francs de récompense,* 1934, and *L'Intervention,* 1951). All of them have been performed, especially the last two pieces.

Theatre: Romantic theatre and Victor Hugo. A peculiar quirk in literary history is our perception of what is important, as opposed to the emphasis put on certain issues by contemporaries, an emphasis differing from our own. A case in point is that of Romantic theatre: the battle of Romanticism versus classicism. This battle was fought in the theatre with

(1) a slow modification of classical strictures (Mercier's *Christophe Colombe*, for example) and a classical reaction; (2) the famous 1827 *Préface de Cromwell* (*see Cromwell, Preface to*), which can be seen as the Romantic answer to Nicolas Boileau-Despréaux's codification of Classic doctrine in his *Art poétique*; and (3) the victory of *Hernani** with, for the moment, a decisive rout of the classicists.

Yet, of all aspects of Romanticism, its theatre is the least accepted. The heroes and heroines of the Romantic theory (with perhaps the exception of Alfred de Musset's* play *Lorenzaccio*) seem two dimensional, driven by an idée fixe, such as revenge or ambition, but always overwhelmed by a sense of fate or destiny leading them to a Romantic denouement of doom and death. *Hernani* is a good example. There is, from the point of view of classical psychology, not one good reason for Hernani* and Doña Sol de Silva* to poison themselves when the black domino arrives at the end of their wedding banquet to claim his due. For a long time the sense of Spanish honor has been the only explanation. Nowadays it appears as an example of modern psychology and may also have a symbolic meaning.

Thénardier family. If ever there was a family of brigands and thieves, it has to be the Thénardier clan from Hugo's *Les Misérables.** A mixture of underworld figures—grotesque, crafty, pathetic, and dangerous—they are certainly derived from the medieval French tradition of the farce and the fabliau. At times they appear even comical. Unlike the medieval approximations, they descend to the level of evil, the source for which is found by Hugo in the unequal division of society into classes, the "haves" and the "have nots." In this light, they are partially redeemed from the extremes to which they seem to be driven.

They have, especially in the role of their patriarch, Monsieur Thénardier, the street smarts of the deprived, but not the innate goodness of one equally deprived, Gavroche, who has run away from the family and who possesses a Gallic spirit (*l'esprit gaulois*), unknown to the more serious child outcasts found in the novels of Charles Dickens, little Joe, for example, in *Bleak House*. Joe and Gavroche, however, are honest, and the Thénardiers are not; their quasi-animality puts them at the lower rank of the human ladder.

The Thénardiers form an important and integral role in the binding of the narrative of *Les Misérables*. They are essential in the intertwining of the coincidences (a basic structure in Hugo's novels) that lace together this very long novel. They are first presented as the guardians of Cosette* whom Fantine* places in their hands for safekeeping, for which she pays them increasing amounts due to their demands for additional funds. Little Cosette becomes, in Cinderella fashion, their servant; in contrast, the Thénardier girls are spoiled by their mother. Cosette is portrayed as frail, homely, and dressed in rags, while the two sisters are gracious, and appropriately adorned with the finest of clothing. The parallel to the Cinderella fable of Charles Perrault in his 1697 *Contes de la dame l'oye* (Tales of Mother Goose) is obvious and must have been known by Hugo.

Thénardier himself is introduced into Hugo's narration of the Battle of Waterloo* in the middle section of this novel. Although he claims to have saved the life of the father of Marius,* it is clear that he is nothing more than a human vulture stealing things of value from the dead or dying soldiers.

The Thénardiers are perpetually in debt, and after their hovel of an inn is closed (an important scene in the musical of *Les Misérables*), they are next seen in Paris where they try to swindle Jean Valjean* of 200,000 francs. The entrapment of Jean Valjean by Thénardier and a group of hardened Parisian criminals reminds the reader of similar dark moments in the London world of Dickens, for example, Fagin in *Oliver Twist*.

Hugo's similes and metaphors, which he groups around this family, aptly betray their low life which seems almost subhuman. In Hugo's view, however, this could be a consequence of poverty and alienation from the mainstream of progressive nineteenth-century society.

Theses on theatrical adaptations of Victor Hugo's novels. Arnaud Laster, professor of modern French literature at the University of Paris III-Censier, is the most eminent authority on the transformation of Hugo's novels into dramatic pieces. His most important work in this regard is *Pleins Feux sur Victor Hugo* (1981). Laster has directed the following very important master's theses in this area: Michel Bernard, *Nerval lecteur de Hugo* (Nerval, reader of Hugo); Michele Petit, *Etudes des adaptations de Notre-Dame-de-Paris* (Study of the adaptations of *Notre-Dame de Paris**); Cécile Cussac, *Les Adaptations des Misérables* (The adaptations of *Les Misérables**); Marie-Alice Dessiotou, *l'Adaptation théâtrale de Bug-Jargal* (The theatrical adaptation of *Bug-Jargal*); Marie Schmidt, *Quatrevingt-treize, l'adaptation théâtrale de Paul Meurice* (*Quatrevingt-treize,** theatrical adaptation of François Paul Meurice*).

BIBLIOGRAPHY

Laster, Arnaud. *Pleins feux sur Victor Hugo*. Paris: Edition Comédie-Française, 1981.

Things Witnessed. *See Choses vues.*

Tholomyès. Tholomyès, the father of Cosette,* led a quasi-debauched life as a student in Paris with the grisette Fantine.* Hugo describes scenes in *Les Misérables** which recall Louis-Henri Murger's *Scènes de la vie de bohème* (Scenes of Bohemian life, 1847–1849). Tholomyès represents the carefree, lackadaisical life of would-be students at the Sorbonne of either the nineteenth century or even earlier types, as found in the late medieval poetry of François Villon (1431–1463?). Unlike Villon, who disappeared from recorded history, the fictional Tholomyès quickly abandons his libertine Parisian days to return, like so many heroes of nineteenth-century French novels, to bourgeois conformity and familial duties. Tholomyès is indifferent to the fact that he has fathered a child, and the narrator, expressing some distaste for this unsavory type, decided to speak no more of him. A judgment is passed: Tholomyès has become nothing more than a fat and rich provincial attorney. Here, of course, he resembles the concluding statements in Murger's novel of Parisian Bohemian life.

To Chateaubriand. *See A Chateaubriand.*

Tomorrow at daybreak. *See Demain dès l'aube.*

Torquemada. This verse drama in two parts, composed of five acts, was written on Guernsey at the height of Hugo's anticlerical feelings, fed by his historical ponderings of the fanaticism of religion, especially during the Spanish Inquisition. The play, composed during the summer of 1869, postdates a poem from *La Légende des siècles** written in 1859, *L'Inquisition,* a satirical piece on Torquemada's relentless persecution of heretics, Jews, and Moslems. The play was published in 1882, but it was never performed during Hugo's lifetime.

While the work, in the interest of dramatic art, manipulates history, reworking it with poetic imagination, it all the same puts on the stage quite a few true historical personages, starting with Torquemada, the Dominican grand inquisitor; King Ferdinand and Queen Isabella; and Pope Alexander VI. Also impressive are the radical changes of place with minute instructions concerning the mise-en-scène, a matter to which Hugo, the painter and dramatist, would usually give great attention. The action moves across Spain, first in Cataluña, then to Italy, then again in Spain, first at Burgos, then at a former Moorish palace in Seville, and then in the king's secret park in Seville.

The plot centers on the intractable religious zeal of the grand inquisitor who has a thirst for burning nonconformists, and this includes those making the slightest deviancy from his idea of orthodoxy. In fact, the denouement is dependent on a minor infraction. Torquemada, at first himself judged as heretical is sealed alive in a tomb at a monastery. He is rescued by two young noble lovers, Sanchez and Rosa, to whom he will be indebted. At the marriage of the young couple, the king, who lusts after Rosa, banishes them both to monasteries. Sanchez's uncle, the marquis de Fuentel (grandfather of Sanchez), intervenes on their behalf throughout the play. In the final act, in the king's secret garden, he fretfully plans their escape from Spain. Meanwhile, the court jester Gucho, out of fear of Torquemada, reveals the king's tryst with the presumed abducted Rosa and gives Torquemada the key to the garden. There, he encounters the young lovers and learns of their fate. In gratitude for their help in the past, he helps them and even marries them. He learns, however, that they had used a cross to move the stone blocking him within the tomb. This sacrilege can be answered only by death, and the play ends with the arrival of the band of followers of Torquemada, who will lead the couple to their immolation.

The personage of Torquemada is the most intriguing, especially his monologue which ends act 2 of part 2. As he watches the burning of the Jews, the monk becomes transfixed on these fires of salvation. He truly believes that the liberated souls will find paradise as soon as their earthly suffering has ended, a kind of purgatory on earth, in Spain. Against this strong characterization is opposed that of the weak and erotic Ferdinand, first subservient to his wife, but the two of them live in total fear of the grand inquisitor.

The play has many aspects of the spectacle with the processions of priests, monks, and bishop, the parade of the penitents; and the presentation of the persecuted Jews before the king and queen. It has been criticized as lacking in verisimilitude, but "realism" per se, as understood later in the century, is not a possible intent for Hugo. He fuses history with imagination and with his tendency to hold onto stage devices inherited from Gothic romances. The play is successful and saved from banality by its verse form, written at the height of Hugo's poetic maturity.

Translations of Hugo's works. All translations are enormously difficult to make, giving assent to the old saying that to translate is to betray. In the case of Victor Hugo, he has been fortunate enough to have been very well rendered into English both in Great Britain and in the United States. Certain errors, however, do creep into the best of texts, and some should be cited as illustrations of the pitfalls to be encountered by anyone undertaking such work, regardless of the individual's proficiency in the target language.

Such is the case, albeit a minor one, in the excellent translation of Hugo's *Les Misérables*,* made by Lee Fahnestock and Norman MacAfee (New American Library, 1987), based on the classic translation of Charles E. Wilbour (A. L. Burt Company, New York, 1862, and authorized by Hugo), published in the same year as the European editions.

The errors are small, but they should be called to attention if only to indicate the difficulties encountered by anyone trying to render, from one language to another, any piece of literature, especially with such a long and difficult text as *Les Misérables*.

In Book Three of this translation, entitled *In the Year 1817*, chapter 5, *Bombarda's*, the reader is in the act of witnessing the conclusion of an idyllic Sunday excursion to Saint Cloud, with nice river breezes refreshingly arising from the Seine. The important character in this interlude is Fantine,* soon to be the mother of Cosette,* fathered by Tholomyès,* a carefree and lazy student at the Sorbonne.

At the conclusion of their outing, the four couples arrive at the restaurant of Bombarda on the Champs-Elysées exhilarated, no doubt, by their ride on the Russian Mountains. Any modern reader could be confused by what could possibly be meant by a Russian Mountain. It is easily explained by recourse to any standard French-English dictionary: *Attraction foraine constituée d'une serie de montées et de descentes rapides sur lequelles on se laisse glisser dans un wagonnet*. Simply put, in plain English, a Russian Mountain is a roller-coaster.

Likewise, any reader could also be confused by Javert's* confrontation with Jean Valjean* concerning "Father Champmathieu," a man accused of stealing apples. The American or English reader might readily think that the narrator is referring to either a Roman Catholic or Anglican priest, since the appellation is commonly used by those communions to describe their male clergy. A better translation would be "old man Champmathieu." French terms of familiarity such as *le père* and *la mère* for neighbors, either in a Parisian quarter or in the provinces, meaning someone who may be eccentric, or simply amusing, or even considered with respect and affection is almost impossible to render in English. A case in point is Balzac's novel *Le Père Goriot*, translated as "Old Goriot." Father, of course, would not fit.

These are minor irritations which beset any translator. So much depends not only upon linguistic proficiency, knowing both languages intimately, but also on a solid assimilation of the culture from which the material is derived.

Translation of the work of another nineteenth-century writer, Ernest Renan (1823–1892), a former Roman Catholic seminarian who abandoned Christianity after his philological studies of ancient languages convinced him otherwise, gives us another example of mistranslations caused by misunderstandings of the culture of the target language. Thus a nineteenth-century translation of Renan's famous autobiography *Souvenirs d'enfance et de jeunesse* (Memories of childhood and youth) startlingly renders *le petit seminaire*, at Saint-Nicolas du Chardonnet in Paris, as "the Little Seminary." An informed person would know that, in Roman Catholic parlance, the proper wording in English is "minor seminary."

French, despite its claim to being the clearest and most precise of all the Romance tongues (*Tout ce qui n'est pas clair n'est pas français*—What is not clear is not French), still presents enormous obstacles that demand minute scrutiny, not only of the literal or figurative meaning, but also of the social and cultural contexts. Such thorny problems most certainly are magnified in moving from Western to Eastern cultures (Chinese or Japanese), without speaking of the lesser problems of moving from a Romance to a Germanic (English) tongue. Therefore, let the reader beware.

Travailleurs de la mer, Les. *Les Travailleurs de la mer* (The toilers of the sea), published in March 1886, is derived from Hugo's long exile on the Channel Island of Guernsey whose culture, customs, and language he assimilated with study, observation, and a certain amount of surprise. There is a submotif running throughout this novel which views the Channel Islands and their inhabitants as a new cross-breed between England and France. As Hugo so aptly put this question in his long introduction to the narrative: *Les îles de la Manche sont des morceaux de France tombés dans la mer et ramassés par l'Angleterre* (The Channel Islands are pieces of France fallen into the sea and picked up by England).

The narrative of this sea novel is not complicated, and, unlike its title, it has next to nothing to do with the fishing industry. The narration starts on a Christmas Day in 1820 (?) in which we see the beautiful Deruchette who mysteriously writes Gilliatt's* name in the snow, the meaning of which remains symbolically unclear. Gilliatt lives on an isolated street of Saint-Sampson with his mother who is disliked and disapproved of by the neighboring gossips. With his mother he occupies a *maison visionée** (a visionary house), a place thought to be for witchcraft. The whispers, all negative about the hero, assume that he is in league with the devil, that he protects animals and talks with toads. He is also supposed to be a *guérisseur*, a healer. His qualities are enumerated: he is ambidextrous, an excellent swimmer, and a good sailor, in short, a man of many talents. He is also rumored to be a *visionnaire*: a witch, fortune teller, and predictor of the future.

The narrator then turns his attention to a secondary protagonist, Mess Lethierry, the uncle and protector of Deruchette, who invests in the new steamboat type of navigation. A native son of Guernsey, he is a good man, but a terrible sailor. Mess Lethierry is cheated out of 50,000 francs by a so-called friend, Rantaine. The reader learns that Mess Lethierry is anticlerical (like Hugo), and his steamboat is considered by the local clergy to be an instrument of the devil; this modern boat is a *libertinage* (a licentious invention).

A most complex part of this novel concerns the personality of Gilliatt and his attitude toward women. He appears to be a virgin; he scorns the company of women, even old ones, yet he spies on them when they bathe in the channel. This is perhaps the most difficult and deepest part of the novel as the narrator tries to unravel Gilliatt's personality.

The novel then introduces the character of Clubin who becomes the captain of the steamboat owned by Mess Lethierry. Clubin is the ultimate hypocrite, whom all see as an example of probity and virtue. During a crossing from Saint-Malo to Guernsey, a terrible storm arises and the helmsman, who is drunk, seems responsible for the perilous condition of the ship, the *Durance*. There is a shipwreck, the passengers are saved, but the whole event seems to have been a prearranged scenario by Clubin to escape with the fifty thousand francs which he had taken from the original thief, Rantaine. He is dragged into the sea, however, and killed by an octopus.

The second half of the novel is dedicated to Gilliatt's efforts to salvage whatever remains of the *Durance*. He succeeds, against almost insurmountable odds, to raise the essential sections of the ship, in the course of which he does battle with an octopus. As the novel concludes Gilliatt is a hero to Mess Lethierry who wants him to marry his niece. Gilliatt knows that this is impossible, and through a series of manipulations, he arranges the marriage of Deruchette with the Anglican clergyman who then sail for England. As Gilliatt watches the ship disappear on the horizon, the tide rises, and he allows himself to drown: a heroic suicide* in the name of impossible love.

The invention of the steamboat by Robert Fulton is a pivotal point in this novel. It is changing the modes of maritime navigation, and it is also a means for the enrichment of Mess Lethierry, ruined by the wreck of the *Durance* but saved by the salvage efforts of Gilliatt. The comparison of old and new modes of navigation seems to anticipate similar conflicts to be found in the novels of Emile Zola, such as *Au Bonheur des dames* (A woman's happiness), in which small merchants see themselves destroyed by the advent of the department store. The steamboat is feared by the peasants and condemned by the church.

The novel also presents a typical Hugolian long digression on the manners and mores of the island of Guernsey. Any reader of Hugo has to expect and accept this as his principal novelistic mode. The narrator gives a geological, geographical, and botanical introduction to the archipelago of the English Channel. This is followed by a minute description of the principal city, Saint Peter-Port. There is a long dissertation of religious evolution since the time of the Reformation, including not only the official Church of England, but also the free churches of the Methodists. The reader is further informed about the customs and laws of the island. A major section of the introduction deals with the superstitious beliefs of the islanders, visionary houses, the presence of witches, and a written record of a conversation of phantoms, certainly derived from the spiritism* he experienced when he first arrived on Jersey. A curious piece of "expressionism," or visionary aspect, is found in the description of the windowless houses (that is houses without windows on the sea side for obvious protective reasons), presented by Hugo as living, blind creatures, anticipating a similar bunker structure found in Samuel Beckett's play *Fin de partie* (Endgame).

Hugo's interest in the island extends to philological exercises with which this novel abounds. It is clear that Hugo knew Old French. In addition he playfully intertwined English and French and gave etymological explanations of the Guernsey dialect. Although his linguistics may at times appear defective and incorrect, most of his intuitions in this regard hit the mark.

The main motif, however, deals with the destructive power of the ocean; the English Channel is well known as a most vicious stretch of water. Thus the sea is seen as a graveyard, for ships and sailors; it is only Gilliatt, in epic manner, who is able to overcome the odds. The visionary, hallucinatory presentations of the sea, its reefs, and its promontories are well illustrated by Hugo's drawings,* and it presents linguistically what will later be found in painting as abstract expressionism.

This novel then is rightfully called visionary, or expressionistic, in style. Its motif certainly announces the maritime seascapes to be found in the novels of Pierre Loti, especially in his *Pêcheur d'Islande*.

While it never attained the popularity of *Notre-Dame de Paris** or *Les Misérables*,* it is all the same one of the most abstract and pictorial of all Hugo's prose. It deserves to receive more attention than it has been accorded.

BIBLIOGRAPHY

Bromberg, Victor. *Victor Hugo and the Visionary Novel*. Cambridge, Mass.: Harvard University Press, 1984.
Hillsdon, Sonia. *Jersey: Witches, Ghosts, and Traditions*. Norwich, England: Jarold Colour Publications, 1984.

Travels. Hugo, possessed of an innate sense of curiosity and as a writer always intent on expanding his horizons, liked to travel, perhaps more than most nineteenth-century French people. He was fascinated by new things and places. Part of his travel experiences come from the fact that he was the son of a general in the Napoleonic wars; also, however, from his exile from France to the Channel Islands starting in 1852 and lasting to the fall of Napoléon III* at Sedan in 1870.

He was a great walker both on the islands and in Paris; in his old age, he liked to ride on the new omnibus from one side of Paris to the other. There were moments when his traveling could bring great sorrow, however. He learned of the death of his daughter, Léopoldine Hugo,* and her husband, Charles Vacquerie,* who drowned at Villequier while he was reading a newspaper in a café in the small village of Soubise, near Rochefort, on the Atlantic coast (September 1843).

Born in Besançon in 1802, he was taken as an infant to Corsica, Elba, back to Paris, and on to Naples, while the family followed the Napoleonic military meanderings. In 1808 he was in Naples and in 1811 in Madrid, where he gained a fine proficiency in Spanish. As a young man he traveled throughout France, especially the Loire Valley where his father resided at Blois. He also made trips to Normandy and Brittany, itineraries which would soon be imitated by Gustave Flaubert* as recorded in his *Par les Champs et par les grèves*. His exile brought him first to Brussels, but then to the Channel Islands. He also had a fondness for Luxembourg, where he stayed for a while in 1872.

It may be surprising that Hugo never planned any travels to either the United States or to Central or South America. With the exceptions of Chateaubriand and Alexis de Tocqueville, these trips seemed too long for most nineteenth-century writers.

His attitude may be similar to that of Stendhal,* who never thought of going beyond his beloved Italy. While Hugo was interested in humanitarian causes—for example, he sent a letter to the president of the United States pleading that John Brown* not be executed—he may have thought, as did Stendhal, that America was simply a new country filled not just with immigrants, but ignorant ones at that, whose public opinion, as Stendhal so aptly put it at the conclusion of chapter 1 of the *Red and the Black*, is rampant with bigotry.

It is rather perplexing that, after Chateaubriand and Alexis de Tocqueville, there was almost no interest on the part of French writers to move out of Europe. There was hardly any difference in the twentieth century despite the interest in New York by the Swiss-French writer Blaise Cendrars (*Les Pâques à New York*—Easter in New York, 1912) which may be nothing more than the cosmopolitan spirit found in such writers as Federico García Lorca, whose New York adventures inspired his *Poeta en Neuva York* (Poet in New York), which was published in 1940 after his death.

Victor Hugo traveled a great deal, but never out of the pan-European geopolitical limits.

Triboulet. Triboulet is the principal personage in Hugo's drama *Le Roi s'amuse** (The king has a good time) of 1832. Triboulet is an ugly and deformed jester in the court of Francis I. His virgin daughter, Blanche, is sexually assaulted by the king, giving a certain irony to the title of the play, and her father vows revenge. By an unfortunate turn of events, Blanche, dressed in the clothing of a man, disobeys her father and returns to the decrepit inn where a trap has been laid for the king to be killed. It is Blanche who is murdered and who dies in the arms of her father. Royal censorship closed the play down. If the play did not succeed in the form given it by Hugo, it was, nevertheless, an enormous success as Giuseppe Verdi's opera *Rigoletto* (1851).

The personage of Triboulet is in line with a literary tradition, mainly from Hugo, which combines the sublime and the grotesque (Quasimodo* in *Notre-Dame de Paris** is another example). A similar type, equally serious, but in a solitary manner, is the play *Fantasio* by Alfred de Musset* (1810–1857). Fantasio is part of the genre of ugly or misunderstood court jesters, clowns, and buffoons, who under a mask reveal a heart filled with love. Thus Triboulet, Quasimodo, Fantasio, and Pagliacci of Leon Cavallo (1857–1919) fit into the same category.

Triboulet's dilemma stems, in part, from his fanatical devotion to his sixteen-year-old daughter Blanche (Bianca), and here he joins a long line of fathers with an unusual attachment to their offspring, usually female; including William Shakespeare's *King Lear* (1605) and Honoré de Balzac's* *Le Père Goriot* (Old Goriot) of 1835.

It should be noted that Hugo did not invent the name Triboulet. There was such a court jester at the time of Louis XII and Francis I (who appears as the villain in this play).

Tristesse d'Olympio. *Tristesse d'Olympio* (Olympio's sadness), from *Les Rayons et les ombres,** remains the most cherished of Hugo's poems written before the exile. Olympio was the poetic name Hugo gave himself, with egotistical echoes to Mount Olympus, and it was used by André Maurois for his biography, *Olympio, the Life of Victor Hugo* (1956). For Pierre Albouy, in his notes to volume 1 of the Pléiade edition (Gallimard, 1968), this poem stands as the major poetic achievement of French Romanticism between 1820 and 1840. This enthusiasm was not shared by André Gide,* who finds the poem to be overpraised. For Gide, Hugo's poem is not much more than pure rhetoric, which may explain why he chose to cite only two verses (10 and 33) in his *Anthologie de la poésie française* (Gallimard, 1949).

Tristesse d'Olympio is dedicated to the abiding love of his entire life, Juliette Drouet. The manuscript reads: *pour ma Juliette, écrit après avoir visité la vallée de Bièvre en octobre, 1837* (for my Juliette, written after visiting the valley of Bièvre in October 1837).

Contrary to other Romantic poems uniting the themes of love, nature, and remembrance, *Olympio* does not speak either of a love ended by death (Alphonse de Lamartine's* *Le Lac*) or love destroyed because of new liaisons (Alfred de Musset's* *Souvenir*). Hugo's poem expresses the sentiment that this love has had a springtime which is past, a honeymoon that will be enshrined in the heart of the poet. Thus this poem, written in 1837, has none of the elegiac feeling of *Le Lac* and certainly little of the sniffling sentimentality of Musset's *Souvenir*. There were many years left for Hugo and Juliette, some of which were tumultuous. The poem's formal structure consists of thirty-eight strophes divided into two parts, the first consisting of eight verses, each of six lines, interspersing twelve and six syllables. Therein is recorded the narrator's walk through a nature which had been shared with the beloved, seeking out whatever may remain of the past. The second part, with thirty strophes of four-line alexandrines, poses philosophical and theological questions about the nature of the human experience, especially love, focusing almost obsessively on the material spaces of the forest which may or may not retain some memory of what had taken place between the two lovers.

Looking across such a long poem, many lines and derivative thoughts stand out even for the modern reader. In the first part, nature refutes any idea of John Ruskin's "pathetic fallacy," for, contrary to the uncertainties in the poet's soul, nature is in a happy mood; it is a splendid, sun-filled autumn day (strophe 1). The second part begins the Romantic philosophical and existential questioning of the nature of human experience. Nature has overwhelmed favorite past sites; the poet's work is almost that of an amorous archaeologist digging for relics of love amongst the ruins. This part's long philosophical meanderings have allowed anthology editors to cut segments of the poem, without any apparent damage to its progression. If nature has covered up the amorous past, then Hugo can derive from this sad fact that life starts here but ends elsewhere. Life is or was but a dream: *N'existons-nous donc plus?* (Do we no longer exist?); *Avons-nous eu notre heure?* (Did we not have our time?). The poem concludes, however, with an affirmation that this remembering of things past, this souvenir, will give a certain eternity or permanence to what had been. In this sense, Hugo anticipated a similar meditation by the twentieth-century novelist Marcel Proust.

Tristesse d'Olympio is based squarely on the real-life, intimate relationship of Hugo and Juliette Drouet in the Vallée de Bièvre* in the years just before the composition of the poem. By contrast with Lamartine's *Le Lac*, in which it becomes textually impossible for us to comprehend the past relationship between the poet and his Elvire (Madame Charles), Hugo's poem is filled with veiled erotic allusions, putting this poem within the full-blown Romantic zeitgeist, and outside the Petrarchian tradition which Lamartine may have stumbled upon in his early Romantic poem of remembrance.

Tristesse d'Olympio is a major text for understanding poetic and ideological evolutions within the Romantic movement, from Lamartine's *Le*

Lac (1820), through Hugo's poem (1837), and then three years later de Musset's lament *Souvenir* (1840).

BIBLIOGRAPHY

Levaillant, Maurice. *Victor Hugo, Juliette Drouet et 'Tristesse d'Olympio'*. Paris: Delagrave, 1945.

Twilight Songs. *See Chants du crépuscule, Les.*

U

United States of America and Victor Hugo. Victor Hugo's reputation in the United States parallels its development in the United Kingdom. Translations, at least of his novels, were slow in being made, and the selections seem eclectic, namely the novel *Bug-Jargal*,* which must have produced trepidation in the South where slave insurrections were always feared, and *The Hunchback of Notre-Dame*, a silly title that persists today in translations and in movie versions (the latest is a cartoon version produced by the Disney Studios). The American emphasis seems to have been on Quasimodo,* stressing Hugo's theory of the grotesque. There were also translations of *Le Rhin* (the Rhine Valley tours—1838 and 1842), which can be explained in general by the vogue for literary itineraries that have dominated the Western imagination since the later years of the eighteenth century, augmented by Romanticism itself (witness the travel documents of both Chateaubriand and Washington Irving at the Alhambra in Spain). There were also translations of *Han d'Islande*,* in 1843, and some subsequent translations of it in 1862, 1870, and 1883. The most important translation, however, was that of *Les Misérables*, which appeared right on the heels of the French edition.

As for his theatre, it had much less success in America, although there is evidence of translations of *Marie Tudor*,* *Lucrèce Borgia*,* and *Angelo, tyran de Padoue*. The famous American actor, Edwin Booth (of the same family as John Wilkes Booth, who assassinated Abraham Lincoln), wrote a preface to a translation of *Ruy Blas*,* and translations of this play, as well as those of *Hernani*,* were sponsored both in England and New York by the publisher Samuel French, which remains to this day the most important house for the publication of dramatic works.

Poetry proved more difficult to translate, and it might even be considered inaccessible, not only for translating from French into English but from any language to another. Poetry presents enormous difficulties of vocabulary, rhyme, rhythm, and meter, especially given the regular cadence of the French alexandrine which Hugo used, but not classically.

As the study of modern foreign languages developed in the United States, particularly under the auspices of Henry Wadsworth Longfellow (1807–1882), who is considered the father of modern language studies in America especially of the Romance tongues, student reading manuals were in great demand. As the nineteenth century moved into the twentieth, there were, and still are, myriad editions, some bilingual, of Hugo's prose works, often in truncated form, designed to develop reading skills in American high school students and institutions of higher learning.

Today, Hugo is a major part of the curriculum in college departments of Romance Languages or departments of French and Italian, and in comparative literature programs. For the general public, he remains little known for his poetry or theatre, but he is very well known for the Gothic novel about Notre-Dame and, of course, for the musical adaptation of *Les Misérables* (*See Misérables, Les* [musical play]).

Two aspects of Hugo's reputation in America should be underlined. First there was an enormous journalistic curiosity about the strange amorous odyssey of Hugo's daughter, Adèle Hugo,* who followed her imagined lover, Lieutenant Albert Pinson,* first to Canada, and then to the Caribbean. These antics were fully published in both the Canadian and American press. Even Adèle's demise in 1915, thirty years after the death of her father, was duly noted in the American press.

More important, however, and this remains probably the most singular aspect of Hugo's personal reputation in the United States, is his involvement in the treason trial of the abolitionist John Brown.* Hugo was an adamant and stubborn enemy of capital punishment* and slavery, and he did try, to no avail, to intervene to stop the hanging of John Brown. The letter on behalf of Brown was addressed to the editor of the *London News*. In any case, it arrived too late, and it would have had no effect whatsoever as America prepared for war between the northern and southern states.

Concerning biographical information, there have been no important original biographies by American scholars, but there have been translations of the French works; two by Alfred Barbou were translated into American English in 1881 and 1882 and the important work attributed to Hugo's wife, *Victor Hugo raconté par un témoin de sa vie* (Victor Hugo's life told by a witness of his life) in 1868. Judged in comparison with other nineteenth-century French writers, it honestly can be said that Hugo had by far the greatest reputation in the United States during that period.

By far the most important source on Hugo in America is Monique Lebreton-Savigny's *Victor Hugo et les Américains* (1971). The text is an example of minute and disciplined scholarship. Aside from the text itself, its enormous bibliography, which includes items traced through the American press across all the states and the District of Columbia, Lebreton-Savigny's work includes dates of publication of Hugo's novels, theatre, and poetry; Hugo's inclusion in French readers, in literary magazines, and in reference works; productions and adaptations of Hugo's plays performed in America; operas and ballets based on Hugo's works; comments in the American press on Hugo's reaction to the coup d'état of Napoléon III,* in December 1851; Hugo's return to Paris in September 1870; and reports of Hugo's death on May 22, 1885.

BIBLIOGRAPHY

Lebreton-Savigny, Monique. *Victor Hugo et les Américains (1825–1885)*. Paris: Editions Klincksieck, 1971.

Ursus. Ursus is the itinerant caravan driver of Hugo's *L'Homme qui rit*.* Ursus frames the story because the opening chapters are dedicated uniquely to him, to his character, and to his general good will toward all mankind. It is he who takes in the shivering disfigured little boy, Gwynplaine,* and the little blind infant girl, Dea.* It is also Ursus and his wolf Homo* who frame the final scenes of this novel as they sail for Holland, left in bereavement over the death of Dea and the suicide* of Gwynplaine. Man and wolf are again alone as they were in the beginning of the narration. Ursus is an extraordinary creation of Hugo; he is a man of multiple talents—a witch doctor in the Western sense of healer or *guérisseur*, ventriloquist, and actor.

Ursus does not like the company of other humans; he prefers the open road, a solitude which is meditative, with only the company of the wolf Homo. It is not that he is a true misanthrope, for his character and actions prove the contrary. It is he who takes in the abandoned children and infant and becomes their adoptive father. His big mistake, perhaps, was taking his troupe of comedians in the Green Box (a rolling caravan) to London which exposed Gwynplaine's true identity as a peer of the kingdom, and resulted in their expulsion from England in order to spare the life of the wolf. Ursus, which sounds a bit like "Bear-man" (as "Homo" the wolf sounds like a human being), is one of the quiet heroes of Hugo's novelistic world, somewhat in the character of Gilliatt* in *Les Travailleurs de la mer*.* In a novel that has not had much success either in France or elsewhere, he remains one of Hugo's finest creations, the incarnation of Hugo's humanitarian impulses.

V

Vache, La. *La Vache* (The cow), from *Les Voix intérieures** of 1837 reveals a Hugo at age thirty-five still smitten with eighteenth-century or even early Romantic sentimentality. Yet, by its descriptive beauty, equivalent to that found in the 1829 *Les Orientales,** it seems to announce a nineteenth-century meditation before the beauty of nature, especially as found in animal* creation. It is thus a forerunner of Parnassian poetry,* proving Hugo to be entirely and completely of his century.

The poem as a panegyric to nature seems derived from eighteenth-century sources, namely the Comte de Buffon and Jean-Jacques Rousseau, but above all the sentimental painter Jean-Baptiste Greuze (1725–1805), who stressed a purity found in the countryside but never in the city. Hugo's sentimental meditation of the mystical cow seems almost manneristic today. The poem, however, is redeemed by the lyrical voice of the poet which sings above a prosaic argument.

It is divided into two parts. The first part describes a cow in a barnyard, a mother-nature type, surrounded by Romantic barnyard figures of chickens and roosters. To this is added, in a startling manner, the hunger of young children who seek the udder of the cow, a faint echo to the story of Romulus and Remus, the legendary founders of Rome.

The second part adds, somewhat like the tercets of a well-formed sonnet, a type of textual explication or response to the first part. What was seen as a picturesque bucolic scene in part 1 is transformed into a general meditation on the human condition in which the poet sees that nature, conceived at once as spiritual and carnal, nourishes mankind's aspirations.

The poem concludes with a message, Buddhist in intent, that like the cow, we stand as made, without anxiety, dreaming about infinity: *sans te déranger, tu rêves à ton Dieu* (without interruption you dream about your God).

Vacquerie, Auguste. Auguste Vacquerie (1819–1895) was the brother of Charles Vacquerie,* who married Hugo's daughter Léopoldine Hugo.* Auguste was a fervent believer in Romanticism and a devotee of Victor Hugo. A second-rate writer whose style has been seen as affected and even eccentric, he is important today for his intimate contact with the Hugo clan. His *Les Miettes de l'histoire (trois ans à Jersey)* (Morsels of history: Three years on Jersey), of 1863, is an important and intimate document on various aspects of the poet's exile on that Channel Island.

Auguste Vacquerie's devotion to both Hugo and his causes made him the subject of two of Hugo's poems; poem twelve in Book Four, *La Religion est glorifiée* (Religion is glorified), *A Quatre Prisonniers* (To four prisoners) is in honor of Hugo's two sons, Charles and François-Victor, and François Paul Meurice* and Auguste Vacquerie, all of whom were condemned to the Conciergerie by the courts for their outspoken writings in *L'Evenement* against capital punishment,* an essential aspect of Hugo's ideas about liberty and democracy. Hugo also dedicates the opening poem of Book Five, *En Marche* (On the road), of *Les Contemplations,** to Auguste, back to back with the last poem of Book Six, *Pauca meae*, dedicated to Charles Vacquerie.

BIBLIOGRAPHY

Vacquerie, Auguste. *Les Miettes de l'histoire (trois ans à Jersey)*. Paris: Pagnerre, 1863.

Vacquerie, Charles. Charles Vacquerie was the husband of Victor Hugo's elder daughter Léopoldine Hugo* and the brother of a fervent admirer of Hugo and his work, Auguste Vacquerie.* Charles married Léopoldine in Saint Paul's church in Paris on February 15, 1843. Auguste, the more interesting and versatile of the brothers, was secretly in love with Léopoldine but he remained silent and promoted the cause of his brother. The marriage was of short duration because of an accident at Villequier in which both Charles and Léopoldine perished in the Seine. A mythology has developed around the Romantic notion that Charles, an excellent swimmer, chose deliberately to drown with his wife. It cannot be proven. This legend was propagated by Alphonse Karr in his reporting of the event in *Les Guêpes*, on September 10, 1843, just six days after the fatal accident took place on September 4.

BIBLIOGRAPHY

Karr, Alphonse. *Les Guêpes*. Paris: Michel Levy, 1862.

Valéry, Paul. Paul Valéry (1871–1945), a symbolist poet (*see* Symbolism), wrote a significant essay in his *Etudes littéraires* entitled "Victor Hugo créateur par la forme" (Victor Hugo, creator through form), which was broadcast on August 15, 1935, by Les Cahiers de Radio-Paris on the occasion of the fiftieth anniversary of the death of Hugo. It is a significant tribute made by a Cartesian symbolist in which Valéry explained the greatness and endurance of Hugo's poetry, which can be summed up as Hugo's absolute commitment to poetic form. Borrowing from the Provençal poet Frédéric Mistral (1830–1914), Valéry cites this important phrase: *Il n'y a que la forme; la forme seule conserve les oeuvres de l'esprit* (There is only form; form alone conserves the works of the mind). He defined the attributes of form as rhythm, rhyme, number, symmetry of figures, and antitheses; and Hugo is noted as the poet who mastered all these categories. It is through these forms that his passions are preserved.

For Valéry, Hugo was important inasmuch as form was generally neglected by the other major Romantic poets of the time, namely Alfred de Musset,* and to a lesser degree, Alfred de Vigny* and Alphonse de Lamartine.* Lamartine is quoted somewhere as writing to Hugo that great poets did not need to pay attention to grammar, with the commentator stating that a difference between the two poets is that Hugo did know his grammar and Lamartine did not.

Valéry thought that Hugo's cult of form derived from his study of classical Latin authors such as Virgil and Horace, and the great classical poets of France in the seventeenth century. Valéry was impressed by Hugo's rigorous work habits while he lived on the island of Guernsey. He worked on his art from five in the morning until noon, not allowing any interruption, not even, it would seem, for the death of his son (see Valéry's letter to Paul Souday, October 1923, cited in the Gallimard edition of *Oeuvres de Paul Valéry*, pp. 1732–33).

Some concluding phrases attest to the "classical" discipline of Hugo which seems to fulfill Nicolas Boileau-Despréaux's dictum in the *Art poétique* concerning inspiration and hard work, the latter being the most important in literary output. Valéry concludes by saying that Hugo traveled throughout the universe of vocabulary (*Il a parcouru tout l'univers du vocabulaire*), which seems to verify the general statement that Hugo had the largest vocabulary of any nineteenth-century poet, and adding that Hugo's true mistress was form (*Chez lui la forme est toute Maîtresse*).

BIBLIOGRAPHY

Oeuvres de Paul Valéry. Annotated and edited by Jean Hytier. Paris: Gallimard, Bibliothèque de la Pléiade, 1954.
Valéry, Paul. *The Art of Poetry.* Introduction by T. S. Eliot. New York: Random House, 1958.

Valjean, Jean. In the novel *Les Misérables*,* Valjean was a former convict, who had been unjustly imprisoned in the galley ships of Toulon. Once freed, in a last unconscious act of stealing, his conscience surmises what is good and what is evil. His innate intelligence and goodness cause him to make many social reforms. He saves Cosette* from the malevolent Thénardier family* and grows deeper in quietude and contemplation.

Pursued for years by Javert,* a man who fights for law and order, Jean Valjean finally dies, surrounded by Cosette and her husband, Marius.* Hugo's intent must have been to contrast redemptive possibilities in the personage of Jean Valjean with the despair of Javert who commits suicide.* The idea of a stolen loaf of bread may recall the multiplication of loaves for the hungry followers of Jesus.

Van Tieghem, Philippe, and the *Dictionnaire de Victor Hugo*. This is one of the most useful reference works on Hugo in French. Published in 1970 (Librairie Larousse in Paris), it was edited by Van Tieghem, one of the most important and prolific French scholars in the field of both national and comparative literature. This work, amply illustrated, contains several hundred entries on Hugo's life, family, friends, and writings. Two items merit particular note: a detailed chronology covering Hugo's entire life, its main events, and dates of the publication of his writings; and two maps, one tracing Hugo's voyages, and the other, his places of residence in Paris. The work contains an alphabetical list of all of Hugo's poems, dates of publication, and the collections in which they appear. Victor Hugo's most often cited lines of poetry are also presented, and finally there is a thorough bibliography. Indispensable for those who can read French, this work is complementary to, but quite different in approach, content, and concept, from this encyclopedia.

Vigny, Alfred de. Alfred de Vigny (1797–1863) was one of the most important of the French Romantic poets. He was often, erroneously, called the "philosophical" or "symbolic" writer, mainly because of the facile, yet beautiful, allegories he put in such poems as *Moïse* (Moses) and *Le Mont des Oliviers* (The Mount of Olives) and his touching Romantic lyric *La Mort du loup* (The death of the wolf), all of which should be ranked among the best poems of the French Romantic movement. De Vigny's off-and-on relationship with Victor Hugo remains one of the intriguing circumstances of French Romanticism—an intimacy between a writer who will eclipse the century while de Vigny will slip into solitude and obscurity, perhaps willed, as some of his poems suggest.

Hugo and de Vigny met in 1820, when they were both aspiring young poets, the one eighteen, the other, a military officer of twenty-three. They quickly became close friends, and de Vigny was the best man at Hugo's marriage to Adèle Foucher in the church of Saint-Sulpice on October 12, 1822. The mutual admiration of two young writers continued, especially on the part of de Vigny, who saw in *Han d'Islande** the French equivalent to, or even superiority over, the novels of Sir Walter Scott.

Yet the friendship waned for reasons that are not totally clear. Charles-Augustin Saint-Beuve* seems to have had a hand in the events, perhaps out of his own persistent, latent bitterness toward Hugo and Hugo's friends. What had started out as a very close, if not intimate, friendship between de Vigny and Hugo became, if not an alienation, at least a distancing.

De Vigny is important in understanding the early years of Romanticism, above all his close friendship with the Young France movement. If he remains in the background of French Romanticism, it is not because of his short relationship with Hugo but perhaps because of the limited range of his own literary productivity which, while admirable in itself, could never match the energetic productivity of the young Hugo.

Villequier. This small town at the mouth of the Seine river (Seine-Maritime) is the site of the home of the Vacquerie family (now a Hugo museum), and the tragic site of the drowning of Léopoldine Hugo* and her husband Charles Vacquerie* on September 4, 1843. This catastrophe engendered a major section of an 1856 collection of poetry by Hugo, *Les Contemplations,** divided into six books, the most lyrical of which is Book Four, *Pauca meae*. Most of the twenty-seven poems in this book concern the loss of Léopoldine. It is in this book that one finds the poem *A Villequier*, perhaps the longest, most poignant elegy in French literature since Francois de Malherbe's *Consolation à Monsieur du Périer sur la mort de sa fille* (Consolation for Monsieur Perier on the death of his daughter), written in the early seventeenth century.

Composed of forty strophes, defying a latter-day injunction of T. S. Eliot that lyricism cannot be maintained over a long poem, it stylistically and thematically reiterates the grieving father's inability to come to terms with the loss of the beloved daughter, married on February 15, 1843 (poem two of Book Four) and dead a little less than seven months later. The poem is typical of Hugo's meditations on the human condition, destiny, the will of God, human strife, and the interplay of good and evil; and it concludes, after a crescendo of high emotion, on the quiet sobbing of a father who cannot or will not be consoled for this enormous loss, the daughter who had made the joy of the home and of the soul: *Lorsqu'on a reconnu que cet enfant qu'on aime/Fait le jour dans notre âme et dans notre maison* (When one has recognized that this child whom one loves/brings daylight into our soul and into our house) (verse 39).

Structurally, the poem can be seen as a dialectical argument the poet engages in with himself but mainly with God, an interlocution of lyrical existential and theological pleading as Hugo the Romantic attempts to understand paternal loss.

BIBLIOGRAPHY

Claudel, Paul. *Oeuvres complètes*, vol. 15, *Positions et propositions*. Paris: Gallimard, 1959. See pp. 27–36 for an incisive stylistic analysis of *A Villequier*.
Frey, John A. *Les Contemplations of Victor Hugo: The Ash Wednesday Liturgy*. Charlottesville: University Press of Virginia, 1988.
Nash, Suzanne. *Les Contemplations of Victor Hugo: An Allegory of the Creative Process*. Princeton, N.J.: Princeton University Press, 1976.

Visionary house. *See Maison visionée.*

Voix intérieures, Les. Les *Voix intérieures* (Interior voices), the third in the four volumes of the July monarchy, published on June 26, 1837, contains thirty-two poems preceded by an interesting preface in which we see Hugo's penchant for the magical number three, which is used to explain, simplistically, the order of life and the universe. The threes of the preface, looking like a fake paradox, present man as heart, nature as soul, and events as mind—thus the triple aspects of life: for man the domestic scene, the fields representing nature, and the street representing events. This last named phenomenon would certainly be important in describing the uprising depicted in *Les Misérables*.* The preface underlines the civilizing role of the poet, and also his moderation. Hence the poet has great respect for the people, but only scorn for the crowd; he can salute the tricolor flag of the revolution, but he will not insult the fleur de lys of the Bourbon monarchy. True to the title of the collection, Hugo states that everyone has music within if only we could learn to listen to it. Thus the interior voices are another manner of communication, but this requires meditation.

By the time of *Les Voix intérieures*, it has to be admitted, Hugo was adept at producing long lyric poems; consequently, poem two, *Sunt Lacrymae rerum*, rambles on with multiple digressions for 399 lines. The famous *A l'Arc de Triomphe*, one of the most popular of the collection, has 446 lines. Other inordinately long, digressive poems are the three-part *Dieu est toujours là* (poem five); poem seventeen, *Soirée en mer*; the very beautiful *A des Oiseaux envolés* (poem twenty-two); and *Olympio* (poem thirty). Such long lyrics are not necessarily to be negatively criticized, but they are especially irksome when treating subjects of ephemeral value to the modern reader, that is, the subjects frequently tied to a particular historical moment.

Thematically, there is great range in this collection. Without enumerating in detail, we should note some of the varieties. There are some themes that persist from previous collections, such as the poet's love for Juliette Drouet (poems seven, eight, nine, and eleven; as well as one poem that just plainly exalts love in general, poem twenty-six).

There are dazzling accolades to family life, especially to the joy of children, which was previously seen in *Lorsque l'Enfant paraît**: poems twenty, twenty-one, twenty-two, twenty-three, and twenty-five. This particular voice of the poet will continue across future collections, ending with the very famous late collection *L'Art d'être grand-père.** Also there is Hugo's great love of nature and his fear of it when manifest in the engravings of Albrecht Dürer (poem ten), or when nature is seen in its fearful rage in the symbol of the ocean (poems seventeen and twenty-four), or when it is manifest in a positive manner as in poem fourteen, dedicated to the painter Louis Boulanger.

Ridiculed by some as too sentimental and anthropomorphic, the poem *La Vache,** poem fifteen is, in addition to carrying a symbolic message of the nurturing role of nature, an example of Hugo's Parnassian poetical* inclination (the so-called school of objective poetry founded on the heels of Romanticism and usually seen as having its roots in Hugo's *Les Orientales**). It is also vividly pictorial, for Hugo had an eye and a talent for the plastic arts (*See* Drawings).

There are, however, several pessimistic pictures of the nineteenth century in this collection, especially Hugo's abiding concern for the welfare of the poor (*Dieu est toujours là*, poem five) and the contrast he makes with the idle, cynical, and decadent rich (poems six and nineteen).

Recall of bygone days is achieved through the contemplation of ruins, or of structures, such as a Chateau (*Passé*, poem 16), or the very poignant tribute made to his insane brother Eugène, who died in a clinic in Charenton in February 1837. While the poem concentrates on Eugène's genius as a poet, a faculty disturbed by the onset of a nervous breakdown on the very day of Hugo's marriage, it is a touching tribute of brotherly love, of moments shared together on the grounds of the Feuillantines* convent when they were but very small children.

The collection also increases the tempo of Hugo's religious difficulties, his meditations on destiny and providence, his own fears about his faith which seems to be crumbling (poem one), but above all *Pensar, dudar* (Think and doubt), dedicated to that calm in the eye of the storm, Louise Bertin (*see* Bertin family).

Finally, we have two appearances of Hugo's alter ego, Olympio. Poem thirty, *A Olympio*, presents the poet persecuted by his enemies as does poem thirteen, *Jeune homme, ce mechant fait une lâche guerre* (Young man, this wicked man wages a cowardly war), an invective against two well-known adverse critics of Hugo.

If this collection opens with an affirmation of a belief in progress for the nineteenth century, in the terminal poem, *O muse contiens-toi! muse aux hymnes d'airain* (poem thirty-two), the poet accepts the challenge to be a leader of his time, fighting each and every battle against injustice. This last poem seems to announce the engaged spirit which we will find in *Les Châtiments** of the 1850s.

The value of the four collections of the July monarchy is certainly found in the delineation of the major themes found across the entire poetic work of Hugo: love, nature, family and children, religious faith and religious doubt. These volumes do not have the rigorous conceptual unity which will be found in *Les Châtiments, Les Contemplations,** and *La Légende des siècles.** These three collections will stand in contrast to the volumes of the July monarchy by their organic unity of bitter satire, the intermingling of exile with thoughts of the death of Léopoldine Hugo,* and the rewriting of history from a poetic perspective.

W

War to the Scaffold. This verse monologue, in alexandrine, written by Lozes-Preval, is a theatrical adaptation of Hugo's *Le Dernier Jour d'un condamné*, which had been published in 1859. Impossible to perform in France because of official censorship, the author had it presented in Switzerland where the death penalty had just been abolished. Hugo, who had a lifelong passionate interest in the abolition of the death penalty, heartily approved Lozes-Preval's project, with the provision that the author's share of the profits be given to the poor. This is an interesting point since Hugo, as many modern humanitarian thinkers, saw the relationship among poverty, imprisonment, and capital punishment,* as in the case of Mr. Tapner, the last person executed on Guernsey (*see* Tapner, the execution of Mr.).

Waterloo, Battle of. Situated to the south of Brussels, Waterloo was the site of the victory of the English and Prussian armies against Napoléon Bonaparte on June 18, 1815. If Waterloo figures in the writings of Hugo, it is because of Bonaparte's almost hypnotic influence on him, first negatively, then positively, and finally with a certain ambivalence. Waterloo is a main ingredient in the Napoleonic myth exploited by French Romantic painters and writers. In the case of Hugo, two examples of the Waterloo theme are sufficient to demonstrate its role in Hugo's thinking, while keeping in mind that his complete work continues additional commentaries on this conflict.

Waterloo, which takes up about fifty-eight pages of *Les Misérables*, is incorporated into the main thread of the narration with the so-called saving of the life of the father of Marius* on the battlefield by Thénardier, the rascal of rascals (*see* Thénardier family). In fact, Thénardier was stealing from the pockets of the dead and wounded, but Pontmercy (Marius' father) interpreted his action as humanitarian, thus indebting Marius to the man through a good portion of the novel. It serves, however, as a fine excuse for Hugo to make his usual historical digression, and it is, as fiction, convincing. Hugo's historical account of Waterloo is more epic in its proportions than, say, the single vision of the battle as seen in Stendhal's* novel *The Charterhouse of Parma* (1839) for it is only through the eyes of its hero, Fabrice del Dongo, that we witness the battle. Stendhal's technique is similar to that used in Stephen Crane's novel *The Red Badge of Courage* (1895), which recounts civil war battles through the eyes of a simple, ordinary soldier.

Hugo wants to tell the whole story and, for him, this means geography, study of the terrain, and then a temporal progression in which he describes moods and perspectives not just of Bonaparte but also of the English and the Prussians. In a chapter entitled "Should We Approve of Waterloo?" Hugo speculates on its meaning and concludes that it is not just Europe against France, but Europe trying to undo the French Revolution.

For the Waterloo sequence in *Les Misérables*, however, the prose passage is rather different from the heroic rhythms found in the eighty-eight lines of descriptive poetry of the battle in the second part of *L'Expiation** from *Les Châtiments.** The prose version from *Les Misérables* seems almost placid and philosophical compared with the subjective and panoramic vision presented in the poem. The opening two lines are filled with an ominous symbolism: *Waterloo! Waterloo! Waterloo! morne plaine! Comme une onde qui bout dans une urne trop pleine* (Waterloo, Waterloo, Waterloo mournful plain/Like a wave which boils in a too-filled urn). The poem indeed follows the prose version from the viewpoint of temporality and markings of the changes from day to night. The poetic narrative rises above any simple accounting of military maneuvers and could be classified as epic or heroic rhapsody.

The second part of *L'Expiation* may be aesthetically preferred to the prose account given in *Les Misérables*, which was derived from an actual visit by Hugo to the battlefield. However, both are important in measuring Hugo's evaluation of Napoléon.

What the Mouth from the Shadow Says. See *Ce que dit la bouche d'ombre.*

When the Child Comes into the Room. See *Lorsque l'enfant paraît.*

Will They Eat? See *Mangeront-ils?*

William Shakespeare. Hugo perhaps knew fewer than one hundred words of English, but he knew, as a Romantic, the importance of shaking French theatre free from classicism by using a foreign and northern

model. In this he was preceded by both Madame de Staël and Stendhal*
who wrote an important short treatise in the 1820s comparing Jean Racine with the English bard. It was certainly through the heroic and assiduous translations of Shakespeare made by his son François-Victor
(replacing the inept Letourneur translation) that Hugo himself started
his meditations on art in general which was finally produced between
1858 and 1864, and entitled *William Shakespeare*.

In the work on the English Renaissance dramatist, he ponders genius
across the ages, going from the Greeks through Miguel de Cervantes,
and François Rabelais, certainly not a myopic vision.

Hugo must have admired most in the tragedies of Shakespeare the
mixture of comedy and tragedy, which Hugo had advocated in his *Préface de Cromwell* (*see Cromwell, Preface to*), but also the ability to create
myth out of national history, something Hugo himself had tried in *Hernani*,* *Ruy Blas*,* and *Les Burgraves*.*

Shakespeare who, for seventeenth-century France, was the antithesis
of the classical ideal became for the Romantics the ideal playwright, and
Hugo's work, although coming late, perhaps due to his exile on Guernsey, was a major continuation of the new French wave.

Z

Zola, Emile. Zola (1840–1902), the chief practitioner of naturalism in the novel, theatre, and criticism, was the author of the twenty-volume series *Les Rougon-Macquart* (well-known individual novels within the series are *Germinal, L'Assommoire,* and *Nana*). He shared with most French writers of the time a youthful enthusiasm, which has been dampened by artistic maturation and judgment demanding new directions, far afield from the Romanticism that dominated most of the nineteenth century.

The adolescent Zola, like Gustave Flaubert,* was filled with admiration for the poetry of Romanticism; two authors stood out as exemplary for him; Victor Hugo and Alfred de Musset.* Aesthetic admiration was accompanied by republican zeal for Hugo, the exiled poet, to whom Zola wrote, at Hauteville House on Guernsey (1860), a letter of praise for his literary productions and liberal viewpoints. Zola's early enthusiasm would wither, however, as he developed his own literary doctrines which placed him squarely in the tradition of Honoré de Balzac.* Zola's alienation from Romanticism meant alienation from Hugo. Thus an article on *La Légende des siècles* harshly judged Hugo and Romanticism as ephemeral episodes in literary history.

Zola's motives emanated from his belief that an artist must be of his own time and that art should be revelatory of contemporary society. While recognizing Hugo's revolutionary innovations made to French theatre in 1830, he now called for new directions for a stagnant French theatrical scene (*Le Naturalisme au théâtre,* 1881).

It has been suggested that Zola was not unhappy to see Hugo's funeral procession (May 1885), the end of the glorification of Romanticism, and perhaps a moment of triumph for the new and modern school of Naturalism. If such is the case, it is an irony that Zola's remains (transferred from the Montmartre cemetery on June 3, 1908) were to be reinterred next to Hugo's in the Panthéon on Mont Sainte-Geneviève where the French government inscribed over the great portal, *Aux Grands hommes, la patrie reconnaissante* (To its great men, a grateful country).

Zubiri. *Zubiri*, a one-act entertainment, was derived from a narration in Hugo's *Choses vues** (1887 and 1900). *Zubiri* was the product of the theatrical imagination of Georges de Porto-Riche (1849–1930), the author of many passionate and sentimental plays at the end of the nineteenth century and the beginning of the twentieth century. Porto-Riche dedicated this theatrical diversion to his friend, the socialist politician Léon Blum (1872–1950), and he easily admitted that the dialogue was entirely that of Victor Hugo. A bit racier than the plays of Eugène Labiche (1815–1888), whose most famous farce was *Un Chapeau de paille d'Italie* (1851) (An Italian straw hat), Porto-Riche's work draws heavily upon the real-life amorous feelings of both Hugo and his son Charles for a famous Parisian beauty, Alice Ozy, alias Zubiri, in this ribald play in which the best of the French Gallic spirit with its double-entendres is expressed.

Charles Hugo, who was twenty-one years old in 1847, was enamored of Alice Ozy. This beauty had expressed a desire to have in her autograph album some poetic lines of Hugo. When Hugo arrived at her home and saw her magnificent and suggestive bed, he wrote the following: *A cette heure charmante où le couchant palit,/Où le ciel se remplit d'une lumière blonde,/Platon souhaitait voir Venus sortir de l'onde;/Moi, j'aimerais mieux voir Alice entrer au lit* (At this charming hour when the sun wanes, when the sky is filled with a blond light/Plato wanted to see Venus come out of the sea,/I, I would prefer to see Alice getting into bed). (Cited by Escholier, 1953, 279). The audacity of Alice is recorded by Hugo as he contemplated the state of Europe in 1849, a year in which the Church lost Rome, Louis-Philippe was in exile in London, and Alice Ozy played the role of Eve, completely nude, in the theatre of the Porte-Saint-Martin.

These are the elements which make for the naughtiness of Porto-Riche's one-act play, presented on January 24, 1909. The play has the rococo "esprit" of the eighteenth century, particularly of Voltaire who liked a dirty twist of words, provided they were recited with elegance. Porto-Riche's play contains elements of Hugo's love poems and lines, such as, "Which would you prefer, a seat in the French Academy or the chaise-longue of your mistress?," or *Ce n'est pas ces dames de la Comédie-Française qui vous ont de ces seins-la!* (It is not the ladies of the Comédie-Française who present these breasts [seins, but also in the sense of scenes] there). Porto-Riche obviously captured a jocular and semilewd aspect of Hugo's sexuality and his appreciation of the female body.

BIBLIOGRAPHY

Excholier, Raymond. *Un Amant de génie, Victor Hugo.* Paris: A. Fayard, 1979.

Selected Bibliography

The general reader should consult the annual German bibliographical information supplied in the work of Otto Klapp, *Bibliographie der Franzossichen Literatur Wissenschaft*, and the annual bibliography of the Modern Language Association of the United States and Canada.

MANUSCRIPT SOURCES ON VICTOR HUGO

Most Hugo materials are found in the National Library in Paris. Special collections are contained in the *Spoelberch de Louvenjoul* collection, also found in Paris. Some manuscripts are located in the Hugo museum, no. 6 Place des Vosges, Paris. Other manuscripts are found in private collections not available to the public.

BIBLIOGRAPHY

Barrère, Jean-Bertrand. *La Fantaisie de Victor Hugo*. Paris: José Corti, 1949, 1950, 1960.

Baudoin, Charles. *Psychanalyse de Victor Hugo*. Geneva, Switzerland: Mont Blanc, 1943.

Bowman, Frank Paul. "The Intertextuality of Victor Hugo's *Le Dernier Jour d'un condamné*." *French Forum* (Lexington, Kentucky), 1993.

Brombert, Victor. *Victor Hugo and the Visionary Novel*. Cambridge, Mass.: Harvard University Press, 1984.

Chauvel, Ad., and M. Forestier. *The Extraordinary House of Victor Hugo in Guernsey*. Guernsey Historical Monographs, no. 14. Saint Peter-Port: Tucan Press, 1975.

Chenay, Paul. *Victor Hugo à Guernsey*. Paris: Juven, 1902.

Drouet, Juliette. *Mille et une lettres d'amour à Victor Hugo*. Paris: Gallimard, 1951.

Escholier, Raymond. *La Vie glorieuse de Victor Hugo*. Paris: Plon, 1928.

Selected Bibliography

Gaudon, Jean. *Le Temps de la contemplation*. Paris: Flammarion, 1969.

Glauser, Alfred. *La Poétique de Hugo*. Paris: Nizet, 1978.

———. *Victor Hugo et la poésie pure*. Geneva, Switzerland: Droz, 1957.

La Gloire de Victor Hugo. Paris: Editions de la réunion des musées nationaux, 1985.

Grossman, Kathryn M. *The Early Novels of Victor Hugo*. Geneva, Switzerland: Droz, 1986.

Gueriac, Suzanne. *The Impersonal Sublime*. Palo Alto, Calif.: Stanford University Press, 1990.

Guille, Frances Vernor. *Le Journal d'Adèle Hugo*. Paris: Lettres modernes, 1968.

Hillsdon, Sonia. *Jersey: Witches, Ghosts, and Traditions*. Norwich, England: Jarrold Colour Publications, 1984.

Houston, John Porter. *Hugo*. New York: Twayne, 1974.

Ionesco, Eugène. *Hugoliad or the Grotesque and Tragic Life of Victor Hugo*. New York: Grove Press, 1987.

Laster, Arnaud. *Pleins feux sur Victor Hugo*. Paris: Comédie-Française, 1981.

———. *Victor Hugo*. Paris: Pierre Belfond, 1984.

Lebreton-Savigny, Monique. *Victor Hugo et les Américains (1825–1885)*. Paris: Editions Klincksieck, 1971.

Massin, Jean. *Victor Hugo, oeuvres complètes*. Paris: Le Club français du livre, 1967–1970.

Maurois, André. *Olympio, ou, la vie de Victor Hugo*. Paris: Hachette, 1954.

Richardson, Joanna. *Victor Hugo*. New York: St. Martin's Press, 1976.

Said, Edward W. *Orientalism*. New York: Pantheon Books, 1978.

Seebacher, Jacques. *Hugo le fabuleux*. Paris: Seghers, 1985.

Swinburne, Algernon Charles. *A Study of Victor Hugo*. Philadelphia: R. West, 1978.

Ubersfeld, Anne. *Paroles de Hugo*. Paris: Messidor, 1985.

Index

The page numbers set in **boldface** indicate the location of a main entry.

About the Author

JOHN ANDREW FREY was Professor Emeritus of Romance Languages and Literatures at the George Washington University. A specialist in French literature of the 19th century, he wrote books on French symbolism, Emile Zola, and Victor Hugo, along with major articles on Chateaubriand, Balzac, Washington Irving, and André Gide.

ISBN 0-313-29896-3

HARDCOVER BAR CODE